*"The history of mankind is a history of
repeated injuries and usurpations
on the part of man toward woman."*

Declaration of Sentiments, 1848

Praise for **GIVEN NO CHOICE**

"This is a must read book on the history of abortion politics in the US. If, like me, you think you know it all, you will be blown away by the intimate and absolutely accurate history of the movement, the leaders on both sides and the paths they took to either block or provide access to safe abortion. If you are new to the issue–perhaps concerned now that Roe has been overturned and every woman has lost all right to end a pregnancy—you will be inspired by those who have gone before and the struggle that lies before us. Frankly, it is the best book on the issue I have ever read—and I've read them all."

—**Frances Kissling**, president, The Center for Health Ethics
and Social Policy

"Finally! A rights-based approach to the history of abortion in the United States. This book tells the abortion rights story at the right time, giving us an accurate view of where the fight has come from and where we have to take it to secure sexual and reproductive freedom for now, for all, forever."

—**Dazon Dixon Diallo**, founder of SisterLove

"*Given No Choice: A History of Abortion Rights* is an engaging and authoritative account of one of the central stories of our time—the struggle for and against abortion rights. This book is valuable beyond the story of where we've been and how we got here. It also surfaces important lessons learned—many by those who dedicated their lives to the cause. These lessons may very well inform our current political moment as well as generations to come. Whether you have a passionate, passing, or professional interest, *Given No Choice* is a good read and an essential reference."

—**Frederick Clarkson**, senior research analyst,
Political Research Associates

"Cody McDevitt's book illuminates the complex history of a woman's struggle to maintain bodily autonomy in order to protect her life, health and ability to maintain economic equality with men. By understanding the past, McDevitt's important, well-documented work can help men and women work together to create a more just and enlightened nation on this issue."

—**Bill Baird**, reproductive rights pioneer

"A sweeping, deeply researched book of feminist history, which exhaustively details how reproductive rights in the U.S. have evolved over the years and how we got to where we are today. The battle over abortion is far from over, and *Given No Choice* is compelling, important reading for anyone who wants to better understand the past in order to keep fighting for access in the future."

—**Rebecca Grant**, author of *Access: Inside the Abortion Underground and the Sixty-Year Battle for Reproductive Freedom*

"Cody McDevitt's book, *Given No Choice*, is an important addition to the library of publications concerning the long and tortured fight for women to have the freedom to have safe abortions in the United States. His book is well-written and highly readable. It contains many valuable details about the history of this struggle including dynamics of the U.S. Supreme Court. It includes the individual personal and professional struggles of important pro-choice leaders such as Margaret Sanger, Alan Guttmacher, Gloria Steinem, Dick Lamm, Patricia Maginnis, Frank Susman, Sarah Weddington, Karen Mulhauser, Judy Widdicombe, Fran Kissling and others over the years in carrying on this historic effort. As involved as I have been in over 55 years with these events and leaders, many of them close friends, I learned a lot in reading Cody's book."

—**Warren Hern**, longtime abortion provider and
reproductive rights champion

Cover photo by Bettye Lane and permitted to be used by her nephew and family.

Cover and interior design by David Provolo

ISBN (Hardback): 979-8-9941126-2-5
ISBN (Paperback): 979-8-9941126-1-8
ISBN (Ebook): 979-8-9941126-0-1

First edition.

Printed in the United States of America.

GIVEN NO CHOICE

A HISTORY OF ABORTION RIGHTS

CODY McDEVITT

CONTENTS

FOREWORD

By Karen Mulhauser

It is evident to anyone who knows me that an unintended pregnancy in 1964 while in college has defined the rest of my life. I self-induced an abortion and thought I had been successful. However, I fainted in the bus terminal on my way back to college. I awoke in the terminal office in a pool of blood. They must have known what happened and just wanted me to leave as soon as possible. They allowed me to wash, change my clothes and leave.

I had not spoken about this much until 2022, when the Supreme Court reversed *Roe v. Wade*. Then it seemed that those of us who had pre-*Roe* abortions needed to tell our stories in an effort to make it clear that we must not return to those days when it was common for women to get sick or suffer complications from self-inducing or going to a back-alley "doctor," who may, in fact, have not been medically trained at all. This book offers a history that many young people may not have learned about or of which they are unaware. This book, in part, helps explain why so many of us fought for abortion access and how challenging it was throughout the last 50 years.

How did this experience change my life plans? While teaching high school and middle school science in the late 1960s, I found myself spending a great deal of time talking with students about sex and how to prevent pregnancy. Since then, I have counseled hundreds of women and girls with unintended pregnancies. I've trained family planning professionals and was the executive director of the National Abortion Rights Action League (NARAL), and the president of the local Planned Parenthood.

When I opened the Washington lobby office of NARAL in 1973 and then became the CEO in 1975, it became obvious to me that if women could not decide when or if to have children, they could not avail themselves of the education and economic opportunities available to those who cannot get pregnant. It's that simple. It is central to achieving gender equality.

NARAL relocated its national office to Washington, D.C., in 1975, as the organization was shifting its focus to Congress and becoming increasingly political. I helped it establish its political action committee and trained activists to open chapters in nearly all states. Our mantra became "If it does not bring workers to campaigns or voters to the polls, just don't do it!!!"

Today, my personal mantra is reflected in my email signature: "If we don't like the policies, we have to change the policymakers!"

I have worked for abortion rights and gender equity my entire adult life and thought I knew a great deal about the movement. After reading Cody's manuscript, I now know a great deal more. This book is overwhelming and important. Women have had abortions throughout history—whether self-induced or with assistance. And clearly, lives are protected if abortion is available legally in communities that value a woman's freedom.

People and governments that misname themselves "pro-life" deny this freedom. I call them pro-birth because they do not support lives after birth, and they seem to believe that embryos have more rights than women.

This history both informs and frightens. With every page and chapter, it reminds me that people who support reproductive freedom are those who can make abortion legal and safe. We must work to elect officials at the local, state and national levels who agree that abortion is both a health issue and a human rights issue.

The Supreme Court's decision to overturn *Roe v. Wade* reminded the country of the importance of elections. The president and the Senate determine who is on the Supreme Court. Now we are reminded just how important state and local elections are, because it is at these levels that decisions are made to determine whether women have bodily autonomy.

Abortion was on the ballot in 2022, and it surprised some that so many young people registered to vote for candidates who support legal abortion. It was again on the ballot in 2024. Elections at all levels of government will galvanize both sides. Still, those who support the freedom to have abortions are in the majority and can make a difference in local, state and national elections—if they register and vote.

I smiled when I saw the names of colleagues and NARAL board members—people like Sarah Weddington, Gloria Steinem, Pat Maginnis, Frances Kissling, Harriet Pilpel, Dr. Ken Edelin, Frank Susman and so many more. In the 1970s, abortion rights were not a partisan issue. My young friends today find it hard to imagine that Republicans were some of our strongest congressional advocates. Today, I find it unusual that many right-wing voters so often speak of freedom as part of a democracy. Yet, they do not recognize the freedom to determine what to do with a pregnancy as one of our central liberties.

I conclude by reflecting on a successful voter engagement initiative that I launched, called "Trusted Sources."

I have worked with nonprofit leaders to help them get their members to register and vote. When someone trusts a leader, they are more likely to follow their suggestions than a stranger's. I have worked with dozens of groups, including Vote Run Lead, the Coalition of Labor Union Women, the League of Women Voters, the NOW Foundation, the Black Women's Roundtable, and many more. I helped them work with Target Smart, a data firm that enables them to identify which of their members are registered to vote and how frequently they should. This allows them to tailor their messages effectively. They get the updated data after the election and learn its effectiveness. In each case, they had greater impacts than national averages.

Both men and women know that abortion is a personal decision—not one to be made by politicians. But if they do not vote, anti-abortion politicians could be making those choices instead of individuals.

INTRODUCTION

The purpose of this book is to provide the next generation of feminists with a primer on reproductive rights history. I hope to help tell the story of how we got to where we are, with an eye to regaining what has been lost and taking the fight forward. I want people to place themselves in that history—a history still being written, and one that provides context for the lived experience and the stories of our ancestors, relatives, friends and communities.

For the past six years, I have been immersed in abortion research. I began by reading extensively. Following the publication of an academic paper, I turned it into a full-length book. I tracked down living members of the pro-choice movement for the last 50 years. In dozens of conversations over the phone and in person, I realized that the people who had fought for the right to choose were as impassioned as they ever had been.

The book draft itself was completed in 2022, but it sat unpublished for three years as I sought a traditional publisher. After realizing that I wouldn't get one, I started editing for self-publication. In the time between its first version and now, there was a revolution in research methods that permitted me to flesh out the story in much greater detail.

The end of *Roe v. Wade* demonstrates that reproductive health care must not be taken for granted. In America, abortion was at one point legal, at another illegal and then legal again after a century of struggle. It's now partly legal and partly illegal.

Still, for most Americans, it is not a black-and-white matter, but shifting shades of gray. It often depends on who you talk to. I've heard the stories of women who lost the ability to bear children because of back-alley abortions. I've talked to women who suffered attacks on their clinics. I have learned of the toll that this debate takes. The vast majority of Americans who are pro-choice need to be just as vigilant as their opponents—if not more so—in defending and advancing their cause.

I want readers to share what they learn with others who are or should be interested. I hope this stimulates discussion in rural areas as much as urban ones. A belief in a woman's autonomy is universal and not bound by religion, party, region or demographic.

This book is intended to serve as a starting point for feminists before reading more in depth on specific topics. Therefore, I've highlighted what I thought were the most valuable parts of this history and the leaders who played important roles in them. For those who want to learn more, I have cited essential works of scholarship and references to other sources of information.

The book is written from both a journalistic and scholarly viewpoint. It's intended to be readable while at the same time serving as a roadmap for further exploration. It is rich material, variously disturbing, shocking and inspiring. I feel honored and humbled to be able to tell this story.

While reading, keep in mind that the terms and descriptions given to abortion have evolved. I wrote this book to place readers in the time frame in which the events took place, so the lingo reflects that. I did make an effort not to use anachronisms at later points when the language had changed to reflect new perceptions.

We have reached the end of *Roe's* legal protections. With that comes the possibility of harsh punishments for those who receive and provide certain forms of reproductive care. The war over reproductive freedoms is far from over. As we've seen in the last few years, there is a never-ending impulse to rob women of their ability to chart their own destinies in life. Whatever gifts we have—whether as a writer or filmmaker or as a political strategist or leader—should be used to advance human dignity and self-determination. That's what I hope to do here.

PREFACE

In 1962, Sherri Chessen's family life was idyllic. Chessen was the popular host of "Romper Room," a children's television show that aired throughout Phoenix.

She was also the mother of four children and was expecting a fifth. Her husband, Bob Finkbine, was a high school teacher. One morning, before filming her 11 a.m. show—an hour-long program featuring six preschoolers drinking chocolate milk, eating cinnamon rolls, running around and playing games—Chessen tried to ease her morning sickness with tranquilizer pills Bob had brought back from Europe.

The pills were thalidomide, a sedative then used to treat depression. Earlier that year, Australian doctor W. G. McBride had discovered the drug caused severe fetal deformities. The Food and Drug Administration had subsequently banned its use in the United States, a decision President John F. Kennedy publicly praised.

Not long after taking the pills, Chessen read an article in *The Arizona Republic* about doctors in England euthanizing newborns with deformities linked to thalidomide. She realized the pill she had taken might have the same effect and immediately sought medical advice.

Chessen's fears were justified.

Her doctor—speaking, she recalled, as if advising his own wife—recommended terminating the pregnancy. He told her she would need to write a letter to a three-man medical board at the local hospital and assured her the abortion would be approved.

He also gave Bob an envelope of photos showing infants with thalidomide-related deformities—only heads and torsos, black bars drawn across their eyes. He instructed Bob to show them to Chessen only if she wavered, but Bob showed them immediately.

"To this day, I can see those babies," she told me from her retirement community in San Diego. "For 25 years, I had a recurring dream of those babies lined up, but they would have the head of my second son. And I knew … the kids I already had were my fiduciary responsibility."[1]

Sherri Chessen was one of the first people I interviewed for this book. She spoke with the unhurried candor of someone who has recounted the same story for decades and understands its historical weight. Her recollections moved easily between the personal and the public, unfolding less like an interview and more like an oral history—rich with detail, reflection and the emotional texture of a life-altering decision.

She knew she needed an abortion.

"For that child—potential child—and for the children I already had, I had to be strong. Intellectually, I had to have it together. I never wavered. But emotionally, my heart broke. You fall apart."

Wanting to warn other pregnant women in Phoenix about thalidomide, she called the newspaper and asked for a story focused on the drug's dangers.

Instead, the next morning's front page proclaimed that a "baby-deforming drug may cost an unidentified woman her child." The article centered on the abortion rather than the drug—and despite the paper's withholding Chessen's name, readers easily identified her from the details.

When she arrived to film "Romper Room," she was fired. Station executives claimed she was no longer competent to work with children because she planned to have an abortion. Soon after, her doctor informed her the hospital board had canceled the procedure.

Chessen then sought to challenge Arizona's abortion law on mental health grounds. The judge sent her to two psychiatrists. One questioned whether her husband was the child's father, prompting a heated exchange.

---

1 Chessen, S. (2020, May 29). *Interview with Cody McDevitt* [Personal interview].

He concluded she should be denied an abortion, sterilized and separated from her existing children. The second psychiatrist was more sympathetic and told her they had already decided in her favor.

The judge still ruled against her.

"So there I am—thrown out of the hospital, thrown out of my doctor's office, thrown out of Arizona," Chessen told me.

The story soon drew national and international attention. Readers overseas sent letters. *Life* magazine published an extensive spread. Threats against her family multiplied. Chessen received photos of herself with daggers drawn through her eyes. The FBI intervened; agents escorted her children home from school because some threats described cutting off the children's limbs.

Amid the harassment, others offered questionable help. One person suggested she drink ammonia to end the pregnancy. Another claimed he could induce a miscarriage through hypnosis.

The Vatican's newspapers labeled her a prospective murderer.

Chessen learned that Americans could obtain abortions in Japan by simply hiring a taxi driver for $20 to take them to a hospital. Seeking privacy, she traveled to Los Angeles to visit the Japanese consulate disguised in a blond wig over her brunette hair, with towels stuffed under her clothing to simulate advanced pregnancy. She walked through the airport alone, fearing Bob would be recognized. She passed the assembled newspapermen unnoticed.

But consulate staff refused to issue a visa, fearing anti-Japanese protests.

A Swedish reporter then offered assistance in exchange for exclusive coverage. In Sweden, however, hospital officials interrogated Chessen for three weeks before approving the abortion. The international press followed her every move.

When she and Bob returned home, she discovered someone else was hosting "Romper Room." Her television career was over.

Chessen's ordeal marked a turning point in the struggle for abortion rights. Previously hidden in the shadows, the issue was thrust into public view. The case galvanized reform efforts across the United States. While

Catholic leaders continued to denounce abortion, her experience persuaded many Protestant and Jewish denominations to reconsider their positions. A movement led by religious organizations and secular feminists grew, eventually culminating in the Supreme Court's recognition of a constitutional right to abortion—a right that stood for 50 years and has now been lost.

CHAPTER 1

As Old As Civilization

Abortion wasn't new to politics or the law when Chessen first made news.

As far as human records go back, scholars have found evidence of humans seeking reproductive control. Historians attribute Emperor Shen Nung, who reigned in China from 2737 until 2696 B.C., with the oldest mention of an abortifacient. Nung recommended mercury to end pregnancy. Chinese folklore included many methods for abortion in 48 volumes of handwritten text, though there are fewer recipes in printed medical books. Ancient Chinese remedies featured both mild oral prescriptions and external procedures.

The Code of Hammurabi, the Sumerian Code and the Assyrian Code each lay out penalties for people who caused a miscarriage. In Assyria, authorities punished women who had an abortion with crucifixion and impaling, according to theologian Roger Huser. Hippocrates, in his famous oath, warned against making abortifacients available to pregnant women, yet he himself indicated methods to terminate a pregnancy. Over the centuries, people have misread the Hippocratic Oath and used it to justify anti-abortion policy. The Oath itself merely discourages the use of pessaries or suppositories.

Romans also used helleborus and castoreum to end pregnancies.

Dioscorides wrote that gentian induced abortion, and Soranus of Ephesus—a Greek physician practicing medicine in ancient Rome—performed abortions.

The Kahun Gynecological Papyrus, dating back to 1800 B.C., is the oldest known Egyptian medical text dealing with women's health issues such as birth, contraception, fertility and disease. It prescribed crocodile dung, sour milk and honey to make a dough that was inserted into the woman as both a contraceptive and a means to induce abortion.

In 1550 B.C., the Egyptian Ebers Papyrus offered remedies for a wide range of ailments. In it, abortion was achieved through a mix of crushed dates, acacia gum and honey coating a plant-fiber tampon. Additional abortifacients included silphium—now extinct—and pennyroyal, which was highly toxic yet used by the ancient Greeks, Romans and Egyptians.

In Turkish culture, the prince's harem always had a midwife who performed abortions.

Philosophers also addressed the topic. The followers of Pythagoras saw a fetus as human life that women should preserve from conception. They believed abortion stopped the soul's journey to enlightenment. Aristotle knew of contraception and abortion methods. In his writings, he analyzed the soul and the gestation process, and although his theories on abortion are not entirely consistent, he mentioned in *Historia Animalium* that abortion within the first 40 days seemed acceptable, but in the second trimester a change occurred in the embryo that presented a moral quandary.

Some Jewish theologians and those crafting the Old Testament saw abortion as a minor infraction, depending on the circumstances. Exodus indicates that men would suffer a fine from a husband if he caused his wife to suffer a miscarriage. It was designed to compensate for the loss of future labor. The fetus wasn't seen as a human, and so the commandment against murder didn't apply. The Talmud permitted abortion when the life of the mother was in danger. Jewish religious documents discussed the ordeal of bitter water, which was an abortifacient administered to women who were suspected of adultery.

Jewish scholar Rachel Biale writes about abortion in *Women and Jewish Law: The Essential Texts, Their History and Their Relevance for Today.* Biale discusses how both the Torah and Halakhah, or totality of Jewish law, treated the issue. Fetal personhood wasn't recognized in early Jewish literature. If someone accidentally caused a woman to miscarry, they weren't punished for a capital offense, but they did have to pay a debt to the father of the fetus. It was seen as property damage. Some Jewish commentators even argued that abortion may be legal to save the woman from public disgrace should a baby be conceived out of wedlock. Ben Zion Uziel, who was a chief rabbi of Israel, called for abortions to be practiced by knowledgeable doctors so the procedure itself wouldn't be dangerous.

Other modern scholars have also discussed the issue and given presentations on the Jewish treatment of abortion. Rabbi Danya Ruttenberg spoke at the 2022 Sacred Gathering conference, which was a first-of-its-kind convening of religious leaders who advocate for reproductive rights and justice. As part of a panel, Ruttenberg said her organization, the National Council of Jewish Women, focused on reproductive justice.

"Literally in Judaism, it's my body. So in Judaism, this is the basis for our approach to pregnancy," she said at the event.

In the first millennium A.D., Christian leaders didn't treat homicide and abortion as equal crimes. In the Eastern Orthodox Church, the institution created by the Apostle Paul, leaders distinguished between a formed and an unformed fetus. St. Basil the Great, in the fourth century, said that a woman who destroys her fetus is answerable for murder, and didn't distinguish between formed and unformed. But the distinction prevailed among Church councils between the fifth and 12th centuries. Gratian said, "He is not a murderer who brings about abortion before the soul is in the body."

St. Antoninus, who was the archbishop of Florence, wrote about abortion in the 1500s. He argued that abortion was permissible to save a woman's life. That happened frequently at the time, according to Catholic theologian Daniel Maguire, who has written extensively about abortion within all organized religions.

"Both sides of the issue are represented," Maguire said. "And the pro-choice side, as we call it today, was part of the recognition in all the world religions. In some circumstances, it called for abortion. The termination of fetal life in those circumstances is morally good and in some cases morally mandatory."

The Catholic Church's current position didn't become doctrine until the 1830s, during the reign of Pope Sixtus V, when he issued some penalties for it. In 1869, Pope Pius IX eliminated any line between formed and unformed fetuses as the standard for when the church condoned abortion. He said he would excommunicate abortionists and women who got abortions. Popes thereafter followed the same line, although the rhetoric about kicking women out of the church for having an abortion generally softened.

Much of what historians understand about abortion in early America is owed to the foundational scholarship of Leslie J. Reagan and James C. Mohr, whose works established the documentary and analytical frameworks that continue to shape the field. Reagan's *When Abortion Was a Crime* (1997) excavates the lived experience of women, midwives, physicians and criminal defendants from the mid-19th century through *Roe v. Wade*, showing how abortion shifted from a commonplace part of reproductive care to a target of state surveillance and punitive enforcement. Her meticulous use of court records, hospital files and public health archives reveals the human costs of criminalization and the social worlds in which reproductive decisions were made.

Mohr's *Abortion in America: The Origins and Evolution of National Policy, 1800–1900* (1978) remains the definitive political and legal history of 19th-century abortion regulation; he traces how a profession-driven campaign by physicians transformed abortion from a widely tolerated practice into a crime, illuminating the cultural anxieties, professional rivalries and gendered power dynamics at the heart of the emerging laws. Together, Mohr and Reagan established the historical foundations on which modern research (and the contemporary political struggle) still relies.

Prior to 1800, abortion laws in America followed the English custom that had permitted abortion until the quickening, the first fetal movement. It was a crime to get an abortion after that. American lawmakers codified the earliest statutes regarding abortion between 1821 and 1841, in order to protect the health of the mother. In 1821, Connecticut enacted the first anti-abortion law to prevent maternal poisoning from the inducement of abortion.

Protestant churches accepted abortion when pregnancy threatened a woman's life up until the same year Catholics condemned it. The issue became politicized around that time, as discussed later in this book. But even as it did, abortions were commonplace among the Protestant laity. Since there was a great deal of intolerance directed toward Catholics, there was pressure among Protestant ministers to condemn abortion to keep the moral high ground.

African slaves and Native Americans had their own abortion methods, including the use of herbs, plants and other remedies. Some enslaved people saw abortion as a form of resistance against the enslaver. A Black woman was more likely to get an abortion if a plantation owner raped and impregnated her. Enslaved women used cottonwood to abort those pregnancies, as well as pennyroyal, tansy, juniper bush, Seneca snakeroot and ergot. Indigenous tribes had a range of views on abortion. The Chippewas strongly opposed it. The Dakotas employed various herbs, which often resulted in the mother's death.

Beginning in the 1830s, Americans changed the way they looked at reproduction and sexuality thanks to lecturers and advertisers who distributed information in newspapers, magazines and pamphlets. The country grappled with the two concepts as it struggled to balance moralism with controlling family size.

Physicians who sought to regulate abortion during that era were not motivated solely by concern for the health of the mother or because of anti-abortion views. Rather, they feared economic competition from non-medical abortion providers and only later became part of a medical reform to eliminate a relatively dangerous procedure.

During this same period, newspaper advertisements described different abortifacients or agents that cause miscarriages. Publications also listed abortion services, usually expressed in a euphemistic code, like eliminating a pregnancy that was described as an irregularity—in reference to missing a period. Abortion became one of the first medical specialties.

Madame Restell

Madame Restell, who was born Ann Trow in 1812, later Ann Lohman after marriage, became a debutante in New York City after she decided to be the most brazen abortionist in the country. Puritanical lawmakers, police officers and prosecutors targeted her throughout her career. Newspaper accounts in the mid-19th century vilified her and said she was responsible for multiple murders of the unborn.

Restell was born in England and started working as a maid when she was 15 years old. She married a tailor, Henry Summers, when she was 16. They had a daughter in 1830, and then the family sailed to New York, settling in Lower Manhattan. Henry died in the fall of 1831. About five years later, Restell met Charles Lohman, who worked as a printer at the *New York Herald*. With his help, she began publishing information on population control and contraception.

Restell's reason for becoming an abortionist is not known, but she likely began as someone who worked at a compounding pharmacy and then became an abortion provider. She eventually developed a pill that supposedly prevented conception or ended pregnancies. That medication sold well. If the pills failed, she performed surgical abortions, charging rich women five times what poor women paid.

She and her husband first advertised the business in the *New York Sun* on March 18, 1839. They promised financial prosperity with more adequate family planning and a reduction of childcare burdens. She said that people might prosper more with fewer children.

At the height of her career, the 35-year-old Restell drew attention with her elaborate dress and piercing black eyes. She was well known for riding around the city in a showy carriage with four horses.

Madame Restell went on trial in 1840 for performing an abortion. Mary Purdy, a 21-year-old who was dying from tuberculosis, admitted to her husband on her deathbed that she had been pregnant and visited Restell on Greenwich Street and obtained a vial of medicine, as they had a 10-month-old baby and she was not prepared to have another child so quickly. Purdy had a doctor look at the medicine, who told her not to take any more after noting that it contained turpentine and tansy oil, which made it dangerous. She visited Madame Restell again, who said she could do the procedure. Purdy agreed and later became ill, certain her sickness came from her abortion.

Purdy's husband went to the police, who arrested and charged Restell. The newspapers dubbed her "the monster in human shape."

Restell was found guilty, but on appeal, she successfully argued that the deathbed statement was inadmissible. The court overturned the verdict because such evidence was only permitted in civil lawsuits. Her legal victory strengthened her resolve, and she opened additional offices.

The Age of Medical Reform

Abortion remained dangerous until around 1857, when Louis Pasteur discovered that minute invisible organisms caused liquids to ferment. Later he discovered that contamination could occur via the atmosphere. Lord Lister, for whom Listerine is named, saw Pasteur's discovery and revolutionized surgical practice by using carbolic acid to exclude atmospheric germs, creating antiseptic surgery. Until 1867, abortions were inherently dangerous because surgeons didn't know what caused infection. One estimate indicated the death rate from abortion fell to one-fiftieth of what it had been once antiseptic techniques were adopted.

When medical reform regarding abortion reached its apex in the 1860s, a number of doctors, researchers and authors produced tracts explaining why politicians should criminalize the procedure. Edwin M. Hale, the author of *The Great Crime of the Nineteenth Century*, argued that the Ten Commandments ordered followers not to kill, and linked the abortion procedure to that religious tenet. Hale said the prevailing laws, which permitted abortion until quickening, were ungodly.

Hale criticized some other reasons given for abortion, notably that women sought to maintain beauty in this way, which he thought was vain. He felt women didn't want to give up bachelorette lives. He said adultery didn't justify abortion.

Horatio Storer, a gynecologist who crusaded to ban the procedure, was the most famous anti-abortionist of his time. Storer criticized new social roles for women. He infused that with his traditional gender views.

Storer was with the American Medical Association (AMA) in 1856. Only a year later, he started the Physicians' Crusade Against Abortion. He wrote to doctors across the country to learn about abortion laws. In Suffolk County, Massachusetts, he urged fellow members of the Suffolk District Medical Society to condemn the procedure.

Storer published a tract on the subject in which he argued against the quickening threshold. Storer said the fetus and the mother were separate entities and were each entitled to the same rights of personhood. Storer believed the procedure could kill the mother. To him, abortion was murder, and everyone should be punished accordingly.

Storer thought delaying marriage among "literary women" was one of the reasons for the uptick in abortions. He shamed women who thought of getting one. But this did not stop women from approaching Storer for abortions. In 1860, he reported that 15 women had asked for one in six months.

The AMA took his cue and became one of the main opponents of abortion in the late 19th century. It wanted to professionalize medicine, to elevate its jobs above midwives, herbalists and others, even though those professions had been involved in pregnancy care for centuries. In 1910, the Flexner Report, a book-length, landmark report of medical education in the United States and Canada, pushed for higher medical education standards, more rigorous certification exams to practice medicine, and stricter state laws.

In Victorian society, between 1837 and 1901, Protestant and Catholic churches joined with the medical establishment in demonizing abortion providers and the women who sought them. Victorian society saw a woman who got an abortion as someone evading motherhood duties, and as immoral and selfish. If a woman was deathly ill after an abortion, law enforcement officials forced her to testify against both her lover and the abortion doctor before she could receive care at a local hospital.

All this may have been the result of abortion proliferating after the Civil War. Around 400 abortionists reportedly operated in New York City. The quality of care varied, as some were in mansions while others were in the slums. In Michigan, one man's correspondence with doctors led to an estimate that a third of the pregnancies of Protestant women ended in abortion.

Publications focused on the procedure's dangers. In September 1871, *Harper's Weekly* reported on the unfortunate case of Alice Bowlsby. A railroad worker discovered Bowlsby's body in a trunk after she had been killed by a back-alley abortionist. The report indicated few women's bodies were found because abortionists threw them into the Hudson River if they died. *Harper's* took issue with abortion advertisements.

> *There is no other civilized country where the procuress, the libertine and the abortionist are allowed to flaunt themselves before the public in this shameless manner. This is an abuse of the freedom of the press, which calls for immediate abatement.*

The publication called for the prosecution of people who published such material. However, their contention that America was the only country with abortion ads was wrong. A medicine company in England sold tonics masquerading as abortifacients,

That's when Anthony Comstock, a member of the Congregational Church, who hated female expressions of sexual freedom and liberty, arrived. Leaders of the Young Men's Christian Association (YMCA) applauded his efforts, but his targets—those who trafficked in birth control, abortion methods or pornography—thought him the bane of their existence.

Comstock, a bald man with a horseshoe mustache, served in the infantry during the Civil War before moving to New York City, which teemed with prostitutes and obscene publications. In the late 1860s, he investigated vice and then told police about it. In 1872, he got Congress to pass the Comstock Act, which defined contraceptives—as well as information on them and abortions—as obscene. Comstock's clout derived from his role as the leader of the New York Society for the Suppression of Vice, a heavily influential organization in the Victorian era. The Act made it a federal crime to disseminate birth control through the mail or across state lines.

Comstock targeted Restell early in his career.

In January 1878, he rang the bell at Restell's basement office and asked to see her. During his meeting, he asked for and received a contraceptive. After springing the trap, Comstock left but returned the next day with five more men, including officers, a deputy, and two local newspaper reporters from the *Tribune and World*. Comstock identified himself. They searched the premises and found abortifacients and birth control devices.

Afterward, Restell rode in her carriage to the court, where a crowd met her. Newspapers sensationalized the arrest and trial. Reporters described her as "the wickedest woman in New York."

The negative publicity wore on her. In 1878, Restell's chambermaid found her dead in the bathtub after she had committed suicide by slitting her throat from ear to ear. While many at the time were either happy about or indifferent to her death, others felt as if they had lost someone whose legacy promoted oversight and safer standards for abortionists. Her facility had been safe. Stricter state abortion laws drove more women into dangerous situations. Comstock died in 1915, but his legacy endures to this day.

By 1900, all states had laws outlawing abortion. In 1912, federal officials launched a nationwide raid against abortionists and disseminators of birth control information. They worried about "race suicide," as the *Chicago Tribune* put it when it described the roundup of 173 people suspected of violating the state's Comstock laws. The concept—the self-elimination of one's racial group—came from the eugenicist movement, then popular nationwide. Most of the fear-mongering promoted the idea that the white race would disappear through the use of birth control and abortion while communities of color would grow without them.

A significant development related to reproductive rights and eugenics theory emerged when American Charles Davenport and Englishman Francis Galton communicated their theories of evolution developed from the work of Gregor Mendel, who was Galton's cousin.

Davenport experimented with animals and plants at his lab in Cold Spring Harbor in Long Island to create selective traits in their offspring. He thought the same method could be used to improve humans.

Later, he and a team of researchers collected wide-scale data. They sent out family-history questionnaires, studied medical records, gathered family pedigrees and argued that humans passed on inherited traits. The central question was whether desirable characteristics could be bred and undesirable ones bred out. They felt that social problems were caused by genes, and so eliminating those would diminish things like poverty and crime.

The Industrial Revolution coincided with the eugenics movement, bringing with it rapid changes in demographics. It created slums, crime and disease. Progressives felt they could use programs to solve some of these problems. So they supported eugenics.

Davenport focused on low intelligence, which was known as feeble-mindedness. Fellow researcher Henry Goddard wanted to connect it with antisocial behavior. His charts delineated between idiots, imbeciles and morons. Mental deficiency and immorality became connected. He argued feeble-mindedness caused two-thirds of society's problems. Identifying it was key. The next step was to prevent its passing on to future generations.

Davenport brought the idea to Mary Williamson Harriman, a wealthy woman, that eugenics was a better solution than charity for issues such as poverty. That view became common. Harriman funded the Eugenics Record Office, which Davenport ran and used to gather genetic information on the American population. His staff conducted research among various communities and institutions to develop theories. Those men and women then found places at universities where the ideas became popular. Davenport lectured across the country and argued that human genetic strains had caused poverty and crime, just as genetics had created descendants with attractive characteristics.

Americans, by and large, agreed with Davenport. Teddy Roosevelt commended him. Davenport encouraged government action to prevent parenthood among lower intelligence people through institutionalizing and sterilizing them. Such an action would protect America, he and his supporters said.

While genetic research at the time lent support to the idea that plants and livestock could improve through selective breeding, other experiments revealed a more complicated picture of how traits passed down to successive generations of plants and fruit flies. American biologist Thomas Hunt Morgan tested his theories on fruit flies and found that although some genes passed down through chromosomes as part of packages, the process wasn't entirely predictable. This finding led him to believe that eugenics had no part in shaping government policy and decision-making, and he left the eugenics movement.

Part of the problem with eugenics is that it was used to preserve hierarchies of race, class and religion. The sense of moral superiority higher groups had over lower socioeconomic communities was supported by arguments for selective breeding. According to their view, they were the ones who should reproduce while reproduction by others should be limited or eliminated. Along with that was the concern that those with lesser pedigrees were reproducing at a far faster clip and could supplant them simply by outnumbering the higher classes.

Madison Grant, an American eugenicist, argued in his tract, *The Passing of the Great Race: Or, The Racial Basis of European History*, that people of white European ancestry were superior to other groups. He discouraged mating with what he termed "inferior races."

The theory was later appropriated by the Nazis. Grant supported existing laws preventing interracial marriage and sex. He feared native-born Americans would reproduce with immigrants. He wanted to preserve the Nordic race by limiting immigration.

All this is connected to policies and views regarding birth control, abortion and sterilization.

Edward Ross, a famous sociologist at the time, who had coined the phrase "race suicide," also opposed birth control because he felt it broke down the bonds of marriage and promoted sex out of wedlock.

"Knowledge of birth control would lower the moral standards of the youth of this country," he told a reporter in 1922. "The chief obligation of marriage is procreation. Unfortunately, the tendency of today is to devote too much time to frivolous pleasure."

Curiously, Ross later said that the world nevertheless had to control its human population through some means. He felt that overpopulation led to war and misery.

Eugenicists often believed in the racial and cultural superiority of white Protestant Americans, and they feared higher reproductive rates in minority communities. The Protestant birth rate, particularly among white, U.S.-born women, declined in the late 1800s. Abortion and birth control were unpopular among Protestant white men because they saw those things as reproductive controls that disempowered white people by disproportionately limiting population growth among that group. Contemporary feminists have criticized President Theodore Roosevelt for racism and classism rooted in his opposition to "race suicide."

Chicago tolerated abortionists during the Teddy Roosevelt administration. The president of the Chicago Medical Society concluded at an AMA conference in 1908 that the medical profession and the public didn't want an aggressive campaign against criminal abortion. Medical experts who were called to testify against abortionists failed to appear, but they regularly testified in defense of accused abortionists. Jury selection was difficult for prosecutors because, in a group of 12 men, one of them had likely gotten a woman pregnant and had expressed interest in paying for an abortion.

Abortion attitudes shifted. As a result, magazines published letters and articles calling for liberalized abortion laws.

It was a changing world—with women calling for greater independence amid a transition from an agrarian to an industrial economy. This included an expanded role for women in social settings and changes in public attitudes about sex. While many abortions happened within marriages, many also occurred outside them. It was a situation that demanded visionary feminists—and that's precisely what America got next.

CHAPTER 2

An American Rebel

Margaret Sanger operated in a world where birth control information was considered obscene. Doctors refused to give people family-planning advice because of the Comstock laws.

"Women came to me and asked me what they could do," Sanger told CBS later in life. "Parents, mothers, fathers wondering what they would do so they wouldn't have to have as large families as their parents had. And I bumped up against this very arrogant, old-fashioned, stupid law, which had to be changed. But it was going to take a long time to change it. And I decided the best way to change it was to break it."

According to author James Reed, when Sanger moved to New York City before World War I, the poverty that the city's women endured left an imprint on her. The push for economic independence drove her advocacy in the decades ahead. Socialist political leader Eugene Debs inspired her. Police arrested her several times when she picketed for workers' rights in Hazleton, Pennsylvania. But she left her greatest mark on sexual matters.

In 1912, a young New York truck driver, Jake Sachs, came home to his wife, Sadie, on the Lower East Side. She had had an abortion that brought complications. Sanger and a doctor attended to her and helped her recuperate. Sanger carried water up three flights of stairs to help.

Sadie survived, but a few months later, Sanger returned to find her languishing from another abortion. Sadie died that time, which left Sanger in tears and made her wonder what would have happened had Sachs known about contraception.

Sanger later said it was the death of Sachs that made her rebel against social mores regarding birth control—a term she coined and popularized throughout her career.

Around then, birth control and abortion appeared in popular culture. In "Where Are My Children?"—a 1916 film—an actor portrays a district attorney who discovers that his wife had multiple abortions before his prosecution of an abortionist. The movie was an argument for why abortion and birth control were evil.

Sanger was undeterred and opened America's first birth control clinic on Oct. 16, 1916, in Brooklyn, New York. She couldn't recruit a licensed physician, but 45 women lined the sidewalk on its first day. Nine days later, a female police officer went undercover and paid 2 dollars for a pamphlet. Officers later arrived to seize the clinic's supplies. They jailed Sanger and her aide, Ethel Byrne.

A jury convicted them, and the judge sentenced both to 30 days in jail. Sanger's lawyer, Jonah Goldstein, appealed the decision. Though the appeals court upheld the convictions, New York's highest court ruled that the state's law banning contraception could not prevent a doctor from prescribing birth control to a married woman for whom it would prevent disease, which was defined broadly.

Sanger continued her work, and soon women returned for advice.

Sanger, in both speeches and letters, argued that abortion wouldn't be necessary if contraception were available to women of all socioeconomic backgrounds. In one lecture, she acknowledged the illegal abortion operations or rings that police had discovered. She said many who underwent abortion were married and had too many children.

"These women are in desperate circumstances," Sanger said. "The laws make it difficult for women in conditions of poverty to obtain contraceptive advice, and they turn upon the abortionist to whom these women appeal in despair."

In her seminal work *Woman and the New Race*, published in 1920, Sanger decried the use of abortion when contraceptives were available. That book called for the sexual liberation of women—and contraception was a central part of her argument. In film and in society, women could choose to embrace their sexuality largely because of Sanger's writing and speeches. The 1920s—with their flappers and speakeasies—laid the groundwork for the sexual revolution that came four decades later.

In 1921, Sanger wrote a pamphlet titled "Facts on Abortion and Legislation in Relation to Birth Control." She said birth control laws repressed women and that one to two million women a year had abortions in America. Most were married, according to a social scientist she quoted:

> *When society holds up its hands in horror at the "crime" of abortion, it forgets at whose door the first and principal responsibility for this practice rests. Does anyone imagine that a woman would submit to abortion if not denied the knowledge of scientific, effective contraceptives? Does anyone believe that physicians and midwives who perform abortions go from door to door soliciting patronage?*
>
> *The abortionist could not continue his practice for twenty-four hours if it were not for the fact that women come desperately begging for such operations. He could not stay out of jail a day if women did not so generously approve of his services as to hold his identity an open but seldom-betrayed secret.*

Sanger said that lawmakers should reform birth control laws:

> *The woman who goes to the abortionist's table is not a criminal but a martyr—a martyr to the bitter, unthinkable conditions brought about by the blindness of society at large. These conditions give her the choice between the surgeon's instruments and the sacrifice of what is highest and holiest in her—her aspiration to freedom, her desire to protect the children already hers. These conditions—not the woman—confront society with this question: Contraceptives or abortion— which shall it be?*

It's common to see anti-abortion activists describe Sanger as an intolerant eugenicist who educated the Ku Klux Klan about birth control. While she did speak to them—as she spoke to anyone who invited her to promote the use of birth control—she also worked directly with Black leaders such as W.E.B. Du Bois and Mary McLeod Bethune to spread information about birth control and reduce deaths among pregnant Black mothers. Bigoted eugenicists of the time focused on limiting access to birth control among wealthier white classes because they feared losing their status to minority groups reproducing at a higher rate. Sanger disagreed with that sentiment.

She criticized a eugenicist editorial in *American Medicine* that called for social Darwinism. Sanger didn't advocate for larger families among the rich. She did, however, believe in population control and felt the world was overpopulated; she thought birth control could address that. Sanger's views on birth control among African Americans were identical to those of Du Bois, who felt that only intelligent Black people should reproduce.

In July 2020, Planned Parenthood of Greater New York made the consequential decision to remove Margaret Sanger's name from its flagship Manhattan clinic. Leaders of the affiliate acknowledged that while Sanger had played a formative role in the birth control movement, her association with eugenics and discriminatory beliefs could not be ignored. The organization described the change as part of a larger reckoning with systemic racism, particularly in the wake of the George Floyd protests, and emphasized the importance of building trust with the Black and Latino communities it served. Board chair Karen Seltzer called the step "long overdue," framing it as both a symbolic and substantive move toward aligning the organization's mission with its present-day values.[2]

The announcement led to debates across the country. News outlets such as *Time* highlighted how the removal of Sanger's name reflected broader struggles over history, racial justice and the legacies of once-celebrated reformers. Planned Parenthood's statement did not deny Sanger's

2 Planned Parenthood of Greater New York. (2020, July 21). *Planned Parenthood of Greater New York Announces Intent to Remove Margaret Sanger's Name from NYC Health Center* [Press release]. Planned Parenthood. https://www.plannedparenthood.org/planned-parenthood-greater-new-york/about/news/planned-parenthood-of-greater-new-york-announces-intent-to-remove-margaret-sangers-name-from-nyc-health-center

pioneering role in reproductive rights, but it made clear that her contributions could not excuse her record of supporting ideas rooted in racial hierarchy. The decision was portrayed as an institutional acknowledgment that reproductive freedom could not be disentangled from the ongoing work of confronting racism.

Reaction to the move revealed the fault lines around Sanger's memory. Many racial justice advocates praised the announcement as a long-delayed recognition of the pain Sanger's legacy caused, particularly among communities of color. Staff members within the New York affiliate, who had been pressing for change, saw the decision as a victory that would strengthen their ability to connect authentically with patients and colleagues. Local leaders welcomed the step, describing it as a meaningful gesture toward equity in public health and reproductive services.[3]

At the same time, critics charged that Planned Parenthood was erasing history rather than contextualizing it. Some defenders of Sanger argued that her achievements in championing birth control deserved more weight than her missteps, while opponents of abortion rights seized on the decision as vindication of their long-standing criticisms. For them, the disavowal was proof that Planned Parenthood itself had finally conceded the validity of claims tying its origins to racism. The controversy ensured that the debate over Sanger's legacy—whether she should be remembered primarily as a pioneer or as a flawed figure implicated in harmful ideologies—would remain unsettled long after her name disappeared from the clinic facade.[4]

Alexis McGill Johnson, the current president of the Planned Parenthood Federation of America, criticized Margaret Sanger for her connection to white supremacist and eugenicist groups in an op-ed that appeared in *The New York Times* in April 2021. Johnson also said that Sanger focused on white womanhood.[5]

Johnson concluded that Sanger had harmed generations of women with her beliefs.

3 *The Journal News.* (2020, July 22). [Article on Planned Parenthood's removal of Sanger's name]. p. A9.
4 *The Buffalo News.* (2020, July 22). [Article on Planned Parenthood's removal of Sanger's name]. p. 4.
5 Johnson, Alexis McGill. "I'm the head of Planned Parenthood. We're done making excuses for our founder," *New York Times.* April 17, 2021. (Accessed via https://www.nytimes.com/2021/04/17/opinion/planned-parenthood-margaret-sanger.html on July 31, 2022)

Sanger wrote in her autobiography about her 1926 experience speaking to the women's branch of the Klan. Sanger's assistants accepted any invitation she received during that time in her effort to promote birth control. Sanger said it was the strangest experience she ever had and that she feared for her life. Unbeknownst to the Klan, Sanger had begun a birth control clinic in Harlem where Black doctors trained before treating the Black community, which had been denied care by white physicians. *The Pittsburgh Courier*, the leading Black newspaper at the time, said that Sanger was "one of many white persons who have done much constructive work in New York's celebrated Negro sector."

During the early part of Sanger's career, Americans had widely embraced eugenics. County fairs held "human stock" competitions, where judges determined who was of the best breed. Sanger wanted to tie her birth control advocacy to anything that would increase the chances it would be accepted. So she wrote *The Pivot of Civilization*, in which she criticized child labor and the need for charity as products of overpopulation and poverty resulting from parents having too many children. The book is problematic because of its ableist language, typical of the time, yet it remains the basis for much of the contemporary criticism today.[6]

Anne Finger, a prominent disability activist who has been heavily involved in the reproductive rights movement, explained why writing a complete and accurate account of Sanger's life is crucial.

"I don't think it can really be reconciled," Finger said. "I mean, I think we have to say, there was this movement, it was enormously important in women's lives, it was enormously important in children's lives.

"And it has this very mixed history, and I think to try and reconcile it means it's going to be somehow smoothed out and taken care of. And I think really what we have to do is to look at it and acknowledge it honestly."

It's important to realize eugenics permeated the culture in the 1920s. Movies like "Are You Fit to Marry?" perpetuated the theory. It became an almost religious belief to not breed with people deemed less fit. Eugenics became a household term. As time went on, genetic researchers

---

6 Alfred, Bruce. *Margaret Sanger.* Films Media Group. 2011.

continued to find flaws in eugenics theory. In 1926, Hermann Muller, who worked with Thomas Hunt Morgan, found that X-rays could cause mutations in fruit flies. Mueller criticized the eugenics theory because he felt that people couldn't accurately predict which genes were the superior traits.

Later in life, Sanger wrote "Love or Babies: Must Negro Mothers Choose," an article that appeared in *Negro Digest*. In it, Sanger said birth control would reduce mortality and disease among mothers and the babies that they delivered.[7]

Sanger's opinions have often been misrepresented. Quotes belonging to other people of her time have been attributed to her by anti-abortion writers. It's a method that has been used to discredit and misrepresent the historical legacy of Planned Parenthood and reproductive rights activists.

George Grant, perhaps the anti-abortion movement's most formidable writer, compared Sanger to Hitler, Mussolini and Stalin. Sanger did not, however, share the politics of any of them and was not aligned with any American groups that were. Sanger criticized Mussolini in 1938, for example, for his policies promoting population growth in Italy. She argued that countries with high birth rates were more likely to go to war—and she singled out Japan, Germany and Italy

"Excessive birth rates mean not only a few advantages for children but sow the seeds of war," she said at a world peace conference in New York.[8]

Sanger saved the life of Ernst Gräfenberg, a Jewish obstetrician imprisoned by the Nazis, by paying a ransom that led to his release from prison. She helped rescue other Jewish refugees from Nazi rule.[9]

In his book *Killer Angel: A Short Autobiography of Planned Parenthood's Founder Margaret Sanger*, Grant falsely attributes an objectionable line at a conference to Sanger. The Sixth International Neo-Malthusian and Birth Control Conference was held in 1926 by the American Birth Control League. Grant quotes the following passage:

---

7 Sanger, Margaret. "Love or Babies: Must Negro Mothers Choose," *Negro Digest*, August 1946. Pg. 3-8.
8 Mrs. Sanger Proposes Limitation of Babies as Antidote for War," Ashville Citizen-Times, May 23, 1938. Pg. 2. (Accessed via newspapers.com on May 8, 2022)
9 Grossman, Anita. *Reforming Sex: The German Movement for Birth Control and Abortion Reform.* Oxford University Press. 1997.

The dullard, the gawk, the numbskull, the simpleton, the weakling and the scatterbrain are amongst us in overshadowing numbers—intermarrying, breeding, inordinately prolific, literally threatening to overwhelm the world with their useless and terrifying get.[10]

Grant attributes the quote to "they," which gives the impression that it was either said in unison or issued as an official statement. On his website, he went further, directly attributing it to Sanger herself.

But in reality, the quote belongs to Max G. Schlapp, a doctor who was invited to speak at the conference, which also featured presenters who decried race prejudice and nationalism. While Sanger expressed ableism herself, this is an example of how historical misrepresentation can occur—whether accidentally or on purpose.[11]

In other interviews, Grant falsely claimed that Sanger was part of the occult, addicted to drugs, and a paid communist operative. He contended she was closely connected to anarchist groups that advocated assassinations.[12] There is no historical evidence that pro-choice researchers or women's historians have acknowledged that supports that portrayal.

The smear campaigns and historical revisionists notwithstanding, history tells a different story. Nonetheless, it's been difficult to portray Sanger accurately given the climate and decisions made recently by major leaders. I once attended a Zoom presentation led by a Black woman who spoke about Margaret Sanger and Planned Parenthood. In her view, the birth control movement was not a matter of reproductive autonomy but a form of genocide against Black people.

I had joined the group hosting the talk as part of my ongoing membership, which began when I published my book *Banished from Johnstown*—a history of the 1923 Rosedale Banishment, in which Black and Mexican residents of Johnstown, Pennsylvania, were forcibly expelled under threat of violence. That work connected me with

---

10 Grant, George. *Killer Angel: A Short Autobiography of Planned Parenthood's Founder Margaret Sanger,* Highland Books, Nashville. 1995. Pg. 95-105.

11 Sanger, Margaret. *The Sixth International Neo-Malthusian and Birth Control Conference: Volume 3, Medical and Eugenic Aspects of Birth Control,* New York, 1926. American Birth Control League. Pg. 129.

12 Parker, Kim. "The Legacy of Planned Parenthood," *Concerned Women,* June 1988. Pg. 3.

numerous social justice and civil rights organizations, leading to moments like this one, where history and current debates over race and reproductive rights collided.

During the presentation's Q&A, I tried to set the record straight about Sanger, offering historical context and challenging the idea that she had set out to exterminate Black communities. I asked a series of careful, well-researched questions but soon realized the limits of what I could accomplish in that space as a white man. My efforts were further undermined by the fact that Planned Parenthood itself had publicly distanced from Sanger, which only reinforced the speaker's framing.

Later, in a conversation with Dr. Willie Parker—an African American abortion provider who practiced for years in some of the most dangerous states in the Deep South, he told me, "You and I both know I can say things to them that you can't."

That observation reinforced my view that we need to involve more Black men and women in community outreach to groups like this so that opinions on PPFA and on Sanger can be shifted with greater credibility and impact.

The women's rights movement between the Declaration of Sentiments in 1848 and the passage of the 19th Amendment in 1920 focused primarily on two issues—voting rights and the prohibition of alcohol, which feminists believed was the root of many problems besetting American women, including marital rape and domestic abuse. After politicians granted women suffrage, they turned their attention to other issues, including reproductive freedom.

Mary Coffin Ware Dennett, a suffragist from Worcester, Massachusetts, also advocated repealing the Comstock Laws. She published a sex education pamphlet that soon became popular, titled *The Sex Side of Life: An Explanation for Young People*. It featured diagrams, proper medical terminology, and explanations of the effects of sex, both physiological and emotional. Dennett created it for her 14-year-old son because she found most educational materials about sex to be inadequate and shaming. At the time, such material was filled with euphemisms and vague explanations because it was considered obscene to discuss sex openly.

Her work was published in the *Medical Review of Reviews* in 1918. Dennett then issued the pamphlet to a wider audience. The YMCA distributed it, and it was used in public schools and at Union Theological Seminary, one of the most prominent Protestant seminaries in the United States.

Between 1918 and 1928, more than 35,000 copies were sold to individuals and institutions.

By 1922, the U.S. Post Office declared the pamphlet obscene and unmailable. Dennett approached several attorneys but ultimately chose Morris Ernst, one of the leading liberal legal minds in the country. Ernst believed that the law needed to be reshaped. Like many great lawyers, he was media-savvy and understood the role publicity played in swaying judges and juries.

Ernst took the case pro bono and corresponded with Dennett for several months. Later, a postal employee entrapped Dennett by requesting a pamphlet, and she was charged with violating the Comstock Act. The trial featured puritanical testimony on behalf of the government and scientific-based arguments for the defense. A jury convicted her, and she was fined $300.

The case dominated headlines across the nation. Generally, editorials saw the laws as archaic and unscientific. Eventually, the verdict was overturned by Judge Augustus Noble Hand, a respected liberal jurist, who said that material must be reviewed as a whole instead of in parts when judging its obscenity.

Sanger, along with Katharine Martha Houghton Hepburn, founded the American Birth Control League in 1921, which became Planned Parenthood in 1942. Houghton—known as Kit—was a leading feminist and the mother of actress Katharine Hepburn.

At the instigation of New York City Roman Catholic Archbishop Patrick Hayes, police removed a speaker from the stage and arrested Sanger at the League's first conference. The resulting publicity helped attract new members to the organization, which eventually had several state affiliates and a central office.

While Dennett's trial worked its way up the legal ladder, police raided Sanger's New York clinic. Ernst's defense of the clinic began a long relationship with Sanger, during which they developed the political and legal strategy to liberalize birth control laws nationwide. The case received massive press coverage. Five hundred spectators crowded into a small courtroom. Judge Abraham Rosenbluth ruled in favor of the clinic. Afterward, the number of birth control clinics in the country rose from 55 to 374 within eight years.

While birth control was the main focus at the time, abortion was always an underlying theme. Dr. Charles Flippin, an abortionist whom newspapers described as "notorious," worked in Nebraska. Journalists sensationalized his seven trials for criminal abortion between 1910 and 1926. As a Black man, he faced entrenched racism. He performed abortions for low-income women of all races. The disapproval wasn't universal: Three thousand people signed a petition supporting him when he appeared before the Nebraska State Department of Welfare to request reinstatement of his license.

Ruth Barnett, an Oregon woman known for draping herself in diamonds and furs, operated during that period. Author Rickie Solinger—a trailblazing feminist historian, writer and curator—described her as the "queen of abortionists in the Pacific Northwest." Barnett performed an estimated 40,000 procedures between 1918 and 1968. She never lost a patient. She cared for incest and rape victims, jilted girls, careless teenagers, unfaithful wives, battered women, perimenopausal women, exhausted mothers and mistresses. Barnett's practice was an open secret. She socialized with politicians, newspapermen, gamblers and pimps in her lavish house in the Southwest Hills.

While there were many reputable practitioners during this period, others were less so, and engaging their services could be risky. In Bangor, Maine, in 1925, the local newspaper reported the trial of Dr. Charles Edmunds, an abortionist who perforated a woman's uterus during the procedure. She later died of septic shock.

Similar sensational trials occurred throughout the country during the 1920s. A mistress of Mississippi Gov. Lee Russell sued him, claiming he was responsible for an illegal abortion. She contended that she could not work because of complications from it. The governor denied the accusations. There was a subsequent civil trial. An all-male jury cleared Russell.

Abortion was also a topic within literary circles. Ernest Hemingway wrote about it in his 1927 short story "Hills Like White Elephants." In the story, a man and woman discuss the operation. The dialogue is poignant:

> *"And you think then we'll be all right and be happy."*
>
> *"I know we will. You don't have to be afraid. I've known lots of people that have done it."*
>
> *"So have I," said the girl. "And afterward they were all so happy."*
>
> *"Well," the man said, "if you don't want to you don't have to. I wouldn't have you do it if you didn't want to. But I know it's perfectly simple."*
>
> *"And you really want to?"*
>
> *"I think it's the best thing to do. But I don't want you to do it if you don't really want to."*

William Faulkner explored the topic in *As I Lay Dying*, with Dewey Dell's character consumed by her need for an abortion. She ends up being coerced into sex with a pharmacist from whom she seeks an abortifacient. In a later work, *The Wild Palms*, one of Faulkner's characters dies from a botched abortion. Some scholars claimed Faulkner once procured an abortion for a woman he impregnated.

It made sense for both iconic writers to address the topic: abortion was widespread. Their novels resonated with readers who had dramatic, life-changing stories of their own. But the people who sought out abortionists often didn't fit the stereotype. During the Great Depression, married women obtained abortions more frequently than single women, primarily for economic reasons.

During the 1930s, notable abortion rights advocates emerged. Dr. William Robinson published *The Law Against Abortion: Its Perniciousness Demonstrated and Its Repeal Demanded* in 1934. He argued that the right to birth control extended to abortion and that abortion was a necessary evil in certain circumstances. Robinson believed the best way to eliminate abortion was to reduce the need for it by addressing its causes. He wanted to abolish the Comstock laws.

A. J. Rongy, a leading physician of that era, contended that the 2–3% of doctors in the 1930s who were abortionists had significantly reduced the procedure's risk through antiseptic and aseptic methods. Rongy argued it was cruel to force women to continue pregnancies resulting from rape or incest. Mental defectiveness was another circumstance in which Rongy said abortions should occur because the mother could not properly care for the child.

He cited financial hardship as a valid reason for abortion, noting the case of a widow impregnated before her husband's death, who had no means to support the child. He argued that limiting family growth for fathers unable to provide for their children would be beneficial. Some of Rongy's reasoning may seem outdated in an era when both parents often work, but his underlying rationale—financial planning and autonomy— still informs many people's decisions to end pregnancies.

It's fair to criticize Rongy because he argued on classist and ableist grounds, which was common then. He said leaders should limit reproduction among what he considered the criminal element of society. Rongy supported the *Buck v. Bell* Supreme Court decision, which permitted sterilization of people deemed mentally handicapped. He also characterized lower-class people as dirty.

Even as the Catholic Church resisted and demonized Sanger, she saw the potential to expand her influence by building alliances with other religious organizations. She wrote letters to religious leaders and sought opportunities to speak at churches and synagogues. She attended religious conventions annually. Ministers who supported birth control acted as delegates for her with other clergy and rabbis. As those leaders came around, so did their congregations.

The American Unitarian Association issued a resolution supporting birth control in 1930. In March 1931, the mainline Protestant Federal Council of Churches of Christ in America, which had 23 million members, issued a statement calling for the repeal of laws prohibiting the spread of birth control information. Father Charles Coughlin, a Catholic demagogue with a radio show—and a precursor to modern radio and television evangelists—lambasted the Protestant council, calling it "a surrender to the ideals of paganism."

Sanger appealed to many religious leaders because her message relied on concrete, observable examples of suffering. It evoked empathy through real-world stories rather than abstract theology. She called for practical solutions instead of doctrinal arguments. While Catholics took a staunchly anti-abortion stance, other religions held more progressive or moderate positions on whether it should be permitted. American rabbis and Jewish doctors framed arguments for choice around protecting women's lives, promoting social welfare and aiding the poor. Protestants occupied a middle ground between prevailing Jewish and Catholic views.

At the beginning of the 1930s, Margaret Sanger established the National Committee on Federal Legislation for Birth Control to lobby Congress to repeal the Comstock laws at the national level. When that failed, she declared, "Men are men, and senators are cowards."

Ernst advised her to seek reinterpretation rather than repeal, leading to the strategy of securing reproductive rights through court challenges. The first victory came when Sanger attempted to import contraceptive devices and literature from Japan, in violation of postal laws forbidding it.

Dr. Sakae Koyoma of Osaka, Japan, had sent a pessary—or diaphragm—to Sanger for testing at her clinic. Customs officials seized it. Ernst told them to return the devices to Japan because he knew he would face a tougher verdict if Sanger were the plaintiff. And then, he arranged for the devices to be sent to Dr. Hannah Stone, a physician at the clinic.

United States v. One Package of Japanese Pessaries was a landmark case that advanced reproductive rights. It was heard in 1936 by District Court Judge Grover Muscowitz, who ruled that a doctor's intent mattered, and allowed the use of contraceptives for reasons beyond preventing pregnancy.

The government appealed. Ernst enlisted Harriet Pilpel, one of his associates, who later became one of the most influential lawyers in the birth control movement. Pilpel surpassed her mentor, laying the groundwork for legalization of birth control and, eventually, for the right to abortion. She, in turn, mentored younger generations of lawyers, including the late Supreme Court Justice Ruth Bader Ginsburg, who built on Pilpel's work for gender equality long before joining the bench.

The appeal was heard by a three-judge panel of the Court of Appeals—Learned Hand, Augustus Hand, and Thomas Swan. The appellate court upheld the ruling. Ernst and Pilpel called Augustus Hand's opinion the "Bill of Rights" of birth control.

The attorney general declined to appeal further. The customs office subsequently issued a memo stating that imported contraceptive devices would not be detained if the consignee was a reputable physician seeking to protect a patient's health.

The decision effectively allowed doctors to prescribe and distribute birth control whenever they believed pregnancy would endanger a woman's health. Public-opinion polling showed that most Americans believed birth control should be legal and accessible to married couples.

The victory wasn't total. While the verdict essentially nullified federal laws about birth control, regulations and rules regarding it remained on the books in several states. Until the 1960s, many state and federal judges upheld those rules.

Ernst's and Pilpel's cases, over time, established the legal precedents used in arguments for the right to privacy, resulting in the *Griswold* decision of the Supreme Court, which was the basis for *Roe v. Wade* and subsequent jurisprudence that favored abortion rights. As the reader will see in later chapters, Comstock laws and those dealing with the mailing of abortifacients have come into play again, as contemporary anti-abortion legal scholars have pointed out they were never repealed. Supreme Court decisions eventually nullified most of them. But that nullification itself is now gone as the *Roe v. Wade* precedent was overturned.

While the term "abortion ring" may seem outdated now, it accurately describes the networks through which many women obtained abortions before *Roe v. Wade*. Newspapers in the early 20th century revealed that powerful figures—and often members of organized crime syndicates—profited from abortion services. Since these groups also traded in other vices like prostitution, they needed ways to terminate pregnancies. As word spread, people unaffiliated with their criminal enterprises but in need of abortions likely sought them out through word of mouth.

In 1941, the Kings County district attorney in Brooklyn, New York, convened a grand jury to investigate abortion rings. The testimony revealed the general structure of an abortionist's practice. The abortionist typically had a well-paid secretary who screened patients and set prices based on how much she thought clients could afford, judging by their attire and demeanor. A typical abortion ring also had a business agent who managed salaries, bribes and split fees. Nurses assisted abortionists, and accomplices helped obscure the practice's details. Pharmacists, taxi drivers and family members referred patients. Women were often taken to meeting places blindfolded before being escorted to the abortionist, so they couldn't later identify the location if police made arrests.

A 1935 article in *Forum Magazine* reported that between 100,000 and 250,000 women a year underwent illegal abortions in New York City. While some respectable doctors performed therapeutic abortions, others profited by referring women to less reputable midwives and back-alley abortionists, often in exchange for half the fee. Bribes to police were common.

Law-enforcement tactics were inconsistent. Some officers participated in shakedowns, while others genuinely sought to dismantle abortion rings. Corrupt detectives often used decoys—pregnant women given cash to pose as patients. Once the abortionist accepted payment, detectives would burst in, demanding money to avoid arrest.

Other officers conducted legitimate investigations. They typically sent a woman and an undercover officer posing as a pregnant couple. They would let the abortionist begin preparations before making an arrest. But actual trials with witnesses were rare. Prosecutors called on Charles G. Norris, New York's first appointed chief medical examiner and an expert in forensic toxicology, to testify only once in 31 years. That case involved a woman whose body was found in a politically connected physician's office in the Lower East Side. Norris discovered her uterus had been perforated, but despite the evidence, the jury acquitted the doctor.

Politicians at the federal level largely avoided the issue. President Franklin Delano Roosevelt's staff occasionally discussed abortion, but he mostly declined to engage. Catholic prelates criticized Eleanor Roosevelt for her pro-choice views.

In 1935, the White House hosted a conference on abortion and its dangers. The president commissioned Dr. Frederick Taussig, a gynecologist, to study the problem. In his report, Taussig estimated that the United States had 681,000 abortions annually, resulting in 8,179 deaths. He urged the president and lawmakers to legalize abortion as Russia had done the previous decade. Taussig proposed allowing abortions performed by licensed practitioners in hospitals and argued for broad discretion when the fetus was not viable outside the womb.

In 1936, Sanger visited Roosevelt at his home in Hyde Park with a delegation of women, as war loomed and authoritarian leaders abroad encouraged higher birth rates among women. Neo-Malthusians like Sanger believed population control could reduce the likelihood of fascism and conflict.

"How can the country avoid war without a population policy?" Sanger asked.

The president waved Sanger off, a cigarette in his hand.

"Don't worry, neighbor," Roosevelt said. "I'll get an answer for you."

Lana Phelan, who would later become a prominent abortion rights activist, recounted her experience during the Great Depression in the documentary "When Abortion Was Illegal: Untold Stories." She asked a co-worker at the Walgreen Drug Store where she worked whether there was someone who could give her an abortion. She couldn't even say the word because it was so stigmatized—but the woman knew. She referred Lana to an abortionist who charged $50. Phelan sold everything she owned to raise the money. The abortionist used a piece of slippery-elm bark, which she inserted into her uterus. The abortionist told her it would swell and that she would develop a fever. Two days later, Phelan was in such pain that she returned to the shack where the woman lived. The abortionist held her and said, "Did you think it would be so easy to be a woman?"

Abortion soon made world headlines after a sensational case in London. One evening, a 14-year-old girl named Nellie Hales was walking with two friends past the Horse Guards when one of the guardsmen invited her inside to see "a horse with a green tail." The teenager foolishly went in. Guardsmen stripped off her clothes and held her down. They raped her twice.

Afterward, her mother took her to a Catholic hospital, where a doctor refused to perform an abortion and told her that the unborn fetus might one day be a prime minister. Desperate, she wrote to Dr. Joan Malleson, who worked at St. Mary's Hospital and belonged to the Abortion Law Reform Association—England's only pro-choice organization at the time. Malleson brought the case to Dr. Aleck Bourne, a respected obstetrician and gynecologist, and asked him to admit the girl to his ward at St. Mary's. In a letter to Bourne, Malleson noted that the girl's parents did not know a respectable abortionist. Bourne replied that he had no hesitation in performing the procedure.

In his autobiography *A Doctor's Creed: The Memoirs of a Gynecologist*, Bourne wrote that he kept the girl in bed for eight days. When he examined her for infection from the rape, she wept. Bourne decided she needed relief. There were no complications from the abortion.

Bourne then invited prosecution, asking the attorney general to act against him.

About eight hours later, two police officers came to the hospital to see him. They told him the operation should not have been done and that they wanted the girl to testify against the guardsmen. Bourne informed them he had already performed it.

England's abortion law at the time, dating to 1809 and incorporated into the Criminal Law Amendment Act of 1861, prescribed life imprisonment for performing an abortion illegally.

Bourne was committed for trial in the Central Criminal Court. Reporters and journalists harangued him until the proceedings began about a month later in Courtroom No. 1 at Old Bailey. Letters arrived from all over the country, offering both praise and condemnation.

The attorney general, Donald Somervell, argued that doctors could justify an abortion only to preserve the mother's life and that mental health was not a valid reason. The judge instructed the jury on English abortion law, noting that lawyers and judges had never considered whether a doctor could terminate a pregnancy for mental health reasons. That connection—between a woman's life and her mental health—formed Bourne's defense. The vast majority of medical experts at the trial, known as *Rex v. Bourne*, testified that the operation was justifiable under those circumstances.

According to records at the National Archives, Bourne's barristers contended that "preserving life" must include preserving health in all its aspects.

In his closing argument, Somervell emphasized that the law was based on the sacredness of human life and that there was a fundamental difference between preserving life and preserving health. He argued that mental health did not justify termination.

Judge Malcolm Martin Macnaghten disagreed.

"If the doctor is of the opinion, on reasonable grounds and on adequate knowledge, that the probable consequences of the continuation of the pregnancy would indeed make the woman a physical or mental wreck, then he operates, in that honest belief, for the purpose of preserving the life of the mother," the judge said.

The jury deliberated only 40 minutes before returning a verdict of not guilty. Bourne's acquittal led to changes in legal interpretation and gave abortion rights advocates around the world a concrete precedent for mental health exceptions.

In recent years, I have been adapting the Aleck Bourne story into both a stage play and a screenplay, exploring the moral, medical and legal dimensions of one of the most consequential abortion trials in modern history. The play dramatizes the courage of Dr. Joan Malleson, the compassion of Dr. Bourne, and the plight of Nellie Hales, whose case reshaped British abortion law in 1938.

To develop the project, I have worked with London Playwrights, a creative organization that supports emerging and established dramatists in refining structure, dialogue and character through workshops and mentorship. This collaboration has allowed me to bring the historical record to life on stage, weaving archival research and testimony into a human narrative that examines conscience, autonomy and justice in a society on the brink of change. It has yet to be staged or produced into a movie.

The British government formed a committee to study the issue after the trial. Newspapers throughout the country editorialized in favor of liberalized abortion laws. The effort might have gained more traction if the impending war with Nazi Germany had not diverted national attention. Still, reformers resumed their work after the war.

The Abortion Law Reform Association (ALRA) lobbied Parliament for reform. Although the trial and its aftermath dominated global headlines, Britain did not change its abortion laws until 1967, when Parliament legalized the procedure by a registered practitioner to protect the life or health of the mother or in cases of fetal abnormality. The timing coincided with growing activism in the United States. As so often in the history of abortion rights, international developments reshaped the American feminist narrative.

In recent years, British prosecutors have charged women for taking abortion pills outside the strict regulations of the 1967 Act. Detectives have gathered evidence from online orders and clinic records—more than 100 such cases. Activists urged Parliament to amend the law following the prosecution and acquittal of Nicola Packer, a 45-year-old who self-managed an abortion after receiving medication via telehealth. In June 2025, Members of Parliament amended the law: Women can no longer be prosecuted for self-managed abortions.

CHAPTER 3

Headline News

A Chicago squad car patrolled the city on the first day of February 1941. A dispatcher told them that a woman at 801 Drexel Square needed help. When they arrived, they found a woman named Jacqueline Circle in distress. She told them that she had paid $50 for an illegal abortion and had suffered complications. Paramedics took her to Chicago Hospital, where doctors confirmed it. The police set out to arrest the people responsible. Their investigation led to Ada Martin.

Martin, who had been in the abortion business for 25 years, had helped 18,000 women obtain abortions between 1932 and 1941. Records indicated that the ring brought in millions of dollars.

Martin operated one of Chicago's most active underground abortion clinics in the early 1940s, though she was not an abortionist herself. After acquiring the clinic from Dr. Josephine Gabler, Martin became its primary organizer. She managed scheduling, payments and patient intake while coordinating with physicians—most notably Dr. Henry J. Millstone—who performed the procedures. Martin enforced strict privacy protocols, sometimes blindfolding patients and using aliases to protect both clients and staff.

Though not medically trained, Martin played an essential role. She handled logistics, referrals and police payoffs, becoming the clinic's public face. Arrested during police raids in 1940 and 1941, she avoided conviction after courts ruled key evidence inadmissible. Martin's case illustrates how nonmedical actors played vital roles in abortion access during an era of widespread criminalization.[13]

Doctors, pharmacists and beauty-shop operators from southern Wisconsin, northeastern Illinois, Indiana and southwestern Michigan referred women to her. The ring charged patients whatever they could afford. They kept their books in code. Unethical doctors had founded the abortion ring nearly a quarter century earlier. The leaders quashed any complaints that reached law enforcement through bribery.

A few days later, 18 officers stormed Martin's office. They moved couches and tables and went through all the cupboards. Officers drilled through the iron door of a vault. They seized books, records and papers containing the names of women who had received abortions.

Sex, murder and corruption were all central to Ada Martin's trial, which became the climax of a story that included two suicides, the suspension of a detective and the dismissal of two assistant state attorneys. The prosecution was part of the state's effort to clean up the abortion racket. Martin warned that she would take down public officials with her if they imprisoned her.

The judge ruled that the officers had acted without a search warrant, rendering the evidence inadmissible. But the testimony of witnesses found because of the search was allowed against Martin and her co-defendant, Josephine Kudor, who served as her receptionist.

Two months later, Daniel Moriarty, an officer from Cook County, entered Martin's home on Lake Park Avenue. Martin had paid Moriarty for years to quash criminal prosecutions against her. Moriarty wanted to silence Martin before she could expose the bribery and public corruption involving elected officials. He carried a loaded revolver. When he met the maid, he said he wanted to see Martin. The woman told him she was asleep.

---

13 Reagan, L. J. (1997). *When abortion was a crime: Women, medicine, and law in the United States, 1867–1973*. University of California Press.
Retrieved from https://publishing.cdlib.org/ucpressebooks/view?docId=ft967nb5z5; Indiana Historical Bureau. (2022, July 15). *Chicago's Underground Abortion Clinics and the Ada Martin Case. Indiana History Blog.*
Retrieved from https://blog.history.in.gov/tag/ada-martin

"I'll deliver my own message," Moriarty said, pushing past her.

He ran upstairs and burst into Martin's bedroom. Moriarty tossed $3,000 on the bed.

"This is the end of this dirty business," he muttered before emptying the gun into the woman sleeping there.

He had mistaken the woman's daughter for Ada, whom he wanted to murder.

Ada saw her daughter on the floor.

"Mother, I am shot," Jennie said.

"Morry, you shot Jennie," Martin told Moriarty.

Martin's husband confronted Moriarty, who beat him over the head with the revolver and attempted to shoot himself. The gun jammed, and Moriarty fled.

Jennie later died at Chicago Hospital.

Around the same time, Dr. Henry Millstone, a 44-year-old abortionist associated with the ring, committed suicide, leaving behind a note detailing his involvement.

As law enforcement detained Martin and her husband, they ransacked her house—searching dresser drawers and private compartments. They took seven envelopes containing the names and addresses of witnesses.

At the trial, Martin's attorneys argued that police had illegally gathered evidence. A jury convicted her in April 1942. The judge sentenced Martin and Kudor to one to five years in prison. The state supreme court overturned the verdict in November, agreeing with Martin's attorney's argument that the evidence had been unlawfully obtained. The court granted her a new trial. Prosecutors declined to retry the case. Martin died of a heart attack in 1946. Moriarty died in prison that same year.

Police raids on abortion rings were common in Chicago in the 1940s. To make arrests, officers had to catch women and abortionists in the act. To bolster their cases, they seized operating equipment and medical logs listing patients' names, then threatened to expose those women to newspapers unless they cooperated.

Until the late 1930s, most trials lacked the testimony of women who had undergone abortions. In earlier decades, many had died from infection or perforated uteruses. But advances in medicine allowed more women to survive.

In Meyersdale, Pennsylvania, 18-year-old Viola Lenhart sought an abortion from two men in 1939. She was hospitalized with complications but eventually testified against her abortionist and his accomplice. When the case was heard before the local magistrate, more than 200 people crowded in to watch. The judge sentenced the men to between one and a half and seven years in prison. The punishment equated to the sentence for malpractice or manslaughter. No higher court had recognized fetal personhood in American history—abortion was not legally considered murder.

Media coverage during World War II and the years immediately afterward sensationalized criminal abortion. An article in the Jan. 22, 1944, edition of *Collier's* magazine described the procedure's prevalence. Its lead illustration depicted an abortion doctor as the Grim Reaper, hovering in darkness before a woman. The article highlighted the dangers of back-alley abortions and the high rates of maternal deaths, injuries and infections.

Around that time, medical professionals adjusted their approach to reproductive care. Alan Guttmacher, a birth control expert, pushed for hospital committees to approve or deny therapeutic abortions. Religious organizations offered little opposition.

Guttmacher's interest in birth control had begun in the 1930s, when he practiced obstetrics in Baltimore. He believed that every woman had a basic right to decide whether to have a child and that poor women deserved the same access to contraception as the wealthy. He felt abortions should be a decision between a woman and her doctor. Guttmacher became one of the preeminent leaders of the reproductive rights movement. Some viewed him as an evangelist. He traveled widely—including to Africa, where he distributed contraceptives—and raised money for clinics in Pakistan. Predictably, he was condemned by Catholic leaders. Even within the birth control movement, some found him egotistical but admitted he was persuasive; his folksy demeanor helped win support.

By the late 1940s, one in three pregnancies ended in abortion. A third of those were therapeutic or spontaneous miscarriages, but the rest were self-induced or illegal. The Food and Drug Administration (FDA) campaigned against abortifacients, investigating 60 manufacturers in a multimillion-dollar market. Ninety percent of all illegal abortions at the time were performed on married women between the ages of 25 and 35.

The medications used varied widely, containing ingredients from ergot to quinine. Doctors frequently admitted women to hospitals for poisoning caused by these drugs. Merz & Company, a corporation based in Frankfurt, Germany, introduced an abortion paste to the United States that Germany had banned because it had killed or disabled so many. Within months of its introduction in New Jersey, it sold $150,000 worth—used by abortionists in place of curettes because it left no evidence.

In the 1950s, the forces driving McCarthyism—named for Sen. Joseph McCarthy of Wisconsin, who led a witch hunt against alleged communists—portrayed abortion as subversive. Hospitals continued to establish the kinds of abortion committees Guttmacher had advocated in the 1940s. Mental health was a frequent consideration, and psychiatrists often served on these committees.

It remained difficult to secure approval. Even threats of suicide often failed to persuade hospital boards. Physical health was another criterion, but this required multiple physicians to confirm necessity. Some states required police certification of a sexual-assault report before an abortion could be authorized.

Most women approved for abortions were longtime patients of the doctors involved. They also needed the financial means to cover both the procedure and the lengthy approval process. Only a small minority were public-ward patients; most were privately treated.

The American Law Institute (ALI) studied abortion during the late 1950s, developing guidance for state legislatures on criminal reform. This resulted in the Model Penal Code, released in 1962, which recommended legalizing abortion in cases of severe fetal abnormalities or when the mother's physical or mental health was at risk. The code also recognized rape, incest and other criminal sexual acts as potential grounds for legal abortion.

Dangerous abortions affected women across ethnic groups. In 1951, a judge sentenced Dr. Cyril Babb, a Harlem physician, to four years in Sing Sing Prison after he accidentally removed several feet of a woman's intestines during an abortion. Babb earned roughly $25,000 annually from his practice—equivalent to about $258,000 today. *Ebony* magazine ran a January 1951 story about Black women who died from botched abortions. Black abortionists practiced throughout the country.

Around that time, Sanger and Katharine McCormick met Gregory Pincus, who was researching an oral contraceptive. Sanger had dreamed of such a pill for years, and Pincus needed both funding and test subjects. He began clinical trials for Enovid—the first birth control pill—in Puerto Rico, recruiting poor women desperate for family planning. Participants were not told they were part of an experiment. Delia Mestre, a Puerto Rican participant, later criticized the doctors for conducting the trials in secrecy. Anti-abortion critics of Sanger have cited the experiments as evidence against her and Planned Parenthood's legacy. Aside from funding and supporting Pincus, she did not oversee the research or design the trials.

Pincus eventually developed an effective pill that helped spark the sexual revolution, making family planning a practical reality for millions of women. The mixed legacy—unethical testing methods versus transformative social progress—remains a difficult issue for reproductive rights scholars to reconcile.

The Planned Parenthood Federation of America (PPFA) hosted a conference on abortion-law reform in New York in 1958. Panelists described abortion as both a social and human problem as well as a legal and medical one. Milton Helpern, New York City's chief medical examiner, spoke about performing autopsies on women who had died from criminal abortions. Many cases went before grand juries, which often rejected indictments due to lack of evidence. This inability to prosecute successfully created an environment that encouraged illegal abortions, as providers knew they could operate with impunity.

Another panelist noted that abortion costs were inflated because the price of doing business included bribes to police, district attorneys and judges to avoid arrest and prosecution. There were also numerous accessories—parents, siblings, boyfriends and husbands—who were often aware of a woman's plans and could be charged as accomplices. That reality discouraged many prosecutors. As a result, investigators tended to focus on large abortion rings and a few high-profile providers.

Helpern described the coroner's role as that of a fact-finder. He examined perforated uteruses and foreign objects found inside women who had died. The causes of death had evolved over his career: Once dominated by infection and tetanus, they now more often involved gas gangrene, anesthetic complications, hemorrhage or shock. Some women died after corrosive substances were inserted into their cervixes. By the mid-1950s, Helpern noted, deaths from illegal abortion had dropped dramatically compared with 15 years earlier.

In 1953, the Institute of Sex Research, led by Alfred Kinsey, surveyed 5,293 white women and 572 Black women about pregnancy, birth and abortion. The prevalence of illegal and medically dubious abortion was difficult to gauge. While estimates ranged from 500,000 to one million, statisticians like Kinsey emphasized that reliable data were nearly impossible to obtain because of abortion's criminal status. Most people were not forthcoming, given the stigma and legal risk. Kinsey argued that statistics from police departments and state agencies were unreliable and that self-reported surveys offered a truer picture. He studied abortion partly to determine whether its incidence was higher within specific ethnic communities.

The Mechanics

Among African Americans, respondents reported attempting abortions with water containing a rusty nail, tansy tea, ginger tea, horseradish, turpentine, bitters, whiskey and bluing.

In Detroit, Dr. Edgar Keemer began performing abortions in 1937. A Black physician who had marched with Dr. Martin Luther King Jr., Keemer performed more than 30,000 abortions before his arrest in the late 1950s. He used a thick, foamy medication resembling soap. If a patient required hospitalization, Keemer admitted her under another doctor's name. He served three years in prison. Keemer championed abortion access for Black and poor women because he believed they lacked the options available to wealthier patients.

Ruby Caril, a Black woman who had migrated to Detroit from Georgia, sought Keemer's care. She spoke about her experience in the documentary "Back-Alley Detroit: Abortion Before *Roe v. Wade*."

"I'd tell my girlfriend, and she'd tell her girlfriend," Caril said. "Look, he was always busy."

The *Saturday Evening Post* launched a major investigation into the abortion racket in May 1961, beginning with the case of Brenda Blonder, a pregnant 16-year-old from Beverly Hills who had eloped. Blonder's mother had contacted a nurse, who referred them to a doctor. The procedure cost $650.

Brenda died. Edgar Schrater, a real estate salesman posing as a doctor, had injected her with too much anesthetic. He drove her body to a hospital, dumped it on the lawn, and phoned to report it. Schrater was later convicted of involuntary manslaughter.

At the time, the Los Angeles district attorney prosecuted fewer than a dozen abortion-related homicides each year. He told the *Saturday Evening Post* that few cases succeeded because of the difficulty of proving intent and causation.

In the early 1960s, Los Angeles detectives ran a sting operation targeting Frank Rollins, known as "Doctor Parker." Police referred to abortionists like him as "mechanics," slang for untrained abortion providers. Most abortionists were not physicians—they might be bartenders, aircraft technicians or real estate agents who saw the work as lucrative. They paid kickbacks to restaurant workers, drugstore clerks and hairdressers who referred patients.

The *Saturday Evening Post* claimed that criminal abortion was the third-largest racket in the United States at the time. Police told reporters that a few abortionists were licensed doctors who began by helping a friend and, through word of mouth, built profitable practices.

Journalist John Bartlow Martin interviewed a 50-year-old abortionist from Newark who described his career. The man had been jailed once but had studied gynecological surgery before his imprisonment. After his release, he moved to Chicago, where a nurse began referring patients to him. He performed four abortions a week, charging $300 each, and split the proceeds with the nurse. Most of his patients were married—some from high society, others showgirls. He perforated one woman's uterus and bowel during a botched procedure and was arrested.

"It's a history of someone well-intentioned that's gone wrong," the abortionist told Martin. "I'm classified as a criminal now, but it doesn't seem possible to me. I never had any criminal intent. I never had the reputation of cheating my patients. I always tried to be considerate of humanity."

When an ethical surgeon performed an abortion in that era, it cost as little as $75 to $125. Criminal abortionists, however, charged up to $2,000—whatever they thought a woman could afford. The average fee in Chicago was $400–$500. In Los Angeles, a midwife might charge $25, a male nurse $100 and a doctor $500. Some abortionists earned as much as half a million dollars a year.

Even as journalists and politicians condemned illegal abortionists, many respected physicians and psychiatrists advocated expanding access in safe, sanitary settings. In the early 1960s, the number of therapeutic abortions for psychiatric reasons rose sharply, the most common justification being the prevention of suicide.

At the time, abortion was permitted only when the mother's life was at risk. Dr. Jerome Kummer, a Santa Monica psychiatrist, told Martin he believed abortion was warranted if a woman was mentally ill enough to require institutionalization. Kummer and Zad Leavy, a Los Angeles deputy district attorney, advocated creating consultation centers where social workers could counsel women about adoption and contraception.

Some hospitals were more permissive than others. Margaret Hague Maternity Hospital, a Catholic facility in Jersey City, performed only eight therapeutic abortions out of 150,000 deliveries in 1961. In contrast, Mount Sinai Hospital in New York City performed one for every 174 pregnancies, while 26 California hospitals averaged one for every 418.

Many deaths in the early 1960s resulted from abortions, though they were often recorded under other causes. The Los Angeles County Medical Association worked aggressively to drive abortionists out of the city.

In 1953, the California Legislature passed a law granting minors the same access to reproductive care as adults—the first such law in the nation. It allowed minors to consent to treatment without parental approval, a precedent that became a flashpoint in later debates between abortion rights and anti-abortion advocates.

For those who had to seek abortion care, the memories of the complications could be difficult to recall.

In 1958, Mary Litman became pregnant by a man she couldn't marry. She shared her story decades later on NPR. Litman, 20 years old at the time, came from a large family in Pittsburgh, where she worked for a major corporation. She couldn't return to her job as an unwed pregnant woman, and she didn't want to burden her parents financially. Her partner told her there was a "safe" abortionist in Youngstown, Ohio— "where all the guys took their girlfriends."

It was a ramshackle house in an alley. People gambled in the front room. Litman left her two companions and entered a room where an old man stood beside a table under a wall calendar from the year of her birth.

"So much of it is a surrealistic experience," she told NPR. "I was so very frightened. I'm not sure where reality left off, because I don't remember anything. I don't remember the man touching me."

Litman and her friends drove back to Pittsburgh. Her roommate, Leigh, stayed with her through the pain and hemorrhaging. Leigh urged her to go to a hospital, but Mary refused, fearing arrest for criminal abortion.

The hemorrhaging stopped, but she developed a severe infection that produced a strong odor. A doctor admitted her to the hospital, where physicians discovered she had undergone an abortion.

"I thought, you break the law, you go to jail, period," Litman told the host. "So, I went on with my life, sort of pushing it back. I never told anyone except my roommate. I got married in 1961 and tried for years to get pregnant but never could."

Though the illegal operation had left her infertile, Litman spent the rest of her life fighting for safe, legal abortion.

"It's unbelievable how brave women are," she said. "When people ask me whether the anti-choice people in front of our clinic make any woman change her mind, I say, 'Absolutely not. Women used to risk their lives to terminate an unplanned pregnancy. They would walk over the backs of those anti-choice protestors if they had to.'"

Karen Mulhauser became pregnant in 1962 at age 19. Even though her parents were supportive, she felt ashamed to tell them. So she took a knitting needle and self-induced a miscarriage. But when she reached the Boston bus station to return to college, she fainted and collapsed in a pool of blood.

"When I woke up and was conscious again, I was in an office and I felt okay," Mulhauser said. "I felt embarrassed. I think everyone knew what had happened. And I asked if I could clean up and go."

They persuaded her to stay. Mulhauser later said she was grateful for the care she received—and for surviving without infection or long-term complications.

"It obviously helped shape who I became for the rest of my life," said Mulhauser, who went on to become a prominent figure in the abortion rights movement for the next 60 years.

Mulhauser wasn't alone in joining the burgeoning movement. Sherri Chessen's case had helped ignite a new wave of feminism, galvanizing both men and women to fight for safe and legal abortion. Even within law enforcement, many officers, coroners and prosecutors no longer saw much justification for continued criminalization.

There are lots of stories. Here are a few:

Retired Baltimore Police Lieutenant Gary Woodcock saw firsthand how the criminal abortion racket endangered women's lives. Raised a devout Catholic, Woodcock later became a strong supporter of abortion rights. He recounted his experience in a 2018 letter to the editor of the *Tampa Bay Times*.[14]

Maryland General Hospital fell within his assigned foot-patrol area. The facility served poor neighborhoods to the west, an avant-garde community to the east and a wealthy district to the north. Downtown lay to the south.

In 1959, Woodcock received a call to respond to an injured woman. When he arrived, a car was parked in front of the emergency-room entrance with its rear passenger door open. A small pool of blood stained the pavement and more soaked the backseat. He followed the trail into the treatment room, where blood covered the floor, the doctor and three nurses. Woodcock thought the patient had been gutted.

He later learned that the bleeding had resulted from an abortion. He notified the abortion squad, a specialized unit within the department that investigated abortion rackets.

Abortion squads had informants everywhere. Emergency-room staff were required to report abortions. Catholic Church officials shared information. Parents reported their daughters. Priests sometimes violated the confidentiality of confession to alert police.

Once investigators identified an abortionist, they searched for physical evidence—sometimes sifting through garbage and, on occasion, discovering a discarded fetus.

Woodcock later testified in court.

"The abortion had been performed literally *in a back alley*—in the back seat of a car under the bright security lights of a warehouse," he said in the editorial.

The abortionist was a former midwife who had lost her license for alcoholism and malpractice. She had nicked a vein while removing the fetus and couldn't stop the bleeding. The young woman had wanted to end her pregnancy so she could enjoy Christmas.

When women were hospitalized, they were often reluctant to tell doctors the truth, fearing arrest or exposure. That silence frequently led to misdiagnosis and fatal complications.

---

14 Woodcock, G. (2018, July 11). *This Is What Back-Alley Abortions Were Really Like* [Column]. *Tampa Bay Times*. Retrieved from https://www.tampabay.com/opinion/columns/Column-This-is-what-back-alley-abortions-were-really-like_169865016/

Dr. Cyril Wecht, a renowned coroner and forensic pathologist from Pittsburgh who passed away in 2024, performed multiple autopsies on women who had died after illegal abortions.

"I don't know if it shaped my views on abortion, but it certainly strengthened them," Wecht said. "Seeing a woman on the autopsy table who tried to abort herself with a coat hanger or by taking some strong stuff—yes, that undoubtedly deepened my conviction intellectually and emotionally."

When I interviewed Dr. Wecht, he described performing four such examinations over his career. These included women who had tried to terminate pregnancies with dangerous self-inflicted methods—such as using a coat hanger or ingesting toxic chemicals—and another who had died after a botched procedure by an unqualified practitioner.

These tragedies underscored for Wecht the dire consequences of restricting access to safe abortion care. He spoke with both professional precision and personal conviction about their significance. His perspective, shaped by decades of medical-legal experience, was rooted in the realities he witnessed firsthand in the morgue.

It was Wecht who first set me on the path of researching abortion in depth. In 2018, as Justice Anthony Kennedy announced his retirement from the Supreme Court—a moment many feared would shift the balance on abortion rights—I approached Wecht about writing a story for a local Pittsburgh alt-weekly.

I hoped to connect his autopsy work to the modern political and legal climate surrounding abortion. Despite my efforts, the piece proved difficult to place. When I told Wecht I was considering expanding the topic into a book, he encouraged me and opened his archive to me—a collection that became the foundation of my research.

Wecht had a lifelong habit of reading five newspapers a day and clipping stories that interested him, which he stored in organized boxes. Abortion was one of those topics. Over 60 years, he amassed an extraordinary archive—news clippings, correspondence with local feminist organizations and case files on abortion-related litigation from across the country.

His collection served as both a chronicle of public discourse and a record of the legal and medical battles over reproductive rights. Access to this trove, combined with Wecht's insight, gave me the impetus and the primary sources to begin what would become a sustained, deeply researched project on abortion in America.

Wecht eventually commissioned me to write an academic paper on abortion-investigation methods for his forensic-science compendium. Neither of us anticipated how timely that research would become.

CHAPTER 4

A Right to Privacy

Planned Parenthood had focused on birth control since its founding. Margaret Sanger believed abortion was unnecessary when contraceptives were widely available. Sanger and others sought to distance themselves from abortion because it was deeply unappealing to much of the country. Debates erupted over whether birth control should be free, since it was least accessible to poorer and minority communities. But some groups resisted public funding, arguing that their taxes should not support something they considered immoral.

In 1962, CBS News aired a special titled "Birth Control and the Law." The segment focused on Cook County, Illinois. It showed poor and Black women entering local hospitals seeking artificial methods of pregnancy prevention. At the time, birth control advocates framed their rhetoric around controlling population growth and reducing poverty. The argument was that if children were born to parents without the means to care for them, the resulting poverty would perpetuate social problems that proper pregnancy planning could prevent.

At Cook County Hospital, an entire 40-bed ward—"Ward 41"—was dedicated to septic abortion cases. Women were frequently admitted with horrific injuries and complications. Death was common.

In American slums, birth rates ranked among the highest in the world. Some population-control advocates argued that limiting births would reduce the welfare rolls. Dr. Alan Guttmacher spoke to CBS about this advocacy:

"We want each child born a desired child, a wanted child, into a home which is emotionally, spiritually and economically prepared for this child," Guttmacher said. "That doesn't mean that we think that people with limited means shouldn't have children. But I think each child should be the result of thoughtful planning on the part of parents."

CBS reporters interviewed several Black residents of Chicago. One mother of five said she had heard of birth control but didn't know where to get the pills. She asked a welfare worker about family planning, but the worker offered no useful information. Cook County Hospital banned its doctors from providing family-planning advice.

The Rev. Edgar Ward, a Black Presbyterian community activist in Chicago, appeared in the special to describe how the lack of access to birth control affected Black families who had migrated north. Ward pushed for birth control to be made available to minorities, noting that they faced many of the same racial barriers they had experienced in the South.

"They seek security in each other. And I think as a consequence of seeking security in each other, children are born," Ward said. "They don't necessarily want these large families, but they don't know where to turn to seek some help in preventing them."

When Alan Guttmacher became president of Planned Parenthood in 1962, he brought a deep background in medicine and a strong belief in the power of science to drive social change. A respected obstetrician-gynecologist and former vice president of the American Eugenics Society, Guttmacher was already well known for advocating birth control as a cornerstone of women's health care.

His appointment marked a turning point for Planned Parenthood, transforming it from a network of clinics into a nationally recognized leader in public health and policy. He emphasized integrating family planning into mainstream medical practice and expanding services for low-income women nationwide.

During his tenure, Guttmacher guided the organization through a period of major growth and increasing political influence. He was instrumental in creating Title X, the federal family-planning program established in 1970, which provided funding for contraceptive services to underserved populations. In 1968, he founded the Center for Family Planning Program Development, which later became the Guttmacher Institute—Planned Parenthood's independent research arm.

This reflected his conviction that reproductive policy should be guided by rigorous data and public health priorities. Guttmacher's leadership helped position Planned Parenthood not only as a health care provider but also as a policy and research leader in the reproductive rights movement.

Although Guttmacher played a central role in the emerging abortion rights movement, his first priority was expanding access to birth control. Soon, however, the organization would find itself at the center of another controversy—this time in Connecticut.

By 1964, Massachusetts and Connecticut still had laws prohibiting the distribution of birth control. Many other states also retained such restrictions under the Comstock Act.

Connecticut's statute was among the nation's most stringent, based directly on Comstock's language. The legislature followed federal lawmakers in equating contraception with obscenity.

The Supreme Court had first examined the issue in its 1960 case *Poe v. Ullman*. Connecticut's law, rarely enforced, made it a crime to provide medical advice on reproductive planning or contraception.

A married couple, known by the pseudonyms Pauline and Paul Poe, used contraceptives to prevent their fourth pregnancy after losing their first three children in infancy. In another case, a plaintiff known as Jane Doe sought contraception because pregnancy could endanger her life. Both the Poes and Jane Doe received counseling from Dr. Lee Buxton, a respected obstetrician-gynecologist in New Haven. Connecticut's state attorney, Abraham Ullman, threatened to prosecute Buxton if he provided such advice.

The plaintiffs—Buxton and his patients—sued, arguing that the law violated the 14th Amendment's guarantees of equal protection and the privileges of citizenship.

Although the statute had existed for 70 years, Connecticut had prosecuted only three people under it. The Supreme Court dismissed *Poe v. Ullman*, finding that the plaintiffs lacked standing because the law had not been enforced against them.

Justice William Brennan, a liberal appointee of President Dwight Eisenhower, noted that the state had sought to prevent the large-scale opening of birth control clinics, rather than policing private use by married couples. In June 1961, the Court refused to rule on the law's constitutionality, calling it a "dead letter" because of its lack of enforcement.

However, this "dead letter" would soon come back to life—in the case of *Griswold v. Connecticut*.

In September 1961, Planned Parenthood opened a birth control clinic in New Haven. Local officials disagreed with the Supreme Court's assessment. Police raided the clinic and closed it after 10 days.

The first complaint had come from James G. Morris, a conservative father of five who compared birth control to prostitution. He called the police, the prosecutor and the press, pressuring authorities to file charges. Prosecutor Julius Maretz issued arrest warrants for Estelle Griswold, Planned Parenthood's executive director, and Dr. Buxton, who treated patients there.

Their conviction followed the testimony of three married women who said they had received contraceptive advice. The court fined Buxton and Griswold $100 each.

Buxton told CBS that Connecticut had one of the lowest birth rates in the country, showing that many residents were already using birth control privately.

"If a woman can afford to go to a private doctor as a private patient and pay a fee, she can get contraceptive advice in Connecticut," Buxton said. "But if she hasn't the money to go to a private doctor, if she's a patient in our clinic here, she can't get contraceptive advice here.

"She needs to go to a family planning clinic. And they're the ones who really need contraceptive advice from a socioeconomic as well as a health point of view. They're being discriminated against because of their economic status."

Griswold said she would continue her education and referral program despite the warrant. Over the previous four years, Planned Parenthood counselors had referred 20,000 women to out-of-state clinics, subsidizing care for low-income patients. She doubted police could enforce such a law effectively.

"I think if you had a policeman under every bed in Connecticut, they still could not prove anything," Griswold told CBS.

Pharmacies throughout the state continued to sell contraceptives. The law's contradictions were glaring—it was illegal to use or prescribe birth control pills, but not illegal to sell them. Pharmacists simply claimed they were for "other purposes."

The Long Arm of the Law

The case drew support from Yale University faculty and became known as the Yale Project. Law professor Fowler Harper defended Griswold and Buxton, appealing their convictions. He argued that their rights to due process and First Amendment freedoms had been violated.

"When the long arm of the law reaches into the bedroom and prohibits what a man and his wife want to do, and what many medical advice suggest that they do, it seems to me that this is a merciless invasion of the freedom and liberty of the citizens of this country," Harper told CBS News.

An appeals court upheld Griswold's and Buxton's convictions in January 1963. Later that year, the Connecticut Supreme Court affirmed the law's constitutionality. Planned Parenthood's lawyers then appealed to the U.S. Supreme Court.

On that bench sat Justice William O. Douglas—a liberal firebrand, appointed by Franklin D. Roosevelt and known for his passionate defense of civil liberties. He had written more opinions and dissents than any justice in the Court's history.

According to biographer Bruce Allen Murphy, Douglas drafted his initial opinion for *Griswold* in longhand—five pages, double-spaced, completed in about the time it once took him to commute to work. Ten days after the justices' private conference, he had produced a concise, forceful defense of the right to privacy.

Justices Hugo Black and Potter Stewart dissented, arguing that privacy was not explicitly mentioned in the Constitution. Douglas, however, found protection for it in the "penumbras" of other amendments.

"The prospects of police with warrants searching the sacred precincts of marital bedrooms for telltale signs of the use of contraceptives is repulsive to the idea of privacy and of association that make up a goodly part of the Constitution and Bill of Rights," Douglas wrote.

After lobbying by Justice Brennan, Douglas revised his reasoning to ground the right to privacy in the Third, Fourth, Fifth, Ninth and 14th Amendments.

Douglas' majority opinion in *Griswold v. Connecticut* (1965) became a landmark victory for reproductive rights and established a foundational precedent: that the Constitution protects a right to privacy.

This decision would later serve as the cornerstone for *Roe v. Wade*. It is impossible to understand how abortion rights were granted without understanding *Griswold*, which first articulated the constitutional basis for privacy in matters of reproduction.

Lawyers fighting for abortion rights later used that judgment as the basis of their arguments that abortion access extended from the right to privacy. This opinion became a flashpoint in the debate on the role of the judiciary in America. When conservatives say they don't want activist judges, they usually refer to Douglas' jurisprudence. Liberals have lionized Douglas because he protected civil liberties.

Seeking Help Where They Could Find It.

The momentum continued. In 1965, CBS News aired an hour-long special titled "Abortion and the Law." It featured women discussing their abortions, and interviews with leading medical and legal figures.

Anchor Walter Cronkite reported that criminal abortion was the third-largest illegal racket in the United States, generating $350 million a year. Dr. Robert Walter said on the program that he was tormented when patients pleaded for help.

"And I feel something should be done, but my hands are tied,"

Walter told CBS. "The law says I cannot and the patient sits there and pleads and works on my sympathy as well as rationally and logically. She says, 'I'm going to go out and have an abortion if you don't do it. It probably will be done badly. I may die. What kind of law is it? What justice is there if you let me go when I know you can do it?'"

At the time, Puerto Rico was a popular destination for abortions. CBS estimated that 10,000 American women traveled to San Juan each year. They rarely needed prior arrangements—cab drivers, bellhops and newsstand vendors arranged everything for a fee. Women on the West Coast often went to Tijuana, where roughly 75 abortionists operated throughout the week and saw their busiest days on weekends.

Lawmakers across the country were pushing for abortion reform. John Knox, a California assemblyman, heard the story of a woman who had a child through rape. In 1961, he introduced a bill for reform on abortion to the state legislature. Knox's bill died in committee, but it would be the starting point for future reform proposals in California. The bill itself did not garner much media attention, though it inspired Patricia Maginnis to join the cause after she saw a small article in the newspaper.

Maginnis grew up in Oklahoma in a Catholic family, and her parents sent her to boarding school as a teen. She worked in a lab and then joined the Women's Army Corps. While there, Maginnis worked as a medical provider in the pediatric and obstetrics ward, where she saw women in all aspects of pregnancy. She saw women with horribly deformed children and others infected because of botched back-alley procedures.

She had her own experiences with abortion. A man impregnated Maginnis while she was at San Jose State College, and she went to Mexico to get an abortion. In 1959, Maginnis self-induced another abortion. She botched it and had to go to the hospital. The San Francisco homicide squad visited and interrogated her to find out if she had given herself an abortion. She immediately told them that she had and cheekily asked them if they wanted her to demonstrate the procedure in court.

In 1962, Maginnis started the Citizens Committee for Humane Abortion Laws, otherwise known as CCHAL. Maginnis met Rowena Gurner the same year. In 1965, they formed the Society for Humane

Abortion, the new name for the CCHAL, as a nonprofit organization in California. The Society for Humane Abortion fought for elective abortions and proper medical care before, during and after abortions without harassment. Maginnis ran the group from her San Francisco apartment.

"No woman should have to grovel before a board of directors or anyone else for the right," Maginnis once told a newspaper.

Maginnis received threats when she traveled the country to advocate for abortion access.

Maginnis, Rowena Gurner and Lana Phelan were at the center of the Society for Humane Abortion. Collectively, they were known as the "Army of Three."

The Society for Humane Abortions sponsored meetings with doctors, published a quarterly newsletter and held a speaker series that provided additional literature to family planning clinics. At these panels, doctors discussed what procedures were safest. As part of their education about the topic, Maginnis and Phelan authored *The Abortion Handbook*, which recommends various methods women can use to get an abortion. Among them was to feign mental illness or, as they put it in the book, "Act Psychotic."

California lawmakers sought to change the statutes six years after the American Law Institute recommended liberalizing abortion laws. The legislature studied the subject for seven years. In February 1965, Assemblyman Anthony Beilenson authored and introduced a bill to liberalize it. Representatives of the Catholic Church, which operated 40 hospitals in the state, said that the 14th Amendment protected the unborn. Beilenson said that the fetus had no rights and criticized the due process for fetuses argument when he spoke to CBS.

At the bill's hearing, Beilenson criticized abortion laws as unnecessarily endangering women.

"The existing law is barbaric because we force women and girls, who could be given expert medical attention by their own physicians, to seek out the services of quacks and criminal abortionists, or to try to abort themselves," Beilenson said. "And we drive thousands of women to their deaths and to serious injury each year."

While Beilenson traveled throughout California in support of the liberalized abortion law, he was approached by women who told him about their abortions.

Meanwhile, existing restrictions prevented many women from obtaining them. A woman had to involve the local district attorney if she requested an exception for a therapeutic abortion on the basis of rape or incest.

While some argued against the bill because they were against abortion totally, others criticized it because it favored wealthier white women in private hospitals. Other women, particularly those of color, wouldn't benefit from its passage as much and the conservative restrictions would not provide enough relief for women in need. That's why Maginnis and her organization opposed it.

In 1966, Maginnis established the Association to Repeal Abortion Laws, known as ARAL, which did much of the same educational work as its predecessor. That same year, the California Board of Medical Examiners, composed mostly of men, met at the University of San Francisco to discuss implementing committees to determine whether women could have their abortions. Maginnis seized the event as an opportunity to spread her message. She passed out pamphlets for approximately six weeks before the meeting. She informed the police ahead of time that she would break the law.

Maginnis raised awareness about the sexual exploitation of women in situations where they had abortions. She prepared a list of people qualified to perform them.

On that morning, Maginnis was passing out the pamphlets near San Francisco's Federal Building. The police arrested her and she went to court, where the judge declared the law unconstitutional and dismissed her case. Maginnis then set her sights on state law.

San Mateo District Attorney Keith Sorensen said he would enforce the California abortion law, which caused Maginnis and Gurner to organize an abortion class there.

On Feb. 20, 1967, a lieutenant from the San Mateo County Sheriff's office went to a meeting attended by 20 people in Redwood City. They arrested Maginnis and Gurner. While awaiting a trial in Redwood City, the two said they searched for a rental to hold more abortion classes for up to 50 people on Thursday nights.

A jury convicted them, and they appealed the decision to the California Court of Appeals in the First District. Attorneys for the women said the law violated the First Amendment.

As the case went forward, the Army of Three spoke against the Therapeutic Abortion Act in California. They wanted abortions to be available in all circumstances. Maginnis provoked thought by passing out pamphlets that asked whether Congress would ever consider requiring men to get approval from a panel of female doctors before they could get vasectomies.

In 1967, after great debates and scrutiny, California's legislature enacted the Therapeutic Abortion Act, which allowed abortions for up to 21 weeks into the pregnancy if it was a result of incest or rape or if it endangered the physical or mental health of the mother. Gov. Ronald Reagan signed the bill.

A committee of at least two or three licensed physicians or surgeons of a hospital's medical committee had to approve an abortion. It was intended to bring abortion laws into congruence with advances in medical practice while controlling illegal abortion. At that time, a study had shown that about one-third of maternal deaths in California were due to illegal abortions.

Clergy Consultation Service

By 1967, Karen Mulhauser taught at a junior high school. Students asked her about abortions. She wanted to teach a sex education course, but the school's higher-ups initially declined. She kept talking to the students anyway. That was when she realized there was a serious need for programs where young people could get the information they couldn't from their parents. She joined a group in Boston called the Problem Pregnancy Council. In Massachusetts at that time, women couldn't even get contraception. She talked to eight to 12 girls a day about their unwanted pregnancies.

If women could afford it and they wanted to terminate a pregnancy, they would put them on a charter plane to go to London, where abortion was legal. If they couldn't afford it, Mulhauser referred them to the Clergy Consultation Service, which consisted of ministers and rabbis who helped women get abortions.

Outsiders view the abortion debates as pitting devout people against socially liberal secular women. But in the early years, some parishioners and churchgoers lobbied for legalizing the procedure and even helped women get abortions.

In 1964, the General Assembly of the Unitarian Universalist Association called for abortion to be legal in all circumstances. Driven by the civil rights movement and other causes like feminism, some mainline Protestant denominations supported the abortion rights movement because church leaders associated it with social justice.

In the mid-1960s, before *Roe v. Wade*, Lawrence Lader emerged as one of the most visible advocates for repealing the nation's abortion laws. A Manhattan activist and author, he made the case forcefully in his 1966 book that abortion should be legal and accessible. The book struck a nerve, prompting a flood of letters from women desperate for help. Lader's advocacy did more than highlight the scope of the problem—it suggested new avenues for action. He began to argue that ministers, with their moral authority and the trust of their congregations, could act as intermediaries for women seeking abortions, providing counsel and safe referrals at a time when such options were scarce and dangerous.

Lader's entry into the abortion rights movement began through journalism and historical research that evolved into advocacy. A Harvard graduate and former *Look* magazine writer, Lader's early reporting on population control and reproductive health drew him into collaboration with Margaret Sanger.

He chronicled her life and work in *Margaret Sanger and the Fight for Birth Control* (1955), which positioned him as one of the first male writers to treat contraception as a civil rights issue. Under Sanger's mentorship, he came to see abortion not merely as a medical concern but as central to women's autonomy and equality.

By the early 1960s, Lader's intellectual curiosity became direct activism. He co-founded the National Association for the Repeal of Abortion Laws (NARAL) with Dr. Bernard Nathanson and others, channeling his research into political organizing. His 1966 book *Abortion* was pivotal—it broke a long-standing public silence by exposing the human cost of criminalized abortion and framing the issue in constitutional and feminist terms. The book inspired both grassroots organizing and legal challenges that would culminate in *Roe v. Wade*. Lader's mix of scholarship and agitation reflected his belief that social reform required public education as much as courtroom strategy.

Throughout his early career, Lader blended literary craft with movement leadership. Though sometimes dismissed as a polemicist, he insisted that moral passion and factual precision were inseparable. A *Los Angeles Times* profile from 1995 described him as "a champion of choice" who saw abortion rights as a continuation of Enlightenment ideals of liberty and bodily sovereignty. His beginnings were marked not by institutional power but by persistence—one man using the tools of journalism, biography and protest to make reproductive freedom part of America's moral vocabulary.

Howard Moody, senior minister at New York's Judson Memorial Church, was a clergyman who responded to Lader's call. Judson was no ordinary congregation; rooted in social justice, it had long been involved in progressive causes, including youth outreach and resistance to the Vietnam War. Moody embraced the church's mission to be "a church for the world," active wherever pain, injustice and inequality were present. His leadership, moral conviction and willingness to take calculated risks made him an ideal spokesperson for CCS. By leveraging Judson's activist culture and his own reputation, Moody helped legitimize the idea of clergy openly aiding women in accessing abortion, framing it as both a moral duty and a public statement against unjust laws.

The partnership between Moody and Lader was key to the service's creation. The idea for a clergy abortion referral network emerged during a September 1966 lunch Lader had with Moody and two Episcopal priests. Lader recognized Moody as the ideal collaborator—someone who combined a deep commitment to social responsibility with pragmatic realism. Lader pushed the group toward public action, believing that openly referring women for abortions would advance the cause of legal reform. Moody, in turn, mobilized clergy contacts and infused the project with the activist energy of Judson Memorial Church. Their alliance exemplified the merging of strategic advocacy with moral leadership, laying the groundwork for a network that would eventually span the country.[15]

Convinced that the church had a pastoral responsibility to address what he saw as a public health crisis and a matter of justice, Moody moved quickly to put the idea into practice. In 1967, he convened a group of ministers to create the Clergy Consultation Service on Abortion, an openly named referral network that sought to destigmatize abortion and ensure women could access competent medical care. Moody's decision to embrace the word "abortion" in the group's name was deliberate, an act of defiance against both the legal restrictions and the shame surrounding the procedure. In this way, Lader's conceptual vision—clergy as active participants in securing reproductive freedom—was transformed by Moody into a concrete, organized service that spanned multiple states and changed the landscape of abortion access before legalization.[16]

The Clergy Consultation Service on Abortion (CCS) emerged in the late 1960s as the first organized effort in the United States to publicly offer abortion referrals. Its formation was a direct response to the legal and practical unavailability of abortion in all 50 states at the time. Women seeking abortions could call the group's answering machine, receive the names of two or three ordained clergy on call that week, and arrange a meeting. These clergy would discuss all available options, and if abortion was chosen, provide vetted referrals to licensed physicians willing to perform the procedure—sometimes in neighboring states or

---

15 Dirks, D. A., & Relf, P. A. (2017). *To offer compassion: A history of the Clergy Consultation Service on Abortion*. University of Wisconsin Press

16 Farrow, K. (2018, March 14). *Body and soul: Birth control leaders and their religious allies. The New Republic*. https://newrepublic.com/article/147389/body-soul-birth-control-leaders-allies-religious-groups; Semuels, A. (1989, April 26). Abortion: Once upon a time in America. *The Washington Post*. https://www.washingtonpost.com/archive/lifestyle/1989/04/26/abortion-once-upon-a-time-in-america/dcc01d3a-20eb-49c0-b4a6-6e4769866656/

abroad. The service was free, and while members took precautions to avoid legal trouble, they did not shy away from challenging restrictive laws, motivated by the desperation they witnessed among women facing unwanted pregnancies.

Their collaboration reflected a broader confluence of activist networks in the late 1960s, when religious leaders, feminist organizers and medical reformers found common cause in challenging abortion bans. Lader's work placed the issue in the national spotlight, giving clergy like Moody the intellectual framework and moral justification for open defiance of the law. Moody's efforts, in turn, demonstrated how that framework could be grounded in daily practice—turning theory into tangible services for thousands of women. Together, they embodied a partnership of persuasion and action, one that would help pave the way for the legal and cultural shifts that followed in the years leading up to *Roe*.

The *New York Times* did a front-page article when it was formed. Moody told the newspaper about the various justifications for abortion. The group pledged to work to liberalize the laws.

"In the meantime, women are being driven alone and afraid into the underworld of criminality or the dangerous practice of self-induced abortion," the clergy said in a released statement. "Confronted with a difficult decision and means of implementing it, women today are forced by ignorance, misinformation and desperation into courses of action that require humane concern on the part of religious leaders."

To avoid arrest, they had no actual place of business. They dispersed responsibilities of the service among rabbis and ministers throughout the city. A person working with a telephone service, which was listed, referred women to an abortionist. Arlene Carmen, a church administrator, evaluated an abortionist's practice by pretending she needed an abortion.

The clergy referral service grew to thousands nationwide in most major cities. It referred women to abortion providers outside of New York, including Dr. David Sopher in England, who performed more abortions in that country than anyone. Unethical cab drivers encouraged women who came to England to go elsewhere for abortion and received kickbacks for doing so. The Service warned women about that.

The Rev. Ron Lutz, a Presbyterian, was part of the Philadelphia Clergy Consultation Service. He remembers a father bringing in his daughter. Halfway through the session, the man told him he was a district attorney. Another time, a grandmother brought in her 13-year-old granddaughter. Other consultations simply involved one woman who didn't have any support from a boyfriend, husband or parent. He would talk to them about whether their parents knew they were pregnant. Often one would be aware, while the other was left in the dark.

The director of the Philadelphia service inspected the offices of abortionists. They stopped referring patients to a hospital doctor because he had acted inappropriately toward women. They had to travel to other countries, including Puerto Rico, to ensure the abortion provider was reputable and had a clean healthcare setting.

During that time, Lutz never felt that his advocacy of abortion rights contradicted his religious beliefs.

"Abortion was not a problem for me," Lutz said. "It was not a problem for my theology. But it was for the church. So I decided to take my chances with the church. I don't know what might have happened. I suppose I might have been visited by the district executive for this area. Who knows? I may have been, my ordination may have been taken away from me."

Author and podcaster Gillian Frank researched the Clergy Consultation Service for his forthcoming book *Making Choice Sacred: Liberal Religion and Reproductive Rights in the United States, 1965-1980*, which will be released by the University of North Carolina Press. Much of his research reveals groundbreaking details about the service's operation.

Frank presented some of his findings at Sacred Gathering, a two-day conference in 2022 featuring some of the most prominent names in the religious pro-choice community. He revealed Catholic involvement in the CCS, which he planned on detailing in further depth in his work.

"The Catholic Church needs to be understood as a complex, internally divided entity as an institution, particularly in the mid to late 60s where they were undergoing massive reform," Frank said. "So that's the first thing. And so any sort of unified voice of the church that might be coming from the top down is often met with people who sort of pick and choose or who dissent either vocally or just through their everyday actions."

Liberal ministers, particularly those involved in the Civil Rights Movement, enlisted in the cause for abortion law reform. Following the 1965 march in Selma, which drew 400 clergy, many from Black churches felt they had a moral imperative to push for social justice. For some, that meant advocating for the elimination of restrictive abortion laws, which they said penalized poor women of color.

Others—both Black and white—within the Civil Rights Movement felt the other way. The movement of Catholics away from birth control limitation to abortion restriction eased the way for many anti-abortion Protestant ministers to join their cause. California Episcopal priest Charles Carroll, who opposed the Vietnam war, felt abortion was a "denigration of life."

Martin Luther King Jr. connected the Civil Rights Movement to Margaret Sanger's birth control efforts. When King was in his first parish in Montgomery, Alabama, he joined a Planned Parenthood committee that distributed literature on unwanted pregnancies. He saw Sanger as a model social reformer. When he spoke before PPFA on May 5, 1966, King paid tribute to her legacy.

"There is a striking kinship between our movement and Margaret Sanger's early efforts," King said. "She, like we, saw the horrifying conditions of ghetto life. ... Like we, she was a direct actionist—a nonviolent resister. She was willing to accept scorn and abuse until the truth she saw was revealed to millions."

The Massachusetts Council of Churches voted in May 1967 to support changes in abortion laws. The signers wrote that illegal abortions were numerous and dangerous and forced women to seek out the care of quacks. It would, as they said, "provide relief from unnecessary human suffering."

A number of mainline Protestant denominations adopted pro-choice positions in the years before *Roe*: the United Church of Christ, the 20th century legacy of the Pilgrims (1971), the Episcopal Church (1967) and the Presbyterian Church (USA) (1970).

The annual convention of the American Baptist Church, a small liberal Baptist denomination, adopted a policy statement in June 1968 that abortion was a personal decision. They said that abortion should be permissible in all cases before the 12th week of pregnancy. Later on, it could be permitted if the mental or physical health of the mother were threatened, in cases of fetal deformity, or if there were documented evidence that the pregnancy was the result of rape, incest or other felonies.

That year, a symposium of 25 prominent evangelical physicians and theologians considered the Bible's treatment of human reproductive issues. They formed a consensus that the scripture didn't prohibit contraception or abortion. Birth control wasn't sinful. Abortion could be, but it had to be permitted to safeguard values such as individual health, welfare and social good.

Catholicism continued to be a major exception. The United States Conference of Catholic Bishops formed in 1966. It comprised active and retired bishops. In the late 1960s, as abortion reform measures gained traction across the country, the Conference recognized the need for a more coordinated effort. Their existing campaigns, rooted heavily in doctrinal arguments about contraception, had failed to resonate with a broader public. The bishops understood that if the movement was to survive, it needed a leader who could craft a new strategy—one that emphasized abortion as a human rights issue rather than a purely Catholic concern. They turned to Father James T. McHugh, a young priest from New Jersey who had already distinguished himself in the Church's Family Life Bureau. Intelligent, ambitious and pragmatic, McHugh was entrusted with building what would become the first national anti-abortion organization.

In 1968, McHugh oversaw the creation of the National Right to Life Committee (NRLC), initially headquartered within the bishops' conference. Though the committee began with little more than a shoestring budget, a volunteer staff and a leadership team composed of McHugh's close associates, it soon established itself as the nucleus of the pro-life movement. McHugh envisioned the NRLC not as a traditional lobbying arm but as a coordinating body that would bring together the patchwork of local and state-level Catholic initiatives into a single, coherent national framework.

He pressed bishops across the country to form state right-to-life committees and encouraged them to recruit doctors, lawyers and other respected lay professionals to lead the cause. These figures, he believed, could give the movement credibility in legislative debates that were increasingly dominated by medical and legal voices.

McHugh's strategy was both innovative and deliberate. He urged bishops to keep clergy in the background, recognizing that the Catholic Church's declining political influence limited its ability to sway public opinion. Instead, he promoted a lay-led movement that could attract allies from outside Catholicism. He also encouraged Protestant participation, arguing that non-Catholics must be welcomed into leadership even if it meant compromising on certain legislative details, such as exceptions for rape or incest. For McHugh, the broader goal was paramount: presenting abortion as the destruction of innocent human life, a principle that could unite people across denominational and political lines. This repositioning allowed the NRLC to appeal not only to Catholics but also to Protestants, liberals and secular activists concerned with human rights.

While the NRLC was modest in its early years—operating out of McHugh's office, with volunteers filling key roles—it soon grew into a powerful national organization. State right-to-life groups sprang up under its guidance, many seeded with funds and encouragement from Catholic conferences but structured to appear independent of formal Church control. This delicate balancing act was crucial. On one hand, the bishops provided necessary resources, including annual subsidies, but on the other hand, McHugh emphasized that the committees must distance themselves from being perceived as merely extensions of Catholic hierarchy. He even relocated the NRLC's headquarters from Washington to Virginia to downplay its association with the Church.

McHugh's organizational genius and his ability to reframe the issue of abortion as a universal human rights cause earned him the title of the "father of the pro-life movement in America." By severing ties with debates over contraception and recasting abortion in terms of justice and the defense of the vulnerable, he gave the movement a new ideological foundation. Under his leadership, the NRLC became the umbrella structure that transformed a scattered, mostly Catholic concern into a broad-based national campaign. His vision ensured that, by the early 1970s, the pro-life cause would not only survive but expand, laying the groundwork for the decades of political and legal battles that followed.[17]

The Catholic Church hierarchy's staunch support gave the NRLC strength. Prior to the decision in *Roe v. Wade*, U.S. Catholic bishops created the "Respect Life Program" within the church to "build a culture that cherishes every human life."

October eventually became Respect Life Month. Initiatives by the Catholic Church, primarily men in the Catholic hierarchy and lay people, propelled the anti-abortion issue going forward.

Parishioners and priests within that faith weren't in universal agreement with their views on contraception and abortion. Catholic theologians had begun developing pro-choice and pro-contraception views in the 1930s and 1940s. They argued for them in religious publications and in lectures. Despite efforts among the church's lower-level leaders, the Papacy continued to resist change when it came to family planning.

Pope Paul VI issued his famous encyclical "On Human Life," in July 1968. He rejected the church's birth control commission recommendation of a change in doctrine. American theologians publicly disagreed with the pope and published a statement in the *National Catholic Reporter* in August of that year, which said, "spouses may responsibly decide according to their conscience that artificial contraception in some circumstances is permissible and indeed necessary to preserve and foster the values and sacredness of marriage."

Differences of opinion on reproductive issues continued throughout the institutional church. In 1969, Sister Mary Traupman, who had joined a convent more than a decade earlier, attended a wedding in which a priest gave a homily about the evils of birth control and divorce.

17 Williams, D. K. (2016). *Defenders of the unborn: The pro-life movement before Roe v. Wade.* Oxford University Press.

It turned Traupman off. As a progressive, she disagreed with how much reproductive rights got vilified.

"I have only heard clergy speak about and criticize birth control [by] calling it evil," she told me when I visited her in her retirement home.

"I have never, ever heard an ordained clergy person say, 'Please don't take contraceptives because they could cause cancer. They could cause you to develop a heart condition. We're concerned about your personal health. Please don't take contraceptives.' It was always, 'Don't you dare because it's wrong.'"

Angels of Abortion

Elsewhere in the country, abortion rights providers faced criminal prosecution. In 1966, Dr. Robert Spencer faced a grand jury investigation for criminal abortion. Spencer had previously been in trouble in 1956 for the death of Mary Davies, who had an abortion under his care.

Spencer performed tens of thousands of abortions over more than 40 years. His first came in 1923 when a miner's wife asked him to end a pregnancy. The woman felt they already had too many children. Women from all over the country traveled to Ashland, Pennsylvania, where he practiced. Actresses from Broadway and Hollywood were among his patients.

Ashland sits tucked among the old coal hills, a place you wouldn't likely find yourself in unless you had a specific reason to go. Its main street is lined with modest storefronts, and a statue dedicated to motherhood overlooks a small square—a poignant irony considering the work that once brought women from across the country to this unassuming town. Ashland feels frozen in time, a quiet place with the kind of history most of its residents no longer talk about, but that still lingers in the air like coal dust.

Spencer's office was in an old wooden building with a front refinished with gray-face stone. Women walked into a hallway with one door at the end with a rectangular mirror on it.

One New York City doctor visited Spencer to learn his methods. Spencer injected a paste that softened the contents, loosened them from the uterine wall, and dilated the cervix, according to the doctor's account. The process took a minute or two.

Because one woman died during a procedure, police arrested Spencer, and prosecutors pursued a conviction. A jury cleared Spencer in that trial, and he continued to perform abortions. The doctor wrote about his views regarding it—comparing it to Prohibition, which he considered a failure.

"As a physician, I'm positive that the majority of people believe something like abortion should be legalized," he wrote. "It has been in existence thousands of years, it is here to stay, fear does not eliminate it. If legalized, less harm is done and more good accomplished."

When Spencer died in 1969, the *Los Angeles Times* and *The New York Times* featured his obituary. Susan Brownmiller, a prominent journalist who later wrote the definitive account of rape culture in *Against Our Will: Men, Women and Rape,* paid tribute to him in the *Village Voice.*

The public image of an abortionist, through books, plays, movies, articles, or whatever, was of an evil, leering, drunken, perverted butcher at worst, and a cold, mysterious, money-hungry Park Avenue price-gouger at best. And then there was Spencer with his clinic on the main street of a small American town, who charged $50, who believed in abortions, and who was kind. Knowing about Spencer in Ashland was one irrefutable piece in the logic which led one to the conclusion that the culture was capable of the big lie.

The Second Wave

Around this time, two of the greatest feminist thinkers emerged—Gloria Steinem and Betty Friedan. Abortion dominated their conversations and speeches as they rose to national prominence in the 1960s and 1970s.

Friedan was born to immigrant parents in Peoria, Illinois, in 1921. She graduated from Smith College in 1942 with a degree in psychology and went on to become a psychology fellow at the University of California, Berkeley. However, after a year she moved to New York to be a writer for the *Federated Press,* which was a left-wing news service.

She became more politically active, arguing for labor and union issues—including issues related to women in the workplace.

At her Smith College 15-year reunion, she spoke with many of her classmates and discovered that dissatisfaction with the limited life of a housewife was common among them. She began a five-year interview project, talking to women across the country regarding their lives.

Her research culminated in her bestselling book *The Feminine Mystique,* which discussed the frustration of American women with gender roles and inequality. It was an instant success, propelling Friedan's leadership in the feminist movement.

She later became a co-founder of one of the most important women's organizations at the time and to this day. The National Organization for Women, NOW for short, began June 30, 1966. Friedan was its first president. While pay discrimination and other issues were the initial focus, NOW became one of the most important organizations for abortion law reform and repeal. Friedan was one of the central figures in the abortion rights movement, though a woman who became her rival drew most of the headlines and became most associated with being the leader of the movement.

Gloria Steinem had an abortion after she became pregnant following her graduation from college when she was 22. Steinem was in London and engaged to a man. She broke up with him and didn't know what to do with the unwanted pregnancy. She said she threw herself down the stairs to end it. When that didn't work, Steinem sought out two doctors in the phone book. One agreed to perform the abortion on two conditions, the first of which was anonymity and the second of which was a promise that she would do what she wanted to with her life. Steinem had the abortion. It took her years to publicly speak about it.

Prior to *Roe v. Wade,* Steinem, who wrote for *New York* magazine, reported on an abortion speak-out at Washington Square United Methodist Church. There, she heard women talking about their experiences with illegal abortions. Steinem's feminist career began there.

"I heard women telling the truth about their lives in public in a way I had never heard before," she said in a later interview. "And I also had

had an abortion and not told anyone. And here were women standing up and saying what it was really like and why. I suddenly thought, 'Wait a minute. If one in three women or four of us has had this experience, why is it illegal?'"

After she went back to her newsroom and wrote the article, her male colleagues told her to not associate with the "crazy women" if she wanted to be taken seriously. Once she questioned that, she pondered the other realities women faced, including pay inequity and gender discrimination.

Steinem spoke at Vassar College's commencement in 1970, her first public speaking engagement. In her speech, called "Living the Revolution," she urged the graduates to reject being second-class citizens. She became the most famous feminist in America after that.

In a later speech, she discussed abortion as a political issue.

"The state means to control our bodies," Steinem said. "We produce the soldiers, we produce the workers, and they fear the loss of that control."

The abortion rights movement didn't begin nor end in New York. Feminists throughout the country undertook grassroots efforts to build it. Eleanor Smeal established and built a chapter in Pittsburgh. Mary Jean Collins was pivotal in creating and cultivating chapters of NOW throughout the Midwest, starting in Chicago. Collins slept on couches throughout the region as she started visiting communities large and small. For the most part, Collins and her allies focused on workplace discrimination, but abortion was on the burner too.

"For women who are sexually active, this was a dilemma all the time, every day all the time," Collins said

Our Bodies, Ourselves & The Story of Jane

In 1965, Heather Booth attended a national conference held by the Students for a Democratic Society. They discussed what was known as the women's program. Booth came back to the University of Chicago and started the Women's Radical Action Program, or WRAP for short. They ensured women students were treated fairly.

One of Booth's friends had a sister who was pregnant and suicidal. The friend wanted help finding a doctor to perform an abortion. Booth didn't know where to begin.

Booth went to a doctor who had been in the Medical Committee for Human Rights, which was an arm of the Civil Rights Movement. She asked who she should speak to. The doctor referred her to Dr. T.R.M. Howard, a civil rights champion who performed abortions on poor Black women.

Howard had been an abortion provider since he moved to Chicago years earlier. He didn't use subterfuge or blindfold patients who came to see him, according to a biography written by David T. Beito and Linda Royster Beito. Howard had become an abortion doctor because he felt there was a "crying need."

"I thought that was all my involvement would be," Booth said. "I thought I had done a good deed for a friend." [18]

Karen Mulhauser, whom I had developed a close working relationship with, introduced me to Heather Booth via email. Booth spoke with warm clarity, her voice carrying the calm of experience and the conviction of someone who had lived her values. She told her story with steady rhythm, weaving personal history and political commitment into a natural progression toward activism.

When speaking of the Jane Collective, she conveyed both pride and humility, emphasizing that ordinary people could do extraordinary things. Even when reflecting on the rollback of abortion rights after Roe, her tone carried determination, as if the fight remained an ongoing commitment.

Booth's friend told others that she had helped her. More women approached Booth to arrange abortions. Call after call came in. Soon she arranged a deal with Howard to get him to perform abortions and reduce the fee, which was usually $500. Sometimes women couldn't pay and Howard accommodated the women.

After the police arrested Howard, Booth found someone else named "Mike" who would do abortions.

Later, Booth was too busy and too many women were coming to her for the service and she didn't have time to arrange reproductive care

---

18 McDevitt, C. (2023, February 15). *Interview with Heather Booth* [Interview].

anymore. So she met with 12 women who took over the work. They went on to name themselves "Jane," which became a famous underground abortion network in the city from the late 1960s until the *Roe v. Wade* decision in 1973.

A woman who needed an abortion called Jane's number and spoke to a counselor to talk about her medical history. Once cleared, the counselor provided a date, time and address to arrive at before Jane members took her to the location. They'd check on the patient after it was done.

Eileen Smith was 21 when she got involved with the organization. I met her at the Rewired Pizza Café & Bar in Chicago in the summer of 2021 during a research trip focused on the Jane Collective. In our conversation, she offered an intimate and deeply personal account of her journey from seeking an illegal abortion in 1971 to becoming an active member of the collective. She spoke candidly about her own abortion experience, the trust she developed with the women of Jane, and how that trust later transformed into a volunteer role counseling other women and eventually assisting with procedures.

She had an abortion through the service after she read an underground Chicago newspaper in which Jane advertised. After calling, the woman told her that a procedure cost $500. Smith told her that she could afford $100. They accepted that with the understanding that Smith would repay the remainder at a later time.

A woman called and told her that she didn't live far away. After the meeting, the Jane member told Smith that a woman would call on the day of her abortion and pick her up.

When the time came, a woman drove her blindfolded to the location.

Smith thought Jane was rebellious and hip. The connection between women's liberation and sex appealed to her, so she became a counselor.

"It was cool," Smith said. "It was very cool. It was very satisfying."[19]

Martha Scott was also a member. She joined cautiously at first but soon became deeply involved. An orientation session with several doctors willing to perform abortions reassured her.

"This was a time when not only abortion, but even birth control was

---

19 McDevitt, C. (2021, July 6). *Interview with Eileen Smith* [Personal interview].

not very easy to access," Scott said. "It was a time when you could get birth control from, say, your doctor or from Planned Parenthood. But you could only do it if you were married."[20]

During our interview, Scott came across as practical, committed and quietly courageous—a member of the Jane Collective whose activism stemmed from meeting urgent needs rather than pursuing ideological purity. She described her progression from volunteer counselor—meeting women in her home to prepare them for illegal abortions—to assisting on procedure days and eventually learning to perform abortions herself.

Her recollections conveyed an unpretentious sense of purpose: what they did was not about heroism but about responding to need when the legal system failed women. She spoke of the changing demographics of those they served, the evolving risks and the overlap between abortion rights, civil rights and antiwar activism. She avoided sensationalizing the dangers, focusing instead on structural inequities and lessons for today— namely, that restricting legal abortion would never end it, only make it less safe.

Scott began as a counselor, then transported women, often holding their hands during procedures. Initially, Jane members did not perform the abortions themselves. Once they realized they could safely do so, they trained each other in basic techniques. The procedure, though illegal, was medically simple. They sterilized instruments and used antibiotics to prevent infection.

The group started in Hyde Park, serving primarily that community. According to Scott, half its members were housewives. They viewed Jane as a volunteer activity. Most were white, but Black women also joined.

"It expanded to involve more suburban women, North Side women and more Black women because either they themselves used the service or participated in some way," Scott said.

Jane helped wealthier women too, but never turned anyone away for lack of money. They used a sliding scale, ensuring the work was never for profit.

"If you had a lot of money, you could go to Mexico and things like

---

20 McDevitt, C. (2020, April 26). *Interview with Martha Scott* [Telephone interview].

that," Scott said. "We weren't much cheaper than that. So that population tended to be middle class, very often students, and almost entirely white. But then, as we were able to bring down the price, the people who used our service also changed."

Chicago wasn't the only city experiencing transformation on the reproductive rights front.

In 1969, the Boston Women's Health Book Collective released *Our Bodies, Ourselves*—one of the first books to discuss women's reproductive health in accessible, instructional language. It had begun as a small discussion group on women's bodies, where participants spoke candidly about topics they had never discussed publicly. For many, it was the first time they had shared their experiences with pregnancy, contraception and abortion.

The authors later reflected that understanding abortion laws and access had freed them from the anxiety of unwanted pregnancy. "It has made our pregnancies better because they no longer happen to us, but we actively choose them and enthusiastically participate in them," they declared. "It has made our parenthood better because it is our choice rather than our destiny."

That same year, the Redstockings, a New York women's liberation group, held a now-famous abortion speak-out. The Redstockings broke ground by publicly discussing their abortions and sex lives at a time when women were expected to remain quiet and domestic. Helen Kritzler spoke first. She knew nearly every woman in the audience had likely had an abortion but felt too ashamed to admit it.

Kritzler described her abortion in a dark Chicago room with a doctor she thought was "a nutcase."

The abortionist joked that he was Lenny Bruce, the controversial comedian. He had boarded up the windows to conceal his work. The procedure was agonizing, even after she took a painkiller. When it was over, the doctor asked if she wanted to see the fetus.

"I knew telling my horror story would make them feel better," Kritzler said about her speak-out. "Not alone, not isolated, not ashamed."[21]

---

21 McDevitt, C. (2021, June 2). *Interview with Helen Kritzler* [Interview].

Jenny Brown, author of *Without Apology: The Abortion Struggle Now*, introduced me to Kritzler, helping establish a valuable connection for my research. Brown, deeply engaged in preserving the history and strategies of the women's liberation movement, works to maintain the Redstockings Women's Liberation Archives for Action—a project ensuring that materials and insights from the feminist struggle remain accessible for future generations. The archives, housed online at Redstockings.org, continue to serve scholars, activists and advocates for reproductive freedom.

Women wept when Kritzler spoke. She felt honored to stand on that stage.

"We were as one," Kritzler said. "We weren't individuals. We had all been through it together, but had been separated by our traumas."

CHAPTER 5

Men at the Fore

At the same time that Patricia Maginnis and other feminists made waves, Bill Baird and other men became pivotal figures in the movement to legalize birth control and abortion. Baird, in fact, would play a central role in an eponymous Supreme Court decision on birth control.

Baird's commitment began while he was conducting contraceptive research at Harlem Hospital. One day, he heard a scream. Rushing down the corridor, he saw a woman covered in blood from the waist down—as if someone had splashed her with red paint. A piece of wire coat hanger protruded from her vagina.

After that, Baird dedicated his life to abortion rights activism. He lectured nationwide about birth control and abortion, often facing arrest and imprisonment. *The Boston Globe* once described him as "the Billy Graham of the abortion rights movement," operating with evangelical fervor.

"In my lectures, I wouldn't just talk about birth control. I would also talk about what not to do because so many people thought that if they could just take a piece of coat hanger, break off a piece and put a piece of adhesive tape at the end of it, and gently snake it in …" Baird told me before he trailed off in an interview I conducted with him in 2021.

I first reached Baird by letter, explaining my interest in documenting his role in reproductive rights. His wife, Joni, replied and arranged an interview. That initial exchange became the first of many conversations over the years. Through them, I came to know Baird as blunt, unwavering and deeply principled—willing to endure arrest, public criticism and danger to defend women's autonomy.

Merle Hoffman, a New York abortion provider and second-wave feminist who was Baird's friend, acknowledged his complicated reputation.

"He's a radical and he does what he has to do to get attention," Hoffman said. "And I appreciate that. I appreciate unusual people who were out there by themselves, who were doing the work and saying what they believed. But the women had a lot of difficulty. I mean, there's this whole group of people that thought he was in there for sex."

A recent documentary, *Yours in Freedom, Bill Baird*, directed by Rebecca Cammisa (a two-time Academy Award nominee), chronicles his life, including his feud with Betty Friedan and his fraught relationship with Gloria Steinem.

In press interviews—including one in Kansas—Baird expressed support for underground abortion services and for access later in pregnancy.

At the time, Massachusetts law—first enacted in 1847 and strengthened in 1905—banned the distribution of birth control information or devices to anyone except registered pharmacists or doctors, and only for married couples.

The first attempt to amend the law failed in 1965. In 1966, reformers won a partial victory: registered clinics could counsel married couples and sell contraceptives by prescription, though advertising or vending-machine sales remained banned. Soon after, the legislature approved the state's first birth control reform.

Police met Baird's activism with hostility. At one lecture in Freehold, New Jersey, 50 armed officers confronted him as he arrived in his mobile clinic. All he carried was a can of contraceptive foam, a diaphragm and an IUD, which he demonstrated to mothers inside his van. He was arrested and spent 20 days in jail.

Later, a student editor at Boston University invited him to speak after hearing about his arrest.

In April 1967, Baird lectured there on overpopulation and birth control, holding up a contraceptive pill before distributing a package of Emko vaginal foam to a female student. Police arrested him again. Conviction carried up to five years in prison. After a bench trial—where the judge alone decided guilt—he was convicted and sentenced to three months.

On appeal, the Massachusetts Supreme Judicial Court ruled that his speech was protected under the First Amendment and overturned his conviction for discussing contraception. But by a 4–3 vote, the justices upheld his conviction for distributing it.

Baird appealed to federal court for a writ of habeas corpus—a demand for release from unlawful detention. The First Circuit Court of Appeals granted the writ and ordered him freed.

The Court reasoned that the Massachusetts law infringed on the rights of unmarried couples protected under the 14th Amendment's due process clause. Sheriff Thomas Eisenstadt appealed, bringing the case to the U.S. Supreme Court in 1972.

The case—*Eisenstadt v. Baird*—concerned unmarried individuals' access to contraceptives. Justice Brennan, writing for the majority, declared:

> *If the right of privacy means anything, it is the right of the individual, married or single, to be free from unwarranted governmental intrusion into matters so fundamentally affecting a person as the decision whether to bear or beget a child.*

The Court found that restricting contraception violated the equal protection clause of the 14th Amendment. There was no rational basis for treating single people differently from married couples.

Another key figure was Richard Lamm, a Colorado state representative—and later governor—who introduced a landmark abortion bill in 1967 allowing abortion when pregnancy threatened a woman's mental or physical health, involved fetal deformity, or resulted from rape or incest.

Lamm's views stemmed from a trip to South America in 1963,

where he and his wife learned that illegal abortions were the leading cause of hospitalization among women. After winning election in a heavily Catholic district, Lamm championed reform. The hearings were emotional; anti-abortion advocates brought jars containing preserved fetuses to shock legislators.

At the time, most Colorado women seeking abortions traveled to Mexico. Ruth Steel, a prominent Republican lobbyist, was vital in persuading legislators.

"Ruth went and broke the barriers and talked to these Republican men and explained to them that there was an incredible maternal mortality and morbidity by making abortion illegal," Lamm said.

Gov. John Love, a Republican, signed the bill in 1967 after its passage through a Republican-controlled legislature. Love received about 5,000 telegrams and letters, only slightly favoring the bill. The law required approval by a three-physician panel and restricted abortions to accredited hospitals. Love supported it because the high accreditation standards limited where abortions could occur.

Women later told Lamm about the horrors of illegal abortions—and thanked him. He thought the legislation would end his career, but he went on to serve three terms as governor.

"It was not a partisan issue at all in 1967," Lamm said. "But as soon as the abortion bill passed, the right-to-life movement got together and started primarying the liberal Republicans or the Republicans who had voted in favor of the abortion law. And five or six years later, the Republican Party had generally pretty much been anti-abortion and the Democratic party pretty much pro-abortion."

In 1969, NBC News interviewed Dr. Frans Koome, an abortion provider in Washington State. Koome argued that anti-abortion laws hindered doctors. He described performing abortions to protect women's mental health and appeared alongside several patients who said underground abortionists terrified them, while legitimate doctors offered safety. Despite abortion being illegal in Washington, Koome mailed a letter to the governor confessing he had violated the law for three years, then told the *Seattle Post-Intelligencer*:

Essentially, we are faced here with a tremendous underground problem, underground because the women and girls involved are ashamed to talk about it and the physicians involved are scared to be known to have done an abortion. We are putting our heads in the sand.

A jury convicted Koome for performing an abortion on a minor without parental consent, but the Washington Supreme Court overturned his conviction.

Even as men contributed significantly, the movement remained, at its core, women-driven.

ZPG

Around that time, a new movement emerged to address population growth.

Zero Population Growth (ZPG), as it came to be known, began with the publication of Paul Ehrlich's book *The Population Bomb*, which warned of the dangers of unchecked human birth rates. His thesis was that the world's population was doubling at an unprecedented pace—bringing with it increased risks of pandemics, famine and environmental degradation. ZPG activists argued that birth control and abortion played essential roles in limiting population growth.

Ehrlich, trained as an evolutionary biologist, challenged the prevailing economic belief that perpetual population growth was necessary for prosperity. He linked environmental deterioration—like that described by Rachel Carson—to the strain humans placed on Earth's resources. On his book tour, Ehrlich often faced controversial questions about who "should" be allowed to reproduce. Some Black Americans voiced concerns that population control efforts could target their communities.

Ehrlich, who had helped desegregate restaurants in Kansas earlier in his life, rejected those racist interpretations.

"The problem of the mix of racism and xenophobia with the fact that the planet has too many people on it is a potent and difficult thing that has to be attacked head-on," Ehrlich said as he reflected on his career at his retirement home in Palo Alto, California.[22]

I tracked Ehrlich down through his Stanford University email. When we spoke via Zoom in 2021, he was sharp and articulate despite being in his late eighties. He recalled vividly the reactions to his book—both positive and critical.

Ehrlich said the topic of eugenics came up frequently in public discussions. He considered it more complex than people later portrayed. The idea of cultivating positive human traits, he said, wasn't inherently irrational—but its entanglement with white supremacy made it abhorrent. He noted that modern reproductive technologies, such as in vitro fertilization and abortions following prenatal testing, still raised ethical questions reminiscent of eugenics.

"Would you not do the one that had a known genetic defect?" Ehrlich said. "And it's an ethical question that is very close to eugenics. So it's still a live issue at a totally different level really."

Ehrlich himself never directly tied abortion rights to ZPG but supported abortion access as essential to gender equality. Others, however, argued that women should freely choose how many children to have without social stigma.

ZPG flyers often appeared alongside those promoting abortion rights. The two causes seemed naturally linked, but the overlap raised questions of classism, ableism, racism and discrimination—who was encouraged or discouraged from reproducing.

In later decades, critics misinterpreted ZPG as an effort to reduce Black births. That was never its intent; the movement sought to limit population growth globally to protect the planet's resources.

Looking back over the past 50 years, the environmental damage wrought by overpopulation has largely validated Ehrlich's warnings. Still, discussions of family planning must remain sensitive to the historical injustices that marginalized communities have faced in the name of "reproductive control."

---

22 McDevitt, C. (2021, May 22). *Interview with Paul Ehrlich* [Unpublished interview].

Hawaii

Hawaii legalized abortion in 1970, opening the door to broader reform across the country. The state's population leaned pro-choice, and activists had spent a year lobbying lawmakers to repeal restrictive laws dating back to 1869, which permitted abortion only to save the mother's life.

Patricia Steinhoff, an activist and professor who chronicled the campaign in *Abortion Politics: The Hawaii Experience*, spoke to me about it.

"It was also a new state and very open in its attitudes," Steinhoff said during an interview I had with her. "And so there was a climate that was very different here than in other places."

The rubella epidemic in 1964 led many obstetricians to perform abortions. The disease affects the fetus but doesn't endanger the mother's life. Because of that, many doctors supported liberalizing or eliminating abortion laws.

The two most important figures in Hawaii's abortion rights campaign were State Sen. Vincent Yano and Joan Hayes, a middle-class activist. Along with other grassroots organizers, they managed to turn public opinion against the longstanding ban on abortion.

Hayes testified before the Senate Committee on Public Health, Welfare and Housing, which was chaired by Yano, who had scheduled a hearing on the potential repeal of the abortion law. Hayes supported complete repeal. Later, she sought out several committee members and lobbied them. She played a large role in pushing Yano to his position. So did most middle-class women.

"Many of them may have had abortions, but they didn't say so," Steinhoff said. "But they certainly thought that the law should be changed."

Yano, a Catholic, drew inspiration from Father Robert Drinan of Boston College Law School, who argued that states should have no abortion laws at all—since any law, permissive or restrictive, implicitly condoned "murder."

Repeal, not reform, became Hawaii's strategy.

Opponents warned that Hawaii would become a "destination for abortion tourism."

After 90 minutes of debate, the Hawaii Senate voted for legalization. Women in the gallery applauded. The House passed the bill after adding modest restrictions: abortions had to be performed by a licensed physician in an accredited hospital, and only for residents of at least 90 days.

Gov. John Burns allowed the bill to become law without his signature—a politically cautious move that carried no consequences.

The first elective abortion in Hawaii took place on March 13, 1970. Tourists soon arrived in Honolulu for procedures. Protestors marched on the state capitol with signs reading "Make Babies, Not Corpses."

That year, 15 hospitals performed 3,643 abortions, 43% of them for Hawaii residents.

Anti-abortion activism also took root there. Robert Pearson, an Oahu resident, established the first crisis pregnancy center in 1967. Although not Catholic, Pearson launched the model that spread nationwide: centers posing as medical clinics to dissuade women from abortions.

In Toronto, Louise Summerhill created Birthright in 1968 with help from four priests and 60 volunteers. Funded with a $300 donation and donated office space, the organization expanded into hundreds of U.S. chapters and became the forerunner of today's crisis-pregnancy networks.

On Easter Sunday 1971, Cardinal Terrence Cooke opened a Birthright clinic in New York City, where more than 100,000 abortions had been performed since legalization. A full-page ad in *The New York Times* showed a distressed woman and urged readers to call for "practical, loving help."

New York

New York lawmakers attempted several abortion reforms in 1969. Assemblyman Albert H. Blumenthal proposed a bill permitting abortion for the mother's health and in cases of rape, incest or fetal deformity.

Republican assemblywoman Constance Cook became a key ally after being approached by Betty Friedan and attorney Flo Kennedy.

Initially skeptical that repeal was possible, Cook nevertheless agreed it was morally right.

Public hearings in February 1970 drew crowds and protests. Thirty women picketed outside, handing out flyers that read:

> *The only real experts on abortion are women. Women who have known the pain, fear, and socially imposed guilt of an illegal abortion. Women who have seen their friends dead or in agony from a post-abortion infection. Women who have had children by the wrong man, at the wrong time, because no doctor would help them.*

The hearing featured 15 legal, medical and religious leaders. Only one woman, a nun, spoke. The committee didn't bring in any female doctors or lawyers.

Republican Sen. Norman Lent, who chaired the hearing, attempted to calm the crowd, but some of the women shouted about the lack of women speakers. The senators adjourned their hearing for a closed executive session, with police blocking the door.

The protestors formally requested to testify. The committee responded by allowing two women. But they had to wait until everyone else finished. Six women spent seven hours outside in the hall because the committee wouldn't let them into the room.

The women discussed their experiences with illegal abortions, and spoke about friends who nearly died from getting them. They urged a public hearing solely with women's testimony. Sen. Seymour Thaler ended it in anger.

"You're the rudest bunch of people I've ever met," Thaler said.

As they left, the women yelled back, "Well, we're probably the first women ever to talk about our abortions in public. That's something, anyway."

The winds shifted a year later.

Maryland repealed its laws in April 1970 after the state's House of Delegates voted, 78–43. Democratic delegate Allen Spector, the leader of the abortion rights movement in the legislature, thought it empowered medical authorities.

"Abortion being a medical practice should be a question for a woman and her doctor," Spector said.

Cook and Franz Leichter introduced their repeal bill in New York in March 1970.

It was a dramatic session full of agonizing decisions.

Democratic Sen. Mary Anne Krupsak, a Catholic, cast her vote in favor of passage.

"Mr. Terry, for me life begins at the moment of conception, but I am here as a legislator, and I must represent and give," she said before pausing, "I have an obligation to give a hearing and recognition to the fact that is not the same view of all people under all circumstances."

A Catholic bishop later told Krupsak on the capitol's steps that she "was in need of prayer."

The climax came when upstate Assemblyman George Michaels requested the floor. He had already voted against passage. He hoped the vote would not come down to one person. He decided to risk his entire political career.

"Mr. Speaker, I say to you in all candor," Michaels said at the bill's hearing, "I say this very feelingly to all of you. What's the use of getting elected or reelected if you don't stand for something."

His voice wavered at the end.

New York's legislature passed the Cook/Leichter Abortion Reform Bill by one vote.

And as he anticipated, Michaels, a profile in courage, was not reelected.

Women could get abortions in the first 24 weeks of pregnancy.

The new law went into effect in July. Dr. Hale Harvey established the first abortion clinic in the country with feminist Barbara Pyle in New York City. The Center for Reproductive and Sexual Health, later known as Women's Services, opened on July 1. Clergy referral services in other states sent women there. Hundreds came for abortions.

Planned Parenthood was ready. Their phone lines were perpetually busy. Women from across the nation called to ask where they could get an abortion in New York.

New York City's hospitals anticipated it would perform 100,000 abortions annually. Medical professionals were uncertain how many would be out-of-state women since residency wasn't required. Dr. Shirley Mayer, New York City's assistant health commissioner, told ABC News:

> *From the standpoint of social acceptance, I would think in several years' time, we could look forward to a woman feeling just as much at ease about going into a clinic to request an abortion as she now does to present herself for prenatal care or any other medical procedure.*

The law required clinics to give women birth control information. That rule was designed to make women use other methods of family planning first.

Morton Dean of CBS News reported that medical groups and governmental agencies developed their own residency and hospitalization requirements. They clashed with abortion rights groups about that, and whether doctors could perform abortions in clinics instead of hospitals. Catholic and Orthodox Jewish leaders in the city told their parishioners that they shouldn't be involved with abortions as either doctors or patients.

Medical administrators thought they wouldn't have the staff to meet the demand if out-of-state women were permitted to get abortions. One doctor told CBS that there wouldn't be enough beds in New York City to care for all the women across the country. Lawrence Lader criticized hospital honchos:

> *The hospital hierarchies have decimated the law further. Many require expensive in-hospital abortions. Others demand the committee of approval. One private hospital has even limited its gynecological staff to one abortion per week. Thus the legislature and the people continue to be flouted by the medical establishment whose guidelines and restrictions will preserve abortion for the elite at $600 and $800.*

Dr. Robert Hall, an obstetrician in New York City, thought out-of-state abortions jeopardized reform efforts elsewhere. Hall worried that having to do 500,000 abortions yearly would require opening up separate independent clinics, which frightened him because of the possibility of serious complications.

"It's simply a matter of how well New York City, principally this city and to a certain extent the rest of the state, handles this new law here," Hall told CBS. "If they handle it well, I think we'll have repeal throughout the country within two years at the most. I'm that optimistic. If we botch it, we're going to set back the movement 10 years at least I think."

Dr. Bernard Nathanson, who at that time supported abortion rights, said that the waitlist for a gynecological procedure at a hospital could last up to four to eight weeks. He said such delays would make the procedure more dangerous because it would be performed later.

Meanwhile, a discrete town house on Manhattan's West Side became a center for referrals. In the 10 weeks following the law's passage, the service arranged 6,000 abortions. The agency made $10 on each one. Young women who were mod-looking and soft-spoken answered the phones. Many had had abortions themselves.

Prices ranged from $250 to $900. The service included a hospital bed, a doctor's fee, local transportation and a hotel room reservation if needed. About 90% of the calls came from out of state. Women had to prepay with a money order and then send a telegram to the agency with the order number. Hospitals set aside several beds for the women who called them, according to Dorn Leslie Winter, who ran the service as a 26-year-old graduate student pursuing a Ph.D. in political science. Winter told NBC News that the hospital executives wanted a guaranteed number of patients.

Shortly after the abortion law's passage, New York's Clergy Consultation Service dissolved. It continued to operate in other states, however. Many of its members joined the Religious Coalition for Abortion Rights (RCAR), which was formed after *Roe v. Wade.*

The Wisconsin Historical Society in Madison houses an extensive archive of materials documenting the work of the RCAR and numerous other abortion rights organizations. This trove includes organizational records, correspondence, meeting minutes, publications and campaign materials, offering a rare and detailed view into the strategies, debates and coalition-building efforts of the movement.

By consulting these primary sources, I was able to reconstruct much of the history of religious advocacy for reproductive choice, tracing its evolution from the early years through major political and legal battles. The collection's breadth and depth made it possible to piece together narratives that might otherwise have been lost, preserving the voices and actions of advocates who played a crucial role in shaping the national conversation on abortion rights.

The same month New York legalized abortion, St. John's University sociology professor Paul Marx discovered how to mobilize opposition. Showing students a medical film of vacuum-aspiration abortion, he realized that graphic imagery could move audiences more effectively than theology. His tactic—using fetal photography—became central to the pro-life movement's propaganda.

Frances Kissling directed an abortion clinic in Pelham, New York, in 1970. When Kissling was younger, she had wanted to become a nun. She joined a convent, where she asked questions about divorce, birth control and sexuality. A Mother Superior dismissed her after asking Kissling if she wanted to leave. Kissling moved to Greenwich Village in New York City. She got involved in the antiwar movement before getting into feminism. She later recounted what she had seen to the *Washington Post Magazine.* She arrived at the parking lot at 6 a.m. and saw cars from Kentucky, Maine and Massachusetts with young kids, boyfriends or girlfriends who drove all night.

"Most people I saw knew what they were doing," she told a *Post* reporter. "It was a hard decision, but given their circumstances, it was the best decision they could make."

Kissling later helped operate clinics in Mexico and Rome before becoming one of the most influential voices in global reproductive rights.

Abortion activism spread nationwide. In Philadelphia, Paula Reimers joined Women United for Abortion Rights, an interracial group that demanded abortion be free and accessible.

"We recognized not only that women had a right to control their bodies, but that the price of an abortion was often beyond the reach of many women," Reimers said.

In August 1970, women marched in cities across America demanding abortion access, 24-hour childcare and equal pay. Despite their modest dress and middle-class demeanor, Sen. Jennings Randolph of West Virginia dismissed them as "a band of braless bubbleheads."

In Chicago, one speaker drew cheers when she said abortion should be "taken out of the hands of quacks and butchers."

The second wave of feminism had reached its zenith. Women across the country found purpose in abortion rights work—helping others avoid the suffering they had endured.

In 1971, Claire Keyes volunteered at a referral agency in Pittsburgh, directing women to clinics in New York and Washington, D.C.

When women arrived at a particular airport, they met a van driver who transported them. The bus station had something similar because thousands used mass transit. Wealthy women went to the Bahamas. Poor women in Pittsburgh were often unlucky. They had to get an abortion elsewhere.

"There were loads of places where you could get an illegal abortion," Keyes remembers about the city at the time. "And those were anywhere from mechanics' garages to somebody's kitchen."

Referral agencies advertised nationwide. In New Kensington, Pennsylvania, one billboard listed a phone number and a $250 abortion price—vandals later splashed paint over it. In Florida, a plane flew a banner reading, "Abortion Information," with a Niagara Falls phone number.

Commercial abortion referral agency administrators warned against the danger of eliminating those organizations. Peter Lewine, an owner of one, told NBC News about it:

If you eliminate commercial abortion referral agencies, what you'll have is chaos in the streets of New York. You'll have thousands of people, thousands of women literally every week coming into New York not knowing where to go, not knowing who to contact, being out in the street. An abortion is a traumatic enough time in a woman's life. We strongly believe that it should be made simple and as easy as possible.

Abortion Dominates D.C.

Dr. Milan Vuitch performed abortions in Washington, D.C., long before it was legal. Teenagers, married women and single coeds congregated in the waiting room for Vuitch's services in Washington, D.C., in the 1960s. Vuitch performed a 10-minute abortion for $300.

Vuitch was outspoken, while many doctors in the country were discreet about their support of abortion rights. Police arrested him 16 times for performing abortions, but he never served time in prison. Because determining what constituted a risk to the life or health of the pregnant woman was left to their physicians, Vuitch could legally perform abortions on pregnant women so long as he could justify that in his medical opinion there was a risk to the woman's life or health, according to the Embryo Project Encyclopedia kept by Arizona State University.

Vuitch managed to avoid conviction for criminal abortion for years by asserting, as a physician, that the procedures he performed were medically necessary to protect the life or health of the pregnant patient. Relying on that rationale, he carried out thousands of abortions annually at his clinic. After being arrested for the 17th time, Vuitch was ultimately convicted.

That conviction came in 1969, when he received a one-year prison sentence and a $5,000 fine. Vuitch appealed the decision to the federal district court, contending that the statute under which he was charged was unconstitutionally vague. His legal team argued that the law's failure to clearly define "health" left physicians without a reliable standard to determine whether their actions were lawful. The court agreed, ruling in Vuitch's favor and overturning his conviction in November 1969. As a result, the D.C. abortion law was struck down for its vagueness, effectively eliminating any abortion regulations in the District at that time.

Soon after the district court ruling, the U.S. government announced its intention to challenge the decision before the Supreme Court. In the interim, with no abortion law in effect in Washington, D.C., Vuitch continued performing abortions. His practice quickly grew, and by February 1970—just three months after the ruling—he was reportedly performing around 100 abortions each week. Women from other cities began traveling to Washington specifically to seek care from Vuitch.

In 1971, the situation shifted once more when the Supreme Court agreed to hear the case, *Vuitch v. United States*. The federal government had appealed the lower court's decision that overturned Vuitch's conviction and left the District without an enforceable abortion statute.[23]

It was the first abortion case to go to the Supreme Court. In April of 1971, the Supreme Court found that "health" meant mental and physical well-being, so it was not overly vague. Judges didn't address the legality of abortion. However, it was the court's first foray into the abortion debate. The case galvanized the abortion rights movement further.

During his first term, President Richard Nixon proposed expanding family-planning services. His administration's efforts led to the Family Planning Services and Population Research Act, introduced by Rep. George H. W. Bush (R-TX) and passed with bipartisan support. It funded contraception for low-income families as part of the War on Poverty.

In 1972, Nixon's Commission on Population Growth and the American Future, chaired by John D. Rockefeller III, recommended abortion on request, contraception for minors and sex education in schools. It also urged federal and state funding for abortion. The U.S. Conference of Catholic Bishops denounced the report.

Although Nixon rejected abortion as population control, his campaign aides viewed it politically. Chief of Staff H. R. Haldeman advised him to avoid the issue altogether:

> *If it does become necessary, I think he should take the position that this is a matter to be decided by each state and not reiterate his personal position. The alternative to this would be to moderate his stand which might help him with women and younger voters, but not soften it to the point where he jeopardizes his advantage with some Catholics.*

23 Higginbotham, V. (2018, June 9). *Milan Vuitch (1915–1993). Embryo Project Encyclopedia.* Arizona State University Center for Biology and Society. Retrieved July 21, 2025, from https://embryo.asu.edu/pages/milan-vuitch-1915-1993

Democratic nominee Sen. George McGovern also avoided abortion rights, fearing backlash from Catholic voters. Feminists nonetheless pushed for a pro-choice plank at the 1972 Democratic Convention. Jennifer Wilke, an Alaska delegate, said the majority of Americans supported abortion rights.

"Why then may you ask is this a minority plank?" Wilke said. "Because of fear. Fear of vocal well-financed and often very convincing pressure groups. Fear is trying to silence the true will of America's majority."

The plank was defeated.

At the Republican Convention, abortion proved equally divisive. A subcommittee meeting in a small, hard-to-find room heard gruesome testimony from anti-abortion activists. Knights of Columbus members demanded a constitutional amendment banning abortion, while feminists in the National Women's Political Caucus urged the GOP to support legalization, child care and workplace equality.

Party leaders dodged the issue. But by then, the Supreme Court had already agreed to hear the case that would decide the future of abortion rights: *Roe v. Wade*.

CHAPTER 6

The Case That Changed It All

Sarah Weddington and Linda Coffee were both drawn to the emerging women's rights movement of the 1960s and early 1970s. As Texas lawyers, they faced limited opportunities because of pervasive sexism within major firms. Most male attorneys believed women should remain in subordinate roles and had no place as partners. Both women graduated from the University of Texas School of Law and stayed in touch afterward.

Much of what is known about *Roe v. Wade* comes from two authoritative sources: Marian Faux's *Roe v. Wade: The Untold Story of the Landmark Decision That Made Abortion Legal* and Bob Woodward and Scott Armstrong's *The Brethren: Inside the Supreme Court.*

Weddington first became involved in the abortion struggle through a pregnancy counseling service, whose staff operated openly enough to advertise in local newspapers.

Coffee joined the women's rights movement as a member of the National Organization for Women (NOW) and other Dallas-based advocacy groups.

Weddington wanted to go further. Through a series of phone calls and in-person conversations, she and Coffee agreed that legislative reform in Texas was unlikely. The courts, they decided, offered their best chance.

They needed a plaintiff. Texas law permitted abortion only when the mother's life was at risk—not for rape, incest or other circumstances. Their ideal plaintiff would be a woman with limited income who could not travel to another state for the procedure.

Finding her proved difficult. They searched through their networks and counseling contacts before meeting Norma McCorvey.

McCorvey's life had been turbulent—marked by alcohol, occasional drug use and sex work. Though she primarily had relationships with women, she sometimes slept with men. Pregnant for the third time, she did not want to have another child or place one for adoption. On a friend's advice, she sought help from a doctor.

Her obstetrician informed her that abortion was illegal in Texas and referred her to two attorneys who discussed adoption and abortion. The second attorney referred her to Weddington and Coffee.

The three met at Columbo's, an Italian restaurant in Dallas, where the lawyers explained they would represent her free of charge. Weddington warned McCorvey against seeking an illegal abortion, recounting the story of a New York woman who had bled to death after one.

Weddington told McCorvey that women everywhere should have the right to abortion—but that would require courtroom victories. Although they didn't mention it at first, they planned to make the lawsuit a class action. Weddington anticipated the case might reach the U.S. Supreme Court.

McCorvey falsely claimed that she had been raped. When Weddington found out, she assured her that the detail was irrelevant—their challenge would apply to all abortion restrictions. Still, the lawyers worried the falsehood could undermine their credibility.

Eight weeks later, they filed suit. Precedents were scarce. Coffee and Weddington drew from federal rulings instead of Texas cases. They built upon *Griswold v. Connecticut*, hoping to extend its right to privacy to abortion. They also cited *Vuitch v. United States* and grounded their argument primarily in the 14th Amendment's guarantee of equal protection.

The Eighth Amendment, banning cruel and unusual punishment, was also part of their argument, as was the Ninth Amendment, which states the enumeration in the Constitution of certain rights shall not be construed to deny or disparage others retained by the people. In addition, they felt the abortion laws violated the First Amendment, which protected the right to freely associate because it interceded the doctor-patient relationship.

Coffee thought their case should be heard before a three-judge court. A 1910 law permitted that. The use of special courts had increased during the Civil Rights Movement. In 1973, 183 civil rights cases were argued in front of a three-judge panel. That was up from 49 cases from 1955 to 1959. Coffee and Weddington wanted the fast track to the Supreme Court.

The lawyers were both happy the cases fell under the jurisdiction of the Fifth Circuit Court of Appeals, which was more progressive than others. Their strategy was unique in that it focused on the woman, instead of the doctor, as the lead plaintiff. Most abortion rights advocates had shied away from that approach.

On March 3, 1970, Coffee filed two separate federal lawsuits, *Roe v. Wade* and *Doe v. Wade*. The plaintiffs asked for a declaration of the statute's unconstitutionality and for an injunction against Dallas County District Attorney Henry Wade from enforcing it.

Wade, widely respected, bore no personal animosity toward abortion rights advocates. His office prosecuted few abortion cases—usually when a botched procedure left a woman hospitalized. Still, he assigned Assistant District Attorney John Tolle to defend the law.

Tolle based his argument on fetal personhood—the claim that the fetus possessed legal rights. He misunderstood key precedents, sometimes citing cases favorable to abortion rights. Tolle argued that abortion restrictions were deeply rooted in common law and that society opposed recognizing abortion as a constitutional right.

He failed to address the plaintiffs' core claim: that the right to privacy protected abortion. After consulting physicians, Tolle became even more convinced that fetal life merited protection.

On March 18, 1970, Judge John R. Brown of the Fifth Circuit appointed the three-judge panel. Five days later, Tolle responded, asserting that the plaintiffs lacked legal standing because the statute applied only to those performing abortions, not those receiving them. He also argued that the century-old Texas law was neither vague nor unconstitutional.

The next day, the State of Texas moved to dismiss the *Doe* case.

Their case gained momentum when Dr. James Hallford, already indicted by Wade on two criminal abortion charges, joined the lawsuit— giving them a plaintiff with clear legal standing.

Tolle sought to depose McCorvey, hoping to discredit her or prove she was too far along in pregnancy. Coffee and Weddington feared the news might cause McCorvey to withdraw, but she urged them to continue. Judge Sarah T. Hughes ruled that a deposition was unnecessary, ordering instead that Coffee submit McCorvey's sworn affidavit—which omitted the rape claim and kept her identity confidential.

Coffee and Weddington requested summary judgment, arguing there were no factual disputes and that the issue was purely constitutional. Judge Irving Goldberg, known for his intellect, preferred such clean cases without witnesses.

The hearing, held at the Dallas Federal Courthouse, drew a packed audience of reporters and pro-choice women. Protestors picketed outside. McCorvey did not attend.

The panel consisted of Judge Sarah T. Hughes, Judge William McLaughlin Taylor, and Judge Goldberg, who would prove the intellectual force behind the opinion.

Coffee spoke first since she handled the legal technicalities. She had to argue that the state's law violated fundamental constitutional rights. She started by discussing the relief the court could give. Among the possibilities was declaratory relief, which was a statement indicating that the Texas abortion law was unconstitutional. The panel could also grant injunctive relief, which would force law enforcement to stop upholding the law.

If the court issued both forms of relief, abortion would become legal in the state thereafter. Hospitals and doctors would likely provide abortions. If both were granted, abortion would become legal in Texas, allowing hospitals and doctors to provide it. Coffee argued that the First Amendment protected women's right to associate freely with their doctors—but the judges showed little interest in that claim. Goldberg redirected questioning to the Ninth Amendment. Coffee said the right of privacy was broad enough to include the decision whether or not to terminate a pregnancy.

When the judges asked whether they could simply remand the issue to Texas courts, Coffee objected, arguing that women's constitutional rights should not depend on a doctor's criminal case. She urged the panel to strike down the entire law.

Weddington followed. She argued that life's beginning existed on a spectrum, not at conception. Goldberg pressed her again on the Ninth Amendment. Weddington agreed that Texas law was especially vulnerable there.

Frank Bruner, representing Dr. Hallford, added that the Texas ban drove women to dangerous underground abortions and that overturning it would permit safe medical care.

The attorney general's office offered an unprepared rebuttal. Overwhelmed with civil rights litigation, its lawyers were juggling an average of 50 cases each. Though the office could have declined to defend such an outdated statute, some attorneys insisted the fetus had rights.

Jay Floyd, representing the state, nervously apologized at the outset. He argued that none of the plaintiffs had standing and that abortion was not protected by the First Amendment. Goldberg asked whether vagueness or the Ninth Amendment might apply. Floyd cited *People v. Belous*, a California decision striking down an abortion law—but failed to see that it supported his opponents. Goldberg seized on the contradiction, pressing him on how the state could claim a "compelling interest" from conception.

Floyd's argument faltered.

Tolle attempted damage control in his 15-minute closing, insisting that the legislature—not the courts—should define abortion policy.

Historically, fetal personhood had never been recognized in U.S. law. States issued no death certificates for fetuses, and plaintiffs could not sue for the wrongful death of one not born alive. Centuries of precedent denied damages for fetal death because coroners could not determine cause.

As the hearing ended, Goldberg asked Coffee and Weddington what would happen if the injunction applied only to Henry Wade, not all Texas district attorneys. The lawyers realized their oversight—they had failed to include the others.

"We goofed," Weddington said.

On June 17, 1970, the judges issued their ruling. Copies were sent to the attorneys and the press. The court found that Jane Roe and Dr. Hallford had standing, though the Does did not. The Texas abortion statute, the judges ruled, was unconstitutional: a woman's right to terminate her pregnancy was protected under the Ninth Amendment. The decision allowed for reasonable state regulation concerning safety and medical standards.

However, the court declined to issue an injunction enforcing its decision—granting only declaratory relief. For Weddington and Coffee, that omission felt like a serious setback. Coffee feared Texas would ignore a ruling that lacked enforcement power.

Hours after *The Dallas Morning News* announced the district court's decision, Henry Wade told reporters that his office would continue prosecuting criminal abortions. He instructed Dallas police to crack down, and district attorneys across Texas agreed. The next day, Texas Attorney General Crawford Martin announced that the state would appeal.

McCorvey agreed to continue her case. Weddington and Coffee consulted several constitutional law professors and experts, who told them they had a rare case that may be able to go directly before the Supreme Court. The two lawyers planned to file an appeal in the Fifth Circuit first because of procedural rules. Shortly after filing the paperwork, they learned they could go to the Supreme Court.

Roy Lucas, a prominent abortion rights attorney, joined the effort. He provided research, funding and a network of lawyers who had filed related briefs. His organization—the James Madison Constitutional Law Institute, a Manhattan-based think tank—handled much of the heavy lifting: obtaining the lower-court record, printing jurisdictional statements and submitting materials to the Court. *Roe v. Wade* was formally docketed in October 1970.

Weddington and Coffee reviewed every abortion-related case decided since the Dallas ruling. They knew they would need to address jurisdictional questions. Coffee focused on procedure; Weddington handled the constitutional arguments.

When Lucas' institute failed to complete the brief on time, Weddington wrote it herself—working largely from New York, where law libraries were better than in Texas. She spent long days at the Madison Institute, mailed 40 copies of her finished brief to the Court, and resolved to argue the case personally.

Lucas wanted to deliver the oral argument himself, but Weddington insisted on doing it. Advocates across the movement supported the symbolism of a woman arguing for reproductive freedom before the highest court in the nation.

When she arrived in Washington, she visited the Supreme Court Library. Staffers already had opinions on the case's significance, which was beginning to draw quiet attention—but no protests had yet erupted outside.

Within the movement, lawyers expected support from Justices William Brennan, Thurgood Marshall, and William Douglas, author of *Griswold v. Connecticut*. They assumed Chief Justice Warren Burger and Justices Potter Stewart and Byron White would oppose them. Two vacancies—left by the recent deaths of Hugo Black and John Marshall Harlan—made Justice Harry Blackmun the uncertain swing vote.

Douglas had long wanted the Court to confront abortion directly. He believed liberty included a woman's control over her body and wanted a broad ruling, fearing other justices might dismiss the case on jurisdictional grounds.

Unaware that the Court was focused on procedure, Weddington devoted her argument to a woman's constitutional right to abortion. Douglas listened intently, taking notes and requesting additional legal research from his clerks. Justice Potter Stewart pressed Weddington on jurisdiction. She responded that federal courts could intervene when state laws infringed constitutional rights—abortion included. Justice Byron White, a Kennedy appointee and strict constructionist, took a more skeptical tone.

"We had originally brought the suit alleging both the due process clause, equal protection clause, the Ninth Amendment and a variety of others," Weddington began.

"And anything else that might have been appropriate?" White said.

"Yes, yeah," Weddington said while laughing.

"Well, do you or don't you say that the constitutional right you insist on reaches up until the time of birth, or what?" White said.

"The Constitution, as I see it, gives protection to people after birth," she concluded.

When Jay Floyd, representing Texas, rose to speak, he opened with a sexist quip that fell flat.

"Mr. Chief Justice, and may it please the court, it's an old joke, but when a man argues against two beautiful ladies like these, they're going to have the last word," Floyd said.

No one laughed. Chief Justice Burger simply told him to proceed.

During Floyd's presentation, Justice Thurgood Marshall asked when a fetus gained constitutional rights. Floyd replied, "at the point of impregnation," prompting an incredulous exchange that underscored the state's weak position.

The Court also heard *Doe v. Bolton*, a companion case challenging Georgia's abortion law. Attorney Margie Pitts Hames argued that Georgia's restrictions—residency requirements, hospital committees and physician approval—were unconstitutional burdens.

After oral arguments, no one knew how long the justices would deliberate.

Investigating Jane

Meanwhile, in Chicago, police intensified their investigation of the underground abortion network Jane. Detectives tapped phones, and members noticed background clicks during calls. When they complained, police began photographing them. In 1972, officers raided a Jane apartment under the pretense of maintenance work and arrested seven women.

Martha Scott recalled that many police officers had quietly used Jane's services for friends or relatives, so the group never felt targeted.

"They were surprised at the number of people," Scott said. "They went to the place and the front had all sorts of people-—men, women and children. And they spent a lot of time asking where the abortionist was, saying, 'Where is he?' It's not like they were really aware of what we were doing. It was just a complaint and they were following up on it."

Scott and the others spent one night in jail before being released on bail. The press dubbed them "The Abortion Seven."

Members of the Chicago Women's Liberation Union wore buttons demanding their freedom. Defense attorney Joanne Wolfson deliberately postponed their hearings, anticipating that the pending *Roe* decision might make prosecution irrelevant.

"She knew there were things afoot," Scott said. "She knew things were changing. She said, 'We're going to push this as far as we can as far as timing for two reasons. The people who might be witnesses against us ... the longer you wait, the less likely they'll testify against us.' But she also knew the Supreme Court case might make a whole difference in what position we were in."

Within the Supreme Court, Justice Harry Blackmun emerged as the pivotal figure. The father of three daughters and former legal counsel for the Mayo Clinic, he empathized both with women and with physicians prosecuted under restrictive laws. As counsel, he had advised doctors on the legality of abortions and understood their dilemmas firsthand.

The justices debated how far to go. The previous year, Douglas had argued in dissent in *Vuitch* that courts should not second-guess a physician's medical judgment; Justice Stewart agreed. When the Court met, Douglas, Brennan, Marshall and Stewart voted 4–3 to assert federal jurisdiction over abortion laws.

The next question was whether women had a constitutional right to abortion. Douglas, Brennan and Marshall said yes, under privacy and liberty protections. Burger and White dissented, supporting the state's authority. All eyes turned to Blackmun.

Chief Justice Burger then changed his vote—not out of conviction, but so he could assign the majority opinion. If the chief is in the minority, the senior justice assigns the opinion; Douglas believed it should have been his prerogative. Burger instead chose Blackmun, infuriating him.

Douglas suspected political motives. Nixon's reelection was approaching, and Douglas believed Burger wanted to delay a decision that could hurt the administration. Burger's choice of Blackmun—known to be the Court's slowest writer—seemed calculated.

Blackmun understood the controversy and anticipated the backlash. Yet his reputation as a cautious, non-ideological jurist made him an ideal author for a ruling the public might accept.

Though once close—nicknamed the "Minnesota Twins"—Burger and Blackmun had grown apart philosophically. Still, Blackmun believed he was the right person to speak for the Court.

He favored expanding the rights of medical professionals because of his close connection to doctors during his legal career. He felt hospital committees and other limitations on abortion infringed on their rights.

Blackmun began drafting in the winter and spring of 1972, spending long hours in the Court library. He delved into English common law and the history of abortion in America, discovering that early abortion had been legal up to quickening—the first fetal movement felt by the mother. Only later had laws criminalized it, primarily due to medical risk. With modern antiseptics, abortion had become far safer, and Blackmun questioned whether those old laws still served any purpose.

After five months, he shared his draft with a clerk. The feedback was blunt: the opinion was poorly organized and lacked a coherent analytical framework. It did, however, propose a key principle—viability—as the point at which state interest in potential life outweighed the woman's right to choose.

Blackmun reasoned that before viability, the decision should rest with the woman and her physician. After viability, states could regulate or even prohibit abortion, except when necessary to protect the mother's life or health.

Even with its flaws, the draft contained the seed of what would become one of the most consequential rulings in American history.

Justice Harry Blackmun resisted further edits and circulated his final memo to all chambers. Justice Potter Stewart raised concerns—not only with the opinion's structure but with what he saw as the creation of a new right not explicitly grounded in the Constitution. He chose to write a concurring opinion based on the Ninth Amendment's implicit protection of a woman's right to choose.

Justice William Douglas praised Blackmun's work and joined him. Justice Byron White, however, drafted a dissent, criticizing the majority's reasoning that Texas's abortion statute was unconstitutionally vague.

White's objections unsettled Blackmun. He withdrew his opinion and suggested reargument in the fall. Douglas protested vehemently, comparing Chief Justice Burger's procedural maneuvering to the Soviet system, where the chief justice had two votes.

He prepared a dissent but ultimately withheld it after other justices persuaded him not to publish.

When the Court recessed, Blackmun returned to Minnesota, conducting research in the Mayo Clinic's library, consulting daily with his clerks. It was there that the right to privacy solidified in his draft—but with the caveat that the state could limit that right to protect both potential life and maternal health. The key question became when the state's interest outweighed the woman's.

Blackmun examined the trimester framework of pregnancy. Abortions were safest in the first trimester, still relatively safe in the second and riskier in the third. He noted that fetal viability—the ability to survive outside the womb—occurred around the sixth month. His draft forbade states from regulating abortion until the third trimester.

When the justices reconvened that fall, Blackmun argued passionately for striking down abortion laws. He retained the votes he had before, but Justice Lewis Powell, newly appointed, also sided with him after conducting his own research over the summer.

Powell, though cautious about "creating" new rights, was swayed by the real-world harm caused by criminal abortion laws.

Justice Brennan reviewed Blackmun's draft. He accepted the viability framework but found it risky. As medical technology advanced, he noted, viability would occur earlier—potentially allowing states to restrict abortion sooner. He also worried that Blackmun's opinion emphasized doctors' rights over women's autonomy. Brennan urged separating women's health from the state's regulatory powers.

Masterful at building consensus, Brennan subtly persuaded Blackmun to adopt portions of his reasoning.

To secure a broader majority—and to include Burger—the justices debated what kinds of regulations were permissible in each trimester. Justice Stewart insisted the opinion explicitly reject fetal personhood, warning that if fetuses were recognized as "persons," they would automatically gain the rights to life, liberty and property. Blackmun agreed.

The final opinion grounded itself in rights implied by the First, Ninth and 14th Amendments, as well as precedent privacy cases, most notably *Griswold v. Connecticut*. The Court held that there existed a "right of privacy... broad enough to encompass a woman's decision whether or not to terminate her pregnancy."

Justice White dissented, arguing that abortion policy should remain with the states. He warned that the ruling effectively created "abortion on demand." Justice William Rehnquist also dissented, contending that the plaintiffs lacked standing and that most states had anti-abortion laws when the 14th Amendment was ratified—evidence, he claimed, that no such constitutional right existed.

When the opinion took its final shape, it laid the groundwork by which future legislators could craft abortion laws. Women could get an abortion in the first trimester because the embryo and fetus weren't viable. Lawmakers could require basic safeguards for the woman's health. They could never craft laws because they wanted to prevent abortions. The state legislatures could regulate abortion in the third trimester.

In the second trimester, the interests shift slightly. The Court found that states can impose those restrictions that are reasonably related to maternal health. In the third trimester, Blackmun noted that there is interest in protecting "potential life," so the states could craft laws preventing or limiting abortions. But the statutes had to make exceptions to permit abortions that preserved the life or health of the mother.

Chief Justice Burger ultimately signed on, but delayed the announcement until after President Nixon's inauguration.

When *Roe v. Wade* was released on Jan. 22, 1973, *Time* magazine prematurely reported that the Court had "made every abortion law in the country illegal."

Congratulatory messages and hate mail alike flooded Blackmun's chambers—but news of former President Lyndon Johnson's death initially overshadowed the ruling.

The Library of Congress today houses boxes of Blackmun's correspondence. The negative reactions far outnumber the positive. Some letters called him a "child killer." Others shared wrenching stories: women who had nearly died from illegal abortions, or who had watched friends suffer and perish. One woman recalled the Nazis' execution policy for women who had abortions. Another wrote that during the Great Depression, abortions had saved families from starvation.

Weddington learned of the decision when a friend called to congratulate her. Coffee heard the news on her car radio. Interview requests poured in, but neither woman commented until they had read the opinion in full.

In Laguna Beach, California, clinic counselor and comic artist Joyce Farmer was working on *Abortion Eve*, a comic book designed to educate women about reproductive rights. When she heard *Roe* announced over the radio, she immediately added the news to the storyline.

"Damned if they weren't saying abortion had been made legal throughout the United States," Farmer said.

The comic's cover—a caricature of the Virgin Mary—outraged Catholic readers. Planned Parenthood distanced itself from the publication after internal complaints, though it later became a feminist cult classic.

Shortly afterward, Blackmun traveled to Cedar Rapids, Iowa, to deliver a speech. Anti-abortion protestors picketed outside. He required police protection—a necessity that would follow him for the rest of his life. Death threats became routine.

The Court's decision invalidated abortion restrictions in 43 states, including laws requiring outside approval, residency and hospital accreditation. Attorneys for the ACLU declared that *Roe* had rendered nearly all existing state abortion statutes unconstitutional.

In its wake, maternal mortality dropped by 40–50%. Within a year, Cook County Hospital's notorious septic obstetrics ward—once filled with women suffering from infections after illegal abortions—closed permanently.

In her autobiography *A Question of Choice*, Weddington reflected that the movement's focus soon shifted from legality to accessibility:

> Roe *and* Doe *had obviously changed the legal battles being fought, but those battles—and our victory—would be insignificant if the decisions did not result in pregnant women having access to safe medical care. We had won Round 1, the Supreme Court decision. It was quickly apparent that Round 2 would be a battle to make abortion services available to women.*

The ruling was celebrated as a triumph for reproductive freedom. For many, it felt as though the issue was settled at last.

But the celebration was short-lived. The anti-abortion movement, galvanized by defeat, quickly reorganized. The controversy surrounding *Roe v. Wade* had only begun.

CHAPTER 7
Challenges to New Laws

Frank Susman, a young attorney in the 1970s, built his career defending abortion rights. He was drawn into the fight after befriending two women who worked for a suicide-prevention hotline. Each day, they received calls from women contemplating suicide because of unwanted pregnancies.

At the time, few seasoned attorneys practiced in this area, leaving Susman without mentors or precedent beyond *Roe v. Wade* itself.

State legislators were caught off guard by the *Roe* ruling. Previously, they had debated whether to liberalize abortion laws; now, the Supreme Court had tasked them with figuring out how to regulate the procedure.

Lawyers representing women's health clinics suddenly found themselves on the defensive. The post-*Roe* era marked not just a legal shift but a legislative one. Before *Roe*, reproductive rights had advanced through strategic litigation; afterward, the movement became defined by constant defense—a cycle of fending off restrictive laws in court.

Anti-abortion strategists responded by crafting ever more intrusive regulations, while pro-choice lawyers scrambled to challenge them. As the judiciary grew more conservative, courts increasingly upheld those restrictions.

Lawyers like Susman spent much of their careers in courtrooms defending abortion access. Susman's first major case was *Rogers v. Danforth*, a challenge to Missouri's abortion statute, which permitted the procedure only when necessary to save the mother's life.

Susman ultimately became the only attorney in U.S. history to argue two unrelated cases before the Supreme Court on the same day.

His first abortion case involved Judy Widdicombe, a former hospital nurse who had witnessed firsthand the trauma and death caused by illegal abortions in the 1960s. Deeply affected, Widdicombe opened Reproductive Health Services, the first clinic in Missouri, shortly after *Roe v. Wade*.

"Because I had been involved with them with the suicide prevention organization, they asked me if I would represent them in establishing a clinic," Susman said. "And I did, and the clinic paid for much of the litigation locally and nationally as well."[24]

Susman represented four physicians, three clergymen and two married women who challenged the law's constitutionality—and Missouri Attorney General John Danforth's authority to enforce it. Dr. Samuel U. Rodgers, a respected physician, was listed as the lead plaintiff, but the case was filed as a class action.

Danforth publicly upheld the statute but instructed prosecutors not to enforce it until the courts ruled. Missouri's abortion law, passed in 1835, was among the nation's oldest. It made it a crime even to advise someone about abortion.

Abortion had long been contentious in Missouri and Kansas. In 1970, the *Kansas City Star* ran a front-page investigation exposing the deadly toll of criminal abortions. The report described women drinking quinine and whiskey, swallowing castor oil or douching with turpentine to induce miscarriages. One estimate suggested that 95% of criminal abortionists were untrained—some were even barbers.

Many women crossed into Kansas after its legislature liberalized abortion that same year. The wait time for procedures quickly reached five weeks, and roughly 200 women per day called one Kansas hospital for information. The law required two letters from licensed physicians attesting that the woman's physical or mental health was at risk.

---

24 McDevitt, C. (2020, June 8). *Interview with Frank Susman* [Personal interview].

Abortions were permitted in cases of fetal deformity, rape, incest or other felonious sexual acts.

A three-judge panel in Kansas City ruled Missouri's 1973 law unconstitutional, citing *Roe v. Wade* and *Doe v. Bolton*. In November 1974, the U.S. Supreme Court affirmed the panel's decision.

Yet victories like this did not make subsequent challenges easier. Each new abortion case presented distinct legal issues that *Roe* and *Doe* had left unresolved.

Susman and other attorneys found themselves litigating a new wave of restrictions: parental-consent, spousal-consent and hospital-approval requirements—laws crafted by state legislatures determined to chip away at abortion access.

"Each case I undertook affected more than just the originally named plaintiff," Susman said.

Missouri's post-*Roe* abortion law introduced new regulations that quickly drew legal challenges from Planned Parenthood and other providers. The statute's definition of viability—as the point when artificial support systems could maintain fetal life—was especially problematic. Other contested provisions included spousal and parental consent, record-keeping mandates and a ban on certain procedures such as saline amniocentesis after 12 weeks. The law also imposed manslaughter charges on physicians who failed to "preserve fetal life" when required.

The district court found that the parental-consent provision was overly broad because it failed to distinguish between pre- and post-viability, but it upheld several other sections. Frank Susman appealed the case to the U.S. Supreme Court, arguing that the statute singled out abortion for restrictions not applied to other medical procedures, thereby placing an unfair and unconstitutional burden on patients and providers.

Spousal consent, he argued, allowed a husband to unilaterally veto a woman's decision to terminate her pregnancy. The Supreme Court agreed. Because the state could not prohibit abortion during the first trimester, the Court held that the decision belonged to the patient and her doctor. The state could not delegate that authority to anyone else—not even a spouse.

If spouses disagreed, the Court ruled, the woman's decision must prevail, as she was the one directly affected. Spousal-consent requirements were therefore declared unconstitutional.

The statute's parental-consent clause applied to unmarried women under 18. Missouri prosecutors argued that the state had a legitimate interest in protecting minors' welfare and could therefore impose greater restrictions. Susman countered that minors already received pregnancy-related medical care without parental consent—no such requirement existed for other procedures. The Supreme Court struck down the provision, ruling that states may not impose blanket consent laws during the first 12 weeks of pregnancy.

The record-keeping section required state officials to monitor every abortion performed and to retain documentation for seven years. The Court upheld this provision, finding that reasonable public health record keeping was constitutional so long as it did not violate patient privacy.

Overall, the justices upheld most of Susman's challenges to the statute—a major victory for abortion rights advocates.

The Edelin Trial

The trial and appeal of Dr. Kenneth Edelin became one of Susman's most significant cases, testing *Roe*'s viability standard, which had never defined the exact point at which a fetus could survive outside the womb. The Supreme Court had left that determination to the states.

In Boston, a heavily Catholic city still reeling from *Roe v. Wade*, abortion dominated public discourse. Local politicians recognized its political potency.

Thomas Connelly, a prominent Boston anti-abortion leader, began protesting outside hospitals in early 1973. Conducting his own investigation into Boston City Hospital, he interviewed nurses who mentioned Dr. Kenneth Edelin, a Black physician who often treated low-income women seeking abortions. Connelly alleged that the hospital used fetal tissue from abortions for medical research. He and fellow activists held a press conference to publicize their claims.

In September 1973, the Boston City Council convened hearings on abortion practices at city hospitals. Monsignor Paul Harrington of the Roman Catholic Archdiocese of Boston testified that abortion was morally indefensible under any circumstances, even comparing it to the Holocaust.

Other anti-abortion witnesses demanded a criminal investigation. Bowing to pressure, Assistant District Attorney Newman Flanagan, an ambitious young prosecutor, convened a grand jury to investigate Boston City Hospital.

Prosecutors called Dr. Edelin to testify. Earlier that year, he had performed an abortion later in pregnancy on a 17-year-old Black woman whose pregnancy was estimated between 20–28 weeks. After his testimony, the district attorney's office charged him with manslaughter, arguing that the fetus had been viable. The case drew both local and national attention.

Religious groups played a major role in shaping public opinion. On the anti-abortion side, the National Right to Life Committee (NRLC) intensified its campaign for restrictions and bans. The organization's momentum was driven by Dr. Mildred Jefferson, the first Black woman to graduate from Harvard Medical School.

Denied many professional opportunities because of racism, Jefferson became one of the most visible leaders of the anti-abortion movement. Journalist Joshua Prager, in *The Family Roe: An American Story*, emphasized her overlooked influence, noting that historians often portrayed the movement as dominated by white men. Jefferson strongly condemned Edelin and framed the case as emblematic of *Roe*'s moral dangers.

On the pro-choice side, ministers and rabbis formed the Religious Coalition for Abortion Rights (RCAR) in 1973. The coalition, which had earlier lobbied for repeal of restrictive laws, sought to counteract the rising tide of conservative religious opposition. Its leaders believed that a theological voice in defense of reproductive freedom could serve as a moral counterweight to the anti-abortion narrative. The RCAR publicly supported Edelin, portraying his prosecution as a threat to both women's rights and physicians' medical autonomy.

During the trial, Assistant District Attorney Newman Flanagan called a series of anti-abortion medical experts, who testified that the fetus could have survived outside the womb and that Edelin had a responsibility to save it.

Flanagan explained his reasoning to ABC News:

A woman has a right to have an abortion. But after the termination of the pregnancy, which is the abortion, what rights does the individual that becomes alive and on its own systems have following the termination of the pregnancy?

William Homans, Edelin's defense attorney, countered with expert witnesses who testified that the procedure was permissible under *Roe v. Wade* and consistent with accepted medical standards at the time.

Homans argued that Dr. Edelin had acted in the best interests of poor Black women—the group most likely to die from dangerous back-alley abortions.

Judge James McGuire, however, cautioned against introducing issues of class into the trial, saying he wanted to focus solely on the legal questions at hand. During the proceedings, McGuire admitted a photograph of the aborted fetus into evidence—a decision Homans protested as highly prejudicial to the jury.

In his charge to the jury, Judge McGuire explained the legal definition of "personhood." He drew a sharp line between the born and the unborn, emphasizing that the law recognized rights only after birth.

"A fetus is not a person and not the subject of an indictment for manslaughter," McGuire said. "In order for a person to exist, he or she must be born. Unborn persons, as I said, are not the subject of the crime of manslaughter.

"Birth is the process which causes the emergence of a new individual from the body of its mother. Once outside the body of its mother, the child has been born within the commonly accepted meaning of that word."

In his closing argument, Flanagan insisted that the fetus was viable and independent. Homans countered that it was not a person under the law. The jury retired with those arguments in mind—and later returned a guilty verdict.

As the decision was read, a man in the courtroom shouted a racial epithet directed at Edelin. Anti-abortion advocates denied that racism had influenced the outcome, claiming that "no one could tell" the light-skinned Edelin was African American.

Judge McGuire sentenced Edelin to one year of probation, but delayed enforcement pending appeal. Edelin returned to Boston City Hospital, which soon adopted a policy of referring women seeking abortions to other facilities.

After the conviction, the Boston Area Socialist-Feminist Organization organized a protest. Two thousand women flooded the streets of downtown Boston. Gloria Steinem spoke to the crowd as demonstrators carried handmade signs demanding that the state "Keep Your Hands Off Edelin."

Officials at Boston City Hospital publicly expressed support for Edelin. Most abortion-clinic directors in the city, including Bill Baird, believed the verdict would mainly affect late-term procedures; earlier abortions, they said, would likely remain protected even if the conviction were upheld.

A *McCall's* magazine survey of 97 abortion providers, all of whom performed procedures beyond 12 weeks, found that only 45 continued to do so after the verdict.

When Edelin returned to work two weeks later, he found his desk piled high with letters of support. His staff greeted him with a handwritten sign reading, "Welcome Home."

Edelin read one note for CBS News cameras.

> *I feel tremendously shocked and angry at the guilty verdict given to you. And the injustice of making up laws about the life of a fetus inside the courtroom by non-medical people is ludicrous.*

Doctors across the country began to fear prosecution for performing later-term abortions. In New York, one woman filed a $250,000 damages lawsuit against a hospital that refused to perform her abortion because she was three and a half months pregnant.

Dr. Mitchell Rabkin of Beth Israel Hospital called it an untenable situation—for the Supreme Court to affirm a constitutional right to abortion while prosecutors simultaneously pursued manslaughter charges against physicians exercising that right.

"Consequently since no one wants to be hauled up for manslaughter, he will tend to be more and more conservative," Rabkin said.

Rabkin predicted that this climate of fear would disproportionately harm younger and poorer women. Beyond pre-teens, he noted, it would especially affect women who discovered fetal deformities late in pregnancy, when procedures were more complex and already stigmatized.

Almost two years later, the Massachusetts Supreme Judicial Court overturned Dr. Edelin's conviction. The justices ruled that the verdict was inconsistent with the evidence and that nothing about Edelin's procedure had been reckless or unlawful.

The Court further held that Flanagan had prejudiced the jury by arguing that the fetus was a "person," a claim unsupported by Massachusetts law.

Edelin told ABC News that the controversy wasn't going away.

> *I'm not sure it's ever going to end. The people who are against abortion have some valid arguments for their side. The people who are for freedom of choice for women have valid arguments on their side. And I think the arguments are going to continue for a very long time. I'm not sure the arguments will ever end.*

Other, similar cases emerged throughout the 1970s. In Pittsburgh, Dr. Cyril Wecht, serving as county coroner, convened an inquest into the case of Dr. Leonard Laufe, a gynecologist accused of performing a late-term abortion for a woman who said she had been impregnated by a rapist. Manslaughter was listed as a potential charge.

A coroner's inquest is a formal judicial inquiry conducted by a coroner to determine the circumstances surrounding a person's death, particularly when the cause is sudden, unexplained, violent or occurs under suspicious or unusual conditions. The inquest does not assign criminal or civil liability but seeks to establish key facts: the identity of the deceased, the time and place of death and the medical cause and manner of death—whether it was natural, accidental, suicidal or homicidal. Witnesses may be called to testify under oath, and evidence such as medical reports and police findings is presented. The coroner or, in some jurisdictions, a jury then delivers findings or recommendations to help prevent similar deaths in the future.

Although a coroner's inquest does not determine criminal guilt, its findings can carry significant weight. Prosecutors are often under pressure to align their charging decisions with the inquest's conclusions, especially when the inquiry has drawn public attention or established a clear narrative about how the death occurred.

Dr. Laufe, a highly respected obstetrician-gynecologist, faced a panel that deliberated for just one hour before clearing him of all wrongdoing.

For a socially conservative city like Pittsburgh, Wecht found the verdict telling. It revealed, he believed, a shift in public sensibility about abortion—an acknowledgment, even among conservatives, of its necessity in certain circumstances.

"I can't tell you what was on the jury's minds," Wecht said. "I have no way of knowing that. I will say my thoughts, and it's just my conjecture. Based upon what I think people feel, I think that could well have been a factor in Dr. Laufe's favor in the fact that the woman had been raped and didn't want the baby."

Criminal prosecutions for manslaughter charges stemming from abortions declined sharply in the years that followed.

Nonetheless, in the decades ahead, anti-abortion activists continued to distort the debate by exaggerating the prevalence of third-trimester abortions. They had learned from the Edelin trial how potent public reaction could be to graphic imagery of later-stage fetal development— and how such imagery could be wielded to sway public opinion against abortion rights.

The legal battles that followed *Roe v. Wade* revealed how fragile the new constitutional protections were and how quickly opponents adapted to challenge them in courtrooms and legislatures. Each victory for reproductive freedom prompted an equal and opposite campaign to restrict it—setting the stage for the next era of struggle, defined by the Hyde Amendment and the political rise of the religious right.

CHAPTER 8
Access for All

While doctors were largely protected from prosecution after *Roe v. Wade*, making abortion accessible remained a central challenge for abortion rights activists. One case in particular dominated headlines in the mid-1970s.

Rosie Jimenez, a 27-year-old Texas woman, was studying to become a special education teacher when she became pregnant. A single mother on welfare, she could not afford another child. Unfortunately, by 1977, the newly passed Hyde Amendment barred Medicaid from covering abortions performed by licensed physicians.

Unable to pay for a safe procedure, Jimenez turned to an illegal abortionist in McAllen, Texas. The operation led to a fatal infection.

Many blamed her death directly on the Hyde Amendment. Abortion rights advocates argued that it forced poor women back to unsafe back-alley providers—reviving the dangers *Roe* had sought to end.

Representative Henry Hyde (R–IL) had sponsored the amendment, first passed in 1976 as a rider to the federal appropriations bill for what later became the Department of Health and Human Services. A former trial attorney and devout Catholic from a wealthy Chicago suburb, Hyde persuaded his colleagues to support the measure—comparing abortion to the Holocaust.

"The only virtue to abortion is that it is a final solution," the lawmaker said at the time. "Believe me, it is a final solution, especially to the unborn child."

The Hyde Amendment prohibited the use of federal funds and government insurance plans to cover abortion costs. Under the law, Medicaid recipients could receive funding for an abortion only if the pregnancy resulted from rape or incest, or if the woman's life was in danger. Over time, Congress made the law even more restrictive, eliminating coverage in many of those exceptions as well.

That meant that even if a doctor recommended abortion because of serious health risks to the mother or fetus, federal funds could not be used. If a fetus could be carried to term but born without brain tissue, Medicaid still would not cover the procedure. The policy placed a crushing burden on low-income women and communities of color.

Despite decades of criticism, Congress has renewed the Hyde Amendment every year since its passage.

Before Hyde, approximately one million women each year had Medicaid-funded abortions. The practice began in New York State in 1970 and spread nationwide after *Roe v. Wade*. Anti-abortion advocates mounted an aggressive letter-writing campaign that successfully shifted political sentiment, especially among moderates.

Republicans, including Sen. James Buckley of New York, argued that Medicaid-funded abortions forced taxpayers to subsidize a procedure they opposed. Health experts countered that wealthy women would always have access to abortion, while poor women would simply resort to unsafe methods.

In the mid-1970s, a CBS News segment featured three Black women who said they could no longer afford legal abortions and feared being forced back to unsafe back-alley providers. Another woman pointed out that many of the resulting births would end up on welfare, ultimately costing taxpayers far more than funding abortions through Medicaid.

The Department of Health, Education, and Welfare (HEW) estimated that Medicaid abortions cost $55 million annually, but that eliminating the funding would result in over $500 million in additional welfare expenses in the first year alone.

The Hyde Amendment galvanized a new wave of feminist activism, particularly among women of color who had often been sidelined in mainstream movements. Some of the earliest pioneers in the fight for reproductive justice were Black women who demanded to be heard.

Among them was Byllye Avery, who since the 1970s has fought to ensure women of color are included as fully as their white counterparts in the reproductive rights movement.

In 1974, Avery and two other women founded the Gainesville Women's Health Center, a first-trimester abortion and gynecological clinic. The experience was eye-opening for her; she saw firsthand how frequently Black women sought abortions—and how deeply structural inequality shaped those choices.

"A large part of it was really not having access to contraception and not knowing how to use it because it's not such an easy thing to do," Avery said. "Everybody just thinks that 'Oh, you just do this. You just do that.' But a lot of women had a lot of trouble."

She reflected on the differences between white women's health concerns and those of Black women. They shared many of the same struggles, she observed, but their priorities and lived realities often diverged.

"While white women were talking about reproductive health, black women were really talking more about psychological issues that had to do with racism, sexism, classism and all of the feelings of being left out," Avery said.

Congressman Robert Drinan (D–MA), a Jesuit priest elected on an anti–Vietnam War platform, emerged as one of the most vocal opponents of the Hyde Amendment.

Although Drinan personally opposed abortion, he believed that legality and morality were distinct issues. He supported a more lenient version of the ban proposed by the Senate, arguing that government policy should not impose religious or moral doctrine.

Drinan called it hypocritical that businesses and taxpayers could deduct portions of their health-insurance premiums that covered abortion services, while the Hyde Amendment denied poor women access to the same medical care through Medicaid.

"There is no such thing as one Catholic position on abortion," Drinan said. "Many Catholics say they don't approve of abortion, but they would not impose their views on others. People who think this is wrong have a right to influence public morality."

When the Hyde Amendment passed, Dr. Richard Sweet, chief of OB/GYN at San Francisco General Hospital, opened the city's first clinic offering both family-planning services and abortions. The facility provided care for women who needed later-term abortions or who relied on public insurance that no longer covered the procedure.

Polling in 1976 showed that most voters did not view abortion as a decisive issue in the presidential election. President Gerald Ford opposed a constitutional amendment banning abortion outright, but favored one that would allow individual states to decide.

He told CBS News anchor Walter Cronkite that he considered himself a moderate on the issue—opposed to unrestricted access but also uncomfortable with overturning *Roe v. Wade*:

I think we have to recognize that there are instances when abortion should be permitted. The illness of the mother, rape or any of the other unfortunate things that might happen. There has to be some flexibility. I think the court decision went too far. I think a constitutional amendment goes too far. If there was to be some action in this area, it's my judgment that it ought to be on the basis of what each individual state wishes to do under the circumstances.

Ford said that although he disagreed with the Court's ruling, he would uphold its interpretation of *Roe v. Wade*. The Supreme Court had largely forbidden states from imposing broad restrictions, which was why Ford favored an amendment allowing state legislatures to regulate abortion as they saw fit. It was a subtler challenge to abortion rights than a nationwide ban—one that would allow individual states to take either a liberal or conservative approach.

Ford recognized that abortion had become a volatile political issue, and many of his advisors adopted a cautious tone when discussing it. First Lady Betty Ford, however, publicly broke with her husband's moderation, calling *Roe v. Wade* "a great, great decision."

Federal law left the funding of abortions to the states. As a result, anti-abortion leaders concentrated on lobbying state and local legislatures to restrict or eliminate public funding for abortion after *Roe v. Wade*.

In 1977, the Supreme Court ruled 6–3 in *Beal v. Doe* that although women had a constitutional right to abortion, they did not have a right to have the state pay for it. Justice Lewis Powell, writing for the majority, held that states and the federal government could choose to fund abortions if they wished, but were not required to do so. He concluded that Pennsylvania's Medicaid restrictions did not interfere with physicians' ability to offer medical opinions or treatment options simply by denying coverage.

Elsewhere, medical professionals condemned the government's stance on Medicaid-funded abortions. Dr. Newton Long of Grady Hospital in Atlanta warned that thousands of women who had previously relied on safe hospital procedures would now return to backrooms and unsafe abortionists.

"Our mortality rate would go back up," Long told CBS News. "When I came to this hospital, there was never a time that we didn't have at least three critically ill patients from the consequences of illegal abortion. Last year, we had two the entire year. So no question that will go up."

Financial aid covered roughly 300,000 abortions per year out of approximately 1.1 million total procedures, according to CBS News.

Frances Kissling, then the executive director of the National Abortion Federation (NAF), was among those most shaken by Rosie Jimenez's death. The NAF, a Washington, D.C.–based trade association of abortion providers, viewed the tragedy as emblematic of the Hyde Amendment's deadly consequences.

For Kissling, Jimenez's death brought several realities into focus. She believed the Hyde Amendment should be repealed and that Medicaid must once again cover abortion costs.

Many others in the movement, however, felt that activism should center on preserving abortion's legality rather than fighting over funding.

Kissling warned that this approach risked abandoning poor women and creating a two-tiered system in which wealth determined access to reproductive rights.

"The decision had its reasons in terms of the movement at that time, mostly as a fundraising strategy," Kissling said. "To focus on the threat of a constitutional amendment, which would affect every woman in the country, was more sellable than a massive effort to protect poor women because, basically, the public doesn't like poor people."

In the Jimenez case, local police took minimal action. Although early investigations revealed that Jimenez had gone to a lay midwife known for performing unsafe abortions in Texas, police made no serious effort to follow up—even ignoring leads from two women who had accompanied her.

It was activists, not law enforcement, who ultimately exposed the midwife. They organized a sting operation in which the woman was recorded offering to perform an abortion for $125. The evidence led to the only legal consequence: the midwife was sentenced to three days in jail and fined $100. Notably, she was never charged in connection with Jimenez's death from septic complications.

Kissling, one of the activists involved, was outraged by what she viewed as law enforcement's negligence. She joined forces with Ellen Frankfurt, a feminist author, to investigate Jimenez's death themselves. Together, they carried out the sting operation against the back-alley provider in McAllen, Texas, gathering the proof that authorities had failed to pursue.

"What was amazing in my mind was that the police department was not interested enough to do this," Kissling said. "These are the kinds of things that get neglected. When they relate to abortion or women's health, or when they relate to Latinos in McAllen, there's a lot of prejudice."

"It's much easier to say, 'Oh this didn't happen in our community. There's nothing that happened in our community. She did it in Mexico.'"

In late 1977, the U.S. Senate debated for four months over the wording of the Hyde Amendment, with several senators holding out for more liberal language. In November, they approved a compromise allowing Medicaid to pay for abortions in cases of rape or incest—but only if the incident had been reported to law enforcement or a health agency. Coverage was also permitted in cases where pregnancy threatened severe and long-lasting physical damage to the mother's health. The House of Representatives subsequently approved the revised language.

That same year, three Supreme Court cases—*Maher v. Roe, Poelker v. Doe*, and *Beal v. Doe*—established lasting precedents for how judges would interpret the Medicaid abortion-funding debate. The pseudonyms Roe, Doe, and Poe were used to protect the identities of the women involved. All three cases were decided on the same day.

In *Maher v. Roe*, the Court considered whether a state participating in the Medicaid program was constitutionally obligated to fund elective abortions. The case stemmed from a Connecticut regulation limiting Medicaid reimbursement for abortions to those deemed "medically necessary," effectively denying coverage for elective, nontherapeutic procedures.

A woman identified as Roe challenged the policy, arguing that by funding childbirth but not abortion, the state was violating the constitutional protections recognized in *Roe v. Wade*, particularly for low-income women dependent on Medicaid for healthcare.

In a 6–3 decision, the Court upheld Connecticut's policy. It ruled that while the Constitution protects a woman's right to choose abortion, it does not guarantee a right to government funding to exercise that choice.

The decision drew a clear distinction between state interference with a right and state inaction. By choosing to fund childbirth but not abortion, the Court said, Connecticut was expressing a policy preference—not imposing a direct obstacle.

The ruling solidified a crucial principle: governments may lawfully encourage childbirth over abortion through funding mechanisms. It also laid the foundation for future restrictions on public funding, ensuring the continued enforcement of the federal Hyde Amendment.[25]

In *Poelker v. Doe*, the Supreme Court examined whether a city

---

25 Oyez. (n.d.). *Maher v. Roe*. Retrieved July 30, 2025, from https://www.oyez.org/cases/1976/75-1440

government could constitutionally refuse to provide publicly funded, nontherapeutic abortions in its municipal hospitals. The case centered on St. Louis, Missouri, where the city's mayor—an openly anti-abortion official—had ordered public hospitals not to perform elective abortions.

A woman identified as Jane Doe, who was indigent and sought an abortion at one of the city's hospitals, filed suit. She argued that the policy violated her constitutional rights under *Roe v. Wade* by effectively denying poor women access to abortion services that wealthier women could obtain in private facilities.

In a 6–3 decision, the Court upheld the city's policy. The justices ruled that there was no constitutional obligation for a municipality to provide elective abortions in public hospitals.

The majority reasoned that while the Constitution protects a woman's right to choose abortion, it does not require the government to actively facilitate that choice through publicly funded institutions.

The Court further emphasized that elected officials may reflect their constituents' moral views in shaping public policy—so long as they do not impose direct legal barriers to abortion access.

Like *Maher v. Roe*, the *Poelker* ruling reaffirmed the principle that governments may withhold public funding and facilities for abortion without violating constitutional rights.[26]

In *Beal v. Doe*, the Supreme Court considered whether states participating in the federal Medicaid program were required to fund nontherapeutic abortions as part of their obligation to provide "necessary medical services."

The case originated in Pennsylvania, where the state had implemented Medicaid regulations excluding coverage for elective abortions. Several women—including one identified as Jane Doe—filed a class-action lawsuit challenging the policy, arguing that it violated the federal Medicaid Act and denied equal access to medical care for low-income women seeking abortions.

In a 6–3 decision, the Court upheld Pennsylvania's restriction, ruling that the federal Medicaid statute did not compel states to fund elective

---

26 Ibid.

abortions. The majority held that the law required states to cover only "medically necessary" services, and that states retained broad discretion to define what qualified under that standard.

Together, the *Beal, Maher,* and *Poelker* decisions marked a critical turning point in narrowing federal protections for abortion access after *Roe v. Wade.* They affirmed that while the federal government may fund Medicaid, it is not obligated to cover all constitutionally protected medical options.

The trilogy established the enduring legal foundation for public-funding restrictions on abortion care—a framework that continues to shape reproductive policy to this day.[27]

On the activism front, an increasing number of abortion rights leaders began fighting for the restoration of federal funding for abortions.

Among them was Mulhauser, by then the executive director of NARAL. In 1978, two men broke into her Washington, D.C., home and raped her.

The following year, Mulhauser testified before Congress against the Hyde Amendment, arguing that it forced poor women to carry pregnancies to term—even in cases of rape. She described herself as a "double victim"—first of sexual violence, and then of a system that denied women the means to make their own reproductive choices.

"I said to the elected officials, 'You really need to hear some real human life stories before you make decisions,'" Mulhauser said. "And so of course, the anti-abortion people put out lots of communications about how I made up the whole story. And I actually, of course, reported it to the police."

President Jimmy Carter opposed federal funding for abortions except in cases of rape or incest. He supported family-planning programs, but maintained that "people don't plan for abortions."

Carter drew criticism from pro-choice advocates when they questioned him about his stance on the *Beal v. Doe* decision. His comments revealed a widening gap between the Democratic administration and the

---

27 Oyez. (n.d.). *Beal v. Doe.* Retrieved July 30, 2025, from https://www.oyez.org/cases/1976/75-554

reproductive rights movement, which increasingly viewed access to abortion funding as central to true equality.

"Well, as you know, there are many things in life that aren't fair that wealthy people can afford and poor people can't," Carter said. "But I don't believe the federal government should take action to try to make these opportunities exactly equal, particularly when there is a moral factor involved."

The Supreme Court continued to reaffirm its position on the Hyde Amendment in the years that followed. This became evident in the 1980 case of Cora McRae, a pregnant Medicaid recipient in her first trimester.

McRae sought an abortion that Medicaid refused to cover under the new restrictions. She joined Planned Parenthood and several hospitals in suing the secretary of Health, Education and Welfare—a case initially titled *McRae v. Mathews.*

At the district court level, Judge John F. Dooling Jr. issued a preliminary injunction in January 1980, ruling that the Hyde Amendment likely violated the due process clause and the establishment clause of the Constitution. He found that denying Medicaid coverage for medically necessary abortions coerced poor women and infringed upon their constitutional rights.

The case was later appealed to the Supreme Court, where it became known as *Harris v. McRae.*

Patricia Harris was the U.S. secretary of Health, Education and Welfare, the federal official responsible for administering Medicaid. She was named in *Harris v. McRae* not because of any personal role in crafting abortion policy, but because the lawsuit challenged the federal government's enforcement of the Hyde Amendment, which she was legally obligated to implement in her official capacity.

McRae's case was argued by Rhonda Copelon of the Center for Reproductive Rights, who contended that the Hyde Amendment unconstitutionally coerced women's reproductive decisions by restricting abortion access based on financial means—and that it violated both the due process and establishment clauses.[28]

28 Center for Biology and Society. (n.d.). *Harris v. McRae (1980).* Embryo Project Encyclopedia. Arizona State University. Retrieved July 30, 2025, from https://embryo.asu.edu/pages/harris-v-mcrae-1980

They argued that by withholding Medicaid coverage for abortion—except in rare circumstances such as when the pregnant person's life was endangered—the federal government was effectively coercing poor women into carrying pregnancies to term, while wealthier women retained full access to abortion services.

In a 5–4 decision, the Supreme Court rejected these arguments, ruling that the government's decision not to fund abortion did not impose an unconstitutional burden on the right to choose. The majority reasoned that the Hyde Amendment merely reflected a policy preference for childbirth over abortion and did not prevent anyone from obtaining an abortion with private funds.

The Court reaffirmed the principles established in earlier funding cases such as *Maher v. Roe* and *Beal v. Doe*, emphasizing that a woman's constitutional right to abortion does not extend to a right to government assistance in exercising that choice.

The ruling cemented the legality of public-funding restrictions on abortion and had enduring consequences for low-income women's access to reproductive healthcare.[29]

In 1978, the Planned Parenthood Federation of America entered a new chapter in its history with the appointment of Faye Wattleton as president. At 34, she became both the youngest person and the first African-American to hold the position—a choice that reflected the changing face of the women's movement and the organization's recognition that its leadership needed to speak to a broader, more diverse America.

Wattleton's background in nursing and public health, combined with her experience as executive director of the Dayton, Ohio, affiliate, gave her both the clinical insight and the administrative acumen to steer Planned Parenthood through increasingly turbulent political waters.

From the outset, Wattleton made it clear that her presidency would be defined by action and advocacy. She inherited an organization that had grown in size and influence but now faced mounting political and cultural challenges in the post–*Roe v. Wade* era. Rather than keeping Planned Parenthood at arm's length from these battles, she insisted on

---

29 Oyez. (n.d.). *Harris v. McRae*. Retrieved July 30, 2025, from https://www.oyez.org/cases/1979/79-4

placing it squarely at the center of them.

To Wattleton, safeguarding reproductive rights was inseparable from providing reproductive health care. Under her leadership, the federation would not simply respond to attacks—it would proactively shape the national conversation and push for policies that expanded access to contraception, family planning and abortion services.

Her vision extended far beyond Planned Parenthood's traditional constituency. Wattleton sought to bring the organization's services into underserved communities—rural areas, low-income neighborhoods and regions where women of color had historically been denied access to reproductive care. She understood that the movement's credibility depended on its ability to serve all women, not just those with the means or proximity to established clinics.

By building coalitions across racial, economic and geographic lines, Wattleton reframed reproductive freedom as an issue of social justice. In doing so, she ushered Planned Parenthood into a new era—one defined by unapologetic defense of reproductive rights and by a determination to meet women wherever they were.[30]

Wattleton had witnessed firsthand the dangers of self-induced abortions during her early career at a hospital in Harlem. According to her autobiography *Life on the Line*, roughly 6,500 women were treated for abortion-related complications during her tenure there.

Wattleton brought both clinical experience and moral urgency to her role. She attended the *Harris v. McRae* hearing at the Supreme Court and later reflected on the decision's far-reaching significance for reproductive rights and the fight for equitable access to abortion care.

"The truth was that abortion was no longer secure, and it was the beginning of the end for all women," she wrote in her autobiography. "The court had declared that when it came to funding, the government did not have to remain neutral between childbirth and abortion—the opposite of its ruling in *Roe*. The government could push interest in the fetus, using dollars to back its position."

---

30 The Plain Dealer. (1978, May 21). *[Profile of Faye Wattleton's appointment as president of Planned Parenthood]*. *The Plain Dealer* (Cleveland, Ohio), pp. 253–254, 257–260, 262. https://www.newspapers.com/image/1065435640/

Religious Opposition Begins to Take Shape

During the 1976 presidential campaign, leaders of the U.S. Conference of Catholic Bishops met with President Carter at the White House to discuss abortion. They disapproved of Carter's position, which neither supported abortion rights outright nor fully rejected them. After the meeting, Church leaders said the president's explanation was "encouraging" but ultimately unsatisfactory.

Reporters later asked Archbishop Joseph Bernardin to compare Carter's and Gerald Ford's views. Bernardin criticized Carter for refusing to support any constitutional amendment—whether a total ban or one allowing states to regulate abortion individually.

Catholic leaders were unimpressed with the "states' rights" approach, arguing that it failed to meet their goal of an outright national prohibition.

The Catholic Church was, and remains, highly organized in the politics of abortion. Each diocese maintained a pro-life committee, often mirrored in local parishes. These committees coordinated nationwide efforts to push for a constitutional amendment recognizing fetal personhood. They meticulously tracked abortion-related votes by incumbents and challengers in every congressional district across the country.

Anti-abortion demonstrators shadowed Carter throughout his first campaign. Protestors carried signs accusing him of "discriminating against the unborn."

In one instance, Carter had to move a scheduled speech from a Catholic church to a Lutheran church in Philadelphia amid concerns that he would discuss abortion.

Cardinal John Krol, the Archbishop of Philadelphia, told ABC News that he was not partisan, but nonetheless criticized Carter's position on abortion, saying it fell short of the Church's moral expectations.

"When he says, and he said this, that as far as he is concerned, a decision from the Supreme Court right or wrong is something that he accepts, then I have to say we have to wash out the Nuremberg trials because those people at those trials appealed to the law of the land to justify some of the worst types of atrocities," Krol said. "The killing of the defenseless unborn child, in my judgment, is of utmost importance."

Carter sought to appeal directly to Catholic parishioners rather than seeking approval from their leaders. He drew a large crowd in Pittsburgh's Polish Hill, a devout Catholic neighborhood, where he confronted the abortion issue head-on with a parish priest standing nearby. Carter emphasized the importance of family values, striking a tone that blended personal faith with political pragmatism.

Despite his tensions with Catholic leaders, polls showed that many Catholic voters—the laity—generally supported him.

Democratic vice presidential candidate Walter Mondale largely avoided the topic during the campaign, focusing instead on Watergate, the scandal that had led to Richard Nixon's resignation. President Ford's pardon of Nixon still lingered in the public's memory and dominated voter sentiment.

At the same time, the U.S. Conference of Catholic Bishops met in Washington, D.C., and reaffirmed that their support for fetal personhood extended through all stages of pregnancy. While critics accused them of single-issue politics, the bishops maintained that if they were to stand for one principle, it would be the defense of developing human life and all that sustained it.

The political and religious rhetoric surrounding abortion grew increasingly inflammatory. Archbishop Fulton Sheen, a nationally known Catholic broadcaster and theologian, described abortion rights supporters as "lovers of death" and "necrophiliacs."

In response, Rabbi Richard Sternberger of the Religious Coalition for Abortion Rights (RCAR) called Sheen a demagogue and urged a return to rational dialogue.

In its early years, the RCAR focused heavily on Medicaid funding for abortions. When engaging opponents, its leaders often asked whether anti-abortion activists supported Medicaid coverage for abortions in cases of rape or incest. To oppose such exceptions, they argued, revealed a lack of empathy and undermined claims of moral consistency.

Around that time, there was an uptick in anti-abortion violence. An arsonist had set a St. Paul abortion clinic afire. Someone fired bullets into another facility and then attempted to bomb it. In Omaha, another arsonist threw four bottles of gasoline through a clinic window that ignited and caused $35,000 in damage. The perpetrator sent a letter to a local newspaper with glued letters that said, "You'd bomb a concentration camp—why not abortion centers?"

The rise of conservative evangelism catalyzed part of religious radicalization. Theologians formulated extreme views on abortion. Francis Schaeffer, an evangelist for a conservative Presbyterian splinter group, campaigned vigorously against abortion and secular humanism. Schaeffer and his wife ran L'Abri, a Christian community in Switzerland. The evangelical community greatly respected Schaeffer, and he had even drawn left-leaning musicians and thinkers to his retreat, including Timothy Leary and Jimmy Page. Eric Clapton praised his study retreat while not commenting on his later anti-abortion work.

Several years after abortion was legalized, Schaeffer's son Frank persuaded him to take a stronger stance against it. The pair filmed a documentary series, "How Should We Then Live?," in which the final two episodes focused on abortion. The thrust of the whole work was that secular humanism had supposedly destroyed the Christian foundation on which Western civilization had been built. Abortion was the prime example of that erosion, Frank Schaeffer explained in his autobiography *Crazy for God*.

Francis Schaeffer hadn't wanted to focus on abortion, but he acquiesced to his son's demand. Following the film's release, Schaeffer toured the U.S. to promote the documentary and its related book. They showcased it in Madison Square Garden.

Schaeffer followed that documentary series with another called "Whatever Happened to the Human Race?"

Pediatric surgeon C. Everett Koop and the young Frank Schaeffer developed the series together. Koop had been a leading pediatric surgeon and surgeon-in-chief of the Philadelphia Children's Hospital. Koop was an ardent pro-lifer and a member of the same conservative Presbyterian sect as the Schaeffers (the Presbyterian Church in America). The series focused on infanticide, abortion and euthanasia. They didn't use images of dead fetuses. Instead, they used allegories and metaphors that incorporated plastic dolls and actors.

The films galvanized the evangelical community around abortion. The Schaeffers traveled the country and spoke to increasingly larger audiences, stressing the need to actively resist the secularization of Western culture. They helped increase the number of crisis pregnancy centers.

Schaeffer influenced early leaders of the Christian Right, such as Pat Robertson and Jerry Falwell, who railed against "secular humanism" and the supposed attack on Christian Western civilization. Schaeffer argued that living peacefully with secular people was unacceptable and ungodly. He came to see abortion as the embodiment of his argument.

Within anti-abortion literature, Randall Terry, founder of the militant direct action group Operation Rescue, credited Schaeffer with inspiring him. Terry became the face of the anti-abortion movement in the next few decades, taking a confrontational approach to blockade and harass abortion providers. Terry said during his career that anyone who wanted to understand Operation Rescue had to read Schaeffer's book *A Christian Manifesto*.

Around this time, anti-abortion lawyers began adopting the incrementalist approach to challenge abortion rights. Rather than attempting sweeping reforms all at once, this strategy focused on making many small policy changes over time to reduce abortions and the number of clinics. Some of these restrictions were subtly worded, but they had a profound cumulative impact on abortion access. Incrementalism relies on passing laws that chip away at abortion rights—often appearing minor or technical, yet steadily eroding protections.

Popular incrementalist tactics included parental and spousal consent laws, waiting periods, record-keeping and reporting mandates, hospitalization requirements, counseling scripts, funding restrictions, exclusions for emergency exceptions, and limitations on second-trimester procedures. Some bills bundled multiple restrictions into a single piece of legislation.

Record-keeping requirements proved especially intrusive, as anti-abortion organizations employed private investigators to obtain information through open-records requests and database searches of clinics and patients. For clinicians, compliance was time-consuming and expensive.

As the federal judiciary grew more conservative, many of these laws began to withstand legal challenges. Legislators later applied the incrementalist strategy to other social and civil rights issues, including voting rights, LGBTQ+ equality and racial justice.

Incrementalism also reduced political backlash. By advancing restrictions in small, seemingly technical steps, lawmakers could gauge public reaction, avoid large-scale protests and make each successive measure appear modest. Conservative think tanks such as the Heritage Foundation and Americans United for Life developed and disseminated model legislation that advanced anti-abortion objectives in piecemeal fashion.

Over time, these measures became increasingly invasive. For example, Kentucky recently enacted a law requiring women to obtain a death certificate and make funeral arrangements for embryonic tissue expelled after using abortion medication.

One way incrementalists sought success was by creating inconsistencies among federal district and circuit courts. For instance, if an abortion restriction passed in a liberal state, courts might strike it down as unconstitutional. But if the same law passed in a conservative state, appellate courts might uphold it. The result was a split among the circuits—for example, a law deemed unconstitutional in the Ninth Circuit (California) but upheld in the Fourth Circuit (North Carolina). Such conflicts increased the likelihood that the Supreme Court would step in to resolve the discrepancy, giving anti-abortion strategists an opening to re-litigate *Roe v. Wade*.

In the 1970s, Missouri lawmakers passed statutes requiring spousal consent for abortions and parental consent for minors under 18. In *Planned Parenthood of Central Missouri v. Danforth* (1976), the Supreme Court struck down these laws, ruling them unconstitutional because they granted third parties—fathers or husbands—authority the state itself did not possess under *Roe v. Wade*. The Court reaffirmed that states could not delegate power over a woman's body to others any more than they could exercise it directly.

As these incrementalist restrictions accumulated, they paved the way for a new category of legislation: Targeted Regulations of Abortion Providers (TRAP laws). These measures focused on reducing abortion access by imposing costly or unnecessary medical regulations, rather than banning the procedure outright.

This incremental approach dominated abortion politics for decades—until the Supreme Court's 2022 decision in *Dobbs v. Jackson Women's Health Organization*, which overturned *Roe v. Wade* and eliminated abortion rights as a federally protected freedom. I will discuss later how this incrementalist strategy evolved over the next several decades in subsequent chapters.

CHAPTER 9

Fire and Misplaced Faith

Toward the end of the 1970s, a group of courageous men and women staffed facilities that zealots increasingly attacked and harassed. Charlotte Taft—a lesbian abortion clinic director in Dallas—dealt with homophobia as well as the typical things that came with working at those places.

"Many of the most important organizations, clinics, agencies, in those years, were actually run by lesbians, and most people didn't have any idea of that," Taft said. "You know, it wasn't even in a conversation. This was so many years before Ellen DeGeneres came out. Lesbians, in many ways, were just invisible. They simply were not known or seen."

Anti-abortion advocates didn't discover Taft's sexuality until she went to San Francisco to be on the Democratic platform committee for vice presidential nominee Geraldine Ferraro. Taft's name was published on a list of gay representatives. Reporters noticed. Later, she appeared on a talk show with two anti-abortion leaders, including Bill Price of Texans United For Life.

Part way through the show, Price revealed that Taft was a lesbian. At the time, she hadn't come out of the closet.

"This really caught me off. It hit me sideways," Taft said.

Taft didn't acknowledge their discovery. She didn't know how to handle it. One of Taft's friends was in the audience and overheard someone say she should be killed.

Crisis pregnancy centers had been ubiquitous since Hawaii legalized abortion. One such place in Dallas was the White Rose Women's Center. Taft's abortion clinic was across the parking lot. The White Rose staff misled women who wanted to get an abortion. They advertised that they had information about abortion and financial aid.

The term White Rose came from a group of Christian martyrs in Nazi Germany. The White Rose was a nonviolent resistance group founded in 1942 by students and a professor at the University of Munich who opposed the Nazi regime. The group distributed anonymous leaflets urging Germans to resist Hitler and denounce the persecution of Jews. Their activities were short-lived. After being caught distributing leaflets, several members were arrested and executed in 1943. Though their immediate impact was limited, the White Rose became an enduring symbol of moral courage and resistance to tyranny.[31]

In the 1980s and 1990s, elements of the anti-abortion movement in the United States began invoking the White Rose as a moral and historical parallel, positioning themselves as righteous dissidents resisting what they viewed as a modern-day genocide. Activists and extremist factions claimed that just as the White Rose resisted the Nazi regime's crimes against humanity, they were resisting legalized abortion, which they equated with mass killing.[32]

Some anti-abortion groups have adopted the name "White Rose" for their literature or campaigns, attempting to lend their cause moral legitimacy by aligning with the legacy of nonviolent student martyrs. This appropriation was controversial, as critics argued it distorted the White Rose's original purpose—resisting fascism and state violence—by using it to justify coercive tactics, clinic harassment and, in some cases, violent extremism.

The White Rose staffers in Dallas roamed the parking lots in white

31 Ray, M. (2019, June 24). *White Rose*. Encyclopædia Britannica. Retrieved July 31, 2025, from Britannica website

32 Masucci, S. (2017). *From pacifism to pipe bombs: A history of the extremist anti-abortion movement in the United States* (Undergraduate honors thesis, University of South Carolina). Scholar Commons. https://scholarcommons.sc.edu/senior_theses/498

coats to persuade women to not go into the clinic. When women came in to the Women's Center, according to Taft, the counselors showed them horrifying videos purportedly depicting abortion.

Taft and her staff told everyone who called the clinic that an imposter clinic was nearby. Nevertheless, women still sometimes went to the wrong clinic. Taft knew who they were because they would be shaking and in tears when they came to her.

"It was very, very creepy and horrible," Taft said.

In Dallas, Taft organized candlelight vigils when doctors or clinics were attacked. They had many vigils in those years. Luckily, none of her staff or the nearby providers were harmed when they did.

"It was a frightening time," Taft said. "It was the Ronald Reagan years, which made it worse because we knew that Ronald Reagan was a big part of it."

Reagan had the most anti-abortion rhetoric of any president up to that point. In 1984, he published *Abortion and the Conscience of the Nation*, a manifesto that he co-wrote with his surgeon general, Charles Everett Koop. Reagan expressed support for the Human Life Bill and other pieces of legislation that would eliminate or diminish abortion access. Throughout the screed, Reagan emphasized certain qualities of the unborn—notably their ability to feel pain, which eventually became the basis for anti-abortion state legislation.

Reagan and Koop compared abortion care with the Holocaust. Koop said that the *Roe v. Wade* decision was a slippery slide into Auschwitz, the infamous concentration camp where the Nazis killed 1.1 million Jews.

Reagan's book on abortion alone didn't inflame the debate. At the time, the Fairness Doctrine governed radio and television. The policy required broadcasters to present complex issues honestly, equitably and in a balanced fashion. Reagan pushed for its removal.

"That was the beginning of the far right-wing Christian radio stations," Taft said. "They didn't have to show anything. If you want to ask, 'How the hell did we get into these two countries that we're in now?' I think that would be a big piece of it.

"What Reagan allowed was the ability to create completely separate news. If I'm watching MSNBC, I have one worldview. If I'm watching Fox or one of the other cable networks that are far-right wing, I have a completely different idea of what's true in the world."

Taft remembers one clinic burning to the ground in Dallas. That happened several times. Vandals attacked her center with red paint. They glued locks shut. Squirting butyric acid into clinics was another favorite tactic.

Butyric acid became one of the quieter but more insidious tools used against abortion clinics in the late twentieth century. Poured into hallways, vents, or entryways, the chemical's overwhelming stench—often compared to rancid butter or vomit—rendered clinics temporarily uninhabitable without causing visible structural damage. The intent was not subtle: to force closures, cancel appointments, and intimidate patients and staff through sensory assault rather than open violence. Though sometimes dismissed at the time as "stink attacks" or pranks, these incidents functioned as deliberate obstruction of medical care, part of a broader campaign of harassment that sought to make lawful abortion access impossible through fear, disruption and attrition rather than law.

"You can't explain anything like butyric acid," Taft said. "We had to send everyone home. People had to go to the hospital because they were throwing up. I think we had to pull up the carpet. It was horrifying."

According to the National Abortion Federation's data, between 1977 and 1988 there were 110 incidents of arson, firebombing or bombing targeting clinics—nearly all (98%) at facilities that provided abortion services. While that series spans 1977–1988, the mass of those attacks occurred in the 1980s—peaking in 1984 with 29 incidents and with elevated levels throughout the decade.[33]

Taft was on the National Abortion Federation board. Not only did she look at Dallas' situation but also the rest of the country. Operation Rescue was a big part of what she studied. Randall Terry had begun the organization in 1986. Terry compared his movement to slavery abolitionists. He described abortion clinics as "fortresses of hell."

---

33 Grimes, D. A., Forrest, J. D., Kirkman, A. L., & Radford, B. (1991). An epidemic of anti-abortion violence in the United States. *American Journal of Obstetrics and Gynecology*, *165*(5 Pt 1), 1263–1268. https://doi.org/10.1016/0002-9378(91)90346-S

The group focused on obstructing access to clinics. Blockades became their hallmark. They also picketed at homes. They shouted at women who sought abortions. They chained themselves to doors and lay across roads to prevent cars from moving. Terry was unlike other anti-abortion leaders in that he was well-spoken when many of them came off as inarticulate and physically unattractive. Terry claimed he took a nonviolent approach, but evidence indicated that his supporters were physically aggressive in protesting. The Feminist Majority Foundation conducted surveys of abortion providers in which they said as much.

He was part of a larger movement within Christian nationalism that took root in conservative America. It was a trend that started during President Carter's administration.

A Profound Movement Within Religious Politics

Carter began his presidency with strong evangelical support. Yet he ultimately became a lightning rod for what would evolve into the religious right—a new bloc of conservative voters pushing for anti-gay, anti-abortion and anti-feminist policies. A moderate Southern Baptist, Carter alienated many white evangelical voters through his support for racial equality and his positions on sex education and abortion.

Years after he had seemed the embodiment of evangelical life, Carter found himself estranged from that community. It is worth noting, however, that he was never an outspoken champion of abortion rights.

In 2012, Carter joined a group of Democrats urging the party to moderate its stance on abortion. He signed a letter organized by Democrats for Life of America, calling on the Democratic National Committee to support legal abortion only in cases of rape or incest or when a mother's life was at risk. Carter stated that he had always believed Jesus would disapprove of abortion and that, as president, he had worked to reduce the need for it while upholding *Roe v. Wade*. His comments reflected a longstanding discomfort with the Democratic Party's growing embrace of abortion rights and marked one of his few direct interventions in national politics after leaving office.

Meanwhile, Republicans sought ways to defeat Carter in the next election. Paul Weyrich, a conservative activist and political strategist, believed the GOP needed a populist issue to unite evangelicals—who, up to that point, had shown little interest in abortion.

At the time, the Southern Baptist Convention, the nation's largest Protestant denomination, was moderately pro-choice. Weyrich had tried mobilizing evangelicals around pornography, school prayer and the Equal Rights Amendment, but none gained traction.

That changed when he focused on federal policies affecting private religious schools. In the 1960s, White conservative pastors had founded church-run schools for their parishioners—so-called "segregation academies" created in response to public-school integration. In 1971, the Supreme Court's *Green v. Connally* decision ruled that racially segregated private schools were not entitled to tax-exempt status. The IRS soon began sending notices to schools violating the ruling.

Weyrich, an Eastern Rite Catholic critical of what he saw as a too-liberal Vatican, joined forces with evangelical leaders such as Bob Jones Jr. and Jerry Falwell. Together, they reframed the issue as one of religious freedom rather than segregation—an argument that would become the foundation of future Republican victories.

Still, they knew that defending segregation would not inspire mass support. So abortion became their flashpoint issue. Weyrich organized campaign-training conferences to teach religious leaders how to mobilize congregations around conservative causes, with abortion at the forefront.

Ironically, Reagan, the eventual Republican nominee, had signed one of the nation's most liberal abortion laws as California governor in 1967. The law permitted abortion when a woman's mental or physical health was threatened. A year later, Reagan publicly said signing the bill had been "a mistake," claiming the mental health provision was too broad and effectively created abortion on demand, particularly for unwed mothers.

On the 1976 campaign trail, Reagan embraced a strict anti-abortion stance, saying abortion should be allowed only when the woman's life was in danger.

Though not deeply religious himself, Reagan fully embraced the anti-abortion movement. Carter's cautious approach satisfied neither side—it failed to win over anti-abortion voters while alienating abortion rights supporters.

Carter also estranged many pro-choice faith leaders, including members of the Religious Coalition for Abortion Rights (RCAR), after meeting privately with anti-abortion Catholic bishops while ignoring repeated requests to meet with pro-choice clergy. In dozens of letters to the White House, they accused him of marginalizing people of faith who supported safe and legal abortion access.

Within the Democratic primary, most candidates said they personally opposed abortion but did not believe it should be banned. Sen. Ted Kennedy (D–MA) supported funding for poor women seeking abortions, as did California Gov. Jerry Brown. Carter favored financial assistance only in cases involving rape, incest or life endangerment.

By the end of Carter's term, the Christian Right had become the driving force behind Republican rhetoric, policy and platform-making. Its bare-knuckled style of politics soon became the chief antagonist of the reproductive rights movement. It would take equally tough and persistent women to counter its rise.

The Christian Right first took shape through the influence of television preachers, or "televangelists." Hundreds of thousands of new voters registered because of their efforts. They organized lobbying groups in Washington, D.C., state capitals and city halls. Many recruits were motivated by resentment over the perceived advances of feminism and gay rights activism.

By 1978, Christian Right-backed candidates were challenging GOP moderates in primary races. They advocated criminalizing abortion, expanding gun rights and cutting taxes. Their influence outpaced their numbers due to low voter turnout in Republican primaries.

In Iowa's 1978 Senate primary, conservative evangelicals rallied behind Roger Jepsen, who went on to defeat liberal Democratic incumbent Dick Clark.

In 1979, California ministers Robert Grant and Richard Zone launched Christian Voice from a small Pasadena office. Within a year, it had built a mailing list of 150,000 laypeople and 37,000 ministers. Cross-promoted on Pat Robertson's "The 700 Club" television program, Christian Voice sought to unite religious activism on abortion and school prayer with conservative stances on economic and foreign policy.

That same year, Jerry Falwell founded the Moral Majority.

Years earlier, Falwell had denounced Dr. Martin Luther King Jr. for "using the pulpit to advance a political agenda." Yet by the late 1970s, he was doing exactly that—traveling to all 50 states, building local chapters, and turning his Thomas Road Baptist Church in Lynchburg, Virginia, from a congregation of 35 people into a megachurch and media empire.

Through mailing lists, television programs and political outreach, Falwell's Moral Majority became the organizational backbone of the religious right, shaping Republican politics for decades to come.

Eventually, Falwell began preaching to an audience of 4,000 every Sunday, along with a television audience of 20 million. With their donations, Falwell built the Liberty Baptist College for $16 million. His network included 72,000 preachers. It dominated politics in less populated states. In Alaska's 1980 Republican primary, Falwell and his allies elected 80% of the delegates to the Detroit convention. The major issues for Falwell were abortion, gay rights and the Equal Rights Amendment— which his members had adamantly opposed. They had to support school prayers and strong national defense.

"All the moral issues that count today are in the political arena," Falwell told ABC News. "There's no way to fight these battles except in that arena."

Falwell called for a coalition of "moral people" who might not theologically agree but who did agree on abortion, pornography and drug trafficking. They registered 14 million voters before the presidential contest between Reagan and Carter. Supporters sent Falwell $52 million yearly to politically mobilize the Moral Majority.

Falwell held "I Love America" rallies at state capitals. He invited politicians to speak with him. Some—like Sen. Jesse Helms (R-NC)— talked about school prayer and national defense. Falwell reaffirmed the officeholder's integrity.

The Religious Roundtable became the third major organization of the late 1970s rooted in religious conservatism. It was founded in 1979 by Ed McAteer, a former Procter & Gamble advertising executive from Memphis, who believed that American Christianity needed to become politically active.

Alarmed by what he saw as the moral decay of the nation—spurred by *Roe v. Wade*, the rise of secular humanism and growing cultural liberalism—McAteer sought to unite evangelicals, conservative Catholics and Orthodox Jews into a single, powerful voting bloc. The organization's mission was to "elect righteous leaders" who would defend traditional values, oppose abortion and restore religious influence in public life.

McAteer's vision placed the Religious Roundtable at the forefront of the Christian Right's emergence. The group hosted rallies, distributed voter guides and coordinated with pastors nationwide to mobilize conservative congregations for political engagement.

Behind the scenes, the Roundtable played a quiet but pivotal role in Reagan's 1980 presidential campaign, collaborating closely with other rising religious-political organizations such as Falwell's.

Together, these movements transformed evangelical Christianity from a largely culturally disengaged community into one of the most powerful and enduring political forces in modern American life.

Beyond the big three, smaller groups like the National Christian Action Coalition had a huge impact on the Republican party. They published the family issues voting index, which rated congresspeople on conservative issues. However, they weren't welcomed by all Republicans, including Sen. Mark Hatfield (R-OR), a born-again Christian.

"They're not basically Republicans as such," Hatfield told *NBC News*. "They're looking for a political instrumentality by which they can advance their cause. So it's a takeover so to speak in many instances to the exclusion of either the traditional Republicans or others who are thinking about coming into the party.

"They've set up new criteria. Not only do you have to be a conservative, but you have to be a born-again Christian conservative."

While white men dominated the headlines, women also played a significant role in the anti-abortion movement. Melody Green did so with her evangelical Last Days Ministries. Judie Brown, with the Catholic-oriented American Life League and the American Life Lobby, eventually attracted more than 300,000 people and nearly $3 million to lobby against family planning facilities. Brown was extreme—she didn't believe in any exceptions for abortion, even in cases of rape and incest.

Brown's group could generate 40,000 to 50,000 letters to any elected representative if she wanted. She focused on other issues aside from abortion, including sex education; she hoped to promote parental authority over their children's sex lives. She felt sex outside marriage was a sin, and she decried the availability of birth control.

The most important women's organization in anti-abortion circles was Concerned Women for America (CWA), founded in 1979 by Beverly LaHaye, a conservative Christian activist and the wife of evangelical pastor and author Tim LaHaye. She created the organization to provide a platform for women who supported traditional family structures and the application of biblical principles to public life. The group quickly grew into a national network described by the *Chicago Tribune* as a "spiritual army" of Christian women organized to promote conservative values in American culture.

From its inception, CWA identified abortion as one of its defining issues. It characterized abortion as a moral wrong and framed opposition to it as a religious duty. Through lobbying, educational campaigns and alliances with other elements of the Christian right, the organization positioned itself as a leading voice in the movement opposing legal abortion.

By the early 2000s, CWA had become one of the most prominent women's organizations in conservative politics. It helped institutionalize the participation of evangelical women in national debates over family, morality and reproductive rights, ensuring that opposition to abortion remained a central focus of the broader religious right.

Right around the time LaHaye began making waves, voters started to link the Republican Party to the anti-abortion movement. That year, Republicans supported a constitutional amendment granting the right to life to the unborn. They pushed for judges who supported overturning *Roe*.

By the election, the Human Life Amendment had become a defining issue for the rising anti-abortion movement. First introduced after the Supreme Court's 1973 *Roe v. Wade* decision, the amendment aimed to overturn the ruling by establishing fetal personhood in the Constitution. Though several versions were proposed—some banning abortion outright, others deferring the issue to states—none gained traction in Congress. Still, the proposals galvanized conservative activists and religious leaders, including Falwell and Phyllis Schlafly of the Eagle Forum, who saw the amendment as a moral cornerstone of their emerging political agenda.

The Republican Party officially endorsed the Human Life Amendment in its national platform. The move reflected the growing influence of the religious right and was strategically aligned with Ronald Reagan's presidential campaign, despite his earlier support for liberalized abortion laws as California governor. The platform shift alienated moderate Republicans but solidified a durable alliance between the GOP and anti-abortion activists. Though the amendment itself never passed, the 1980 convention marked the start of a long-term transformation of abortion politics in the United States.

Anti-abortion demonstrators gathered in Washington, D.C., in January 1979 to lobby Congressional leaders to pass legislation limiting or banning abortion altogether. According to NBC News, most of them felt the courts weren't supportive of their cause. Abortion rights supporters showed up at the same time to express support for the Court's decision and to pressure Congress to support poor women seeking abortions and to oppose any Human Life Amendment. Gloria Steinem spoke to the media to clarify what was at stake:

We are in danger again with this obsessive drive of the so-called Right-to-Life groups of seeing again the slaughter and the maiming that came from this particular intimate Vietnam for women.

Women React to the New Forces of the Right

Faye Wattleton never shied away from speaking about abortion rights during her tenure as president of Planned Parenthood. Despite pleas from others to focus on other aspects of women's healthcare, she declined any engagement in which they asked her not to address abortion.

"The desire for silence seemed to be motivated by the hope that if we weren't so visible, we wouldn't attract controversy," Wattleton wrote in her biography. "Yet all around us was the evidence that we were the focus of the enemies of women's reproductive rights whether we assumed a high profile or not.

"I didn't believe that we would alienate our supporters by standing up for our principles. I believed that we would gain more support if we did not veer from those principles."

Still, the challenges were daunting.

Weyrich's vision of a network of conservative religious organizations driving Republican victories in national elections had succeeded. The party had been rebuilt around an alliance between libertarians, who sought less government regulation and lower taxes, and devout Christians, who felt alienated by society's increasing sexual liberalization.

Polls indicated that the Christian Right had contributed to several Senate defeats for Democrats and to President Carter's loss in 1980. After the election, Falwell vowed to push for a Human Life Amendment in Congress—a measure that, if passed, would have made abortion a capital offense.

The Christian Right viewed the progressivism of mainline Protestant denominations—which had long anchored American religious life—as a major obstacle. In response, a long-term campaign was launched to diminish their influence in both Christianity and public life.

In 1981, Richard Neuhaus, Penn Kemble and Michael Novak founded the Institute on Religion and Democracy (IRD) with this goal in mind. Their strategy was to stage constant policy battles within national and local church bodies to divide and destabilize them from within. When that failed, they sought to encourage schisms.

Authors Sheldon Culver and John Dorhauer, leaders in the United Church of Christ, later coined the term "steeplejacking" to describe this divide-and-conquer strategy aimed at infiltrating and overtaking congregations.

One of the IRD's tactics involved branding a target church as "far-left" and then sowing discord among its councils or lay leadership. Operatives would push out existing pastors and replace them with conservatives aligned with the organization's ideology.

The Institute portrayed itself misleadingly as a middle ground between the Moral Majority and the World Council of Churches (WCC). However, the IRD was instrumental in vilifying the WCC, providing materials to CBS's "60 Minutes" that led to a damaging segment about the council. The producer of the episode later expressed regret for airing it.

The IRD accused the World Council of Churches of supporting Marxism because it funded refugee programs in countries with communist ties. WCC leaders countered that their humanitarian aid was not a political endorsement.

Paul Schrading, a pastor from western Pennsylvania and a WCC member, explained the distinction to *The Pittsburgh Press* following the "60 Minutes" broadcast, clarifying that Christian compassion for refugees did not equate to political alignment with their governments.

"The problem is that if you give humanitarian help to people in a different political ideology, you are seen by critics as supporting that ideology when what you're really doing is responding to the gospel to feed the hungry and clothe the naked," Schrading said.

The IRD and its denominational affiliates waged a war of attrition against mainstream Protestant congregations and denominations. In some cases, they successfully took over local churches, replacing pastors with ones who emphasized anti-abortion messages and condemnations of gay rights.

The constant internal conflict created by these campaigns caused many congregants to grow weary and leave their churches altogether. Within pro-choice denominations, the IRD's sustained pressure eventually severed ties with the Religious Coalition for Abortion Rights, fracturing a once-strong alliance between progressive faith groups and the reproductive rights movement.

The influence of the conservative religious community also reshaped national politics. After Reagan's election, Congress curtailed federal support for abortion. In 1981, lawmakers voted to eliminate Medicaid funding for abortions even in cases of rape or incest.

At the time, roughly 55 women per year qualified for federal assistance by reporting rape, though a CDC official estimated that between 3,000 and 10,000 abortions annually involved pregnancies resulting from sexual assault.

The congressional debate was intensely polarized. Sen. Jesse Helms (R–NC), a right-wing legislator known for racism and intolerance, led efforts to pass new anti-abortion legislation. Sen. Robert Packwood (R–OR), a staunch abortion rights advocate, accused his colleagues of trying to impose a "Cotton Mather morality" on the nation.

"I had thought we stopped burning witches in this country," Packwood said. "Apparently not."

Helms, invoking the Ten Commandments, compared abortion to murder. In response, columnist Tom Braden published a piece condemning Helms and recounting his own daughter's experience of becoming pregnant through rape—a deeply personal rebuke of the senator's moral absolutism.

Meanwhile, Marjory Mecklenburg, an official with the Office of Adolescent Pregnancy, told NBC News that her department's ultimate goal was to prevent abortions in all cases, underscoring the ideological alignment between the Reagan administration and the anti-abortion movement.

"You certainly have responsibility when you are pregnant," she said. "There is another human being involved, no matter how that human being came to be. There is the life of another human being to be considered."

Mecklenburg emerged as one of the most prominent Protestant leaders in the early anti-abortion movement, offering an alternative public image to the Catholic-dominated activism of the 1960s and 1970s.

Along with her husband, Fred Mecklenburg, she co-founded Minnesota Citizens Concerned for Life in 1968—the state's first anti-abortion organization—in response to legislative proposals to reform Minnesota's abortion laws. While both Mecklenburgs initially supported birth control, motivated by concerns about women's rights and global overpopulation, their growing commitment to opposing abortion soon overshadowed their earlier positions.

They expanded their organization, transforming it into a local powerhouse in Minnesota's political landscape, through a mix of grassroots political activism—letter-writing campaigns, lobbying efforts—and community events such as polka dances and bake sales.

Mecklenburg's influence quickly became national. In 1972, she was elected chair of the National Right to Life Committee following her husband's one-year term. Her Methodist faith, youthful energy and photogenic charisma helped project a broader, more mainstream image of anti-abortion activism beyond its Catholic roots.

She also sought to destigmatize single motherhood, advocating for the removal of the term "illegitimate" from birth certificates. However, she often clashed with colleagues who prioritized fetal rights over social support for women. Frustrated by the movement's limited concern for pregnant women's material needs, she resigned less than a year later, criticizing what she viewed as its lack of compassion.

In 1974, Mecklenburg founded American Citizens Concerned for Life (ACCL) in Minneapolis, which she described as a "new kind of pro-life organization" focused on improving conditions for pregnant women to reduce the demand for abortion. Rejecting the confrontational tactics of many anti-abortion groups, she emphasized nonpartisan, service-oriented activism and helped promote the development of crisis pregnancy centers (CPCs) nationwide.

Mecklenburg's model—partly inspired by Canada's Birthright movement—appealed to women who preferred direct aid to pregnant women over political fights to recriminalize abortion. Her organization attracted supporters who valued practical assistance—housing, counseling and financial support—over legislative lobbying, helping to expand CPCs across the United States throughout the 1970s and 1980s.

Although Mecklenburg's opposition to abortion aligned her more closely with New Right social conservatives than with Republican feminists, her service-based approach often placed her on the margins of the broader movement. Her philosophy—less partisan, more compassionate—highlighted a deep tension within the anti-abortion cause: between those focused on restricting abortion through law and those seeking to reduce demand through social support.

By championing CPCs and emphasizing empathetic outreach, Mecklenburg left a distinct and lasting imprint on the movement's strategies and infrastructure.

Over the 1980s and into the 1990s, Mecklenburg became one of the most influential women in the anti-abortion movement. She chaired the U.S. Department of Health and Human Services' Task Force on Teenage Pregnancy and later led the Office of Population Affairs, overseeing Title X family-planning programs. In those roles, she helped shape national policy toward abstinence-based education and expanded restrictions on abortion access.

In October 1981, the Senate Judiciary Subcommittee opened hearings on new anti-abortion legislation sponsored by Sen. Orrin Hatch (R–UT). The proposal declared that the right to abortion was not protected by the Constitution, effectively empowering Congress and state legislatures to restrict or ban abortion outright.

Patricia Gavett, executive director of the RCAR, rejected the proposal, saying it was neither a states' rights measure nor a true compromise—but rather a direct assault on constitutional protections for reproductive freedom

"In fact, it is a back-door approach to prohibiting all abortions by allowing a bare majority in Congress to pass abortion legislation," Gavett said while visiting the Capitol.

Sen. Robert Packwood (R–OR) warned that popular passion could cloud judgment in the abortion debate. Harvard Law professor Laurence Tribe testified that the government had no right to dictate how individuals used their own bodies.

Dr. John Noonan, a prominent Catholic theologian and anti-abortion scholar from UC Berkeley, countered that history would judge abortion rights supporters harshly. "A century from now," he said, "people will wonder how so many distinguished individuals could have defended abortion."

If enacted, the Hatch Amendment, which was officially called the Human Life Amendment, would have given anti-abortion activists a far greater chance of securing a total ban by legally defining when life begins—embedding that principle directly within constitutional and statutory law.

The same year, the RCAR issued a statement that called for education and advocacy within their congregations to maintain legal access to reproductive services.

"It is a proper role of religion to provide leadership and guidance on social and moral issues, and we believe our organizations must now begin to deal with abortion in a more positive and thorough fashion," the statement read. "Too often we have avoided the issue in the vain hope that it would resolve itself."

Hundreds of ministers and rabbis signed a joint letter declaring their opposition to a Human Life Amendment and pledging to do everything possible to prevent its passage. The signatories urged civil discourse and collaboration among faith communities on issues unrelated to reproductive rights, emphasizing the need to avoid sectarian division.

In subsequent hearings, Catholic leaders voiced strong support for Sen. Orrin Hatch and expressed their dedication to seeing his amendment enacted. During one exchange, Sen. Patrick Leahy (D–VT) questioned Terence Cardinal Cooke and Archbishop John Roach on when scripture defined the beginning of life, pressing them on the theological basis for their claims.

"Does canon law treat a fetus as a person from the moment of conception?" Leahy said.

"You're just trying to get the discussion in a philosophical area," Roach said in response.

"Is abortion treated as murder?" Leahy later asked.

"I think it would be inappropriate for us to depart from the kind of moral stance we have taken," Cooke responded.

Politicians debated abortion-related constitutional amendments for years while other key developments unfolded within the broader abortion debate.

In September 1982, Sen. Hatch (R–UT) withdrew his proposed amendment, conceding that he could not secure the two-thirds majority needed in the Senate for passage. A similar effort led by Sen. Jesse Helms (R–NC) also failed when it reached the Senate floor. In both cases, Democratic filibusters played a decisive role in defeating the measures, preserving the existing constitutional protections established under *Roe v. Wade*.

Armed and Dangerous: the New Militancy of Anti-Abortion Activists

Elsewhere, anti-abortion extremism took root. In 1982, radicals kidnapped abortion provider Hector Zevallos and his wife Rosalie in Illinois. They held them for seven days while threatening to murder them if they didn't close the Hope Clinic for Women in Granite City. People suspected the Army of God, a mysterious group of people who masked their identities and advocated stopping abortions by any available method.

There was a manual for people who subscribed to the Army of God philosophy. It was a militant anti-abortion document that outlined strategies for obstructing abortion access through both nonviolent and violent means. It included detailed instructions for sabotaging clinics, blocking entrances and using chemicals or physical tools to render medical equipment inoperable.

The manual encouraged direct action, sometimes outside the boundaries of legality, and it portrayed its authors and readers as participants in a religiously justified war against abortion providers. The language throughout framed abortion as murder and the people involved in providing or supporting abortion services as enemies in a spiritual battle.

The manual includes ideological justifications for violence, presenting acts like arson and bombing as morally permissible under the guise of defending unborn life. It provides a mix of tactical guidance, legal advice for avoiding capture or prosecution, and theological rationalizations for extreme measures.[34]

Investigators found a ransom note for Zevallos in a home in St. Louis. The letter demanded that Reagan denounce abortion. Even after the captors released Zevallos and his wife, the mystery surrounding the kidnapping remained. The perpetrators drove them near their home and let them go. The couple walked home, which surprised investigators. Police arrested Don Benny Anderson, a leader of the Army of God, for the crime.

Helping Anderson was Matthew Mason Moore, who had told people back in Texas that he wanted to go on a mission as a Mormon. His brother Wayne accompanied him. Police arrested the two back home afterward because he instead spent his time in Zevallos' abduction. He had joined the Army of God because of Anderson, who police suspected started the network that eventually continued its anti-abortion terror for the next two decades.

In more than nine months, the three had committed two armed robberies, set two clinics in Florida on fire, and bombed another women's health center in Virginia.

Anderson was convicted of the crime and sentenced to 30 years in prison. During his hearing, Anderson read a 17-minute statement in which he invoked the Ten Commandments and accused the judge of "declaring war on God."

Anderson spoke with ABC News while in prison.

"It is my belief that the answer to violence is total violence," he said. "These people are killing human beings."

The Army of God didn't disappear with Anderson's imprisonment. Police received letters from people claiming to be part of it several times after when abortion clinics got attacked or bombed. They saw themselves as at war and resorted to tactics including bombings, arson and assassination.

---

34 Rochelle, B. (1988). *Pro-life collection of Barbara Rochelle, 1988-1997.* Schlesinger Library.

The Army of God is now an underground revolutionary network with far more support than has sometimes met the eye. Donald Spitz ran its website, which included misrepresentations of Margaret Sanger, pictures of dead fetuses, praise for the murderers of abortion providers, and other writings. It alluded to passages of the Bible that—when accompanying the praise of murderers, vandals and arsonists—give such violence a sense of righteousness, at least among those who adhere to the same mindset.

Some scholars have argued that, despite the Army of God's public posture of "leaderless resistance," key members likely knew each other and coordinated indirectly. For example, when later individuals like Clayton Lee Waagner signed their threats with "Army of God," it suggested a shared identity and symbolism that extended beyond coincidence. This use of common language, tactics and ideological justification pointed to a deeper, if informal, coordination.[35]

In December 2003, a federal jury convicted Waagner on 51 counts tied to a nationwide terror campaign against abortion providers. He had mailed more than 500 threatening letters to clinics, many containing white powder and declarations that they came from a so-called "Virginia Dare Chapter" of the Army of God.

The threats arrived just weeks after the 2001 anthrax attacks, heightening public fear. Though the powder was harmless, the messages warned recipients they might be contaminated and should consider themselves "already dead." The campaign forced clinic closures, evacuations and emergency responses across the country. Waagner was already incarcerated for unrelated crimes when convicted and later received an additional 19-year sentence for his role in the letter campaign.[36]

Figures such as Spitz and Rev. Michael Bray appeared to maintain consistent ideological alignment and mutual endorsement of violent actions, reinforcing the idea that there was some level of communication and solidarity among individuals operating under the Army of God name.

---

35 Clarkson. F.. (2002, January 8). *Our own terror cells*. Salon. https://www.salon.com/2002/01/08/army_of_god/

36 U.S. Department of Justice. (2003, December 3). *Clayton Lee Waagner found guilty regarding threats to employees of reproductive clinics in Eastern District of Pennsylvania and elsewhere*. U.S. Department of Justice. Retrieved from archive of justice.gov

Similarly, the arrest of James Kopp for the murder of Dr. Barnett Slepian, which is detailed later in this book, offered further evidence that Army of God-affiliated actors were part of a broader underground network rather than isolated extremists. Kopp's ties to others who committed or supported acts of violence, including arson and murder, suggested an informal system of support, harboring and ideological reinforcement.

Observers noted that Kopp was not a rogue figure but was enabled by others who shared his views and provided assistance, either directly or by legitimizing such acts through religious and moral arguments. This pattern led scholars and journalists alike to suspect that the Army of God functioned more like a loosely organized terror cell network than a collection of unconnected individuals.[37]

Within early militant anti-abortion circles, three people stood out. Dr. John O'Keefe, who created the clinic sit-in approach, introduced the first widely used method of protesting abortion clinics. While his approach emphasized nonviolence, Rev. Bray, another leading figure, argued for more confrontational approaches. He partook in and provided theological justification for the bombing of clinics. Joseph Scheidler fused both of those philosophies to create the militant wing of the anti-abortion movement. He became famous because he traveled the country championing acts of harassment and voicing support for clinic bombers.

O'Keefe, often credited with pioneering the clinic sit-in approach, helped introduce the first widely adopted tactic for physically obstructing abortion services. O'Keefe's path to activism was shaped by a turbulent personal history. While a student at Harvard, he lost his brother in the Tet Offensive, an event that left him disillusioned with the Vietnam War. Although he initially kept his distance from antiwar groups on campus, he found a spiritual home in the emerging Catholic Charismatic Renewal movement, whose emphasis on emotional worship, personal revelation and apocalyptic overtones resonated deeply. He later applied for conscientious objector status and began seeking ways to translate his

---

37 Clarkson, F. (2001, March 30). *Accused killer part of anti-abortion underground.* Women's eNews. https://womensenews.org/2001/03/accused-killer-part-anti-abortion-underground/

faith and activism into direct action.[38]

Initially unfamiliar with abortion as a political issue, O'Keefe's perspective shifted after an intense conversation with a woman who described her own abortion in terms that he likened to the traumas of war. Following *Roe v. Wade*, he became convinced that abortion was a systemic atrocity requiring an urgent physical response. In the late 1970s and early 1980s, he emerged as a key architect of the rescue tactic—organizing groups to occupy clinics and block access, deliberately courting arrest as a form of witness. While O'Keefe himself did not carry out acts of violence, by the late 1980s he had become one of the most visible advocates of "justifiable homicide" within the radical wing of the movement, offering moral and theological cover for those who killed abortion providers. His background as a physician lent authority to his claims that abortion was a form of genocide, and his rhetoric framed the conflict as a spiritual war demanding uncompromising resistance.

In the 1980s, O'Keefe began gaining prominence within the radical wing of the anti-abortion movement, laying the groundwork for his later, more explicit endorsements of violence. During this period, he operated as both a practicing physician and a public advocate against abortion, delivering speeches and writing articles that increasingly framed abortion as an act of mass murder.

Bray was one of the most prominent and theologically influential figures within the extremist wing of the American anti-abortion movement. A Lutheran minister by training, Bray became widely known in the 1980s, after he was convicted of participating in a series of bombings targeting abortion clinics. These attacks were part of a coordinated campaign across the Washington, D.C., area that caused significant property damage but no fatalities. In 1985, Bray was arrested and served a 46-month prison sentence under federal conspiracy and explosives charges.

After his release, Bray continued to act as a central figure in the radical anti-abortion underground. He authored *A Time to Kill: The Bible*

---

38 Masucci, S. (2022). *From pacifism to pipe bombs: A history of the extremist anti-abortion movement in the United States* (Senior thesis, University of South Carolina). Scholar Commons. https://scholarcommons.sc.edu/senior_theses/492

and Self-Defense, in which he provided a scriptural justification for using lethal force against abortion providers, framing such acts as defensive measures akin to protecting innocent life from murder.

In *A Time to Kill*, Bray argues that women who procure abortions should be viewed not as victims but as morally responsible actors. He criticizes what he sees as a strategic shift in the pro-life movement after the 1960s, when activists began portraying women as misled or coerced rather than culpable. For Bray, this concession to feminist rhetoric diluted the movement's moral clarity and undermined its theological foundation.

Bray draws on early Christian writings that frame abortion as a grave sin akin to murder, explicitly condemning the woman involved. He contends that modern rhetoric, which emphasizes external pressures or portrays abortion as a mistake, obscures the personal guilt involved. Instead, Bray insists that women who choose abortion are complicit in the taking of innocent life and should be held accountable under biblical standards.

He argues that opposing abortion is fully consistent with supporting capital punishment. In Bray's view, defending innocent life requires the just punishment of those who destroy it. He cites scripture to claim that God's law not only affirms the sanctity of unborn life but also commands the execution of those who commit murder. Justice, he writes, demands both the protection of the innocent and the punishment of the guilty.

Bray harshly critiques the anti-abortion movement's embrace of nonviolence, which he labels a false doctrine borrowed from the Civil Rights Movement. He argues that pacifism has pacified the movement, turning it into what he calls a "clinic defense" campaign rather than a battle against mass killing. He likens passivity in the face of abortion to the moral failure of bystanders during acts of violence and accuses nonviolent leaders of weakening the resolve of activists.

He spends much of the book refuting evangelical leaders who allow for abortion in cases like rape, incest or emotional distress. Bray sees these exceptions as a theological compromise, shaped more by public opinion than by scripture. He calls for an uncompromising rejection of abortion in all cases and argues that resistance must be rooted in divine law, not cultural accommodation.

Bray further compares anti-abortion activism to religious warfare. Drawing from biblical and early church examples of militarism, he urges Christians to reject pacifism and embrace the idea of righteous combat. Citing figures like Joshua and Gideon, he portrays abortion resistance as a moral battlefield on which believers are called to fight.

From this militant framework, Bray advances the concept of justifiable homicide—the belief that killing abortion providers can be morally defended as an act of protection. While controversial even within the movement, this idea reframes violence not as murder but as obedience to divine law. In Bray's view, it is a response to a culture that has legalized the destruction of innocent life and abandoned the demands of true justice.[39]

The Army of God connected with his writings. Bray's dual role—as both a convicted domestic terrorist and a theologian of anti-abortion violence—made him a uniquely dangerous figure, as he helped shape a religious and moral justification for violent resistance within the movement.[40]

Scheidler was one of the earliest and most influential leaders of confrontational anti-abortion activism in the United States. A former seminarian and advertising executive, Scheidler turned to full-time anti-abortion activism in the early 1980s, founding the Pro-Life Action League in Chicago. He became a pioneer of direct action tactics, advocating for clinic blockades, sidewalk counseling, graphic imagery and physical presence at abortion facilities to dissuade women from obtaining abortions and to pressure providers. His 1985 book *Closed: 99 Ways to Stop Abortion* served as a tactical manual for activists across the country, outlining methods to disrupt clinic operations and draw media attention.[41]

During this era, Mary Jean Collins organized sit-ins at local clinics as part of her work with NOW. It angered people at Planned Parenthood and NARAL, who wanted to keep abortion workers and clinics out of

39 Bray, M. (1994). *A time to kill: A study concerning the use of force and abortion.* Adroit Press.
40 Winter, A. (2013). *Anti-Abortion Extremism and Violence in the United States,* in *Extremism in America* (UP of Florida)
41 Masucci, S. (2022). *From pacifism to pipe bombs: A history of the extremist anti-abortion movement in the United States* (Senior thesis, University of South Carolina). Scholar Commons. https://scholarcommons.sc.edu/senior_theses/492

the public eye so as not to draw attention to their work, as Collins put it.

"I felt that the violence was partly able to go on because nobody was challenging them back," Collins said. "And it felt to me too much like we were giving into them and giving them too much space and that we weren't defending our turf properly."

Merle Hoffman remembered how the nature of abortion workers shifted during that time. Hoffman said that the pro-choice movement is bifurcated insofar as those who provide abortions versus those who write or discuss them in books or in academia or journalism. When it was first legalized, many second-wave feminists thought working at a clinic was fashionable.

"That changed as the clinics themselves became pariahs slowly within the medical establishment," Hoffman said. "It changed as there were more attacks."

In 1983, the Supreme Court ruled on the legality of several abortion restrictions established in Akron, Ohio, five years earlier. City Council members passed ordinances that changed abortion laws. More than 400 people had marched and cheered around City Hall when it happened. The most controversial provisions of the ordinances were that a woman had to tell her husband or parents when she planned on having an abortion. Doctors had to say to them that the fetus had human features and that aborting it might cause her psychological problems. And women had to wait for 24 hours after first getting a referral to get an abortion. Elsie Reaven, a councilwoman, criticized it when she was at its hearing.

"This dominant male faction in council has had the arrogance to persist against all reason in burdening and possibly encumbering women in the city of Akron," Reaven said.

Norma Goldberger, who ran Akron Women's Clinic, remembered that one of the councilmen had sent his mistress to an abortion provider. And yet, publicly, he had taken a strongly anti-abortion stance. Many on the body were Catholic, and they had tried to become more popular with the ascendant local chapter of the NRLC. Anti-abortion leaders in the area had passed along prototype legislation they hoped would work in Akron so they could implement it elsewhere.

The ordinance passed by one vote. It became the model for laws in 20 states, so its establishment and constitutionality were of great concern to both sides. Stephan Landsman, a lawyer for the local ACLU, approached the abortion providers in the area about representation as part of a court challenge to the Akron ordinance.

Three abortion clinic organizations in the city challenged the law in the Northern District of Ohio, along with the doctor who worked at one of the facilities. The District Court ruled the plaintiffs didn't have legal standing, so the provisions remained. The judge struck down several of the ordinances. Landsman and the abortion providers were happy with the verdict, but the NRLC pressured the city to appeal the ruling.

Lawyers took the case to the Supreme Court, where it became known as *City of Akron v. Akron Center for Reproductive Health*. Several of the nation's medical associations filed briefs, calling the requirement inaccurate and meddlesome.

The Court struck down several of the provisions enacted by the Akron council, including the requirement for a 24-hour waiting period, parental consent, a mandate for disclosure of certain information during the informed consent process, specifications for fetal remains disposal, and hospitalization for second-trimester abortions.

At the same time, the Court upheld a Missouri parental consent law because it was more lenient. It allowed a juvenile woman to get permission from a judge if she didn't want to tell her parents. Other states could follow suit.

Jane Watring, who spoke for the Akron Center for Reproductive Health, said it was a tremendous victory for women in Ohio and nationwide. Faye Wattleton talked to ABC News about it.

"It means that the right to make a decision about an abortion and to receive abortion services has been preserved," Wattleton said.

Outraged anti-abortion leaders quickly said that congressional action was needed if state or local lawmakers couldn't pass regulations to prevent or limit abortion access. They used it as proof that Republican senators and congressional representatives should be required to support the Hatch Amendment passage.

After the decision, Sen. Hatch again tried to pass his Human Life Amendment. Hatch acknowledged that it had little chance of passing. ABC News reporter Brit Hume said the anti-abortion movement was as far as it had ever been from its goal, with the deadlock in Congress on the legislation and the Supreme Court's reaffirmation of Roe *v. Wade*. Despite strong support from anti-abortion activists and a Republican-controlled Senate, the Hatch Amendment again failed to gain the two-thirds majority required to advance a constitutional amendment.

Goldberger experienced more anti-abortion harassment in the years ahead.

"They became more vociferous rather than less. I had some guy from the Catholic cemetery stand in front of our clinic door every single morning," Goldberger told me over the phone. "And finally, he approached me and asked if he could have our fetuses to bury in a cemetery. He would give them a proper Catholic funeral.

"And we had protests around our house. We had to get a lawyer to see if we could get them to stop marching around our house. It affected our children."

Someone went into her clinic and set fire to a trash can in the bathroom. An employee extinguished it, and they called the fire department. Extremists called in bomb threats, to which the police often were unresponsive.

The level of engagement on the other side compared to the pro-choice contingent bothered Goldberger. With so much passion versus complacency, it foreshadowed significant losses for women's rights groups in the decades ahead. There was an unnecessary stigma to getting abortions that made people reluctant to champion the stance.

"Most women think it only happens to them, not to anybody else. They're the only ones that have a lying boyfriend or birth control that doesn't work or a legitimate reason to get an abortion," Goldberger said. "They're the only ones. Everybody else is doing it because they're capricious.

"But for them, it's morally correct. For everybody else, it's morally incorrect. And so with that kind of mindset, they're not going to fight for their sisters."

In 1985, FBI agents investigated a threat on Justice Harry Blackmun's life. Someone shot a bullet through Blackmun's home. The week before, he had received a letter in which the writer said he would laugh at Blackmun's funeral. Blackmun had just left the room when the 9 mm bullet came through the window. The bullet shattered the glass and showered his wife with shards.

The letters sent to Blackmun had gotten increasingly threatening. One writer said he would blow the justice's brains out. A bodyguard accompanied Blackmun during his walks around the court. Throughout the years, he had alternatingly been described as the butcher of Dachau, a murderer, Pontius Pilate and King Herod. Someone sent him a letter saying he would be killed if he didn't change his position. Agents suspected the Army of God was behind it. Blackmun spoke to CNN about the harassment.[42]

"You can think of any name to call someone, and I've been called it," Blackmun said.

Menacing letters to Supreme Court justices were common. ABC News reported that four or five of every hundred letters sent are referred to court police. But security at the court was tighter than it had ever been following the abortion ruling.

Between 1982–1985, 26 clinics were set afire or bombed. On Christmas Day of 1984, anti-abortion militants bombed three Pensacola clinics, which had been the sites of protests. The bombers called it Operation Gideon, after a biblical figure who pulverized a pagan altar on God's orders.

Suspects Matthew Goldsby and James Simmons didn't apologize for the crime.

"If we can stop the killing, whether we stopped it for a period of time or if we could stop it altogether, it would totally thrill the both of us," said Goldsby to a reporter with the *Orlando Sentinel* in January 1985.

---

42 Specter, M. (1985, March 4). *Shot fired through Blackmun's window: Authorities probing possible link to anti-abortion group*. The Washington Post. https://www.washingtonpost.com/archive/politics/1985/03/05/shot-fired-through-blackmuns-window/270a0516-2c7f-4c5e-9002-d017515a5131/; Gorman, S. (1985, March 7). *Shot fired at justice's home believed to be random. United Press International*. Retrieved from https://www.upi.com/Archives/1985/03/07/Shot-fired-at-justices-home-believed-to-be-random/8985479019600/

Newspaper reports and television polls indicated that as many as 52% of Pensacola residents felt they were merely misguided. A neighbor of one of the suspects said his heart was "in the right place."

At the trial, the men's lawyer compared them to Huck Finn and Tom Sawyer. The jury convicted the pair while their wives got sentenced for being part of the conspiracy, making bombs and using them to damage clinics.

Professor Carol Mason, who authored *Killing for Life: The Apocalyptic Narrative of Pro-Life Politics*, argued that the Operation Gideon bombings fused a religious narrative with paramilitary tactics. Mason said that evolution was a logical consequence of the apocalyptic anti-abortion language coming from groups like the American Life League.

The ALL's literature, speeches and campaigns often used intense, emotionally charged terms like "baby killing," "genocide" and "Holocaust" to describe abortion. This framing not only emphasized the absolute nature of their position but also contributed to a culture of fear and urgency within the movement—calling believers to action as if they were engaged in an end-times struggle to save innocent lives and the soul of the nation. Critics, including more moderate anti-abortion advocates, saw this as extreme, fearing it could provoke violence or alienate broader public support.[43]

Similar bombings happened elsewhere in the country in 1984. When I spoke to Gail Frances, an abortion provider in Maryland, she remembered when she heard the news at 6 a.m. that her clinic had been bombed. Before that, protestors had besieged staff and patients coming into the facility. They had to move to a new location because they couldn't renew the lease at an older one. The bomb blew the metal fireproof door on the front of the building 200 yards away.

"It's hard to describe to somebody how you feel when you see that," Frances said. "When I saw how strong that bomb was when the door had been blown across the parking lot into a residential area. The fire was just raging when I got there."

43 Gorney, C. (1998). *Articles of faith: A frontline history of the abortion wars.* Simon & Schuster; Burghart, D. (2012). *Resisting the agenda: Anti-choice activism and the radical right.* Institute for Research and Education on Human Rights;
Ginsburg, F. (1998). *Contested lives: The abortion debate in an American community* (Updated ed.). University of California Press.

Frances remembers walking next to the fire marshal. She faltered, and he caught her before she fell. Television, print and radio journalists extensively covered the bombing. Frances told reporters the rhetoric from President Reagan and Vice President Bush had inflamed the situation.

The destruction of Frances' clinic was part of a rash of bombings in that area during that time. In Washington, D.C., an abortion clinic and a Planned Parenthood office suffered attacks. After the bombings, the tally for total assaults on abortion providers rose to 21 in 1984.

Washington, D.C., Mayor Marion Barry said he was glad the president disavowed the bombers but that he wished Reagan would assign more FBI agents to investigate the crimes, eight of which had happened near Barry's city.

The inadequate federal response bothered a lot of abortion rights activists. Barbara Radford, president of the National Abortion Federation, said the nationwide attacks were orchestrated and federal investigators should look for conspirators.

Harry Hand, an anti-abortion demonstrator in Maryland, told NBC News that he discouraged the use of violence because he felt it wouldn't sway public opinion. After pressure, Reagan condemned abortion clinic bombings. Scheidler was upset that Reagan didn't criticize abortion at the same time.

"Until somebody condemns what goes on inside abortion clinics, the systematic destruction of human life on a routine basis, I just don't see any parity at all between damaged real estate and dead human beings," Scheidler told ABC News.

Scheidler earlier had said that he hadn't shed a tear when he learned about a bombing. In the spring of 1985, Scheidler staged the annual conference of the Pro-Life Action Network (PLAN) in Appleton, Wisconsin. They flew a banner that said, "Welcome Pro-Life Activists: Have a Blast."

At the event, Scheidler announced his book, *Closed: 99 Ways to Stop Abortion*, which recommended picketing doctors' homes and hiring private detectives to dig up information.

"We are going to go back to the doctors' homes, we're going to go to their offices, we are going to go into their clinics, we are going to talk with the young women," Scheidler said. "If somebody wants to call it harassment, so be it."

It was around this time that buffer zones developed. The concept centered on creating a safe space surrounding a clinic where no noise or protests could happen. Bill Baird formed the Pro-Choice Defense League to push for them. Baird developed the idea from restrictions around hospitals that forbade car honking. Those policies had been implemented because car horns could distract medical staff.

"So I said, 'If you can give a zone of privacy from car honking, why not a zone of privacy for people yelling, 'Murder, killer, baby killer,'" Baird told me over the phone. "That would even frighten a doctor more because they'll hear that in the hospital also while he's doing surgery."

Afterward, Baird visited other clinics to push for buffer zones. Boulder, Colorado, passed an ordinance in 1986 that forbade anti-abortion protestors from coming within 4 feet of abortion clinics. Dr. Warren Hern, who performed abortions later in pregnancy, wrote about the topic in his book, *Abortion in the Age of Unreason: A Doctor's Account of Caring for Women Before and After Roe v. Wade*. A dispute erupted in the city that pitted the Colorado chapter of NARAL, now known as Reproductive Freedom for All, against the ACLU, which argued for the First Amendment rights of protestors.

Around that time, Dr. Bernard Nathanson—a cofounder of NARAL who had performed more than 60,000 abortions—dramatically switched sides in the abortion debate.

Anti-abortion activists credited his 1984 film "The Silent Scream" with galvanizing their movement. The film purported to show an abortion in progress, depicting the fetus reacting to pain. However, medical professionals criticized it as misleading, arguing that it distorted both medical facts and fetal development.

In the film, Nathanson described the unborn as "another human being" and declared that abortion was murder. Pro-choice leaders countered that the film misrepresented embryonic development and weaponized emotion over science.

Nathanson sent copies of "The Silent Scream" to every member of

Congress and each Supreme Court justice. President Ronald Reagan even screened the film at the White House, calling it "a chilling documentation of the horror of abortion."

"It's been said that if every member of Congress could see that film," Reagan remarked, "they would move quickly to end the tragedy of abortion—and I pray that they will."

Critics were divided. *The New Republic* compared the movie to a snuff film, while other journalists sought a middle ground, acknowledging its emotional impact but disputing its accuracy. Meanwhile, Falwell's Moral Majority purchased 50,000 videocassette copies of the film to distribute to conservative Protestant pastors across the country, ensuring its wide circulation among religious audiences.

Other works that shaped the anti-abortion movement's fringes came out during that time too. Canadian author Malcolm Ross wrote *The Real Holocaust: The Attack on Unborn Children and Life Itself* in the early 1980s. The book epitomized the anti-semitism that animates some of the anti-abortion movement. Its cover depicted a stereotypical Jewish caricature of burying fetuses outside his abortion clinic. Ross denies the Holocaust in the text. Ross implied that Satan controlled abortion rights activists.

The ideology now widely known as "replacement theory"—the belief that white Christian populations are being displaced by more reproductively prolific groups—has long been embedded in anti-abortion rhetoric. As discussed previously in this book, early 20th-century fears of "race suicide," promoted by figures like President Theodore Roosevelt, warned that white Protestants were failing to reproduce at sustainable levels. This concern was racialized and eugenic in nature: white women were encouraged to have more children, while immigrant and nonwhite women were often targeted for sterilization and other forms of reproductive control. Abortion, in this framework, was seen not only as a moral wrong but as a civilizational threat.

These ideas took their most extreme form in works like Malcolm Ross's *The Real Holocaust,* which framed abortion as part of a Jewish conspiracy to destroy white Christian society. Ross depicted Jewish doctors as orchestrators of mass fetal death, using grotesque imagery to portray them as cultural saboteurs. While such claims remained on the fringes, they reflected a deeper undercurrent of racial and religious paranoia within the anti-abortion movement. In corners where white nationalism and religious fundamentalism overlap, these narratives have persisted—fueling apocalyptic visions of demographic collapse and justifying increasingly militant resistance.

Part of the Mainstream Too

On the 13th anniversary of *Roe* in 1986, 36,000 people marched against abortion in Washington, D.C., in the annual March for Life. Police arrested 10 protestors for breaching a police barricade at the Supreme Court. Reagan addressed the crowd through a speaker.

"Each child about to be born is a unique, unrepeatable gift," Reagan said. "Each child who escapes the tragedy of abortion is an immeasurable victory."

Abortion rights supporters responded by gathering in an alley to connect it with illegal abortions.

That same year, about 100,000 women took part in the pro-choice *March for Women's Lives*. They pushed for greater abortion and birth control access as well as the passage of the Civil Rights Restoration Act, which would have made it sex discrimination for a hospital not to perform abortions. Leaders like Eleanor Smeal connected the need for abortion access to Martin Luther King Jr.'s legacy.

Some important organizations rose to power during that time. The fledgling Catholics for Choice organization became one of the country's most critical groups supporting choice. The group began in 1973, but became influential when Frances Kissling took over. Among their materials were question-and-answer pamphlets and a book about the history of abortion within the Catholic Church. Kissling organized briefings for Congress.

"In almost all other organizations, orthodoxy prevailed, and if you said anything that implied that abortion was serious, complex, and attempted to address the question of fetal status, you were attacked by your own," Kissling said.

Their targets were twofold. They wanted to help women get answers to hard questions about abortion and convince progressive and feminist Catholics to get the institution to accept legalized abortion. Some arguments were accepted by the Women's Church Convergence, a coalition of groups dedicated to feminist positions within the Catholic faith.

In 1987, the Christian Right was embroiled in a scandal of the financial dealings of televangelists Jim and Tammy Bakker, who ran the PTL Club. (PTL stood for "Praise the Lord!") Falwell was asked to take over the ministry. Jim Bakker was forced out for sexual impropriety and dishonest money handling. Bakker said Falwell had attempted to steal his ministry. Falwell disavowed Bakker. Falwell said the Bakkers had looted the organization and demanded $400,000 in lifelong salaries between the both of them, a luxury house, two cars and a security guard. Falwell said he remained firmly in control of the ministry despite the Bakker's threats.

In November 1987, Falwell resigned from his position as Moral Majority leader. He said that he would never work again for a candidate like he did Reagan. He mentioned in a news conference that his active role in politics and the Bakker scandal had hurt his image.

Evangelicals jockeyed for power. By that point, Pat Robertson had become the most famous televangelist in the country. Robertson ran unsuccessfully in the 1988 GOP presidential primary. Out of his campaign's ashes, he created the Christian Coalition, which became the most important anti-abortion organization of the next two decades.

Religious organizations like the RCAR tried to serve as a counterweight, though they were often marginalized by their own side. They wanted Medicaid funding restored to pay for abortions in cases of rape and incest. Executive Director Fredrica Hodges said that rich women wouldn't face abortion discrimination in those instances. As a result of their lobbying, the Senate voted 73–19 to restore funding after anti-abortion forces had caused them to remove it. The effort failed ultimately when President Reagan threatened to veto a spending bill of which it was part.

In the 1988 presidential election, Democratic candidate Michael

Dukakis, a devout member of the Greek Orthodox Church, faced anti-abortion hecklers throughout his campaign. They appeared at most of his events, at first silently. As time passed, they shouted epithets at Dukakis. Fistfights erupted at some of the gatherings.

In Atlanta, at the behest of Operation Rescue and Randall Terry, 1,200 protestors blocked access to clinics in the city beginning at the Atlanta Democratic National Convention and continuing through to the election. They crawled on their hands and knees—with Bibles in hand. Before doing it in reality, the demonstrators practiced at a church rally the night before while a speaker told them to stop once police touched them. If an officer took his hand off of them, then they were supposed to move again.

To get them off the streets, police tied demonstrators' hands behind their backs and carried them with sticks because they wouldn't stand and walk. The protests angered Atlanta's politicians because of the expense of incarceration. The city filed racketeering charges against Terry and Operation Rescue. Anti-abortion leaders called it the "civil rights movement for the unborn."

The protests didn't receive universal support from within their movement. The Rev. Charles Stanley, pastor of the First Baptist Church of Atlanta, distributed a leaflet criticizing the tactics of while disapproving abortion. He supported only lawful demonstrations.

Abortion rights activists counter-demonstrated. NOW president Molly Yard, speaking at a church, said Operation Rescue was, "Immoral because while they are purporting to save lives, they are endangering women's lives."

Operation Rescue officials indicated that one of their goals was to block the criminal justice system as a method of pressuring officials to outlaw abortion. Because they identified themselves as "Baby John Doe" and "Baby Jane Doe," they forfeited the ability to post a bond or be released on their recognizance.

Atlanta Police Sgt. Carl Pyrdum Jr. led efforts to contain the anti-abortion extremists' protest tactics. He singled out Randall Terry in the *Atlanta Journal-Constitution*.

"Mr. Terry's doctrine is to choreograph everything from the police response to the response of the courts, the corrections system, and the media," Pyrdum said. "Not only choreograph it. He wants to control it. I intend to frustrate Mr. Terry."[44]

It served as a place where more violent offshoots developed from the mainstream pro-life community. Law enforcement and abortion rights activists referred to it as the "siege of Atlanta."

Dazon Dixon Diallo, the 23-year-old community relations coordinator at the Atlanta Feminist Women's Health Center at the time, remembered her mixed feelings during the convention. The convention had brought Bill Clinton, Al Sharpton and Jesse Jackson—all people she admired. She lived in defiance and fear at the same time.

"On one hand, it was quite demoralizing to have to go to work every day not knowing if you were going to get home safe that day," Dixon Diallo said. "And at the same time, we were defiant about staying open and providing services and about making sure that the women who were seeking our services got what they needed."

---

44 Sherman, Mark. "Pro-Lifers vow to pack jails in city," *Atlanta Journal Constitution,* August 5, 1988. Pg. 1.

CHAPTER 10

A Heartbreaking Loss

ecky Bell was a 17-year-old Indiana high school cheerleader. An all-American girl of the 1980s, she was obsessed with Marilyn Monroe and had posters of the movie star in her bedroom. She dreamed of going to Purdue to become a veterinarian.

Becky was in love with a young man. She had gotten pregnant, unbeknownst to her parents. She went to the local Planned Parenthood, where a doctor told her that she had to notify her mom and dad if she wanted to get an abortion. Bell could have gone to a local judge to get a waiver about parental notification, but that justice's children went to high school with her and she wanted to keep it discreet.

Because Becky didn't want to upset her parents, she sought out an abortionist in Kentucky. One night, she told her parents that she wanted to go visit a friend who was in trouble and attend a party with her. It wasn't in a safe part of town, but Karen, her mom, acquiesced after Becky pleaded with her.

Becky called home an hour later. Her brother Billy answered the phone and she told him she was lost.

At midnight, Karen heard the keys rattling at one of the doors. She went to the front of the house and saw that Becky's long blonde hair was wet.

"Mama, it was an awful party,'" Becky said. "'Someone put something in my drink.'"

Becky said she felt like she had the flu.

The following day, Becky got up while Karen was in the kitchen. Becky stumbled into the room. She got the milk out of the refrigerator and tilted back and forth. The milk container slipped out of her hand and burst on the floor. Karen and Bill, her father, told her to get in bed. Later that week, they told Becky they wanted to take her to the doctor, which she didn't want to do.

Becky relaxed when she got her period. But she soon collapsed, and her parents took her to the doctor, who couldn't diagnose her cough, fever, and hemorrhaging—a confusing combination for a suspected flu case. The doctor told Bill and Karen Bell to take Becky immediately to St. Vincent's Hospital.

Karen and Becky sat in the back seat.

'Mom, can I lay down and lay my head on your lap?'" Becky said.

"You sure can," her mom said in return.

Karen patted her head.

"I'm so sorry for what I've done," Becky said.

"You haven't done anything," Karen said.

"I ruined yours and dad's night," Becky said.

"You haven't ruined anything," Karen said.

The nurses at the hospital took her to a room. They couldn't draw blood because of how fragile she was. Doctors asked to talk to Becky privately. Becky handed her mom a ring that had been on her finger.

"Forgive me for what I've done," Becky said.

Karen still didn't know what she was supposed to forgive.

Bill and Karen went to another room. The doctors told them they wouldn't want to see Becky in the state she was in. Her lungs had come apart because of an infection.

"We can't save the baby," the doctor told them.

"What baby?" Karen said with tears in her eyes. "I don't want a baby. I want my baby. What are you talking about?"

"Her body is in a state of pregnancy," the doctor said.

He said Becky couldn't be saved and they would have to call the coroner. But he said Bill and Karen wouldn't want to remember her ever looking the way she did at that point.

Becky died on Sept. 16, 1988. The coroner later telephoned the Bell's house and spoke with Bill. It was a botched illegal abortion that caused her death. The abortionist had used filthy instruments.

"We didn't want anybody to know that," Karen said to me over the phone, looking back on the moment. "We weren't going to tell anybody."

They planned on hiding and protecting Becky's reputation, but a minister they knew found out and told them they had to reveal the abortion to the congregation.

"There were two or three of them that were pregnant," Karen said.

Bill and Karen soon began to speak out for abortion rights and against the parental notification law that forced Becky to get an abortion. They got death threats, and older men harassed them with dead fetuses.

I first connected with Karen and Bill Bell by writing them a letter. In it, I described my work in civil rights literature and causes, as well as my earlier two-year project documenting World War II history, in which I spoke with veterans who had fought in different theaters of the war, from the beaches of Normandy to the South Pacific and the Battle of the Bulge. That background, showing both my commitment to historical accuracy and my care in telling deeply personal stories, helped establish trust. Because of that trust, the Bells, along with others in the reproductive rights movement, were willing to share their experiences with me and allow me to tell stories connected to abortion in a way that would honor the truth and the people involved.

The interview was lengthy and deeply personal. Karen spoke in detail about Becky's life, her personality and the circumstances surrounding her death in 1988. Karen's recollections were candid, emotional and often painful, recounting not only Becky's story but also the journey that led the family into pro-choice activism. Bill contributed as well, offering perspective on their testimony before legislatures, their organizing work and the challenges they faced in hostile political environments—including acts of intimidation by anti-abortion extremists, such as the time the lug nuts on their car were loosened after they spoke at an event. He also asked me directly if I had the courage to follow through with telling these kinds of stories, underscoring the personal risk and resolve that advocacy in this field can demand.

After the interview, Karen sent me a photograph of Becky along with a note saying she trusted me to tell Becky's story. It was a gesture that spoke volumes about the connection we had formed and the responsibility I had been given. The conversation left a lasting impression—not just because of the devastating events it recounted, but because of the strength, clarity and conviction that Karen and Bill brought to telling their daughter's story and advocating against the laws that, in their view, contributed to her death. Their willingness to revisit those memories, even in the face of hostility and danger, reinforced the importance of ensuring that Becky's story and the broader issues it represents would not be forgotten.

In the summer of 1990, national abortion rights organizations helped bring Bill and Karen Bell's message to Michigan, integrating their personal tragedy into a broader campaign against parental consent legislation. The Bells' appearance in Ann Arbor was part of a coordinated effort by advocacy groups to mobilize local supporters, connect state-level battles to a national narrative, and humanize the risks posed by such laws.

By pairing the Bells' testimony with grassroots organizing, these groups sought to influence public opinion and legislative outcomes in Lansing, positioning Becky's story as emblematic of the dangers minors faced when legal barriers to abortion access forced them into unsafe alternatives. Those types of rallies involving the Bells happened throughout the United States where these laws existed. [45]

That year, national abortion rights advocates launched the Becky Bell/Rosie Jimenez campaign to spotlight the human cost of restrictive abortion laws. The campaign linked the stories of two young women whose deaths became emblematic of the dangers posed by legal barriers to abortion access. By pairing these cases, organizers aimed to illustrate

---

45 The Ann Arbor News. (1990, August 6). *Becky Bell's parents speak out against parental consent law. The Ann Arbor News*, p. 8. https://www.newspapers.com/image/1180740306/

how different types of restrictions—funding bans and parental involvement laws—could force women and minors into unsafe, often lethal, circumstances.

The Feminist Majority Foundation spearheaded much of the national outreach, producing educational materials, coordinating speaking tours and partnering with local coalitions to press for legislative change. The campaign featured public appearances by the Bells and by Jimenez's friends and family, drawing media attention to the personal narratives behind policy debates. It sought to build a bridge between generational and demographic audiences, framing the fight against restrictive laws as a unified struggle for bodily autonomy across age, class and cultural lines. This strategy gave the campaign national reach, ensuring that both women's names became rallying cries in state-level and federal advocacy efforts.

Through rallies, campus events, and lobbying, the Becky Bell/Rosie Jimenez campaign became a fixture in reproductive rights activism in the early 1990s. Its advocates argued that the deaths of Bell and Jimenez were preventable tragedies caused not by abortion itself, but by government-imposed obstacles. By personalizing the political stakes, the campaign helped energize opposition to new restrictions being debated in multiple state legislatures and reinforced the movement's call to repeal existing measures that threatened safe and legal abortion access.[46]

Anti-abortion groups disputed that Becky Bell had died from an abortion. The Bells produced a letter from a top forensic pathologist to confirm that she had died from a botched procedure. Despite the letter, leaders within the anti-abortion movement continued to dispute it.

Karen couldn't believe the tactics used against them. Karen noticed that most of their antagonists were older men. One such man at another speech said, "The one thing about your daughter is she spread her legs."

Bill was furious at hearing that. They faced such encounters in many places. But he was willing to do it to defend his principles.

Despite their best efforts, Indiana didn't repeal or weaken its parental consent requirement, and the law remained in force. At the national

46 The Birmingham News. (1990, August 16). *Becky Bell/Rosie Jimenez campaign spotlights abortion law dangers. The Birmingham News*, pp. 21, 23. https://www.newspapers.com/image/1153172207/

level, Bell's case was cited in debates and court filings, but it did not trigger a widespread rollback of parental notification or consent laws.

Instead, through the late 1980s and early 1990s, more states either enacted new parental involvement requirements or defended existing ones. The Supreme Court upheld such laws if they included bypass provisions. The legal landscape in the years following Bell's death generally moved toward expanding or entrenching parental involvement statutes, rather than reversing them.

Back at the Supreme Court

While abortion continued to be a divisive issue during the presidency of George H.W. Bush, some women sought to avoid the controversies. Scores of self-help groups around the country taught women how to perform abortions on themselves. The methods were disseminated through articles, videotapes, books and lectures. Much of it was done to prepare women for the possibility that abortion might be made illegal again. Some women's rights groups endorsed it, but others criticized the approach, including Planned Parenthood.

In 1989, the U.S. Supreme Court heard arguments in the landmark abortion case *Webster v. Reproductive Health Services.* The case drew intense national attention and heavy lobbying from political and religious leaders—including President Bush, who urged the Court to overturn *Roe v. Wade.* Both sides organized massive demonstrations outside the Court, underscoring the issue's deep political and cultural divide.

The case's origins dated back to 1986, when the Missouri General Assembly passed House Bill 1596, declaring that "the life of each human being begins at conception."

The law prohibited the use of public facilities or public employees to perform or assist in abortions not necessary to save a mother's life. It also barred the use of public funds for abortion counseling and required physicians to perform viability tests on fetuses at or beyond 20 weeks' gestation before proceeding with an abortion.

The statute reflected the growing momentum among state legislatures in the 1980s to push the limits of *Roe v. Wade* and to test how far the Supreme Court would allow restrictions to go.[47]

William Webster, Missouri's attorney general, was a young conservative who had previously served two terms in the Missouri House of Representatives. He argued that the state had the authority to enact sweeping abortion restrictions under its sovereign powers.

The legal challenge was brought by Reproductive Health Services, a Missouri-based abortion provider, along with several physicians. They contended that the law's provisions violated the constitutional protections established under *Roe v. Wade*.

Reproductive Health Services provided abortions to women throughout the Midwest, often without regard to cost, relying heavily on donations to operate. The plaintiffs argued that the state's declaration that "life begins at conception" intruded on a woman's right to choose and that restrictions on public facilities, employees and funding imposed undue burdens on access to abortion.

Their lawyers maintained that the 20-week viability testing requirement was medically unnecessary and designed to create obstacles to the procedure rather than safeguard patient health.

Lower courts agreed in part, striking down several provisions as inconsistent with the constitutional standards set in *Roe v. Wade* and reaffirmed in *Akron v. Akron Center for Reproductive Health*.[48]

Frank Susman argued for Reproductive Health Services. The state of Missouri hired Charles Fried, former solicitor general of the United States, to represent it. He wanted to overturn *Roe v. Wade*.

Susman's first challenge in *Webster v. Reproductive Health Services* centered on the concept of fetal personhood. Missouri law declared that life begins at conception and therefore granted the fetus the same legal rights as any other person.

In the initial stage of the case, the U.S. District Court for the Western District of Missouri examined the constitutionality of several provisions

---

47 Missouri Revised Statutes, Mo. Rev. Stat. §§ 188.010–188.075 (1986).: *Webster v. Reproductive Health Services*, 492 U.S. 490 (1989).: Cates, W., Jr., & Rochat, R. W. (1990). Legal abortion: The public health record. *Law, Medicine & Health Care*, 18(4), 291–303. https://doi.org/10.1111/j.1748-720X.1990.tb01926.x

48 Reproductive Health Services v. Webster, 662 F. Supp. 407 (W.D. Mo. 1987), aff'd in part, rev'd in part, 851 F.2d 1071 (8th Cir. 1988).

of Missouri's 1986 abortion statute. The court struck down the law's preamble, finding that its declaration that "life begins at conception" conflicted with Supreme Court precedent in *Roe v. Wade*. The preamble, the court held, effectively adopted a state policy favoring fetal rights over a woman's right to choose.

The court invalidated the ban on the use of public employees and facilities for abortions not necessary to save the mother's life, ruling that it imposed unconstitutional restrictions on the performance of a lawful medical procedure. Likewise, it determined that the statute's prohibition on using public funds for abortion counseling interfered with constitutionally protected medical decision-making.

The district court further addressed the requirement that physicians perform viability testing for pregnancies at or beyond 20 weeks' gestation. It found the provision unconstitutional because it forced women to undergo unnecessary and potentially harmful medical procedures not required by prevailing standards of care—thus creating an undue burden on access to abortion.

In reaching its decision, the court relied heavily on *Roe v. Wade* and *Akron v. Akron Center for Reproductive Health*, reaffirming that the state could not place obstacles in the path of women seeking to exercise their constitutional rights.

As a result, the district court issued an injunction barring enforcement of the disputed provisions—setting the stage for Missouri's appeal to the Eighth Circuit and, ultimately, to the U.S. Supreme Court.[49]

Missouri and Attorney General William Webster appealed to the Eighth Circuit Court of Appeals, which upheld most of the rulings of the district court—though with different reasoning. The appellate court agreed that the ban on the use of public funds for abortion was constitutional, but otherwise affirmed the lower court's conclusions.

When the case reached the U.S. Supreme Court, the justices issued a fractured decision that upheld most of the Missouri provisions.

In a plurality opinion written by Chief Justice William Rehnquist, the Court ruled that the statute's preamble declaring that life begins

---

49 Reproductive Health Services v. Webster, 662 F. Supp. 407 (W.D. Mo. 1987).;*Roe v. Wade*, 410 U.S. 113 (1973).; *City of Akron v. Akron Center for Reproductive Health*, 462 U.S. 416 (1983).

at conception had no operative legal effect and therefore did not itself violate the Constitution. The Court also concluded that the state could lawfully prohibit the use of public resources for abortions and require viability testing at 20 weeks—even if these measures practically limited access to abortion.

The majority reasoned that the Constitution did not obligate states to provide facilities or funding for abortion services, characterizing the decision as one of government neutrality rather than prohibition.

Although *Webster* stopped short of overturning *Roe v. Wade*, it marked a significant narrowing of abortion rights, signaling that states had broader authority to regulate the procedure and impose indirect barriers.

The ruling encouraged anti-abortion legislators to pass increasingly restrictive laws, anticipating that the Court might eventually dismantle *Roe* entirely. It foreshadowed the Court's adoption of the "undue burden" standard, which would be more clearly articulated three years later in *Planned Parenthood v. Casey*.

For abortion rights advocates, *Webster* served as a warning that the constitutional foundation of *Roe* was beginning to erode. For opponents, it represented a strategic victory in their long-term campaign to return abortion regulation to the states.[50]

Anti-abortion advocates predicted an avalanche of new regulations. Judith Widdicombe, the Reproductive Health Services clinic's founder, said it would begin a war.

"This is going to become our Vietnam of the 90s," Widdicombe told ABC News. "The people will take to the streets. The people will make their voices known."

Faye Wattleton had attended the Supreme Court hearing in *Webster*, and left depressed afterward.

"The distance had just been cut shorter between the plight of women living under the yoke of the Missouri law as we neared the end of the

---

50 *Webster v. Reproductive Health Services*, 492 U.S. 490 (1989).;*Roe v. Wade*, 410 U.S. 113 (1973).; *Planned Parenthood of Southeastern Pennsylvania v. Casey*, 505 U.S. 833 (1992).; Goldstein, L. (1990). *Webster v. Reproductive Health Services: The Supreme Court retreats from Roe v. Wade*. **University of Miami Law Review, 44**(3), 819–85

twentieth century, and the plight of the women that Margaret Sanger had tried to save in New York City tenements in the early years of this century," Wattleton wrote in her autobiography.

President Bush was on vacation when the *Webster* decision was announced, but he sent his chief of staff, John Sununu, to address the press. Sununu declared that the Court had begun to restore protections for "the unborn."

Bush was pleased that the ruling opened the door to further challenges against *Roe v. Wade.* Sununu told reporters that the decision allowed states to impose additional regulations on abortion—a development the administration strongly encouraged. He added that President Bush supported a constitutional amendment to ban abortion nationwide, signaling that the administration viewed *Webster* as both a moral and political opportunity to advance its anti-abortion agenda.

"The basic thrust of the *Roe v. Wade* decision ought to be reversed," Sununu said. "And he is pleased at any step, including this one, that moves in the right direction."

Operation Rescue leader Randall Terry predicted the court would soon agree to ban abortions.

"I am convinced *Roe* will fall by the end of this presidential term and child killing will be driven back to hell where it came from," Terry said.

Women throughout the country called abortion providers, asking for a procedure before the states made it illegal. The decision permitted states to prevent public money from providing aid for abortions, which was something that concerned poor women who spoke to reporters at the time.

One of the lasting legacies of the *Webster* decision was that it elevated abortion politics to a defining issue for state-level candidates and lawmakers. For the first time since *Roe v. Wade,* state legislators had broad power to enact new restrictions on abortion.

This shift set the stage for what became known as Targeted Regulation of Abortion Providers (TRAP) laws, which, as discussed earlier in the book, grew directly out of the incrementalist approach. Legislators crafted these rules to chip away at the number of abortion providers in their states, disguising them as "women's health" policies.

In reality, the true purpose of TRAP laws was to limit or eliminate access to abortion—forcing clinics to close by making compliance too difficult or too expensive.

Many TRAP laws focus on location, facility, reporting and physician-relationship requirements. Some mandate that abortion facilities be within a specific distance of a hospital, a rule that imposes severe restrictions on clinic placement—particularly in rural areas where hospitals are scarce. Women in those regions are often forced to travel hours or hundreds of miles to reach the nearest provider.

Facility requirements saddle clinics with enormous financial costs, while reporting mandates compel abortion providers to submit private medical data to state agencies.

The physician-relationship requirement—one of the most restrictive TRAP provisions—demands that abortion providers hold admitting privileges at nearby hospitals. Yet many hospitals require doctors to admit a minimum number of patients per year, a threshold most abortion providers cannot meet due to the safety and low complication rates of the procedure.

Both the American College of Obstetricians and Gynecologists (ACOG) and the American Medical Association (AMA) have opposed TRAP laws, stating that they limit or prohibit safe, evidence-based medical care and unnecessarily restrict access to abortion services.

Absolute Strangers

The case of Nancy Klein dominated the abortion debate in 1989. No one thought her pregnancy would become the center of a controversy over abortion.

At the time, Nancy was a 32-year-old woman who lived with her husband, Martin, and 3-year-old daughter, Arielle, in Long Island, N.Y.

Her brother, Arnold Zusselman, described what Nancy was like before her life changed.

"She was the pride and joy of the family," Zusselman said. "She was absolutely the ideal person."

On Dec. 13, 1988, when she was 17 weeks into her pregnancy, Klein slid out and collided with another car while driving on an icy road. The accident put her in a coma. Afterward, she stayed in North Shore University Hospital in Long Island. Her family decided that her pregnancy put additional stress on her body. They all agreed an abortion was the best course. Little did they know how hard that would be to do.

More than 30 years later, the story of Nancy Klein seems as relevant as ever. It raises questions about whether abortion care should be permitted in medically necessary situations and whether women and their families have the right to make healthcare decisions that are in their best interest.

Martin Klein declined to be interviewed for this book. I reconstructed this story through interviews with Nancy's sister, Janet Smuga, her brother Arnold, and abortion rights leader Bill Baird, who became an essential figure in the saga.

In Nancy's situation, doctors faced a dilemma. She alone had the right to end a pregnancy, but she couldn't make that decision given her state of health. Martin sought to get guardianship of his wife so she could get an abortion. He filed a lawsuit at the local courthouse to do so.

Five medical experts testified that pregnancy increased the risks for the comatose patient and could threaten her life. New York State Supreme Court Justice Bernard McCaffrey granted Martin Klein's petition.

But there were soon unexpected—and unreasonable—legal challenges to the decision.

Back then, many reporters covered the judicial branch. One caught wind of Klein's situation and reported it in a newspaper, spreading it to other media. When Nancy's sister, Janet, heard it on the radio while driving, she remembered knowing it would be different than expected.

"As soon as I heard Marty's name, I just … you have one of those moments when your blood freezes," Smuga said.

The story exploded. People sent the family hundreds of cards and notes, offering opinions on Nancy's situation. Most supported the family's decision.

"Out of all those hundreds, there were perhaps a half a dozen that were opposed to the abortion," Smuga said. "There were an awful lot of people who said, 'I'm against abortion. But in your case, I think you should do it.'"

When the incident became national news, Frederick and Anne Zusselman, Nancy's parents, approached Baird for help. Many on the other side of the debate had long been Baird's adversaries. Two men, John Short and John Broderick, took significant roles in Nancy's situation. Short was a retired accountant, and Broderick was an attorney. They had never met Nancy and didn't know the family. Both were from New York and were leaders within the local anti-abortion movement.

Broderick had been involved in the anti-abortion movement primarily as a lawyer who represented activists charged with harassing abortion clinics. Ironically, Broderick had fought for a man to prevent his wife from getting an abortion because he had "father's rights."

In 1975, Short filed to become the legal guardian to all infants born alive after abortions in Long Island. A judge denied his attempt. Short had lost his job at the Nassau County Social Services Department about a decade earlier, after he refused to certify a $10 million state aid claim because he thought it included money for abortions and IUDs. He founded the Long Island Right-To-Life Committee.

Baird had regularly interacted with them. He described them as thugs.

"They were saying to me, 'We're saving her soul. We're saving the husband's soul. And that's the way it's going to be,'" Baird said over the phone.

Short and Broderick filed for guardianship of Nancy to prevent the abortion. In testimony before the appeals court, five medical experts said pregnancy increased the risks for the comatose patient and could imperil her life. Two medical experts testified that the pregnancy was not life-threatening.

Martin Klein said at the time that some physicians advised him that an abortion may help Nancy recover and could save her life.

"All we want to do is save Nancy's life," he said. "Time is precious. Any delay in terminating the pregnancy is only increasing the risks to

Nancy. These people's actions constitute severe harassment and interference with Nancy's rights and my wishes and Nancy's parents' wishes."

Martin expressed his frustration to the national media.

"I'm begging the American people to please help us," Martin Klein said. "We're torn up. These strangers have come off the street and are intruding in our lives. We don't know what to do about it."

While this happened, Smuga was driving back and forth between the hospital and Nancy's home to care for her child. When she visited her sister, she had to pass a police guard outside her room.

The five-member appellate division of the state supreme court in Brooklyn called Short and Broderick "absolute strangers," who had "no place in the midst of this family tragedy."

Short told reporters he was concerned about Nancy Klein's "psychological and emotional state" if she awoke.

"Under our plan, we say the baby's down at the neonatal clinic getting the best care possible," Short said. "Under their plan, they've got to tell her they've killed her baby. Emotionally, that would kill her."

New York's highest court rejected their appeal. The two men then filed a motion to stay with Supreme Court Justice Thurgood Marshall, who also turned down their request.

A Nassau County police officer was stationed in the hospital and a police cruiser was parked out front following the decision, after hospital officials were told the anti-abortion group Operation Rescue might try to stop the abortion, according to a Houston Chronicle report that came out at the time. Officials feared small groups of activists would "infiltrate" the 644-bed facility and chain themselves to vital areas and passageways, attempting to blockade the hospital's surgery wing.

Nancy's parents had been staying with Martin during the court battle and supported his decision to seek an abortion. Afterward, Frederick Zusselman expressed his view of the ordeal.

"Life will never be the same. It was too terrible. And then to have the complications come in and the publicity," he said. "This has been such a horrendous ordeal. I hope no one will ever have to experience what we have. We're really torn apart. We've been up and down on a roller coaster. These people have put us through absolute hell."

Afterward, Nancy came out of her coma, severely disabled due to brain damage. Later, an Emmy-nominated movie starring Henry Winkler and Patty Duke depicted the events. It was named after that judge's comment about Short and Broderick being absolute strangers.

Similar situations to Nancy Klein's have happened recently. In early 2025, Adriana Smith, a 30-year-old nurse in Georgia, suffered a catastrophic medical event that left her brain-dead at approximately nine weeks into her pregnancy. Despite her condition, the hospital reportedly kept her on life support for more than three months to allow fetal development—citing the constraints of Georgia's strict abortion law, which bans abortion after a fetal heartbeat is detected—effectively preventing the family from making their own end-of-life decision. Ultimately, her son was born via emergency C-section in mid-June, and Adriana was taken off life support days later.[51]

Both cases pitted medical judgment and family agency against legal and ideological constraints, highlighting the tragic consequences when reproductive autonomy is entangled with external authority. In Klein's case, judicial processes ultimately affirmed the husband's right to act on behalf of his incapacitated wife—including consenting to abortion— whereas in Smith's case, Georgia's abortion restrictions arguably stripped her family of that decision-making capability even after a declaration of brain death. The contrast underscores how evolving state laws and political landscapes—including the rollback of *Roe v. Wade*—have shifted the balance between personal autonomy, medical ethics and state-imposed restrictions on reproductive decisions.

Reproductive Justice

Byllye Avery formed the National Black Women's Health Project in the early 1980s. In 1983, she put together a conference on Black women's health decisions that was attended by about 2,000 people. Feminist conferences—while now a mainstay—were pioneering then because they permitted women to congregate and discuss things that, up to that point,

---

51 Amy, J., Mulvihill, G., & Thanawala, S. (2025, May 15). *Hospital tells family brain-dead Georgia woman must carry fetus to birth because of abortion ban.* Associated Press.

had been heard mostly by small groups in their homes.

"Women hadn't talked openly about things that were happening to them in the home, like sexual abuse and incest," Avery said. "And then with rapes and all of this and domestic violence … these were things that were on the top of Black women's minds that they wanted to talk about and learn from."

The late 1980s and early 1990s were pivotal years in the formation of what came to be known as the "reproductive justice framework." That's when feminists like Dazon Dixon Diallo, Loretta Ross and Avery started talking about intersectionality, the concept that different intolerances and forms of discrimination converge to hurt women who belong to each respective group affected by those prejudices. Things like food and housing insecurity came to the fore. Infant mortality was significant. They didn't have what they needed to deliver a healthy life for children.

"We didn't have the term intersectionality," Avery said. "But we understood that all of these factors were bearing on us. And we voiced them not using those terms."

In April 1989, the ACLU Reproductive Freedom Project, RCAR, and the Women of Color Partnership Program held a conference in defense of *Roe v. Wade*. It brought together Black, Latina and Native American women, among others, to develop strategies to appeal to people beyond traditional white feminists. Reproductive justice activist Loretta Ross called for a forward-looking movement.

"I want to talk about a reproductive rights movement that talks about poverty," Ross said. "I want to talk about being poor. I want to talk about what it's like."

Ross's career in feminism started when she took a job at the National Organization for Women in 1985. She was tasked with recruiting more Black women to the organization.

She became interested in reproductive issues after she was sterilized in 1973 as a result of a defective IUD. She had an abortion when she was younger, and she had challenges getting her mother's consent.

"I had no intention of becoming a feminist or social justice activist," Ross said. "But these are large, loud door knocks on my consciousness."

Ross saw that white women didn't realize how their race affected their experiences. She coined the phrase "appropriate whiteness" to refer to the type of white-lived experience they would want to live in lieu of white supremacy.

"There's a difference between white supremacy—the ideology—and whiteness as an identity," Ross said. "If you see it as an identity, you get to repurpose what that identity means for you without following the script and ideology of white supremacy. So it almost felt like a strategic breakthrough."[52]

Reproductive justice philosophy emerged between 1989 and 1994. Ross co-founded Sister Song in 1997. The organization was dedicated to helping women of color.

There are some critical lessons to still take from the movement's development. White women then were reluctant to take attention off abortion rights to focus on other issues pertaining to motherhood or feminism. There was a focus on preserving the right rather than on focusing on a more complete picture that addresses all the challenges faced by women of different socioeconomic strata. Ross emphasizes that reproductive justice is about the right to bring healthy children into a world where their health, safety and opportunity are possible.

"A lot of the early fights were about demonstrating to people that abortion rights were within the reach of the reproductive justice framework," Ross said. "It didn't abandon the fight for abortion so much as to contextualize the fight for abortion."

At the 1989 conference, Carmen Luna, a Latina reproductive rights activist, acknowledged some of the more problematic treatment of women of color when she addressed the forced sterilization of Latina women in California. Carmen said they should embrace and acknowledge that history. She had helped build a movement for 10 years in the state, with that as a backdropping topic. The women held conferences to get women excited about being able to maintain the right to choose.

"That was the issue we were able to embrace," Luna said. "It was the issue in our own backyard. An issue that was in the paper."

---

52 McDevitt, C. (2022, May 20). *Interview with Loretta Ross* [Interview].

What emerged from that conference was the beginning of the concept of reproductive justice, which is about seeking greater inclusion of women of color. Dixon Diallo, who spoke at the 1989 conference, said white women initially misunderstood the concept of reproductive justice.

"Anytime people talk about how we came up with RJ because white women weren't including us is not the truth. Right?" Dixon Diallo said. "Abortion and contraception were very much our issue. It's just that it wasn't our only issue.

"And so it wasn't about trying to undo the reproductive rights movement. It was about recreating a different way to organize and make sure that our policy issues were immediately as relevant as the abortion issue."

For the next five years, the concept of reproductive justice developed through conversations and correspondences. Reproductive justice as a formal framework began at the 1994 Black Women's Caucus meeting at the Illinois Pro-Choice Alliance in Chicago.

At that gathering—held just before the International Conference on Population and Development in Cairo—Black women activists, including Loretta Ross, developed the term "reproductive justice" to articulate a broader vision that connected reproductive rights with social justice, economic justice and racial justice. The concept emerged as a critique of the mainstream pro-choice movement's narrow focus on legal abortion, emphasizing instead the right to have children or not to have children, and to raise children in safe and sustainable communities.[53]

The philosophy and movement are still as timely as ever. More than 6.7 million Black women—57% of all Black women ages 15–49—live in 26 states that have banned or are likely to ban abortion, according to a study conducted by the National Partnership for Women & Families and In Our Own Voice: National Black Women's Reproductive Justice Agenda. The report also indicated that nearly 2.7 million Black women living in these states are economically insecure. The inability to access abortion puts them further into poverty.

---

53 Ross, L. J. (2006). Understanding reproductive justice. In *SisterSong Women of Color Reproductive Justice Collective*. Retrieved from https://www.sistersong.net/reproductive-justice

Political climate Continues to Boil

Before the 1990 midterm elections, President Bush sought to moderate his unpopular anti-abortion stance to appeal to a broader range of voters. He believed that the anti-abortion movement could help deliver victory in the 1992 presidential election, but he also recognized the risk of alienating moderates who supported abortion rights in limited circumstances.

Inside his administration, however, the atmosphere was far less moderate. When Bush attempted to fill several scientific and advisory positions, some candidates withdrew their names from consideration after perceiving an informal litmus test on abortion views. Senior officials reportedly pressured staff members not to have abortions, and controversy erupted when Attorney General Richard Thornburgh sent a letter to Justice Department lawyers encouraging them to choose adoption rather than abortion—a move that prompted internal outrage.

Bush banned the use of fetal tissue for medical research, a decision widely opposed by scientists and medical professionals, who argued it would stifle important advances in understanding genetic diseases and developmental disorders.

Simultaneously, NARAL championed the Freedom of Choice Act (FOCA), a proposed law that would have codified the protections of *Roe v. Wade* into federal statute. The bill would have outlawed waiting periods and parental-notification requirements for abortion. Despite strong backing from reproductive rights advocates, the legislation failed to pass Congress, illustrating the deepening political divide over abortion in the early 1990s.

Some abortion rights activists and clinic directors continued to face severe threats. Claire Keyes remembers the horrible trauma she felt after her clinic in Pittsburgh was set on fire in 1989. It would have burned down had the fire station not been two blocks away.

Anti-abortion militants were nothing new in the city. Keyes was director of the Allegheny Reproductive Health Clinic, which had been targeted by Operation Rescue throughout the 1980s. Randall Terry's presence stuck with her.

"I remember when he was very successful for a period of time training people how to blockade clinics," Keyes said. "And after he did that in Pittsburgh, and then eventually, he and all of his followers were jailed. Then they went on to other cities. And eventually, he kind of burned out."

The anti-abortion protestors scared her.

"Every day of my working life," Keyes said. "It was a very fearsome thing to do because all of the people who claimed to be pro-life were actually always threatening, murdering … violence. It was very, very frightening."

CHAPTER 11

Summer of Mercy

In the summer of 1991, anti-abortion protestors threw themselves in front of approaching cars outside abortion clinics in Wichita. Federal marshals carried them off the roads. Police arrested children and clergy. Most were first-time offenders who received a $25 fine for trespassing. Second-time offenders received contempt charges in federal court and faced prison sentences. After receiving death threats, doctors at the clinics in the city arrived with bulletproof vests. Police escorted patients into the clinic for abortion services with blankets over their heads.

Wichita at that time was combustible and politically charged. Anti-abortion protestors swarmed the clinics, especially the one belonging to Dr. George Tiller, Women's Health Care Services, which provided abortions later in pregnancy. Protestors held signs saying "Babies Killed Here" and "Tiller's Slaughter House."

Operation Rescue members sat by the hundreds in front of clinic doorways and blocked women from entering while reading the Bible. Police arrested more than 1,600 people. Operation Rescue's supporters included farmers who drove trucks and tractors with anti-abortion signs throughout downtown Wichita. Militants placed hundreds of crosses outside clinics.

It was called the Summer of Mercy. Protests forced all three of the town's clinics to close for more than a week in late July. Wichita's police chief assigned a quarter of local law enforcement to deal with protestors. Some were on horseback, and even that wasn't enough.

President Bush directed federal marshals to assist. The perception that Wichita was a haven for abortion later in pregnancy was misleading—only 13 or so of the 2,000 abortions performed every year there fit that description.

Peggy Jarman, the clinic's spokeswoman, told *New York Times* reporter Isabel Wilkerson that they felt attacked.

"We feel this entire city is under siege," Jarman said. "Where is the line ever going to be drawn in the name of freedom of speech?"

A federal court banned the blockade. The judge berated Operation Rescue leaders and called them hypocrites. He told them the Justice Department had agreed to send all the marshals necessary to keep clinics open. The U.S. Justice Department, however, submitted a brief in August 1991 that said federal marshals were being used improperly. The brief also argued that federal courts did not have jurisdiction in the abortion dispute in Wichita. Operation Rescue's attorney, Jay Sekulow, said the Bush administration backed them "100 percent."

Bush's Justice Department wanted the trespassing cases to be heard in state court. But the administration's position didn't change the judge's order. Operation Rescue's attorney used the brief to strengthen his appeal later. The protestors violated the judge's order and continued blocking the clinic.

Near the end of August 1991, abortion rights supporters showed up in force in Wichita. They railed against the six weeks of anti-abortion extremism and thanked police officers. Residents joined those protests, and some talked to CBS News, telling the network that the anti-abortion crowd were "lunatics" and that they "wanted them out of town."

Signs described Randall Terry as the Jim Jones of Wichita. Jones was a cult leader who had led a mass suicide in Jonestown, Guyana, in 1978. Abortion rights supporters gathered along the banks of the Arkansas River in Wichita to rally against Operation Rescue's ongoing blockades.

They carried placards that said, "Impregnate Randall Terry." [54]

The event drew national leaders who sought to counter the group's influence and denounce its tactics. Among them was Eleanor Smeal, president of the Feminist Majority Foundation.

"Operation Rescue is a mere footnote, a pathetic miserable little footnote in history," Smeal said during the rally.[55]

NOW's board of directors decided they wanted to have a clinic defense for the providers in Kansas. Abortion rights activists trained extensively before going. It was a little like the game of Red Rover—a line of people held hands while others sought to break through. After realizing that holding hands was too easy to get past, they linked arms as a more steady and reliable defense. Much as Freedom Riders had done in the 1960s, they prepared for vicious verbal insults.

Patricia Ireland, president of NOW, was in the thick of the protests. She had been in the movement for a long time. She had an abortion when she was younger while living in Knoxville, Tennessee. But that wasn't what led to her rise in the women's movement.

When I spoke to her in 2021, Ireland conveyed a blend of personal conviction, legal acumen and hands-on organizing experience that defined her leadership in NOW. She traced her activism to a workplace discrimination case at Pan Am, where she used knowledge from NOW and recent federal policy changes to successfully pressure the airline to alter its insurance coverage.

This formative experience, combined with her legal background, propelled her into leadership roles within NOW during the Equal Rights Amendment campaign and the rise of anti-abortion violence in the 1980s. Ireland spoke in detail about strategic responses to Operation Rescue, from lawsuits to clinic defense, emphasizing nonviolent but physically assertive tactics and the importance of coordination with police.

Her tone throughout the interview was candid and pragmatic, marked by a willingness to describe both victories and setbacks. Ireland

---

54 *Showdown in Wichita: Abortion rights rally hot.* (1991, August 25). The Daily Herald (Everett, WA), p. 3. https://www.newspapers.com/image/1030285015/

55 The Catholic Voice. (1991, September 19). *[Article on abortion rights rally during Summer of Mercy].* The Catholic Voice: Omaha Archdiocesan Newspaper, p. 23. https://www.newspapers.com/image/867826046/

balanced personal narrative—such as her own illegal abortion in 1966—with a strategic overview of the feminist movement's evolving tactics, from RICO lawsuits to the passage of the FACE Act. She displayed a competitive streak in legal battles, pride in grassroots mobilization, and an enduring belief in holding both allies and opponents accountable. By weaving together personal history, legal strategy and on-the-ground activism, Ireland came across as both a seasoned strategist and a committed advocate, deeply aware of the stakes and complexities of reproductive rights battles over the past five decades

Ireland said they had a constant flow of information as spies infiltrated the anti-abortion movement. That's common practice for both sides.

"We found some of our folks because, during the Equal Rights Amendment campaign, we reached out to a lot of religious people," Ireland told me over the phone. "And so we had the people who could, if you will, pass in Operation Rescue and infiltrate."

Because of the spies' work, abortion rights leaders knew which clinics Operation Rescue would harass. Ireland explained how it worked in the Washington, D.C., area. If there were 17 clinics in and around that area, they had to know which clinic was targeted to get there first. Then, they warned the staff and clinic directors.

"It wasn't a game, but it was a little cat and mouse," Ireland said. "Or spy versus spy, I guess from *Mad Magazine*, is a better analogy."[56]

The battle between the feminist forces and groups like Operation Rescue continued into the next year.

In 1992, Buffalo was at the epicenter of the national abortion debate. For about two years, anti-abortion leaders had planned a protest that came to be known as the Spring of Life. Three clinics operated at the time in the city that had many anti-abortion leaders.

Randall Terry was there for it. He had collaborated with other leaders to organize the effort; the Revs. Rob and Paul Schenck, two local activists, had also been part of the planning.

The Rev. Rob Schenck remembers Terry as a compelling figure for several reasons. People treated him as a prophet within the abortion rights

---

56 McDevitt, C. (2021, April 25). *Interview with Patricia Ireland* [Unpublished interview].

movement who argued that they were morally obligated to rescue those who were being taken away to death. Schenck described it as part of the larger "rescue movement" popularized by Randall Terry and bolstered by charismatic Christian leaders who viewed the campaign as a direct moral mission from God.

They cited Proverbs 24:11 as their guiding scripture: "Rescue those who are being taken away to death; hold back those who are stumbling to the slaughter."

Schenck emphasized that within their ranks, this was interpreted literally: they believed they were divinely mandated to physically block clinics, shut down streets and intervene to stop abortions. They portrayed abortion providers as predators.

"That caught fire in the movement," Schenck said over the phone to me.

Across two interviews, Schenck emerged as a reflective and candid figure, openly wrestling with his decades in the anti-abortion movement and the choices that defined them. He recounted his early zeal as a religiously driven activist who embraced confrontational tactics and cultivated political influence at the highest levels.

His recollections revealed an insider's view of the movement's strategies, including its calculated use of public spectacle, moral absolutism and alignment with partisan politics. Yet, in looking back, Schenck framed much of that period with regret, questioning the ethical compromises and the harm caused by the rhetoric and actions he once championed.

Since leaving the movement—particularly after the fall of *Roe v. Wade*—Schenck's perspective has shifted toward reconciliation and moral accountability. He spoke with a confessional tone, acknowledging the personal and spiritual toll of his past advocacy, while also analyzing the broader consequences of the movement's triumph.

Spring of Life was part of an exhilarating mania that anti-abortion activists felt at being imbued with that righteousness. Schenck recalled the movement's internal tensions, including disputes over credit between local Buffalo leaders and national figures like Randall Terry. While Terry later claimed he masterminded the protests, local leaders, including

Schenck, argued that their nuanced understanding of Western New York's social and political landscape was essential to the protest's scale and endurance

Buffalo Mayor Jimmy Griffin, an anti-abortion leader in the city, met with emissaries of that movement. Polls indicated most of Buffalo supported abortion rights despite having a large Catholic population. Still, Griffin gave a tacit nod and described abortion as a scourge. Anti-abortion leaders thought that was a huge moment and victory.

The confrontation in Buffalo coincided with the *Planned Parenthood v. Casey* case. Abortion rights activists hoped that the Supreme Court would address legalized abortion when they challenged a strict Pennsylvania law. Since the *Webster* decision, state lawmakers took the ruling as an invitation to introduce new abortion restrictions.[57]

Pennsylvania had imposed several requirements: a 24-hour waiting period, informed consent, and parental consent of one parent, or a judicial bypass, for juveniles. Additionally, a married woman who sought an abortion had to notify her husband, except in medical emergencies. Further, any clinic that performed abortions must report to the state. The state's legislature had passed the Pennsylvania Abortion Control Act, which called for disclosures on fetal development, paternal support obligations, state financial aid and spousal notification requirements.

Previous challenges to the legislation were addressed in the 1986 Supreme Court case of *Thornburgh v. American College of Obstetricians and Gynecologists*. But the challenges were not over. *Planned Parenthood of Southwestern Pennsylvania v. Casey* became a landmark decision. A group of five physicians who performed abortions, along with five clinics and an independent doctor, filed a lawsuit to challenge the law.

A federal appeals court upheld those restrictions earlier that year. Planned Parenthood took two weeks to file an appeal with the Supreme Court. It was right before a presidential election. Kate Michelman, executive director of NARAL, said the 1992 contest would determine where the country stood on abortion rights.

"For elected officials, this means that the days of dancing and

____
57 Kolbert, K., & Kay, J. F. (2021). *Controlling women: What we must do now to save reproductive freedom*. Hachette Books.

dodging, of hemming and hawing on the right to choose, are absolutely over," Michelman said.

Abortion rights advocates had a two-fold strategy. First, they wanted to see if *Roe* would be overturned. And if it was, they wanted it to be before the election so voters could weigh in.

The court took up the challenge.

Television trucks lined up outside the court on the day of its announcement. Both sides stood outside the court, awaiting the ruling. Lawyers and news interns lined the hallways waiting.

Justices Sandra Day O'Connor, Anthony Kennedy and David Souter wrote the decision. The court upheld the *Roe* precedent, noting how vital precedents were. Justice O'Connor wrote that it is important to adhere to it unless there had been a dramatic change in the topic since the previous decision. She wrote:

> *The Constitution serves human values, and while the effect of reliance on* Roe *cannot be exactly measured, neither can the certain costs of overruling* Roe *for people who have ordered their thinking and living around that case be dismissed.*

In *Planned Parenthood v. Casey*, the U.S. Supreme Court reaffirmed the core holding of *Roe v. Wade*—that the Constitution protects a woman's right to choose to terminate a pregnancy before fetal viability—but replaced Roe's strict trimester framework with a new test. The Court held that states may regulate abortion throughout pregnancy to promote maternal health or potential life, so long as the regulations do not impose an "undue burden" on the woman's ability to obtain a pre-viability abortion. This marked a shift toward giving states more leeway to regulate abortion, provided those regulations did not function as substantial obstacles.[58]

The "undue burden" standard became the central doctrinal change from *Casey*. A law constitutes an undue burden if its "purpose or effect is to place a substantial obstacle in the path of a woman seeking an abortion

---

58 Planned Parenthood of Southeastern Pennsylvania v. Casey, 505 U.S. 833 (1992).

before the fetus attains viability." This was intended as a middle ground between *Roe*'s strict scrutiny approach and more deferential standards. The Court emphasized that while states have legitimate interests from the outset of pregnancy, those interests cannot be pursued in ways that unduly hinder access to abortion services.[59]

Applying this standard, the Court upheld most of Pennsylvania's Abortion Control Act provisions at issue: the 24-hour waiting period, informed consent requirements and parental consent with judicial bypass for minors were all found constitutional. These measures, the plurality concluded, did not constitute substantial obstacles for the "large fraction" of women affected. However, the Court struck down the law's spousal notification requirement, finding it placed an undue burden on women in abusive or coercive relationships, effectively preventing them from exercising their right to choose.[60]

The Casey decision had lasting consequences for abortion jurisprudence. By retaining *Roe*'s central holding but lowering the standard of review to the undue burden test, the Court allowed greater state regulation, leading to a proliferation of pre-viability restrictions in the following decades. The undue burden standard became the controlling test until it was revisited and reinterpreted in later cases, including *Whole Woman's Health v. Hellerstedt* (2016), and ultimately overturned, along with *Roe*, in *Dobbs v. Jackson Women's Health Organization* (2022).[61]

Protest activity in Buffalo escalated during these proceedings, drawing national media coverage. Police arrested hundreds of anti-abortion activists as they attempted to block clinics. The protests created logistical chaos, strained city budgets and angered local residents and businesses. Many church leaders criticized the movement for disobeying civil law, citing biblical calls to respect governmental authority.

Despite the efforts of anti-abortion protestors to thwart care in the

---

59 Planned Parenthood of Southeastern Pennsylvania v. Casey, 505 U.S. 833 (1992).
Chemerinsky, E. (2022). *Constitutional law: Principles and policies* (7th ed.). Wolters Kluwer.
60 Greenhouse, L., & Siegel, R. B. (2011). Before (and after) Roe v. Wade: New questions about backlash. *Yale Law Journal, 120*(8), 2028–2087.
61 Siegel, R. B. (2020). The constitutionalization of abortion. In M. Tushnet, M. C. Horwitz, & B. Balkin (Eds.), *The Oxford handbook of the U.S. Constitution* (pp. 1053–1080). Oxford University Press.

city, pro-choice forces surrounded the clinics and kept them open during that time. Abortion rights leaders saw the events in Buffalo during this time as a considerable victory in an era when so many clinics had been successfully blocked.

The protests quickly evolved into a media war. NBC News reported how both sides meticulously staged their presence for the cameras, understanding that public perception was as critical as legal outcomes. Protestors on both sides strategized about how they would look on camera—abortion rights activists were instructed to keep their hands open to appear peaceful, while anti-abortion activists emphasized nonviolent civil disobedience as a sympathy-generating tactic.

Schenck did not expect the number of protestors, which he calculated to be around 5,000 people. They carried signs, blocked doors, crawled on streets and used other obstructing methods. Showing fetal remains to women was part of the approach.

At the time, he knew a laboratory technician in Tulsa, Oklahoma, who worked for a pathologist and had access to fetal remains. One of the more troubling things activists did at the time was use actual fetal remains to harass activists and feminist leaders. One problem they had was in getting through airport security. The man told him that they could strap fetal remains to their body to take with them on flights to places where they held anti-abortion rallies.

"That's what in the end we did," Schenck said. "We had couriers, and the couriers taped these fetal remains to their bodies, passed through the metal detectors at the airports and flew them into various locations."

When Schenck looked back on it, he discussed what he thought the Spring of Life's legacy was. He thought it had some value on the whole to the anti-abortion movement, but he acknowledged that it had a darker side too.

"It prepared the way for the future violence, including the shootings, the murders of both abortion providers and staff people, and others who were both killed and injured and certainly terrified," Schenck said. "I think we were constantly insensitive to the plight of the people at the center of it all, who were women and people."

Residents had grown weary of spending so much money on police protection for abortion clinics and protest control. Businesses expressed to news reporters their frustration with losing business. Seventy-six anti-abortion and three pro-choice protestors were arrested.

Throughout the protests, abortion rights supporters successfully kept Buffalo's clinics open. Katherine Spillar, who was a leader with the Feminist Majority Foundation, described to me how her coalition out-numbered and outmaneuvered Operation Rescue, training thousands in nonviolent tactics and escorting patients through protest lines. The fail-ure of Operation Rescue to close the clinics was widely seen as a turning point for the abortion rights movement—a perception Schenck did not dispute, even from the other side. Spillar said it was a total defeat for Operation Rescue.

"*Time* magazine declared it a defeat," Spillar said. "*The New York Times*, on its front page, declared it a defeat. It was a huge defeat, and that was just days before another big abortion rights march in Washington, DC. So our people were all charged up going to DC for those marches, because we had been so victorious in Buffalo."

When I spoke to her over the phone, Spillar seemed both deeply knowledgeable and strategically minded, speaking with the confidence of someone who has spent decades in the feminist movement and on the front lines of reproductive rights advocacy. She grounded her answers in personal history.

Spillar's team went on to organize clinic defenses at the Democratic and Republican National Conventions later that year, further solidifying abortion rights supporters' ability to out-organize their opponents.

RU-486

In 1992, the U.S. Supreme Court took up a case involving RU-486, the abortion pill. The medication had been banned in the United States, and federal officials seized a bottle from Leona Benten, a California resident, because it was not approved by the Food and Drug Administration (FDA).

"I know that RU-486 is the treatment I want," Benten told reporters.

"It allows me control of my body and removes me from the operating room and surgery."

Generally, the FDA has the authority to block unapproved drugs from entering the country, though it does not prevent the importation of every unapproved medication. The agency attempts to balance patient access to experimental treatments with the need to ensure drug safety.

In 1988, the FDA explicitly banned the personal importation of RU-486 (later known as Mifepristone). By the time the issue arose in the United States, the drug had been used by more than 100,000 women worldwide in five years.

Étienne-Émile Baulieu, a French endocrinologist, developed RU-486 with the French pharmaceutical company Roussel Uclaf. The compound, an anti-progesterone steroid, worked by preventing the implantation of a fertilized egg and inducing a non-surgical abortion. Roussel Uclaf's parent company, Hoechst AG of Germany, was reluctant to distribute the drug in the United States due to pressure from anti-abortion activists and fears that a boycott could extend to the company's other products.

Benten had legally obtained the drug while in England. When she landed at JFK International Airport on July 1, 1992, U.S. Customs agents seized the medication, citing an FDA import alert prohibiting RU-486 for "health reasons." Benten had intended both to terminate her pregnancy and to challenge the FDA's ban.

The Center for Reproductive Law and Policy filed suit on her behalf. Her doctor, Dr. Louise Tyrer, testified that Benten needed to take the medication by July 16, 1992—the eight-week mark—to ensure its effectiveness.

In Federal District Court in Brooklyn, Judge Charles P. Sifton ruled that the government had acted illegally and with political motivation when Customs officials and the FDA confiscated the medication. He ordered the government to return the pills immediately.

The U.S. Court of Appeals for the Second Circuit in Manhattan blocked Sifton's order, and two days later, Benten's lawyers filed an emergency appeal to the Supreme Court. The justices rejected her petition and denied her request to recover the pills. Benten ultimately underwent a surgical abortion.

Despite the case's outcome and Hoechst AG's reluctance to distribute RU-486 in the United States, clinical trials continued, and the FDA formally approved the drug in September 2000.

The Supreme Court's rulings in both the Benten case and *Planned Parenthood v. Casey* dominated the national conversation during the 1992 presidential election between President Bush and Arkansas Gov. Bill Clinton.

Anti-abortion activists argued that the Supreme Court should have overturned *Roe v. Wade*, while abortion rights supporters believed the justices had essentially weakened or "gutted" *Roe*'s protections.

Clinton made his pro-choice position one of the central themes of his campaign, creating a sharp contrast with Bush, who was reluctant to discuss the issue publicly. Bush maintained that the Republican Party could include both sides.

During the campaign, Bush pledged to continue the ban on fetal-tissue research. Before the ban, women who terminated pregnancies could donate fetal tissue for scientific study. The decision was celebrated by anti-abortion activists but met with fierce opposition from medical researchers and advocates for scientific progress, who saw no ethical conflict in the practice.

In the early stages of his campaign, Bill Clinton sought to appeal to both moderates and liberals. He emphasized that abortion should remain "safe, legal, and rare," a carefully crafted message designed to defuse Republican attacks while appealing to voters who supported abortion rights but held moral reservations.

At the same time, Clinton's record as Arkansas governor—including his prior opposition to public funding for abortion and support for late-term restrictions—came under scrutiny. Critics questioned his consistency and sincerity on the issue.

Facing pressure from abortion rights groups to take a firmer stance, Clinton's campaign highlighted his opposition to mandatory parental-consent laws and his support for public programs aimed at reducing unintended pregnancies. His team worked to portray him as pragmatic rather than ideological.

Republican strategists depicted Clinton as an extremist aligned with the Democratic Party's platform, which opposed virtually all abortion restrictions. Clinton, however, aimed to strike a delicate balance—projecting a strong pro-choice position without alienating centrist swing voters.

Some activists on the left remained wary of Clinton's moderate tone, especially his emphasis on making abortion "rare," which they feared could reinforce stigma surrounding the procedure.

Nevertheless, Clinton's strategy proved highly effective. He maintained broad support from reproductive rights advocates while presenting himself to the general electorate as a centrist capable of bridging moral and political divides.

This approach helped Clinton neutralize Republican attacks and transform abortion from a divisive political liability into a winning issue—a dramatic reversal of the dynamics that had shaped American electoral politics since the 1970s.

Anti-abortion activists disdained Clinton. When he got into a limousine at the Inter-Continental Hotel in New York at the 1992 Democratic National Convention, 37-year-old Operation Rescue member Harley David Belew confronted the Arkansas governor and asked for an autograph on a newspaper. He had a newspaper and pen in one hand.

"Would you sign my newspaper?" Belew asked

Clinton got out of his limo and obliged. Then, Belew opened the newspaper and exposed a fetus.

"What about the babies, Gov. Clinton?" Belew asked.

Belew claimed that Clinton threw the newspaper at his feet, went back to his limo and then threw the pen back at Belew afterward.

The Republican party split on the abortion issue during that election cycle, with iconic conservative Barry Goldwater saying Bush would lose the election if he held his strongly anti-abortion views.

"There is no way in the world that abortion is going to be abolished. It has been going on ever since man and woman lived together on this earth," Goldwater wrote to Mary Crisp of the National Republican Coalition for Choice.

By early 1993, anti-abortion violence had escalated further. According to the Feminist Majority Foundation's national clinic violence survey, 50.2% of clinics experienced severe anti-abortion violence in just the first seven months of 1993. This trend illustrated a worrying rise in both the prevalence and severity of harassment, transforming it into a persistent, multi-pronged threat to providers and access to reproductive healthcare.[62]

The urge for violence came from somewhere. It was not serendipitous. It was organized. Part of this was a proliferation of underground literature. Mark Crutcher, through his writings and organizations, promoted a strategic approach to anti-abortion activism that blended legal tactics with a paramilitary mindset. In 1992, he authored *Firestorm: A Guerrilla Strategy for a Pro-Life America*, an underground manual explicitly marked as confidential and intended for a targeted audience of committed activists. While *Firestorm* did not advocate outright illegal acts like bombings, it promoted "guerrilla legislation"—using legal and legislative maneuvers to harass, stigmatize and demoralize abortion providers, with the goal of making abortion services increasingly difficult to sustain. The manual showed its alignment with extremist thinking even if it focused on ostensibly lawful means.

Crutcher operationalized his strategies through two nonprofit corporations based in Denton, Texas—Life Dynamics Incorporated (LDI) and National Lifesource. LDI functioned as a front organization, publicly portraying itself as a clearinghouse for educational materials while covertly coordinating decentralized, independent campaigns in multiple states. These campaigns were broken down into labeled components (G-1 through G-5), each focused on specific regulatory, legislative and public relations objectives. By dispersing responsibility to loosely connected operatives, LDI created a structure that made it difficult to trace accountability for any aggressive or potentially unlawful actions back to the central organization.

The *Firestorm* plan emphasized harassing abortion providers through tactics such as mandatory malpractice litigation, exposure campaigns and

---

62 Feminist Majority Foundation. (1993). *1993 National Clinic Violence Survey Report*. Arlington, VA: Feminist Majority Foundation.

exploiting medical regulations. Campaigns were designed to appear as independent, local efforts while in reality being monitored and coordinated to ensure cumulative national impact. Publicly, Crutcher claimed that the decline in doctors willing to perform abortions was an unintended consequence of the movement's activism, but his writings suggest that these pressures—and providers' resulting feelings of fear and isolation—were part of the strategy. The overall approach blurred the lines between lawful activism and extremist harassment, embedding a militant, guerrilla ethos into the anti-abortion movement's legal strategies.[63]

Some scholars connected this decentralized, cell-based operational model directly to the leaderless structure adopted by anti-abortion terror cells, which sought to insulate central figures from liability while enabling lone actors to carry out targeted violence or sabotage under a shared ideological framework.

During this time, violent actors continued to harass abortion workers, particularly doctors who performed abortions later in pregnancy, like Warren Hern and George Tiller. Shelley Shannon, a member of the Army of God, attempted to assassinate Tiller in 1993. Police dug up a copy of an Army of God manual in her backyard. It provided a tutorial on how to attack and even destroy a clinic. Some of the methods were less drastic, like using syringes to inject butyric acid, a profoundly foul-smelling liquid, into clinics. However, the appendix further described how to destroy cars and commit worse vandalism. The final section included a call to action.

Not everyone will be blessed with this opportunity. With family ties, it would be most difficult … You may not be afraid to die. You are afraid of a lifetime of living in bonds. Understandable. Yet you have faith. You look forward to meeting our Lord face to face. The time has come … It would only take a few activists practicing terminal courage to drive the entire killing industry underground. Maybe the Spirit of God has been hounding you to take certain actions on behalf of his children and you have not obeyed. Here is your last chance.

---

63 Mason, C. (2002). *Killing for life: The apocalyptic narrative of pro-life politics.* Cornell University Press.

Religious leaders on the pro-choice side were quick to condemn the Army of God in the years that followed. Lynne Landsberg, associate director of the Religious Action Center of Reform Judaism, said in organization letters, "Religious behavior means using our time, our talent, and especially our moral leadership to sanctify life and condemn violence," Landsberg said. "This manual preaches not peace but poison. This manual promotes not community but conspiracy, not creation but chaos."

CHAPTER 12

A Tragic Death

r. David Gunn delivered babies and terminated pregnancies throughout his career. He had to prop up his leg while performing abortions because polio had crippled him during his childhood. He was a diminutive 130 pounds at best. In 1993, Gunn was divorced and had two children, a 22-year-old son and a daughter who was 17.

During his career, he told friends he thought it unfortunate that so many women had to provide for children even at 15. Gunn was passionate about two things—his family and women's rights. He felt abortion should be done safely by a trained practitioner.

"It wasn't that he didn't value life," his friend George McCormick told a Pensacola newspaper. "He was just sophisticated enough to know that circumstances are not the same for everyone."

Gunn opened his first OB/GYN practice in Brewton, Alabama in 1977. He focused on prenatal care and delivery. Eventually, he learned abortion methods. With those lessons, he began treating women throughout the South. Gunn also worked at a Pensacola clinic because there weren't many abortion providers in the region.

Gunn was tracked and became the target of Old West-style "wanted" posters. Because he knew the threat was real, he carried a weapon when he drove the back roads to get from one clinic to another. Gunn knew that he could be attacked.

The use of wanted posters featuring abortion providers' personal information stood out to people like Katherine Spillar as particularly dangerous. These posters, she argued, were not protected free speech but a legitimate peril, designed to encourage violence.

"Those are true threats," Spillar said, reflecting on that era. "The only time wanted posters have been used is in the Old West. It's wanted dead or alive."

The courts eventually agreed. In *Planned Parenthood of the Columbia/ Willamette v. American Coalition of Life Activists*, the Ninth Circuit Court of Appeals ruled that it was unprotected by the First Amendment. The court found that, though the posters did not explicitly call for violence, they were issued in a context where similar posters had preceded the murders of abortion doctors.[64]

Listing names, addresses and photographs and accusing the doctors of "crimes against humanity," the posters sent an implicit message of violent reprisal. The court concluded that a reasonable person would interpret the materials as a serious expression of intent to harm.

This decision marked a significant limit on speech that incited fear in a climate of violence. The court emphasized that the posters and related "Nuremberg Files" website—which crossed out the names of murdered doctors—were part of a coordinated campaign to threaten providers. By labeling the materials as true threats rather than protected political speech, the ruling reinforced that abortion providers targeted in this way could seek legal remedies against intimidation and harassment.[65]

Even as those protections evolved legally in courts, things worsened after the election of Bill Clinton, whose victory outraged anti-abortion activists. They thought the new president would reverse their victories from the 1980s.

Protestors followed Gunn everywhere, including to his home. Gunn

64 Planned Parenthood of the Columbia/Willamette, Inc. v. American Coalition of Life Activists, 290 F.3d 1058 (9th Cir. 2002).
65 Calvert, C. (2003). *True threats and the issue of intent: Analyzing the American Coalition of Life Activists decision.* Communication Law and Policy, 8(3), 299–329. https://doi.org/10.1207/S15326926CLP0803_01

defied them despite the harassment. He used bullhorns to shout back at protestors, and he sang "Happy Birthday" on the anniversary of *Roe v. Wade*. He played Tom Petty's "Won't Back Down" to rebuke his critics further. Gunn told pro-choice women that they needed to protest outside the clinics as much as anti-abortion people.

On March 10, 1993, Michael Frederick Griffin, a 31-year-old anti-abortion protestor outside Pensacola Women's Medical Services, stepped out of the crowd, chased down, and shot Dr. Gunn three times in the back with his 38-caliber snub-nosed revolver at point-blank range after Gunn got out of his car. Gunn later died in surgery. It was the first murder of an abortion provider in the United States.

After police arrested Griffin, the former chemical plant worker asked to use the Bible as one of his legal documents as he planned to represent himself. He had a checkered past. Griffin's wife had previously accused him of domestic violence.

Steve Powell, an employee at an office park where the clinic is located, said the protestors acted strangely after the shooting, according to the Washington Post.

"It looked like they were just happy," he said.

Loretta Ross studied and monitored hate groups in her work with the Center for Democratic Renewal. It was at that point that she noticed the overlap between the anti-abortion and white supremacist movements.

"The walls between those movements are very porous, and there was a lot of personnel crossover between that white supremacist movement and the anti-abortion movement," Ross told me over the phone. "Particularly this violent vigilante subculture with the wanted posters on doctors and the attacks on clinic staff and the bombings and the arsons and the stalking and things like that."

Ross discovered people who belonged to both movements by looking at different databases. White supremacists like John Burt, a one-time Klansman, had advised Michael Griffin. That proved Ross' point.

While many within anti-abortion circles distance themselves from white supremacy, since beginning to radicalize in the 1980s the movement has sometimes been linked to groups like the Ku Klux Klan. In

1994, the Klan organized several protests outside of clinics in Florida as a response to what the federal government had done in targeting clinic harassment. Organizer John Baumgardner said the Klan's protests had more to do with the buffer zones, which he felt violated free speech ideals.

In opposing abortion, Klansmen adopted some slogans of neo-Nazis and militia groups and took some white supremacist ideas to use through the lens of anti-abortion politics. The concept of racial suicide, or that white people aborted pregnancies more, was a central theme of their arguments. In addition to that, American Klansmen represented abortion care as a profession dominated by Jews, which then was used to make antisemitic appeals to people the Klan attempted to recruit.

Burt, an anti-abortion activist in the community, had raised money for Griffin's family.

"I believe the pro-death people will take care of Dr. Gunn's family," Burt told ABC News. "And as Christians, we're going to reach out to the Griffins and not run away from them because they're in bad trouble."

Burt emerged as one of the most polarizing figures in the anti-abortion movement in Pensacola, blending his past as a former Ku Klux Klan member with an uncompromising evangelical fervor.

He positioned himself as a spiritual warrior, framing abortion not merely as a political issue but as a cosmic battle between good and evil. Burt's public image was built on a mix of theatrical confrontation and paternalistic outreach; he cultivated a small community of wayward girls at his ministry, offering them a strict, Bible-centered life under his authority.

To his allies, Burt was a savior, rescuing vulnerable young women from what he described as the "abortion holocaust" and giving them structure, rules and the "love of Jesus Christ." To his critics, he was a manipulative and dangerous zealot whose activism blurred the line between protest and intimidation.

He stood at the forefront of Pensacola's high-profile clinic blockades in the early 1990s, a period that saw escalating violence, including the murders of Dr. David Gunn and later Dr. John Britton. Burt denied direct involvement in violence but justified extreme rhetoric and maintained close ties to those who committed lethal attacks. His street protests, often staged with oversized graphic signs and war-like casualty boards, were designed to shock and shame clinic patients.

Burt's personal life fed his public narrative. He and his wife, Linda, raised ten children—some biological, others adopted—under rigidly conservative rules, presenting themselves as a model Christian family. But his militant approach, combined with his history in white supremacist circles, made him a lightning rod for criticism and a symbol of how deeply intertwined anti-abortion activism could be with other far-right movements.[66]

In Pensacola's charged atmosphere, Burt thrived on confrontation with the press, law enforcement and anyone he perceived as part of a broader secular enemy. For him, the fight against abortion was not just a cause; it was the central mission of his life, one that justified virtually any means short of pulling the trigger himself.

Burt was part of a fringe element of the Christian right, according to Jerry Reiter's book *Live From the Gates of Hell: An Insider's Look at the Anti-abortion Underground*. Gunn and Burt had squared off many times before, and he had taken Michael Griffin under his tutelage.

Burt protested Gunn's funeral by saying that the murdered doctor was a baby killer who was "burning in hell!"

Investigators and journalists surrounding the case speculated that Griffin had acted under Burt's guidance. Reiter said in his book that leaders seldom wanted to give direct orders to proteges to carry out terroristic violence. They didn't want to be arrested for conspiracy. So, instead, they relied on manipulating the person's emotions.

Burt died in 2013 while serving a prison sentence for molesting a 15-year-old girl.[67]

After Gunn's assassination, a single bouquet marked the spot where

---

66 Houpppert, K. (1993, April 6). John Burt's holy war: One minister's dangerous battle to save the unborn. *The Village Voice*.

67 Feminist Majority Foundation. (2003, June 11). *Anti-abortion extremist arrested on sexual molestation charges*. Retrieved from https://feminist.org/news/anti-abortion-extremist-arrested-on-sexual-molestation-charges/?utm_source=chatgpt.com; Florida Department of Corrections. (2013). *Inmate population information detail: John Allen Burt (DC# R15739)*. Santa Rosa Correctional Institution. Retrieved from https://web.archive.org/web/20130420073914/http://www.dc.state.fl.us/

he was shot. Many anti-abortion advocates in Pensacola condemned the doctor's murder. Still, they said it would save the lives of countless children since Gunn was the only one to perform abortions regularly in that county. That made him the one of the few people that the perpetrators could focus on to commit murder. Abortion rights supporters said that Gunn's murder was the culmination of years of violence from anti-abortion forces.

Anti-abortion terrorism and poor access to abortion services go hand in hand. Because Gunn was the only doctor who performed abortions in that county, his clinic and another he worked with temporarily referred patients to out-of-state clinics.

The shooting outraged President Bill Clinton, who had become the first legitimate champion of abortion access while serving in the Oval Office.

"We must create a climate where people do not believe this kind of behavior is acceptable," Clinton said.

Lobbyists soon began playing a role in the aftermath of Gunn's shooting. Susan Hill, who owned and operated the abortion clinic Gunn worked for, called Ron Fitzsimmons, the executive director of the National Coalition of Abortion Providers. Fitzsimmons had lobbied for the organization for nearly a decade. In the early 1990s, he dealt with anti-abortion violence constantly. People called him to tell him they had been hit with butyric acid or arson attacks or had been bombed. Some doctors told him that the extremists followed them home.

"I was not shocked," he said. "None of us were shocked."[68]

Fitzsimmons emerged as a prominent—and at times polarizing—figure in the abortion rights movement, known for his skillful lobbying and ability to secure key legislative victories on behalf of reproductive health providers. As the longtime executive director of the National Coalition of Abortion Providers, he gained a reputation for being pragmatic, politically savvy and willing to negotiate in high-stakes policy battles.

However, his career was also marked by controversies that alienated some allies, most notably when he admitted in the late 1990s that he had

---

68 McDevitt, C. (2021, March 29). *Interview with Ron Fitzsimmons* [Personal interview].

misstated the prevalence of certain abortion procedures during political debates—a revelation that critics said undermined the movement's credibility. Supporters admired his candor and strategic acumen, but detractors saw these missteps as costly errors, leaving Fitzsimmons with a legacy defined as much by his successes as by the contentious moments that shadowed them.[69]

When I spoke with him in 2021, he came across as a candid, pragmatic and battle-hardened figure whose long tenure in the abortion rights movement was marked by both strategic victories and deep personal exposure to the dangers faced by providers. He blended matter-of-fact recollections of high-stakes lobbying with vivid, sometimes chilling stories of violence, underscoring his proximity to both political power and physical risk.

His willingness to work across ideological divides—even engaging civilly with figures who openly endorsed killing doctors—reflects a complex blend of principle, political acumen and unflinching realism.

At the same time, Fitzsimmons' openness, including frank assessments that sometimes alienated allies, paints the portrait of an advocate more concerned with truth and strategy than strict adherence to movement orthodoxy. The overall impression is of a seasoned operator who navigated moral complexity, legislative battles and threats of violence with a mix of resilience, skepticism and a grounded sense of the costs of the work.

At Griffin's trial in 1994, sharpshooters stood on the roof of the Pensacola courthouse. His lawyers attempted to blame Burt for Gunn's death. The defense claimed that brainwashing incited Griffin to murder. Local abortion providers acknowledged the forces that created the climate for Gunn's murder still existed outside their clinics.

Griffin said during the trial's lead-up that he didn't remember the day of the shooting.

Local anti-abortion leader Rev. Paul Hill praised Griffin during the trial to NBC News.

---

69 *Cong. Rec.*, 105th Cong., 1st Sess., H 643 (Feb. 26, 1997), quoting Ron Fitzsimmons, executive director of the National Coalition of Abortion Providers, admitting that he "lied through [his] teeth" regarding partial-birth abortion claims.

"Michael Griffin, by his actions, has demonstrated the truth that unborn children should be defended with the same force born should be defended," Hill said.

Judge John Parnham told the jury that the abortion issue would bring strong reactions but that the facts of the case shouldn't be obscured. A jail guard overheard Griffin tell his wife that he had killed David Gunn. That was used as evidence against him. In closing arguments during the trial, the prosecution described Griffin as an assassin who stalked and murdered David Gunn. The jury convicted Griffin two weeks later.

Afterward, clinic workers and escorts in Pensacola handed bullet-proof vests to staff and then shielded patients with signs as they entered the facilities. The intimidation had an impact on the number of doctors who wanted to perform abortions everywhere in America. Dr. U.G. Klopfer, an abortion worker, told NBC News that there was no way to stop the violence.

"If someone in this crowd now wanted to pull a gun out and blow someone's brains out, who's going to stop them," he told the reporter.

It's important to note that not all anti-abortion advocates condoned the murders that happened in the 1990s. Cardinal John O'Connor of New York denounced the violence in a news conference. He declared that proponents of violence should attempt to kill him instead of the abortion doctors if they planned on murdering anyone.

As the assassination of Dr. Gunn dominated the news cycle, Susan Hill worked with the slain doctor's children, Wendy and David Gunn Jr.

Eventually, the three found their way onto "The Phil Donahue Show" with Paul Hill, who later killed abortion provider Dr. John Britton and his bodyguard James Barrett.

Before Gunn's death, Fitzsimmons and other abortion rights supporters pushed for legislation to protect abortion providers from the rising anti-abortion militant actions. The Freedom of Access to Clinic Entrances Act (FACE) had stalled in Congress, but as with most noteworthy bills passed, it needed an impetus to garner congressional support. Gunn's death provided that. Fitzsimmons began talking to people about its passage.

"It took a lot of work to pass it," Fitzsimmons remembered. "There were some very serious issues that we dealt with. There was a point where I had a disagreement with [Sen.] Chuck Schumer about language in the bill."

Fitzsimmons wanted to acknowledge that anti-abortion protestors had a right to demonstrate under the First Amendment. Schumer disagreed with him, but eventually, Fitzsimmons' logic won. Fitzsimmons wasn't always popular with his allies for his free speech beliefs, but it was something to which he stuck. The bill prescribed sentences as short as six months to as long as life imprisonment for obstructing clinic access. It permitted civil remedies.

In March 1994, the U.S. House of Representatives opened debate on the FACE Act in response to escalating violence at reproductive health clinics. Supporters of the bill emphasized that the legislation was not about regulating speech or protest but about drawing a line at the use of force, threats and obstruction. The bill was introduced to create federal penalties for those who used such tactics to prevent access to legal medical services. Legislators described the rise in targeted harassment and violence as a national concern requiring a coordinated federal response.

Opponents of the bill argued that federal involvement was unnecessary, since most of the actions targeted by the legislation were already illegal under state law. They raised concerns that the law might chill constitutionally protected protest activity. However, supporters of the bill stressed that peaceful demonstrations and sidewalk counseling would remain legal and untouched by the bill.

The debate centered on whether federal protections should extend specifically to clinics and patients, with backers arguing that existing laws had proven insufficient to deter threats and attacks. The discussion revealed clear divisions over how best to balance public safety, civil liberties and access to health care.

Throughout the proceedings, lawmakers referenced specific incidents—such as clinic invasions and the 1993 murder of a physician—to illustrate the stakes of inaction. Some representatives emphasized the broader implications of allowing politically motivated violence to persist unaddressed.

By the end of the debate, a majority of the House agreed that a federal statute was needed to protect patients and providers. The bill passed the chamber with a vote of 241–174, signaling strong support for a federal response to clinic violence and setting the stage for consideration by the Senate later that spring.

Debate on the floor was limited, with only brief remarks from managers and sponsors. The bill's supporters emphasized the need for federal protections in response to violence and obstruction targeting reproductive health clinics, with members from both parties contributing to the legislative effort.

On May 12, 1994, the Senate approved the final version of the FACE Act by a vote of 69–30. This vote followed the House's passage of the bill earlier that month and cleared the way for it to be sent to President Clinton, who signed it into law on May 26.

Fitzsimmons drove to the White House with Gunn's children, David and Wendy, to watch the president sign the bill. It was a bittersweet ceremony with an audience of roughly 20 people that CNN broadcasted. Vice President Al Gore compared the bill to the landmark *Brown v. Board of Education* Supreme Court decision, which desegregated schools. Attorney General Janet Reno also spoke, and she discussed Gunn's murder:

> *The terrible event focused for me and focused the attention of the nation on the problem of violent attacks against abortion providers, vandalism at abortion clinics, and the efforts by some to prevent women from exercising their constitutional right to choose to have an abortion.*

Reno said her office had reviewed the adequacy of existing laws in protecting abortion providers. Her staff had told her none of the statutes was adequate. She told them to help lawmakers develop the clinic protection bill.

President Clinton spoke last. He said it had been a bipartisan effort, and he said that bill had been a priority. He acknowledged David and Wendy. He addressed anti-abortion protestors by saying they had First Amendment rights.

"Our people have genuinely and deeply felt differences on the subject of abortion," Clinton said. "Even if abortion is safe, legal and rare. But we must all agree as a nation we must be committed to the rule of law. It is what keeps us civilized."

Clinton said they couldn't allow the attacks anymore or permit intimidation of women. He said doctors providing abortions and women seeking them shouldn't have to go through that. He described some on the right as vigilantes. He mentioned Gunn's death and the attempted murder of Tiller.

"Let me say again the awful circumstances which gave rise to this law are the most extreme example of a trend running in this country that is very bad for us as a democracy," Clinton said.

Clinton called for leaders on both sides to diffuse the situation. He said people shouldn't misrepresent others' views or take the law into their own hands. After the media photographed him signing the bill, Clinton took Gunn's children into the Oval Office and spoke with them.

The act had a lasting legacy. It diminished the level of coercion that anti-abortion activists could employ to deter abortions. The threat of imprisonment or lawsuits discouraged those methods.

To protect abortion providers and their patients, some state legislatures have enacted additional laws that prohibit obstructing entrances to clinics and vandalism. A few created bubble zones that prevent protestors from getting within a certain distance of another person without their consent while near a clinic. Other laws include prohibiting telephone harassment, trespassing, having a weapon at a clinic, online harassment, releasing odors or property damage.

Violence didn't decrease after the FACE Act's passage. Paul Hill was the next perpetrator. Fitzsimmons had developed a relationship with him, which he did with many leaders, including the Rev. Flip Benham, a longtime anti-abortion activist who would later lead a schismatic faction of Operation Rescue, Operation Save America. Fitzsimmons tried to be civil.

Hill had developed a belief that homicide was justifiable with abortion doctors. Fitzsimmons asked him why he hadn't committed murder if he thought so. Hill told Fitzsimmons that he had thought about it, but he preferred to be a leader rather than a doer. At one demonstration Fitzsimmons put together in Pensacola, nearly 100 abortion doctors and workers were there. Hill was there at the perimeter with a big sign. He just watched—at least in that moment. But it wasn't long before he took it upon himself to stop abortion by any means necessary.

In July 1994, Rev. Hill shot Dr. John Britton and clinic escort James Barrett outside a Pensacola abortion clinic. Patricia Ireland was horrified. And not just because of the murders. She had helped establish a clinic defense program at the facility, which utterly failed. At his trial, Ireland sat next to a priest who supported the justifiable homicide theory. Though abortion rights had progressed extensively during Clinton's administration, leaders in the women's movement knew that this wouldn't stop violence.

"All of us knew it did not mean the end of clinic attacks," Ireland said. "And it did not mean the end of our struggle. And just having the law is not enough."

In November 1994, prosecutors concluded their case against Hill. Already convicted in federal court for violating the Freedom of Access to Clinic Entrances Act and firearms laws, Hill faced the death penalty if convicted on state charges. Representing himself, he declined to question jurors, cross-examine witnesses or call his own.

Witnesses testified they saw Hill open fire as the victims arrived, and a gun shop clerk identified the shotgun he had sold Hill two days before. Hill was barred from arguing "justifiable homicide," a defense rejected in both trials.

On Nov. 2, 1994, the jury deliberated less than 30 minutes before convicting Hill of two counts of first-degree murder, one count of attempted murder, and one count of firing into an occupied vehicle. The next day, the same jury unanimously recommended the death penalty. On Dec. 6, Circuit Judge Frank Bell formally sentenced Hill to die in Florida's electric chair. Hill showed no remorse, telling a television audience he believed God was "pleased" with his actions and that he expected to "go to heaven."

Supporters of the verdict saw it as a necessary stand against clinic violence; radical anti-abortion activists hailed Hill as a martyr. Years later, Hill called Fitzsimmons from jail, asking him to come to his execution.

"You were at our event a year later with 100 doctors in an open forum," Fitzsimmons asked. "Why didn't you kill us then?"

"Well, I thought of it," Hill said. "But you, over the years, had been very civil with me. We had good conversations, and I just thought I didn't want to interrupt your event."

Fitzsimmons didn't know what to say. The state executed Hill in an electric chair shortly after that.

Pro-Choice President Alienates Christian Nationalists

Clinton had kept his promise to advance abortion access. In March 1993, he lifted the 16-year-old ban on federal funding for helping poor people get abortions. Pro-choice activists praised his decision to eliminate the two-tier health care system, which provided different treatment for wealthy and impoverished patients. Rep. Henry Hyde said Clinton's action would compel and coerce millions of taxpayers who didn't support abortion rights to pay for the procedure.

Anti-abortion activists increasingly despised Clinton for undoing everything previous administrations had done to curb abortions. Joseph Scheidler predicted that Clinton's policymaking would trigger more violence.

Clinton had galvanized the Christian right. Membership in the Christian Coalition more than doubled in his first year in office. Ralph Reed, who was its director, said the president was the best thing they had going for them. Reed had quickly earned himself a reputation as one of Washington's most influential power brokers.

After Pat Robertson's failed bid for president, he chose the 27-year-old Reed to help him create what became the country's dominant Christian right group. Both fiscal and social conservatives agreed to resist Clinton's policy-making. They found common ground in the abortion issue through their desire to cut funds to reproductive rights organizations and to poorer women who might need help paying for an abortion. So the problem became central to the Republican narrative—even though some of their politicians expressed support for legal abortion.

David Wilhelm, chairman of the Democratic National Committee, visited a meeting held by the Coalition in September 1993. He argued that people could be pro-choice and still devout, which was met with jeers. Robertson responded, when he got on stage, by calling for the ousting of Clinton from office.

"We thought we were electing Bubba from Arkansas," Robertson said. "Instead, we got part of the aging Woodstock generation and all the radicals who went along with it."

Controversy about anti-abortion violence notwithstanding, the 1994 midterm elections didn't look promising for President Clinton. Robertson claimed he had attracted 1.5 million people to his cause. His organization distributed millions of half-page paper voters' guides, which proved to be his most valuable weapon against the Democrats. (This was before websites made a lot of paper obsolete.) Churches distributed the documents, which rated candidates on abortion, school vouchers and gay rights.

Many worried that Robertson planned on establishing a theocratic state. Abraham Foxman of the Anti-Defamation League was one.

"They will decide what books your children will read," Foxman told a television reporter. "They will decide what laws will govern America from a point of view of their values, which they say is dictated by God."

Reed said he wanted a pluralistic society welcoming faith into its government. He said his organization was mainstream and not a bunch of people on the fringe. The Coalition raised $21 million in 1994. By then, Reed and Robertson's group had become the constituency the Republicans would pander to the most.

Clinton had tried to maintain his connection to religious leaders. He held an annual Interfaith Prayer Breakfast, where he said he supported a greater amount of religion in public life, including schools.

While Reed ostensibly sought to embrace pluralism, many within the Christian right were revolted by his efforts. Randall Terry called the Christian Coalition the "mistress of the Republican Party" and Terry advocated support for the U.S. Taxpayers Party (USTP) instead. The

USTP was openly theocratic and included many proponents of the dominionist Christian Reconstructionist movement, including Terry himself.

The media focused mainly on Reed, Robertson and others at the Christian Coalition. But several other groups on the Christian right also drove the narrative on the anti-abortion side. Concerned Women for America, Focus on the Family and Coral Ridge Ministries were a few. CWA Chief Beverly LaHaye had a radio talk show, on which she said there should be no separation between church and state. She invited Jeffrey Baker, a leader of the USTP, to speak on the show.

James Dobson, a child psychologist with a national radio broadcast, led Focus on the Family, creating 35 state-level think tanks and lobbying units near state capitals to implement his agenda. Dobson built Focus on the Family into a $100 million-a-year operation.[70]

While extreme to some, the Christian Coalition wasn't nearly as theocratic as those more deeply involved with Christian Reconstructionism, a theological movement that grew in influence in the 1990s. According to that view, LGBTQ+ issues, as well as women's reproductive rights, signaled a shift away from a "biblical worldview" that they sought to reconstruct through church-based activities and—more troublingly— what elected officials could implement within government. As author Frederick Clarkson put it, they wanted to build the Kingdom of God before Jesus returned.[71]

The USTP was a leading promoter of Christian Reconstructionist views. Its founder, Howard Phillips, attacked the idea of public education because he thought it conveyed anti-Christian principles. When he ran for president in 1992, he devoted television ads in Iowa to gory anti-abortion content on cable television. The ads included the photos, names and addresses of abortion providers.[72]

Four years later, the USTP once again ran Phillips, joined by Herb Titus, as its presidential ticket. They argued *Roe v. Wade* was

---

70 Clarkson, Frederick. *Eternal Hostility: The Struggle Between Theocracy and Democracy.* Common Courage Press. Monroe, Maine. 1997. Pg. 32-38.
71 Ibid. Pg. 96-99.
72 Ibid. Pg. 104.

unconstitutional and shouldn't be enforced or obeyed. Titus said they would appoint federal district attorneys to prosecute abortion providers on murder charges if they were elected. Much of their rhetoric about abortion, along with arguments for unfettered gun access, came from the militia movement, which pushed for local and state resistance to federal policies.[73]

The far right demonized their opponents and compared them to satanic forces. Fr. Paul Marx, the founder of Human Life International, said Margaret Sanger was second to the devil in creating moral morass in America. Randall Terry said Planned Parenthood came from Hell. These activists saw abortion as a symptom of a larger trend toward ungodliness.[74]

To this day, Terry argues that theology justifies severe and divine punishment from God. His most recent book, *Divine Correction: How God Gets a Nation's Attention*, published in 2024, has a chapter titled "Don't Kill Children."

He writes that murder is a sin and the punishment prescribed in the stories of both Noah and Moses was death. He cites the Canaanites because of their crimes of killing children, which demanded the most severe reaction from God. He says that child-killing is at the head of a list of demonic and satanic rituals. He cites Deuteronomy chapter 18 and then explains his own reasoning:

> *In the following passage, God not only forbids and condemns child killing, He specifically calls for the execution of the child killer. Beyond that, he threatens to punish those who allow the crime of child-killing to go unpunished—i.e., those who stand idly by and do not stop child-killing.*[75]

Later in the book, he clarifies that he is not quoting similar passages against homosexuality as a call for the execution of people he considers guilty of a sin, which he characterizes as the gay lifestyle.[76] Instead, he

---

73 Ibid. Pg. 118.
74 Ibid. Pg. 128-130.
75 Terry, Randall. *Divine Correction: How God Gets a Nation's Attention.* Kindle Edition, March 2024. Page 142-160.
76 Ibid. Page. 185.

argues that God said you should love your enemy.

Despite Terry and others publicly disavowing the murders of doctors and bombings of clinics, some scholars have written that the anti-abortion rhetoric put forth during this time created a hostile and dangerous environment for people within the reproductive rights movement. Clarkson argued that clinic violence wasn't the result of lone nuts. Instead, it came from cold calculations from the theology of vigilantism or the belief that one had acted on behalf of God. Operation Rescue's early slogan was, "If you believe that abortion is murder, then you must act like it's murder."

The open-ended call to action permitted extremists to justify many actions in the name of doing their God-ordained duty. And while many within the Christian right decried violence in the mid-90s, there was a bit of disingenuousness. They had ignored it for two decades, and some had even condoned it.[77]

One of those groups was Missionaries to the Preborn, a spin-off of Operation Rescue founded by Rev. Matthew Trewhella and Rev. Joe Foreman. Trewhella, along with about 30 others, had signed Paul Hill's statement in support of the idea that the murder of abortion providers was actually a form of justifiable homicide.[78]

Speaking to the *Marshfield News Herald,* he called for criminalizing abortion in all cases, even those involving rape and incest.

"Abortion is a crime like robbery is a crime," Trewhella said. "When you commit a crime, there is a chance you will end up being the one harmed."[79]

Trewhella made news when PPFA released footage of his speech to the USTP of Wisconsin in 1995. He called for church-based militias and used his organization as a suggested template. They held firearms classes for their members. The U.S. Taxpayers Party, which was later renamed the Constitution Party, was a gathering place for some of the most militant and violence-promoting anti-abortion proponents. One

---

77 Ibid. Pg. 140.; Saul, Stepanie. "A Lethal Weapon," Newsday. Oct. 30, 1994. Pg. 20-21. (Accessed via newspapers.com)

78 Southern Poverty Law Center. (1998, September 15). *The Signers*. Southern Poverty Law Center. https://www.splcenter.org/resources/reports/signers/

79 Kallio, Nikki. "Responses to Preborn Rally Mixed," Marshfield News-Herald. July 24, 1996. Pg. 1-2. (Accessed via newspapers.com on April 13, 2022)

speaker at the event declared, "Abortionists should be put to death. They are murderers."[80]

In the mid-1990s, following an alarming wave of violence against abortion providers, Attorney General Janet Reno moved to create a coordinated federal response. After a series of letters and meetings with leaders from Planned Parenthood and other reproductive-health organizations—who had documented escalating threats, arsons and shootings—Reno brought together senior officials from the FBI, the U.S. Marshals Service, the Bureau of Alcohol, Tobacco and Firearms, and the U.S. Attorneys' offices. The goal was to pool investigative resources, improve intelligence sharing and ensure that incidents targeting clinics were treated as part of a broader national pattern rather than isolated crimes.

This effort resulted in the formation of the first multi-agency federal task force devoted to investigating anti-abortion violence. The task force's mandate included identifying extremist networks, providing security assessments to clinics, and coordinating prosecutions under newly strengthened federal laws such as the FACE Act. By centralizing federal attention on the problem, Reno's task force marked a turning point in how the government addressed clinic violence—shifting from a reactive, local approach to a proactive national strategy informed by direct input from reproductive rights advocates.[81]

In August 1994, the FBI began an inquiry into accusations that the use of force against women's clinics and doctors was the work of a conspiracy by anti-abortion militants. Abortion rights groups, including the Feminist Majority Foundation, Planned Parenthood, NOW and the National Abortion Federation, met with the FBI to share information. In a teletype sent to 56 FBI field offices, investigators directed agents that they had information about that. Trewhella and Donald Spitz were on

---

80 U.S. Taxpayers Party–Wisconsin Convention Video Recording, May 27-28, 1994. Planned Parenthood Federation of America records group III (PPFA III), Sophia Smith Collection, SSC-MS-00371b, Smith College Special Collections, Northampton, Massachusetts. https://findingaids. smith.edu/repositories/2/archival_objects/492242 (Accessed July 11, 2025.)

81 Kennebec Journal. (1995, May 2). *Reno vows to fight abortion clinic violence*. Kennebec Journal, p. 4.; Los Angeles Times. (1993, October 30). *Reno meets with abortion-rights, anti-abortion groups*. *Los Angeles Times*.

the teletype, according to *The New York Times*.[82]

It's important to note that Trewhella and Spitz, who denied the allegations, were never charged or convicted with any crime or being part of a criminal conspiracy to kill abortion doctors.

For his part, Trewhella told Newsweek in 1994 that he would never kill a physician who performed abortions. He said that anyone who advocated violence would be asked to leave his organization. He claimed that the FBI investigation was a big joke and his comments about guns on the Planned Parenthood video were lighthearted and taken out of context.[83]

Racketeering

As abortion rights advocates watched mounting instances of clinic blockades, arson, bombings and other violent or coercive actions aimed at shutting down providers, they came to suspect the existence of a coordinated, national-level campaign—what they described as a "pro-life Mafia" intent on systematically impeding access to reproductive health services.

In response, NOW and affiliated clinics brought legal action under federal racketeering and extortion laws, asserting that these violent tactics constituted a conspiracy to deprive women of their constitutional right to abortion by any means necessary.[84]

The feminist leaders felt it was the only way to get the federal government to stop what they saw as a national conspiracy. In 1986, NOW and two abortion clinics filed suit against Joseph Scheidler and associated anti-abortion groups—including the Pro-Life Action League and Pro-Life Action Network—alleging they operated as a nationwide conspiracy to close abortion clinics by means of threats, violence or intimidation. The plaintiffs argued this pattern constituted racketeering activity under the Racketeer Influenced and Corrupt Organizations (RICO) Act

---

82 Johnston, David. "F.B.I. undertakes conspiracy inquiry in Clinic Violence." *New York Times*. Aug. 4, 1994. (Accessed via nytimes.com on July 6, 2025)
83 Liu, Melinda. "Inside the anti-abortion Underground," Newsweek. Aug. 14, 1994. (Accessed via https://www.newsweek.com/inside-anti-abortion-underground-187894)
84 National Organization for Women. (2014, February). *Background on NOW v. Scheidler*. National Organization for Women. https://now.org/wp-content/uploads/2014/02/Background-on-NOW-v-Scheidler.pdf

and extortion under the Hobbs Act, framing the violence as a coordinated campaign with intent to injure clinic operations. The district court initially dismissed the case for failing to allege an economic motive, and the Seventh Circuit upheld that dismissal.[85]

The Supreme Court considered a case in late 1993 that considered the legal questions of whether those behind blockades could be tried for violating RICO. Scheidler was one of the parties in the case known as *The National Organization for Women vs. Scheidler.*

Lawyers for anti-abortion activists argued RICO didn't apply to their demonstrations. They claimed that the law dealt with mobsters and financial criminals. At the heart of the case was whether federal officials needed an economic motive to prosecute. Scheidler said at the time that the anti-abortion movement wasn't at all concerned with financial matters. NOW took the stance that RICO applied to any situation in which organized violence took place.

The law carried civil penalties of up to three times for any actual damage and criminal penalties of up to 20 years in prison. It wasn't likely the court would apply those laws to peaceful protestors, but it was uncertain if the justices thought anti-abortion terrorists should get those penalties.

In January 1994, the court ruled that people blockading clinics could face prosecution under the RICO law. They could receive fines or jail time for both. It was a unanimous decision read by Chief Justice William Rehnquist. Abortion rights activists hailed the decision because it provided a tool they could use against anti-abortion organizers. Jay Sekulow, chief counsel for the anti-abortion American Center for Law and Justice, criticized the decision by saying it would have applied to civil rights protestors had it been issued 40 years earlier. Sekulow felt anti-abortion protestors had the same rights.

Patrick Mahoney, the militant leader of Operation Rescue, lambasted the justices.

"Pro-life activists will not allow the Supreme Court to tell us where

---

85 First Amendment Encyclopedia. (n.d.). *Scheidler v. National Organization for Women (2003).* The Free Speech Center at Middle Tennessee State University. https://firstamendment.mtsu.edu/article/scheidler-v-national-organization-for-women/

we can express our First Amendment rights," Mahoney said. "Will this be challenged in the streets? The answer to that is yes."

Even as those legal victories occurred for pro-choice forces, doctors and medical staff who performed abortions still had to live with the prospect that they could be murdered at any moment. While the nation argued about the myriad abortion-related matters in the 1990s, Dr. Bruce Lucero, a doctor who performed abortions in Birmingham, Alabama, wore a bulletproof vest and carried a gun with him. Lucero traveled like other abortion doctors to provide care.

"I don't know any doctor in this field who isn't carrying a weapon or at least considering carrying a weapon," he told NBC News. "I feel we are under an inevitable siege and that there is violence toward us. Death is all around me. I work at a clinic where James Barrett and John Britton were killed."

Anti-abortion demonstrators sought to change the methods they employed because violence had shifted public opinion in favor of abortion rights. Anti-abortion organizations asked protestors to sign a nonviolence pact. But despite some of their sincere efforts to diffuse the situation, extremists continued to lash out.

On Dec. 30, 1994, John Salvi walked up to a Planned Parenthood Clinic in Brookline, Massachusetts, and pushed the buzzer. After they admitted him, he drew his gun to shoot. Shannon Lowney, the receptionist who permitted his entry, died at the scene. Salvi later drove to Preterm Health Services, another abortion provider, did the same thing and shot Lee Ann Nichols, who was also a receptionist. In total, Salvi murdered two and injured five.

Salvi had been a hairdresser. He was a Catholic with strong views on abortion. He had a poster of an unborn fetus in his truck, according to his employer, Richard Griffin, who was interviewed by NBC News.

A nationwide manhunt commenced. Salvi, the shooter, left a duffel bag at the second crime scene that contained a gun store receipt and a pistol. The next day, Salvi attacked a clinic in Norfolk, Virginia.

A detective saw Salvi fire 23 shots at the Norfolk clinic and then flee in a truck with a New Hampshire license plate. Police pursued him. Salvi stopped, threw his gun out of the vehicle and surrendered.

Staff installed a metal detector at one of the Boston clinics, and in Norfolk, they added more security. Clinton's Justice Department focused on how they could work with clinics to stop the violence, but they didn't connect Salvi to any organization.

J.W. Carney, his attorney, tried to argue that anti-abortion advocates had encouraged Salvi. Investigators traced Salvi's life back to Florida, where they suspected he was guilty of arson and had threatened women and wanted to join an armed militia group. When he moved to Boston, he handed out pictures of dead fetuses outside of churches and attended meetings for an anti-abortion group called Massachusetts Citizens for Life. Its founder said he never fit in.

Neither Nuts nor Alone

Donald Spitz was based in Norfolk when Salvi attacked.

Spitz said after the attack that any action to stop abortion was justifiable, but he wouldn't comment on whether the homicide was. Spitz's name and telephone number were in Salvi's possession. Spitz attempted to see Salvi in prison but denied knowing him beforehand.

Salvi's rhetoric mirrored ideas long entrenched in right-wing conspiracist circles. He claimed a Freemason plot controlled the economy, that the Catholic Church was under siege, and that the Ku Klux Klan, the Freemasons and organized crime worked together. These themes matched the narratives found in the John Birch Society's *The New American*, the *Fatima Crusader*, and other militant Catholic and Protestant publications, where abortion, homosexuality, feminism and education reform were framed as parts of a "New World Order" conspiracy, often with antisemitic overtones.

While living in Florida, Salvi discussed joining a militia and considered attending a bivouac in the Everglades. The militia movement cast the federal government as tyrannical and divided society into "producers" and "parasites"—corrupt elites at the top and welfare recipients at the bottom, often racialized. Abortion providers were folded into this enemy list, making them targets in a moral and political war. This framework reinforced Salvi's self-image as a righteous combatant in a struggle between good and evil.

Militia and militant anti-abortion networks overlapped in media and message. Through shortwave broadcasts, underground papers and fringe conferences, they spread a worldview of imminent tyranny, spiritual warfare and the legitimacy of violent resistance. Salvi absorbed these themes alongside End Times theology from the Book of Revelation, which framed abortion as a satanic assault on divine order. His trajectory shows how interconnected extremist subcultures can radicalize individuals toward political violence.[86]

Frederick Clarkson thinks that attacks on clinics were not generally the work of lone nuts. They were neither nuts nor alone. The attacks were usually, obviously, well-planned and coordinated. Yet, many in the media and law enforcement portrayed the extremists as independent actors.

"They developed a theory of the lone wolf, which allows them to look specifically at an individual without having to look at the concentric circles of support that most of these characters actually had," Clarkson said.

Clarkson suspected that people surrounding the killers, arsonists and bombers had a range of knowledge and complicity. In Shelley Shannon's case, several people provided housing and even cans of gas used in clinic arsons and were named as unindicted coconspirators.

Many of the perpetrators gathered intelligence about their targets by joining in protests at the clinics. That's where they developed an understanding of its layout.

A jury convicted Salvi in March 1996. A mother of one of the victims confronted Salvi after the verdict and described her daughter's last words. Prosecutors had succeeded in portraying Salvi as an anti-abortion terrorist. They cited his purchase of semiautomatic weapons, his attendance at anti-abortion rallies at one of the clinics he attacked, and his efforts to evade capture.

As the violence escalated, Kathy Spillar of the Feminist Majority

---

86 Berlet, C. (1998, March 4). *The increasing popularity of right wing conspiracy theories: Allegations of a Freemason conspiracy and other scapegoating conspiracist theories within the Catholic right, Protestant right, anti-abortion movement, patriot movement, and armed militia movement, including a discussion of statements by John C. Salvi, 3d* (Rev. #14). Political Research Associates.

Foundation closely tracked the anti-abortion movement's leaders. They documented patterns, traveling organizers, the fundraising apparatuses and national networks like the Army of God that connected these extremists. One of their key findings was that these were not spontaneous, isolated actors—they were part of an orchestrated campaign.

Conflict Between the Democratic Party and Reproductive Rights Leaders

Gloria Feldt, who became president of the Planned Parenthood Federation of America in 1996, brought to the role a background steeped in grassroots organizing and reproductive health advocacy. Raised in rural Texas, she began her professional life as a teacher before joining Planned Parenthood in West Texas in the late 1970s.

Feldt's rise through the organization's ranks reflected both her deep commitment to expanding access to reproductive health care and her ability to navigate the political and cultural challenges surrounding abortion and contraception. By the time she assumed the national leadership position, she had earned a reputation as a pragmatic strategist who understood the necessity of blending service provision with public advocacy.

The belief that the organization's mission extended beyond providing clinical services shaped Feldt's vision for Planned Parenthood. She argued it should be a leading voice in molding public policy on reproductive rights while also investing in public education to counter misinformation and stigma. Feldt sought to position the organization as both a trusted health care provider and a powerful political advocate capable of defending reproductive freedom at the national and local levels.

At the heart of Feldt's approach was a conviction that reproductive health was inseparable from women's equality and personal autonomy. She was unafraid to address the growing hostility toward abortion rights in the political arena, warning that complacency could erode decades of progress. Her leadership called for Planned Parenthood to be proactive in litigation, legislation and cultural discourse, insisting that the organization should not simply react to threats but work to control the conversation about reproductive rights.

By integrating community outreach with political engagement, Feldt envisioned Planned Parenthood as a vital force for both direct health care and the defense of fundamental freedoms.[87]

But Feldt's expansive vision sometimes clashed with the more cautious approaches favored by politically powerful allies within the Democratic Party. Feldt did not shy away from holding her political allies accountable. In public remarks, she rebuked the Democratic Party for what she saw as a dangerous lack of resolve in defending abortion rights. Too often, she argued, party leaders sought to sidestep the issue or dilute their positions in hopes of attracting conservative or swing voters, a strategy she believed betrayed the movement's core principles.

Feldt warned that such equivocation risked eroding decades of hard-won progress and emboldening those who sought to dismantle reproductive freedom altogether. To her, abortion rights were not merely another item on a negotiable political agenda but a fundamental human right that demanded unwavering, unapologetic advocacy from the very party that claimed to champion it.[88]

On the conservative side, Republican candidate Bob Dole had sought to make his party's position less rigid on abortion. Four years earlier, the GOP platform included the argument that the unborn child had a fundamental right to life with no exceptions. Dole hoped to have diverse beliefs on the issue within his party.

"My view is that I want to bring people into the party, not keep people out of the party," Dole told ABC News anchor Peter Jennings. "I don't want to build a fence around the party and say that everyone has to agree with me on this issue. I happen to be pro-life, but I've tried to explain to some of the pro-life people that if we're going to win elections and build this party, we can have different views on this issue."

Dole supported having exceptions for abortions in cases of rape, incest and where the health of the mother was at risk. Dole had at one point supported the Human Life Amendment, which made no exceptions for those circumstances. But during his presidential campaign,

---

87 The Mobile Register. (1997, June 4). *Feldt heads Planned Parenthood.* p. 47, 51.
88 Journal Tribune. (1999, November 16). *Planned Parenthood president criticizes Democrats on abortion.* p. 4.

Dole said he was less rigid on the topic.

Dole knew that Republicans were the minority party in America and needed to attract more people. Nonetheless, his position drew the ire of Phyllis Schlafly, who said she didn't want to "water down" the plank. Other members of the party, even those who were anti-abortion, supported Dole because they felt it would increase the chances of their winning the election. Gov. Christine Todd Whitman (R-NJ) said she admired Dole for reaching out to people with other views.

Dole criticized the media for dividing the country on abortion. Ralph Reed gave Dole high marks for his handling of the topic. Pat Buchanan, the iconic conservative Catholic firebrand, also said he supported the statement, though he did so through a news release rather than in person. Dole satisfied pro-choice Republican governors, including Pete Wilson of California. There was controversy at the convention, however, because pro-choice GOP leaders like Whitman and Wilson were not allowed to speak.

A Hit List?

In 1997, Army of God cheerleader Neal Horsley created the Nuremberg Files.

Horsley emerged from rural Georgia into the national spotlight as one of the most notorious figures in the extremist wing of the anti-abortion movement. A preacher's son who once attended Westminster Theological Seminary, Horsley cast his activism as a personal mission from God, shaped in part by the loss of his father before he was born. Living quietly with his wife, Carol, and their daughter, Kathy, he presented himself as a devout Christian determined to "expose the truth" about abortion. Yet behind this domestic façade, Horsley was building one of the most feared and controversial tools in the anti-abortion arsenal—a weapon not of explosives or firearms but of names, addresses and photographs.

That weapon was the Nuremberg Files, an online database cataloging abortion providers, clinic staff and pro-choice advocates with extraordinary detail. Names were accompanied by home addresses, license plate numbers and, in some cases, the birthdates of children. In Horsley's grim ledger, the names of those who had been murdered were crossed out; those wounded were shaded in gray. To supporters, this was an act of "public accountability."

To critics and law enforcement, it was a hit list. The site's notoriety spiked after the murder of Dr. Barnett Slepian, whose name was among those Horsley displayed. Gloria Feldt accused him of inciting the killing; Horsley denied legal culpability but refused to moderate the site, framing it as a constitutionally protected act of speech.

Horsley's influence extended beyond his website. His home became a node in a wider network of radical activists, a place where younger militants could find ideological reinforcement. He cultivated relationships with individuals who embraced the "justifiable homicide" doctrine, arguing that killing abortion providers was morally defensible under God's law. This intersection—between uncompromising theology, conspiratorial worldviews and the mechanics of intimidation—made Horsley a pivotal bridge between nonviolent protest and violent extremism. His work did not simply track the abortion conflict; it escalated it, making him a folk hero to some in the movement and a symbol of dangerous radicalization to the rest of the country.[89]

The Oregon Planned Parenthood affiliate brought a lawsuit against him for violating the FACE Act. After various appeals, the federal Ninth Circuit Court of Appeals said that the website posed a "true threat," and the judges described it as a hit list.

While Horsley may have been a cheerleader, there were plenty others acting out in ways that maimed, killed and destroyed. At the beginning of 1998, glass shattered, and people nearby screamed after Eric Rudolph bombed a Birmingham abortion clinic, killing an off-duty police officer who moonlighted as a security guard. The bomb also seriously injured a nurse. Police suspected that a bombing of an Atlanta abortion clinic a year earlier was connected to the Birmingham explosion because of similarities with the devices. The search for Rudolph spanned several states. Rudolph bombed several other places, including the 1996 Olympics.

89 Voll, D. (1999, February). The righteous man with the hit list rocks on the front porch of his glass house. *Esquire*, 131(2), 111–119. Photographs by B. Smale.

During his terroristic spree, the Army of God claimed responsibility. CNN reported the group wrote letters that said an attack on a gay club was also their doing. It took five years before Rudolph was captured and sentenced to prison. In his guilty plea, Rudolph justified his actions with anti-abortion and anti-gay rhetoric.

Evidence tying Eric Robert Rudolph to the ideological framework commonly associated with the *Army of God Manual* emerges directly from his methods, targets and self-attribution as described in the federal appellate record. According to the court, Rudolph constructed home-made explosive devices designed to maximize casualties, including pipe bombs packed with pounds of masonry nails and triggered by timed or remote detonation, techniques consistent with extremist anti-abortion violence doctrines. His targets—abortion clinics and a nightclub with a largely gay and lesbian clientele—aligned with the categories of institutions he explicitly identified as enemies.

After multiple attacks, Rudolph mailed letters to news organizations claiming responsibility on behalf of the "Army of God," explaining that the bombings were intended to punish supporters of abortion and homosexuality and to target responding law enforcement officers and warning of future violence. These letters framed the attacks as morally and ideologically justified, demonstrating that Rudolph not only acted in accordance with Army of God rhetoric but publicly situated his violence within that ideological tradition, regardless of whether he possessed any specific instructional text.[90]

The Supreme Court's ruling on permitting civil lawsuits against anti-abortion racketeers allowed NOW to sue three prominent anti-abortion activists in 1998. Lawyers argued that the activists had conspired to keep women from accessing abortions through extortion, violence and intimidation. Scheidler was one of the defendants. The federal jury's verdict compared the group to mobsters, and the jury awarded two abortion clinics $86,000 in damages before the amount was tripled under federal racketeering charges. CNN analysts predicted anti-abortion groups would be put out of business.

---

90 United States v. Rudolph, 51-1 (11th Cir. Feb. 12, 2024).

In October 1998, law enforcement officials sent out a warning to abortion providers that there was a significant threat to them on what anti-abortion protestors knew as "Remember the Unborn Children Day."

They targeted Dr. Barnett Slepian, among others. The Buffalo-based doctor had been an outspoken champion of women's rights. On Oct. 23, Dr. Slepian returned home from a synagogue after commemorating his father's death. As he got up from his table, with his oldest son in view, a sniper shot through his home window and killed him. Police suspected James Kopp, the advance man for the itinerant Catholic anti-abortion group the Lambs of Christ. Federal officers couldn't find him when they showed up at his home in Vermont. The attack on Slepian fit a four-year pattern of shootings in Canada and New York and led to a nationwide manhunt.

Kopp had a rap sheet of arrests at anti-abortion protests going back to 1988. While in an Atlanta jail, Kopp got the nickname "Atomic Dog," which appeared in the dedication for the Army of God manual. Kopp sent Slepian's picture with the doctor's face crossed out to a Canadian. After Slepian died, Kopp called the newspaper and told them the next doctor on the list, according to the publication's editor.

After Slepian's murder, Justice Department officials talked about setting up a special task force to investigate anti-abortion violence. Kopp was still on the loose a year later, and concern grew that he would kill again. Abortion providers throughout the country took precautions, including security checks at their homes, carrying guns and wearing bullet-proof vests.

According to FBI investigators, two individuals conspired to help protect Kopp. Abortion rights activists said it exposed a network that enabled and helped extremists. One estimate said there were 100 cells of anti-abortion extremists across the country. Many of those groups communicated through the Internet. Federal investigators believed Kopp remained on the lam in the U.S. and Europe for several years.

John Malvasi, a convicted clinic bomber, was also part of the conspiracy to protect Kopp. A federal complaint indicated that Malvasi and his wife sent Kopp money under false names, planned to buy him medicine, held false identification papers belonging to Mr. Kopp, and planned to put him up in their apartment. The Complaint was based on information gathered by federal agents using telephone wiretaps, intercepted email messages and microphones planted in the couple's second-floor apartment.

Police arrested Kopp in France in 2001. He denied shooting Slepian. French officials were reluctant to extradite him because they don't do it in cases where the suspect would face the death penalty elsewhere. The State Department, under President George W. Bush, promised that the country wouldn't seek the death penalty. In 2003, a judge sentenced Kopp to a minimum of 25 years and a maximum of life imprisonment.

It's troubling that many younger men and women don't know this part of history or the threats to abortion workers that have devastated reproductive health care. It may seem to be a bygone era, but as we will see in later chapters, a newer generation of anti-abortion activists have echoed some of the rhetoric and rationalizations that led to these murders, bombings and attacks. Studying this era, and how we dealt with it, will help us prepare to address the likely rise in violence that will come in the next few decades.

CHAPTER 13

The Culture of Life

During Bill Clinton's presidency, the proposed ban on so-called partial-birth abortions became one of the most contentious flashpoints in the debate. Supporters framed the legislation as a moral imperative to stop what they described as a graphic, late-term abortion procedure, while abortion rights groups argued that the bill was overly broad and threatened access to medically necessary care.

Organizations such as Planned Parenthood, NARAL and the National Abortion Federation emphasized that the term "partial-birth abortion" was not a recognized medical term but a political construct intended to stigmatize abortion and inflame public opinion. These groups launched public education campaigns, organized physician testimony and mobilized supporters to urge Congress to sustain Clinton's expected veto.

Their messaging stressed that late-term abortion decisions—typically involving severe fetal abnormalities or life-threatening complications for the mother—should be made by women and their doctors, not dictated by federal legislation.

Clinton, seeking a middle ground, hoped to avoid signing the bill but also wanted to demonstrate sensitivity to public unease about late-term procedures. Pro-choice leaders identified women who had undergone abortions later in pregnancy due to severe fetal deformities or complications that would have resulted in the painful death of the fetus or serious risk to the mother's life. These women testified before Congress, offering personal and emotional counterpoints to the political rhetoric driving the proposed ban.

"Our response was to try very hard to get the first-hand stories of particular women who had experienced this, so people couldn't just view it in the abstract," Patricia Ireland told me.

Clinton twice vetoed versions of the bill, citing the absence of an exception to protect the woman's health.

Into this tense and carefully managed strategy stepped Ron Fitzsimmons, whose remarks would complicate the movement's unified front. In interviews and congressional testimony, Fitzsimmons acknowledged that doctors performed the procedure—technically known as intact dilation and extraction—more frequently than abortion rights groups publicly stated, and not solely in cases of extreme medical necessity.

Anti-abortion lawmakers seized upon his statements as confirmation of their claims, using them to bolster the push for the ban. His candor clashed with the Clinton administration's and major advocacy groups' emphasis on the rarity and medical necessity of the procedure, a narrative they saw as essential to sustaining public support for the veto.

Critics within the movement argued that Fitzsimmons' comments undermined the president's position and handed a rhetorical victory to the bill's supporters. Fitzsimmons defended his approach as a matter of honesty, even if it risked conceding political ground in the short term. The controversy surrounding his remarks underscored a broader tension within the abortion rights movement: whether to prioritize public opinion messaging or full transparency about clinical realities.

Despite the friction, Clinton's defense of the health exception remained firm, and when the House failed to override his second veto in May 1997, it marked a significant—if temporary—victory for abortion rights advocates, illustrating both the fragility and resilience of the coalition behind him.[91]

---

91 The Republic. (1997, March 5). *Clinton vetoes abortion bill. The Republic* (Columbus, IN), p. 4.' The Plain Dealer. (1997, May 8). *House sustains veto of abortion bill. The Plain Dealer* (Cleveland, OH), p. 35.' USA Today. (1997, May 15). *Abortion foes vow new fight after veto. USA Today* (McLean, VA), p. 6.

Afterward, anti-abortion activists sought to enact state-level bans on the procedure, beginning with Nebraska. At the time, Don Stenberg, Nebraska's attorney general, told a documentarian that the law's wording—graphic and explicit by design—was intended to describe the procedure accurately. Critics, however, argued that the language misrepresented medical reality and was meant to shock the public rather than inform it.

The statute—modeled on language crafted by the National Right to Life Committee and adopted by legislatures across the country—made it a felony for a physician to perform "an abortion procedure in which the person performing the abortion partially delivers vaginally a living unborn child before killing the unborn child and completing the delivery."[92]

Passed in 1997 by Nebraska's unicameral legislature, the law imposed severe penalties: two years in jail and a $25,000 fine for each violation. Physicians convicted under the statute would also lose their medical licenses. The Nebraska law carried no exception for the health of the pregnant woman and imposed penalties of up to twenty years in prison.

Attorney General Don Stenberg maintained that the statute targeted a specific and rarely used procedure known medically as intact dilation and extraction (D&X). But Dr. LeRoy H. Carhart, a Nebraska physician who performed abortions after 16 weeks but not beyond viability, argued that the law's vague and sweeping language would, in practice, ban the far more common dilation and evacuation (D&E) procedure. As a result, he contended, the law imposed an unconstitutional burden on women seeking abortions prior to viability.

Dr. Carhart was both reviled or revered in Nebraska. In 1991, on the night of his daughter's 21st birthday, an arsonist had set fire to his home and horse barn. The blaze destroyed his garage and several vehicles and killed family pets.

The next day, Carhart received an anonymous letter referencing the attack—describing it as divine retribution for his work as an abortion

____

92 Greenhouse, L. (2000, April 23). *Narrow abortion case before court leads to a wider debate. The New York Times.* https://www.nytimes.com/2000/04/23/us/narrow-abortion-case-before-court-leads-to-a-wider-debate.html

provider. Rather than retreat, the experience deepened his commitment to defending abortion rights and ensuring access to safe care.[93]

Carhart performed abortions in Nebraska in a clinical setting. He spoke with ABC News about it.

"I believe that paramount is the health issue," Carhart said. "To me, the woman's health has to be the key factor."

By the time *Stenberg v. Carhart* reached the U.S. Supreme Court in April 2000, similar bans had already been struck down in most of the nearly 30 states that had enacted them.

During oral arguments, the justices expressed deep concern about both the breadth and the intent of Nebraska's law. Justice Sandra Day O'Connor pressed the state's attorneys on whether the statute's wording might inadvertently criminalize the D&E procedure, the most common method used for second-trimester abortions.

Justice Ruth Bader Ginsburg focused on the absence of a health exception, questioning whether the measure advanced any legitimate state interest recognized in the Court's established abortion precedents.[94]

Nebraska's attorney general, Don Stenberg, conceded that the state could not constitutionally prohibit the D&E procedure but argued that the statute should be interpreted narrowly to apply only to D&X.

Dr. Carhart's attorney, Simon Heller, countered that banning any abortion method deemed safest for a woman's circumstances was incompatible with *Planned Parenthood v. Casey*'s principle that a woman's health must take precedence over fetal interests prior to viability.

On June 28, 2000, the Supreme Court, in a 5–4 decision authored by Justice Stephen Breyer, struck down Nebraska's law. The majority agreed with the lower courts that the statute's broad language could encompass D&E procedures, thereby imposing an undue burden on women's constitutional right to abortion.

More significantly, the Court held that even a narrowly written law targeting only D&X would be unconstitutional unless it included an

---

93 *The Sioux City Journal.* (2000, April 5). *[Article about letter sent to Dr. Leroy Carhart following 1991 arson at his home].* p. 22. https://www.newspapers.com/image/336861542/
94 Greenhouse, L. (2000, April 26). *Justices appear set to reject law banning late abortion. The New York Times.* https://www.nytimes.com/2000/04/26/us/justices-appear-set-to-reject-law-banning-late-abortion.html

explicit exception to preserve the health of the pregnant woman.

Citing medical evidence that D&X might, in some circumstances, be the safest procedure available, Breyer concluded that a categorical ban created an unacceptable risk of "tragic health consequences."

Justices Sandra Day O'Connor, David Souter, John Paul Stevens and Ruth Bader Ginsburg joined Breyer's opinion. Justice Stevens, in a concurring opinion, emphasized that it was irrational for a state to prohibit physicians from using the procedure they believed best protected a patient's health.[95]

The dissenting opinions in *Stenberg v. Carhart* revealed deep fractures within the Supreme Court. Justice Anthony Kennedy—a co-author of *Planned Parenthood v. Casey*—argued, joined by Chief Justice Rehnquist and Justices Antonin Scalia and Clarence Thomas, that Nebraska had a legitimate interest in prohibiting a procedure that many Americans viewed as morally abhorrent. Kennedy described what he saw as a "consequential moral difference" between the D&X method and other forms of abortion.

Justices Scalia and Thomas went further, condemning the majority's opinion as a radical overreach and a misguided extension of abortion rights.

For abortion opponents, the ruling represented a strategic setback, weakening the effectiveness of partial-birth abortion bans as a political wedge to erode public support for abortion rights.

For abortion rights advocates, however, it was a narrow but crucial victory—a reaffirmation of the principle that women's health must remain paramount in all pre-viability abortion regulations. That principle, preserved by a single vote, ensured that *Roe* and *Casey*'s core protections survived into the new millennium.

Texas Gov. George W. Bush, son of the president who bore the same first and last names, didn't want to discuss the topic or case during his campaign. In July, he spoke to the National Right to Life Committee via video, saying that they should appeal to the things that unite the country instead of those that divide it.

---

95 Greenhouse, L. (2000, June 29). *The Nebraska case: Court rules that governments can't outlaw type of abortion. The New York Times.* https://archive.nytimes.com/www.nytimes.com/library/politics/scotus/articles/062900sc-abort.html

Vice President Al Gore, the Democratic nominee, sought to challenge Bush and portray him as less than empathetic, in contrast to Bush's portrayal of himself as a compassionate conservative.

Bush wanted to move his campaign toward the center while maintaining his appeal with the Republican base. But with that decision and the possible court vacancies for the next president, abortion dominated the political rhetoric. In the Republican primary, Sen. John McCain (R-AZ) challenged Bush on not having any exceptions for rape, incest or the health of the mother in his platform.

Bush told an audience that states had the right to enact laws limiting and restricting abortions later in pregnancy. Gore reminded voters that Supreme Court seats that would be filled by the next president could determine its direction for decades—including the fate of abortion rights. Chief Justice Rehnquist and Associate Justices O'Connor and Stevens were over 70. Conservative political operatives said Gore would appoint "activist" judges, something that had been a rallying call for evangelical voters since the 1980s.

Bush tried throughout his campaign to be civil, saying that good people on both sides disagreed. But he had said, a year earlier, that he favored a constitutional amendment banning abortion except in cases of rape, incest or when the life of the mother was at risk. He knew the country wouldn't support that effort. So, instead, he focused on reducing the number of abortions in the United States.

Bush's mother, Barbara, was openly pro-choice. His wife, Laura, implied she was. His campaign featured both of them to ease women's concerns. Republican Sen. Susan Collins of Maine said she was confident that Bush wouldn't mount an attack on abortion rights.

Gore himself had cast anti-abortion votes when he served in Congress. In the 1980s, he described abortion as the taking of human life. Gore, a lifelong Southern Baptist, favored federal spending limits on abortion for poor women. During the Democratic primary, rival Sen. Bill Bradley of New Jersey passed out copies of Gore's letters, in which he stated his anti-abortion views. Gore called his positions a mistake. He described himself as a champion of reproductive rights during the campaign.

After Bush won the election, he told CBS News that he wouldn't try to overturn *Roe v. Wade*. He said that his agenda was to reduce abortions and that it wasn't possible to get a constitutional amendment to ban the procedure. He favored a "practical approach" to instituting parental notification laws.

"There's going to be abortion in America," Bush said. "The fundamental thing is, are they going to be safe? Will they be numerous or not?"

Bush worked on advancing the anti-abortion agenda early in his presidency. He signed the Born-Alive Infants Protection Act of 2002, which was presented as an effort to protect any infant born alive, including those after an attempted abortion. Pennsylvania Sen. Rick Santorum and Congressman Steve Chabot of Ohio co-sponsored the bill.

On the 30th anniversary of *Roe v. Wade* in 2003, thousands of anti-abortion protestors showed up at the Supreme Court. President Bush telephoned into the gathering and said he hoped the U.S. Congress would pass a bill banning partial-birth abortion. He didn't say he would outlaw abortion altogether. A CNN poll showed that 66% of Americans thought the procedure should be legal in the first three months of pregnancy. Most felt it needed some restrictions, including suggesting alternatives to patients and waiting periods before an abortion happened. The public largely supported spousal and parental notification requirements as well. Abortions later in pregnancy were unpopular with 70% of the public.

"I'm talking about an ideal world, but we don't live in an ideal world right now," Bush told CNN's Candy Crowley about eliminating abortions. "So in the meantime, it seems to me that we need a leader who shows people the importance of banning partial-birth abortion, having parental notification laws, and not spending taxpayer money on abortion."

Congress approved legislation in October 2003 that made it a crime to perform D&E procedures, which some abortion providers said was a more humane method of abortion than other options in late-term pregnancies. Sen. William Frist (R-TN), a one-time physician who was the Senate majority leader, called the type of surgery "outlandish and ghoulish."

Despite the Republicans' portrayal of the procedure as widespread, the number of women who received it was small; roughly 90% of abortions are performed within the first three months.

The bill indicated that abortion later in pregnancy was never medically necessary. The American Medical Association didn't support the doctor's procedure between the 18th and 20th weeks of pregnancy. Other doctors worried that saying late-term abortions were never necessary for the health of a mother would be detrimental to women's health choices. Some ethicists thought Congress was treading on dangerous ground.

Bush said partial-birth abortion was a violent end to a child's life. He said the bill reflected the compassion and humanity of America. He praised C. Everett Koop decades after Koop had compared abortion to the Holocaust.

"Partial-birth abortion" was a term created by the National Right to Life Committee in 1995, likely for the imagery and emotion the phrase could evoke. Douglas Johnson of the National Right to Life Committee said that they hoped that "as the public learns what a 'partial-birth abortion' is, they might also learn something about other abortion methods, and that this would foster a growing opposition to abortion."

The House Judiciary Subcommittee on the Constitution convened on March 25, 2003, to consider legislation that would criminalize a specific abortion method its proponents described as "inhumane" and "never medically necessary."

Chaired by Representative Steve Chabot of Ohio, the hearing opened with an outline of penalties—fines and up to two years' imprisonment—and a life-of-the-mother exception. Chabot framed the proposal as a moral and ethical imperative, claiming public and medical consensus supported eliminating the procedure.

The legislative backdrop was the Supreme Court's 2000 decision in *Stenberg v. Carhart*, which had struck down the Nebraska ban for vagueness and for lacking a health exception. Chabot said the current measure was crafted to survive judicial review with a precise definition and a narrowly tailored life exception. Omitting a broader health exception aligned with anti-abortion advocates who saw such language as a loophole.

The hearing featured only three witnesses, all supporting the ban. Dr. Mark Neerhof testified on what he viewed as unnecessary risks—hemorrhage, infection and uterine perforation. Supporting materials included statements from members and a 1998 *Journal of the American Medical Association* article co-authored by Neerhof. No representatives from major medical organizations, such as the American College of Obstetricians and Gynecologists or Planned Parenthood, testified to defend the procedure in certain health-related cases.

This absence of dissenting voices allowed the hearing to present an unchallenged case for the ban. Lasting about 90 minutes, the proceedings emphasized moral condemnation and claimed medical consensus. In the following weeks, the testimony and materials became part of the broader legislative push, illustrating how hearings can be structured to reinforce a predetermined outcome while maintaining the appearance of open debate.[96]

President Bush signed the law into effect on Nov. 5, 2003.

"The most basic duty of government is to defend the life of the innocent," Bush said after the bill was signed. "Every person, however frail or vulnerable, has a place or a purpose in this world. Every person has a special dignity. This right to life cannot be granted or denied by government because it doesn't come from government. It comes from the creator of life."

Republicans always cast the abortion debate as pitting atheism, or secularism, versus religion. This false framing of such arguments deliberately obscured the wide swath of the religious community engaged in abortion rights advocacy. Nonetheless, the perception that religious organizations are universally against abortion has generally prevailed among both Democrats and Republicans. Yet many Christian denominations favor maintaining that right. In his speech, Bush mentioned creating a "culture of life," which became synonymous with his anti-abortion policies for the remainder of his presidential administration.

---

96 U.S. House of Representatives, Committee on the Judiciary, Subcommittee on the Constitution. (2003, March 25). *Partial-Birth Abortion Ban Act of 2003: Hearing before the Subcommittee on the Constitution of the Committee on the Judiciary, House of Representatives, One Hundred Eighth Congress, first session* (Serial No. 14). U.S. Government Printing Office. https://commdocs.house.gov/committees/judiciary/hju85987.000/hju85987_0f.htm

This misconception continued throughout later Democratic administrations, which pushed for what became known as common groundism. They sought to reach a compromise with conservative religious people by bargaining away abortion rights. Gloria Feldt criticized Democratic standard-bearer John Kerry in 2004 for his compromising position on abortion.

"He seemed equivocal," Feldt said when she left the organization in 2005. "He ceded the moral high ground to the other side."

Feldt had pushed for a stronger ground game and had unfavorably compared the abortion rights movement at the precinct level to that of Republicans. She encouraged liberal women and their allies to take a cue from Republicans, who she conceded were working more effectively at the precinct level. And under her, the Planned Parenthood organization gave its first-ever endorsement to John Kerry.

President Bush also enacted the Unborn Victims of Violence Act of 2004, which called for criminal punishment under federal law to anyone who causes injury or death to "a child in the womb."

This is in addition to offenses that have to do with the mother. Therefore, if someone causes harm to a pregnant woman within the 60 enumerated federal crimes, such as abuse, they will be held to have harmed both the woman and the fetus and charged for the offenses related to both. The embryo or fetus is now considered a legal victim. Pro-choice activists criticized the act as an attempt to grant fetal personhood. The act does explicitly exclude abortion as grounds for violation and punishment, but it paved the way for future criminal punishment for those who obtain abortions.

Abortion rights advocates filed three lawsuits to challenge the Partial-Birth Abortion law. The hope was that the Supreme Court, after calling the Nebraska statute too vague and not protective of a mother's health, would apply the precedent to the federal law. Both sides wanted to use the new law to galvanize voters. Despite anti-abortion groups' hope that it would lead to bans, President Bush was careful with his words. He told journalists at a news conference that the public wouldn't support a ban. While it had been legally challenged, the ban never took effect for the first three years after Congress passed it. Three lower courts ruled it unconstitutional for not providing an exception for the mother's health.

In *Stenberg v. Carhart*, Justice Sandra O'Connor provided the fifth vote for the ruling. Samuel Alito, an archconservative Catholic, who had upheld abortion restrictions as a lower court judge, replaced O'Connor in 2006. The year before, John Roberts replaced William Rehnquist as chief justice. After the appointments of Roberts and Alito to the Supreme Court, the justices voted to take their first abortion case, which dealt with the Partial-Birth Abortion Act that year. The case was known as *Gonzales v. Carhart*. Carhart once again served as the plaintiff, along with other doctors. U.S. Attorney General Alberto Gonzales was named defendant.

The plaintiffs claimed that the act was unconstitutional under the standards established in *Planned Parenthood v. Casey* because it placed an undue burden on a woman's right to an abortion. Further, the act did not provide an exception to permit abortions when necessary to protect the health of the mother. Therefore, the ban was unconstitutional under *Stenberg v. Carhart*. Congress, in the Partial-Birth Abortion Ban Act, found that partial-birth abortions are never medically necessary. Despite Congress's finding, and based on the rulings in *Casey* and *Stenberg*, the District Court agreed and determined that the Partial-Birth Abortion Ban Act was unconstitutional on both grounds.

After the District Court ruling, the government appealed to the Eighth Circuit Court of Appeals, which agreed with the District Court and determined that an exception for the health of the mother must be included in any abortion procedures. The Circuit Court did not determine whether the Partial-Birth Abortion Ban Act was too broad as to be an undue burden.

The government then appealed to the United States Supreme Court. The Court ruled 5–4 to uphold the Partial-Birth Abortion Ban Act in an opinion by Justice Anthony Kennedy.

Kennedy spent time, in his opinion, fitting the Partial-Birth Abortion Ban Act into the *Stenberg* parameters, differentiating it from *Stenberg*'s Nebraska statute. The decision was especially significant, given its lack of explicit exceptions for when there is a danger to a woman's health.

Bush advocated for a culture of life throughout his presidency. On Jan. 22, 2008, he spoke to the annual March For Life, urging a decrease in the number of abortions and stating that children can live outside the womb earlier and earlier. His religious tilt on the matter was appreciated by the pro-life groups, saying in not so many words that life begins at conception. Throughout his presidency, he aimed to declare fetal autonomy with various bills that would curb abortion in the United States.

CHAPTER 14

Searching for Common Ground

Cecile Richards grew up in the thick of Texas politics, the daughter of Gov. Ann Richards, whose wit and resilience made her a progressive icon in the South. From an early age, Richards absorbed the lessons of grassroots organizing and political tenacity, learning firsthand that power is built not only in statehouses but also in communities and neighborhoods.

Her career followed that trajectory: She began as a union organizer, fighting alongside workers for fair treatment, and later became the founding director of America Votes, a coalition designed to strengthen progressive campaigns across the country. Those experiences gave her both the instincts of a street-level organizer and the strategic insight of a national political leader.

By the mid-2000s, Richards had earned a reputation as one of the Democratic Party's most skilled coalition-builders, able to knit together diverse movements into a coherent political force. In 2006, she was tapped to lead Planned Parenthood Federation of America, a role that placed her at the center of one of the most contested issues in American life.

She approached the position with a clear recognition that Planned Parenthood not only symbolized the fight for reproductive rights but also served a far broader mission by providing basic health care to millions of women who otherwise lacked access. Richards emphasized that her leadership would have to balance political advocacy with the practical realities of health care delivery, reinforcing Planned Parenthood's dual identity as both a service provider and a national advocate.

Her appointment marked more than a career milestone; it represented the passing of a torch. Richards often credited her mother's influence for shaping her political outlook, yet she was determined to define her own leadership in this new arena. Taking the helm of Planned Parenthood, she focused on modernizing the organization's outreach, expanding its advocacy and reminding the public of the breadth of services it offered, from cancer screenings to contraception.

In doing so, she became both the inheritor of a family tradition and the standard-bearer of a movement under siege. Her leadership in 2006 cemented her place in the long struggle over reproductive freedom, embodying the persistence of progressive values and the urgency of a national fight that showed no signs of abating.[97]

Richards' tenure coincided with the rise of the Tea Party and increasing polarization. Rather than adopt a nonpartisan tone, she embraced deeper alliances with progressive causes, aligning Planned Parenthood with movements for LGBTQ+ rights, racial justice and economic equity. This coalition-building approach reflected her belief that reproductive freedom was inseparable from broader social justice struggles.[98]

Critics argued that under Richards, Planned Parenthood became too closely tied to the Democratic Party, risking its image as a health provider and alienating moderates. Some felt that stressing non-abortion services reinforced stigma rather than challenging it. Richards defended her strategy as pragmatic and necessary in a climate of relentless attacks and funding threats.

---

97 The Houston Chronicle. (2006a, May 7). *[Article on Cecile Richards and Planned Parenthood]*. p. 14. https://www.newspapers.com/image/1217216737/; The Houston Chronicle. (2006b, March 11). *[Article on Cecile Richards' appointment to Planned Parenthood]*. p. 19. https://www.newspapers.com/image/1219207261/

98 Time. (2018, March). *Outgoing Planned Parenthood President Cecile Richards Is Not Done Fighting.*

During the 2008 Democratic primary, Planned Parenthood did not formally endorse a candidate. Both Hillary Clinton and Barack Obama had strong records on reproductive rights, but Clinton had a longer-standing relationship with the organization, and many in the Planned Parenthood network were personally supportive of her candidacy. [99] Once Barack Obama secured the Democratic nomination, Planned Parenthood fully embraced his candidacy and mobilized in support of his platform.

Roe *Was* the Common Ground

Obama campaigned on a pledge to seek common ground in 2008. After the American public elected him, religious leaders such as Los Angeles Cardinal Roger Mahony said he wasn't on the same page as them when it came to abortion. The Vatican called Obama's policies disappointing. During his first week of office, Obama signed an executive order reversing the ban on federal funding for international organizations that facilitated abortions in other countries. Unlike most other legislative and executive actions, Obama didn't allow that order's signing to be filmed because he didn't want to antagonize anti-abortion groups.

That plan didn't work because both his opponents and supporters were more concerned with substance than what pols at the time called "optics."

Obama was accused of plotting the infanticide of African children. The FDA's decision to approve embryonic stem cell research with humans further inflamed the abortion divide. Obama responded by telling Republicans to stop listening to Rush Limbaugh.

Pro-choice activists argued that *Roe* was the common ground. Simply maintaining its basic structure was an effort to maintain a balance between each side's concerns. To weaken the decision meant caving into every anti-abortion demand.

In 2009, Obama spoke at the commencement at the University of Notre Dame. His appearance outraged many Catholics—including 70 sitting bishops—who disagreed with the university's decision to honor

---

99 Zenilman, A. (2008, June 10). *Planned Parenthood moving, carefully, to Obama. Politico.*

an abortion rights supporter. Police took hecklers out of the auditorium when Obama spoke, after one of them said the president had blood on his hands. While anti-abortion protestors picketed in their usual way outside, the graduates gave the president a rousing welcome as he took the stage.

"Maybe we won't agree on abortion, but we can still agree this heart-wrenching decision for any woman is not made casually," Obama said. "It has both moral and spiritual dimensions."

Obama said Republicans and Democrats should work together to reduce the number of abortions by decreasing unwanted pregnancies and increasing adoption rates. That was the only point they agreed on. Obama also supported more financial support for women carrying their children. Outside the arena stood anti-abortion militants Alan Keyes and Randall Terry, but inside, his supporters, including the university president John Jenkins, praised Obama for not ducking the issue.

Many Catholics said that while they disagreed with Obama's position, they thought he was a moral and decent man. But Bill Donohue, the incendiary president of the Catholic League for Civil and Religious Rights (which is not an official body in the Church), said Obama couldn't be a champion of social justice and at the same time support abortion access.

"It is so nice to know that Obama thinks abortion 'presents a profound moral challenge.' Is infanticide another 'profound moral challenge?' To wit: When he was in the Illinois state senate he led the fight to deny health care to babies born alive who survived an abortion. That, my friends, is not a moral challenge—it's a Hitlerian decision," Donohue told the Catholic News Agency.

While Catholic leaders publicly criticized Obama, about 54% of Catholic parishioners supported his candidacy. After the election, President Obama rescinded most of the regulations that Bush had implemented. Yet he wasn't robustly supportive of weakening or repealing the Hyde Amendment while in office. Amid heated debates over health care reform, President Obama took a cautious route on the Hyde Amendment—an approach emblematic of his broader strategy to seek common ground on abortion policy.

Rather than challenging Hyde outright, he reinforced its restrictions through Executive Order 13535, which extended the Hyde Amendment's limitations—permitting federal funding for abortion only in cases of rape, incest or when the mother's life is at risk—to the newly created health insurance exchanges under the Affordable Care Act.

Obama sought to appeal to anti-abortion Democrats and center-right constituencies, signaling a desire for neutrality: to preserve essential health care reforms without inflaming cultural divides. This posture reflected his broader vision of abortion politics—not as a partisan battleground but as a realm where public support for contraception, education and societal assistance could bridge ideological divides.[100]

Two weeks after Obama's Notre Dame speech, Dr. George Tiller was murdered in Wichita. Tiller had been subjected to a long-term campaign of character assassination on various right-wing media outlets. Bill O'Reilly of Fox News dubbed him "Tiller the Baby Killer."

At the time, four doctors in the country performed abortions later in pregnancy.

Many of the women who got those procedures were carrying deformed fetuses that had no chance of surviving. Lynda Waddington, one of the women had Tiller treated, talked to CNN's Anderson Cooper. Waddington criticized Obama because the president had said a year before that states could regulate abortions later in pregnancy so long as they made exceptions for the mother's health.

"I think those who are anti-abortion have been very successful at painting a picture of who I am and who other women are who have late abortions," Waddington said. "It kind of ticks me off because it's not accurate. Supposedly, I'm just a person who woke up one day and had a back pain or leg cramp and decided to have an abortion. That definitely wasn't the case. This was a pregnancy that was planned, and that was wanted. It was tantamount to having a loved one on life support and making a decision whether to end that life or not."

Scott Roeder, who had not previously been known for anti-abortion

---

100 Clarkson, F. (2009, Dec. 9). *From right-wing to pro-choice: The shifting goalposts of abortion neutrality.* Religion Dispatches. https://religiondispatches.org/from-right-wing-to-pro-choice-the-shifting-goalposts-of-abortion-neutrality/

activism, walked into the Lutheran church where Tiller was serving as an usher and murdered him point blank. Roeder felt he saved lives by doing it. He showed no remorse when he took the witness stand at his trial, and the jury took 37 minutes to return his guilty verdict. He read from the writings of Paul Hill at his sentencing, when the judge gave Roeder life imprisonment with the possibility of parole. While abortion rights advocates praised the ruling, they felt that the country would return to a period of anti-abortion violence.

When Obama pushed for the Affordable Care Act's passage during his first two years in office, one of the primary points of contention was whether health insurance should pay for abortions. The U.S. Conference of Catholic Bishops supported a proposal known as the Stupak Amendment, which would prevent insurance plans from covering the procedure. Planned Parenthood officials resisted the Stupak Amendment.

It was a delicate issue, as Richards said in her autobiography, *Make Trouble: Standing Up, Speaking Out, and Finding the Courage to Lead.* Ultimately, if Congress banned abortion coverage, the organization had to take a position opposing the health care reform altogether. House Speaker Nancy Pelosi told Richards privately that the bill wouldn't be passed if it included the Stupak Amendment. The politicians supporting the proposal backed down after that pressure.

During the Obama administration, Republican legislatures and governors sought to pass TRAP laws. In Texas, Gov. Rick Perry tried to end abortion with one of those laws, HB 15, which passed in 2003. The law mandated that women meet twice with doctors in person before an abortion. In the first meeting, the doctor performs a sonogram, and in the second, they perform an abortion. As the number of abortion providers dwindled, many clinics have had to book travel and lodging for abortion doctors to go from one clinic to another.

That expense doubled with the new requirement, according to Marva Sadler, an administrator with Whole Woman's Health, the largest abortion provider in the state. After the bill's passage, families came to clinics and slept in RVs in the parking lot to satisfy the two-day process because they didn't have the money to get housing. Couples or single mothers with children couldn't afford the cost of daycare.

The state's most famous TRAP law after that was H.B. 2, which the legislature passed in 2013. The bill banned abortions past 20 weeks and required doctors to have admitting privileges at nearby hospitals.

Democratic State Sen. Wendy Davis filibustered for 13 hours to prevent a vote on the bill. She used a catheter bag early in the morning on the day of the arguments. She wore tennis shoes to prepare for a long standing session. Richards, along with hundreds of other abortion rights supporters, attended the session.

As Davis continued her filibuster, the building became increasingly charged with pro-choice rhetoric and chants. The crowd cheered when the session ended without the bill's passage. Wendy Davis became a symbol of the movement at that moment, saying, "Women here are beautiful. They deserve to live their lives, make full, capable decisions with their doctor and their God."

Texas Gov. Rick Perry called a special session later in the year to pass the bill, however, rendering Davis' filibuster a symbolic victory. Davis' action inspired a new wave of abortion rights support in the state. Lawyers quickly challenged the constitutionality of the law, which began a three-year legal process of judges reviewing it and deciding whether to permit its enforcement. Over the months that followed, 27 of the 42 clinics that performed abortions in the state closed, including all clinics in central Texas, making it extremely difficult for women to obtain an abortion.

Following Davis' filibuster, a group of religious leaders in that state formed Just Texas, which advocates for churches to become "reproductive freedom congregations"—churches that support abortion rights and in which pastors and members undergo months-long training in how to discuss faith and reproductive politics.

During the Obama administration, anti-abortion activists seized opportunities to demonize abortion providers and cast the procedure as evil. Dr. Kermit Gosnell, a Philadelphia abortion provider, who was sentenced to life in prison in 2013 for killing a baby in a botched abortion, provided fodder to the anti-abortion crowd.

His practice, as detailed in the grand jury report, was appalling. Gosnell's clinic reeked of animal feces because cats defecated freely. Furniture and carpets were stained with blood. He didn't dispose of medical equipment properly. Much of the equipment was broken.

I spoke to Claire Keyes, whom I mentioned earlier in this book, about Gosnell. She told me it was an open secret that his practice violated numerous health codes. Many abortion providers in the state warned women not to go to Gosnell. Keyes had unsuccessfully attempted to get the state to inspect their facility, but Pennsylvania regulators were lax. It was a statewide problem. Prosecutors indicated in the grand jury report that the Pennsylvania Department of Health had stopped inspecting abortion clinics after 1993. Gov. Tom Ridge, a pro-choice Republican, had thought inspections would put a barrier up for women seeking reproductive care.

The only reason the state would conduct an inspection was when it received a complaint. But with Gosnell, the state received several of them and didn't do anything. Gosnell had applied to become a member of the National Abortion Federation, which sent an inspector to look at his clinic as part of considering him for a member. The inspector said it was the worst clinic he had ever visited and that they didn't keep records properly, misused anesthesia and had missing equipment, according to the grand jury report that led to Gosnell's indictment.

Philadelphia District Attorney Seth Williams said Gosnell killed seven babies after they were born alive. In Pennsylvania, it is illegal to get an abortion past the 24th week, a time marker that Gosnell ignored. According to the grand jury report, Gosnell induced women into labor, delivered the babies, and then slashed them to death with scissors. Police arrested him after Karnamaya Mongar, a 41-year-old who had come for an abortion, died during the procedure. Pictures of the clinic showed unsanitary conditions with jars and bags of aborted fetuses. None of the employees had medical training. He was convicted of various crimes, including three counts of murder.

In 2011, Pennsylvania's legislature responded to the Gosnell case by passing a law that required routine inspections of abortion clinics.

Anti-abortion advocates seized on the case as an example to show the brutality of abortion, often conflating murder outside of the womb with the termination of a pregnancy inside it. Abortion rights activists countered and said Gosnell's crimes wouldn't have been possible had Medicaid paid for the abortions of women who had been forced to use his services. In fairness, Gosnell was a spectacular exception that proves the rule that abortion is usually carried out by capable medical personnel in sanitary facilities using appropriate equipment safely.

Abortion, when performed legally in a medical setting, is among the safest surgical procedures available—safer than many routine operations and significantly safer than childbirth. Studies have shown that first-trimester abortions, which make up the vast majority of procedures, carry a complication rate of less than 0.5%, and the risk of death is estimated at only 0.4 per 100,000 procedures, making it about 14 times safer than carrying a pregnancy to term.

By comparison, common procedures such as tonsillectomies, wisdom tooth extractions and colonoscopies present higher rates of complications. Both medication abortion and aspiration abortion, the most frequently used methods, are highly effective and carry very low risks, while later-term procedures, though associated with slightly higher complication rates, remain safer than many routine surgeries.[101]

The vilification of abortion activists and providers didn't end with Gosnell. Richards testified before Congress in 2015 after anti-abortion campaigners released deceptively edited videos that showed some Planned Parenthood officials discussing the sale of fetal tissue.

The Center for Medical Progress, an anti-abortion group created by people with a track record of doctoring videos to portray abortion rights supporters negatively, was behind the production. They had spent tens of thousands of dollars to create a fake website. They had posed as biotechnology company representatives at a conference with spy cameras. They sought to portray Planned Parenthood medical staff as profiteers rather

---

101 National Academies of Sciences, Engineering, and Medicine. (2018). *The safety and quality of abortion care in the United States.* Washington, DC: National Academies Press. https://doi.org/10.17226/24950; Raymond, E. G., & Grimes, D. A. (2012). The comparative safety of legal induced abortion and childbirth in the United States. *Obstetrics & Gynecology, 119*(2), 215–219. https://doi.org/10.1097/AOG.0b013e31823fe923

than providing tissue legally for purposes of actual medical research.

Major newspapers, including *The New York Times*, featured the videos. Republicans used the controversy to push for defunding Planned Parenthood. Louisiana Gov. Bobby Jindal alleged that it was an evil and illegal activity.

Elaborate ploys to set up and frame abortion rights supporters, lobbyists and activists had long been part of the anti-abortion movement. Richards said in her book that they had colluded with Congressional representatives. When Richards appeared before Congress, Republicans attacked her while she spoke, and Democrats said the GOP had continued its "war on women" with its attacks on her. Despite the initial issue being the videos, most of the questioning focused on government funding.

"The outrageous accusations leveled against Planned Parenthood based on heavily doctored videos are offensive and categorically untrue," Richards said before the panel.

Congress passed legislation to defund the organization, but President Obama vetoed it.

That same year, 23-year-old Kenlissia Jones was charged with murder in Georgia when she took abortion pills to terminate her pregnancy at 5½ months after breaking up with her boyfriend. She gave birth in the car on the way to the hospital, where the baby died shortly after arrival. A social worker at the hospital called police to the hospital and told them Jones had ordered Cytotec pills online and took four to induce the abortion.

Georgia law did not permit abortions after the first trimester outside of an ambulatory surgical facility, licensed abortion facility or hospital. Police arrested Jones. The charges shocked both anti-abortion and abortion advocates alike. Criminal charges against people who cause the death of a fetus are one common method anti-abortion lawmakers and prosecutors use to establish fetal personhood.

Prosecutors later dropped the murder charge against Jones.

In 2015, tragedy struck Colorado Springs, when Robert Lewis Dear Jr. killed three people at a Planned Parenthood clinic. Dear had lived in a tiny shack in North Carolina before moving to Colorado, where he lived in an RV on a remote land. After the police arrested Dear, he told them that the baby parts he saw motivated him. He also expressed anti-abortion and anti-government views. Richards appeared on Anderson Cooper's show to discuss the case:

> *It is really disturbing to see the kind of hateful rhetoric that's been talked about Planned Parenthood, about the women who come to us, about the doctors who provide health care. It's very hard to see these kinds of violent incidents that I think this rhetoric fuels.*

Richards criticized the Republican presidential candidates in the 2016 race and pointed to increased harassment at women's health centers. Early in the next year, the formerly pro-choice Republican nominee Donald Trump called for some form of punishment for both doctors and women who were part of an abortion.

In October 1999, Trump appeared on "Meet the Press" and discussed his then-liberal social views. When asked whether he would ban partial-birth abortion were he to run for president, Trump said at the time that he was "very pro-choice." Trump said that he hated the concept of abortion, and he cringed when he heard people debating the subject. But he still believed in choice. He said New Yorkers felt differently about the issue than people living elsewhere. Trump said he wouldn't ban abortion or partial-birth abortion.

"I'm pro-choice as far as it goes, but I just hate it," Trump said.

During his 2016 campaign, Trump said no punishment should be levied against the man who impregnated the woman. Later, he said that only the doctor should be held responsible. Democratic candidate Hillary Clinton called the comments horrific. Trump's Republican opponents disagreed about punishment for abortion.

A few days after his comments, *New York Times* columnist Maureen Dowd wrote about Trump's longtime pro-choice stance while he lived in New York City. Dowd had asked Trump whether he had ever paid for an abortion when he was a bachelor. Trump dodged and asked her to move on to the next question.

Trump expressed misogynistic views throughout the campaign and criticized women who brought up any details of his past. He became infamous for telling a media personality that he could grab women by the pussy because of how sexually attractive he was as a famous man. Trump described it as locker room talk. Generally, in his interactions with women on the campaign trail, Trump portrayed himself as a victim of their criticisms.

Trump strengthened his dubious anti-abortion credentials with the selection of Mike Pence as his running mate. Pence, a longtime Christian right activist and politician, had signed one of the most restrictive abortion laws in the country as governor of Indiana.

During this time, abortion rights activists took to the courts to challenge the law passed in Texas. In *Whole Woman's Health v. Hellerstedt*, a group of abortion providers challenged H.B. 2. In defense of the law, Texas argued it protected women's health and limited complications from abortions. The Supreme Court, in hearing the case, found no evidence that the strict new requirements in the law protected a woman's health, though there was plenty of evidence of how the law would harm a woman's health.

The court struck it down in a 5-3 decision, with the reasoning that it was an undue burden under *Planned Parenthood v. Casey*. Only seven or eight facilities that provided abortion would be able to remain open if the arbitrary regulations were put into place, which in and of itself was a substantial burden, as the ability to meet the demand of such a large state would likely be impossible.

The decision thrust the Supreme Court to the front of the election between Hillary Clinton and Trump, particularly for conservatives. During a presidential debate in October, Trump said that *Roe* would be overturned if he was elected because he could appoint several justices to the Supreme Court. He criticized Clinton's support for abortions later in pregnancy.

"You can take a baby and rip the baby out of the womb of the mother just before the birth of the baby," Trump said.

Trump stunned the nation by winning. His views on abortion now had the chance to become the law of the land. Trump won 53% of white women's votes and surprisingly did as well among Republican women as he did among Republican men. The *Wall Street Journal* reported that seven in 10 voters said the Supreme Court was a major factor in their vote.

Some people grew more rigid in their views politically, particularly with regards to abortion. The number of people who wouldn't vote for someone who disagreed with them on abortion had increased from 13% in 2008 to 21% in 2015, according to reporting from *The Atlantic*.

Richard Land, president of Southern Evangelical Seminary and part of Trump's evangelical advisory committee, told *The Huffington Post* that he believed the Clintons' record on abortion had motivated evangelicals to vote in unprecedented numbers. Dr. Ronnie Floyd, the immediate past president of the Southern Baptist Convention, also a member of Trump's evangelical advisory committee, claimed that abortion had been a significant factor in Trump's winning.

"Most evangelicals have believed this was the most significant election in our generation," Floyd told *The Huffington Post*. "Therefore, evangelicals were driven more this year by the platforms more than by the parties and their politicians."

The Pew Research Center indicated 45% of the voting public thought abortion was very important to their ballot decision. However, other issues like the economy, terrorism, foreign policy and health care dominated their worldviews when it came to political conversations. So limiting abortion wasn't as big a factor as some would make it out to be.[102]

Liberal women began the resistance with defiant people challenging the president at every turn. They had no idea how transformative his presidency would nevertheless be. One of the largest and most important social protests happened immediately after the election. As the aging Supreme Court posed a foreboding harbinger insofar as abortion rights, women rallied to show that the feminist movement was still alive and well. It came to be known as the Women's March.

---

102 Pew Research Center. (2016, July 7). *4. Top voting issues in 2016 election*. Pew Research Center: Politics & Policy. Retrieved from https://www.pewresearch.org/politics/2016/07/07/4-top-voting-issues-in-2016-election/

CHAPTER 15

The Anti-Abortion Shift

The Women's March in 2017 unfolded as one of the largest single-day demonstrations in American history, a counter-inauguration to President Donald J. Trump. In Washington, D.C., hundreds of thousands gathered near the Capitol before moving toward the White House. The city's streets swelled into a tide of pink "pussyhats" and protest signs.

There were dueling rallies near the Supreme Court. Celebrities such as actresses Scarlett Johansson, Ashley Judd and America Ferrera expressed support for Planned Parenthood. The outpouring was mirrored nationwide.

The threats to PPFA were real, as they always are when a Republican takes office. Most of the threat comes in the form of funding cuts. Planned Parenthood gets more than 40% of its funding from federal reimbursements. None of it goes toward abortions. Most of it provides basic health care, such as cancer screenings.

Still, the Trump administration tried to bully leaders of the organization to stop performing abortions. The president sent Ivanka Trump and her husband, Jared Kushner—both Orthodox Jews who are pro-choice—to meet with Richards. They told her that the administration would support the organization if it stopped doing abortions. Richards said that wasn't possible.

For the first two years of Trump's administration, Richards often got branded as the leader of "the Resistance," the name given to the contingent of women who protested virtually all of Trump's decisions insofar as reproductive rights and women's issues. But she decided to leave PPFA in 2018. After that, Leana Wen took over.

When Wen was appointed as president of Planned Parenthood in late 2018, she was celebrated as the first physician in nearly five decades to lead the organization. The *Arizona Republic* highlighted that her background as an emergency room doctor and her experience as Baltimore's health commissioner positioned her as a leader who could reframe the abortion rights debate through the lens of public health.

She emphasized that abortion was a fundamental part of comprehensive health care and often spoke of her personal story as an immigrant from China whose family relied on safety-net programs for survival. Similarly, the *Courier-Post* noted that her arrival marked a new chapter in Planned Parenthood's history, signaling a leadership style rooted in medical expertise and personal commitment to expanding access to care.[103]

Wen sought to reorient the national conversation about Planned Parenthood by stressing its role as a mainstream health care provider that offered cancer screenings, contraception and preventive services alongside abortion. She aimed to reduce political polarization around reproductive rights by presenting abortion access as inseparable from broader health care issues.

However, her approach soon clashed with others within the organization, particularly regarding the balance between health care framing and political advocacy. Internal disagreements emerged as Planned Parenthood confronted the Trump administration's restrictions on Title X federal funding, which cut support for clinics that referred patients for abortions.[104]

By July 2019, the conflicts culminated in Wen's abrupt departure. News reports at the time, including the *Akron Beacon Journal,* described

---

103 The Arizona Republic. (2018, November 16). *Planned Parenthood selects Leana Wen as new leader.* The Arizona Republic, p. A3.; Courier-Post. (2018, December 1). *Planned Parenthood names new president.* Courier-Post, p. A8.
104 Ibid; Akron Beacon Journal. (2019, July 17). *Planned Parenthood removes president after less than a year.* Akron Beacon Journal, p. A8.

her ouster as the result of "philosophical differences" between her and the Planned Parenthood board. While Wen emphasized her vision of Planned Parenthood as a trusted medical provider above all else, board members and some staff insisted the organization had to remain a forceful political advocate in an era of escalating state-level abortion restrictions. The *Courier-Post* similarly underscored that her exit reflected tensions between her strategy of depoliticizing abortion and the board's desire to maintain a strong activist stance amid growing national battles over reproductive rights.[105]

Wen's presidency, lasting less than a year, thus became a flashpoint in Planned Parenthood's history. Her appointment had been seen as a bold step toward medicalizing the organization's public image. Yet, her departure revealed the difficulty of separating health care delivery from the political fight over abortion access. Her tenure is often remembered as an illustration of the deep challenges reproductive rights organizations face in navigating the dual roles of service provider and political advocate.[106]

After the sudden ouster of Wen in the summer of 2019, Planned Parenthood named Alexis McGill Johnson as acting president. Johnson, a longtime board member and former chair of the organization, was seen as a steadying hand during a turbulent period.

Johnson's background in racial justice and civic engagement also shaped her arrival. The *Atlanta Voice* highlighted her co-founding of the Perception Institute, a research group focused on addressing bias and discrimination, and noted how her experience in coalition building was expected to strengthen Planned Parenthood's advocacy network. Johnson underscored that her leadership would keep reproductive rights at the forefront of public debate, stressing the need to defend access to abortion as well as the broader spectrum of health services the organization provides. Her emphasis on equity and inclusivity aligned with Planned Parenthood's efforts to serve diverse communities across the country.

Both the Associated Press and the *Atlanta Voice* noted that her leadership was cast as temporary at the outset, yet she quickly emerged as a visible and vocal figure in the national debate. Her appointment

105 Ibid.' Courier-Post. (2019, July 18). *Planned Parenthood president forced out.* Courier-Post, p. A6.
106 Ibid.

reassured many within the reproductive rights movement that the organization would maintain a strong activist posture while navigating one of its most challenging periods.[107]

The AP reported that Johnson's appointment came at a time when Planned Parenthood was facing significant political and financial pressures, particularly after the Trump administration enforced new Title X rules barring providers from referring patients for abortions. Johnson immediately positioned herself as both an experienced leader and an unapologetic advocate, signaling that the organization would continue to fight these restrictions while safeguarding patient care.

Established in 1970 under the Public Health Service Act, Title X remains the only federal program dedicated exclusively to providing comprehensive family planning services—such as contraception, pregnancy testing, STI screening and culturally competent care—to low-income, uninsured or underinsured individuals. By delivering services through a network of public health centers, community clinics and nonprofit providers—all administered through the Department of Health and Human Services—Title X has played a central role in advancing reproductive health equity in the U.S.

Its emphasis on person-centered, confidential care has helped reach diverse and underserved communities, including adolescents (who can access care without parental consent) and immigrants. Importantly, while Title X explicitly prohibits the use of federal funds for abortion, it has nonetheless been instrumental in reducing unintended pregnancies and strengthening women's reproductive autonomy through high-quality preventive care.[108]

Funding for Planned Parenthood again became a political flashpoint. After Trump won, House Speaker Paul Ryan wanted to pass laws that removed federal funding to health care centers that referred women to abortion services.

---

107 Associated Press. (2019, August 21). *Planned Parenthood names acting president after Wen's departure.* *The Times Herald* (Port Huron, MI), p. A2.; The Atlanta Voice. (2019, August 23). *Alexis McGill Johnson named acting president of Planned Parenthood. The Atlanta Voice*, p. 8.
108 Guttmacher Institute. (2025, February). *Features and benefits of the Title X program.* Guttmacher Institute. Retrieved from https://www.guttmacher.org/fact-sheet/features-and-benefits-title-x-program

In March 2019, the Trump administration established a rule that changed Title X's policy about family planning clinics. The goverment distributed about $260 million in grants to those providers yearly that subsidized birth control and family planning for 4 million women nationwide. Previously, the rule had prevented the funds from being used to perform abortions.

The new rule denied clinics money if they so much as counseled women with information on getting one. Doctors at those clinics couldn't refer patients to get an abortion. It was known as the "gag rule" by reproductive rights activists. The first gag rule began under Reagan, and it was upheld by the Supreme Court. The decision faced several legal challenges, but the rules were upheld and took effect. Subsequent Democratic administrations lifted the gag rule only to have it reinstated by Republican ones.

In August 2019, Johnson announced that Planned Parenthood would sacrifice the funds to maintain the services.

"The impact will mean that people will choose to forgo care," Johnson told CBS News. "They may choose to delay their care until this is resolved. And that is what is unacceptable."

With Planned Parenthood withdrawing from Title X funding in protest of the administration's restrictions, Johnson inherited the responsibility of maintaining services without that critical federal support.

Remaking the Supreme Court

Trump did his best to remake the court system from the district level to the Supreme Court. Trump appointed Neil Gorsuch, an anti-abortion judge, to fill the first Supreme Court vacancy following the death of Justice Antonin Scalia. Obama had tried to fill the opening with Merrick Garland, but Republicans had declined to hold a hearing or a vote on the nomination, successfully turning the vacancy over to the next administration.

After Anthony Kennedy retired, Trump nominated Brett Kavanaugh, which brought a massive protest from abortion rights supporters. Christine Blasey Ford, a psychology professor at Palo Alto University, accused

Kavanaugh of sexually assaulting her when the two were in high school. The contentious hearings discussed Kavanaugh's past and drew his ire. Despite the accusation, the Senate voted to confirm Kavanaugh.

Cecile Richards appeared on Anderson Cooper's show during the nomination process and said that abortion didn't begin with *Roe*.

"What happened before *Roe* was that women died routinely," Richards said. "Young, healthy women in emergency rooms across America. And that is essentially what the president is promising to go back to those days. I think women are going to rise up in this country, and they already are."

Leonard Leo, a close outside advisor to the president and a member of the secretive Catholic group Opus Dei, said that he had vetted the nominees and was skeptical that any justice appointed to the U.S. Supreme Court would overturn *Roe*. On ABC's "This Week," Leo described that belief as a liberal scare tactic.

Leo's rise as judiciary reformer is worth detailing further. Born on Long Island in the 1960s, he lost his father young and was raised in a devout household that encouraged daily Mass. At Cornell University, Leo absorbed conservative Catholic thought and founded the school's chapter of the Federalist Society in 1989. What began as a student network soon became, under his direction, a pipeline that recruited conservative law students, groomed them through internships and launched them into influential legal careers.

His ties to Scalia and Thomas reinforced this mission. Leo even delayed his own career to help Thomas through his contentious Supreme Court confirmation, learning that organized money and willpower could overcome controversy and reshape the judiciary.

By the early 2000s, Leo had perfected the fusion of ideology and funding. With backing from donors like David Koch and Richard Mellon Scaife, he turned the Federalist Society into the breeding ground for conservative judges. Its power was clear in 2005, when the group successfully blocked Harriet Miers' nomination and replaced her with Samuel Alito, one of their own. With Roberts and Alito on the Court, Leo proved himself indispensable to conservative legal ambitions.

His reach extended further through ties to Opus Dei and allies Neil and Ann Corkery, who channeled dark money into judicial battles via nonprofits such as the Judicial Confirmation Network. Leo joined the board of the Catholic Information Center in Washington, sending his children to its schools and cementing his role in Catholic conservative networks. These relationships provided spiritual legitimacy and financial backing for his broader campaigns.

Beyond the Court, Leo built a sprawling financial empire. Through CRC Advisors, The 85 Fund and other vehicles, he controlled hundreds of millions in dark money to shape cultural and legal battles. A $1.6 billion donation from billionaire Barre Seid gave him unmatched resources, transforming him from strategist into kingmaker. These funds bankrolled not only judicial nominations but also conservative counter-institutions in education, media and policy.[109] Even Justice Clarence Thomas quipped that Leo was "the third most powerful man in the world"—behind the pope and the president.

During Trump's administration, the court could consider roughly 20 abortion cases. Several states had bills that made abortion illegal. State legislators in deeply anti-abortion states thought they could have the law overturned outright after years of an incremental approach. Richards pointed out that some of the justices opposed funding for birth control as much as they opposed abortion rights.

As Trump's first term ended dramatically, Supreme Court Justice Ruth Bader Ginsburg died two months short of the election. The Court had been divided 5–4 in favor of conservatives. Sen. Mitch McConnell showed no compunction in getting a hearing for his appointment, Amy Coney Barrett, despite having said, in the case of Merrick Garland, that he wanted to let the voters decide who the next Supreme Court judge would be. The Senate approved Barrett's nomination in a 52–48 vote, just days before the 2020 election, giving conservatives a decisive majority and positioning the Court to overturn *Roe v. Wade*.

---

109 Gore, G. (2024). *Opus: The cult of dark money, human trafficking, and right-wing conspiracy in the Catholic Church*. Skyhorse Publishing.

The Fix Was In

The Christian legal group Alliance Defending Freedom (ADF), which is closely aligned with Christian dominionist ideology, developed model legislation intended to challenge the constitutional protections established under *Roe v. Wade*. In early 2018, the group promoted a 15-week abortion ban as a strategic legal vehicle to bring before the Supreme Court, aiming to dismantle the viability framework that had long underpinned abortion rights. This effort was part of a broader plan within the anti-abortion movement to create test cases that could weaken or overturn *Roe*.

The legislation, later enacted in Mississippi as the Gestational Age Act, prohibited abortion after 15 weeks with limited exceptions. Once the law was in place, Mississippi's attorney general used it to directly petition the Supreme Court to overturn *Roe*. The case, *Dobbs v. Jackson Women's Health Organization*, resulted in the Court striking down *Roe* in 2022, completing the long-term legal strategy that ADF had helped set in motion.[110]

It involved challenges to a Mississippi law passed in 2018 that prevented abortions past 15 weeks, save when there is a medical emergency or in the case of fetal abnormalities. Jackson Women's Health Organization was the only abortion clinic left in the state. A doctor from the provider legally challenged the rule and requested an emergency temporary restraining order to prevent it from going into effect.

A district court granted the order because Mississippi had not provided evidence that fetuses were viable at 15 weeks. Given the *Planned Parenthood v. Casey* decision, the judge reasoned that the ban was unconstitutional. The Fifth Circuit Court of Appeals affirmed the judgment.

Thomas Dobbs, state health officer of the Mississippi Department of Health, appealed to the Supreme Court. With a new 6–3 supermajority in the Court, abortion rights leaders worried whether *Roe* would stand. The Supreme Court, after considering the petition a dozen times, granted

---

110 Pitman, A. (2022, July 26). *To rule history with God: The Christian dominionist war on abortion, Part I*. Mississippi Free Press. https://www.mississippifreepress.org/to-rule-history-with-god-the-christian-dominionist-war-on-abortion-part-i/

a review of one question from Mississippi—whether it was a violation of the U.S. Constitution to ban all pre-viability elective abortions.

After the Court announced it would hear the case, Republican governors signed several bills into state law that prevented abortions during the first trimester.

Texas passed S.B. 8., which prevented abortions at six weeks. The bill is the most restrictive, but it didn't call for state enforcement. It permitted anyone to sue abortion providers for $10,000 minimum, plus legal fees, if they performed a procedure. This means that a nosy neighbor, family member, someone watching the clinic and anti-abortion extremists—or any other private person anywhere in the U.S.—may sue anyone said to be aiding and abetting an abortion. Any doctor, staff, rideshare driver or friend who drove the woman can be sued in court for $10,000. The law went into effect on Sept. 1, 2021.

The person accused of aiding or abetting does not need to know in advance that they are bringing the person to the abortion clinic in advance. So, for example, rideshare drivers do not need to be aware that they are taking passengers to an abortion clinic to have someone seek damages from them.

The American Civil Liberties Union, ACLU of Texas, the Center for Reproductive Rights, Planned Parenthood, the Lawyering Project and Morrison & Foerster LLP filed for an emergency request to block the law with the Supreme Court in *Whole Woman's Health v. Jackson*. The Supreme Court let the law go into effect without a response. After the law went into effect, the Supreme Court released the reasoning for its denial, a rare occurrence.

The Supreme Court said that procedural questions had to be addressed before the court gave the case a full hearing. The liberal justices strongly dissented. Justice Sonia Sotomayor said that it was "flagrantly unconstitutional" to let the law stand. She said the court allowed Texas state officials to flout 50 years of federal precedent.

Texas abortion providers released statements that they could no longer perform abortions when fetal cardiac activity is detected, in compliance with the law. Planned Parenthood immediately ceased providing abortions entirely, as it was unable to prepare and undertake the potential costs of liability from the act.

Rallying Against the Right

In mid-June 2022, organizers in Jackson, the capital of Mississippi, gathered at a rally they called their D-Day while the country waited to officially hear the *Dobbs* decision that would decide the fate of *Roe v. Wade*.

Plans for the rally had been in the works for months, but the Supreme Court's rough draft of the decision had been leaked only a few weeks earlier, in one of the biggest security breaches in the institution's history. It seemed clear the Supreme Court would overturn *Roe v. Wade* in one of its most anticipated cases.

Many such rallies were held nationwide in the run-up to the decision.

The Mississippi event started with a rendition of Sojourner Truth's famous "Ain't I a Woman?" speech, read by Michelle Colon, the leader of Sisters Helping Every Woman Rise and Organize, a reproductive rights group based in Jackson.

"I am a proud abortion freedom fighter," Colon said. "I don't care what the Supreme Court says. Abortion is health care. Abortion saves lives. Abortion is sacred. Abortion is love. Abortion is self-care. And my absolute favorite … abortion is liberation."

Her microphone was dialed loud enough that she could be heard over a man with a bullhorn whose backdrop was white men holding placards of fetuses and linking abortion to murder.

Abortion costs there are borne harder by women than in virtually any other part of the country. In Hinds County, where Jackson is located, 44% of the population lives more than 200% below the poverty line. The uninsured rate is twice that of the wealthiest counties in America. Still, most white people here are galvanized more by the abortion issue than by a concern for their own economic well-being.

Derenda Hancock, a clinic escort at Jackson Women's Health Organization, said it may be too late to make a difference in the state.

"There's no possibility in the world," Hancock said of whether they could build a successful movement for abortion rights there.

Half the state didn't even know that the case was happening because their poverty forces them to work multiple jobs, which means they have no time to keep abreast of the news. The clinic staff told their patients about the case and the Supreme Court's consideration.

"What went wrong was the big repro organizations got complacent," Hancock said. "I mean in the late 80s and early 90s, they were still fighting. They were in the streets, where we needed to be all along. And they got comfortable in 1994 when the FACE Act went into effect. Haha. Like it's ever enforced."

In the immediate aftermath of finding out that Roe was overturned, I planned to take a trip to Jackson because it was at the heart of the case. For the previous week, I had visited several civil rights museums and had studied how that movement had become successful.

One of the key takeaways from all the exhibits I looked at was the importance of grassroots organizing and the empowerment of local leaders to make decisions about how to persuade people to support a cause. When thinking of why the reproductive rights movement failed, it struck me that it had become a very top-down movement, with most of the decisions about what direction to take coming from New York City, which I came to realize was far removed from the realities I eventually saw elsewhere in the country for the coming three years as activists developed a true grassroots movement.

Nine days after the Jackson rally, the Court handed down their decision, written by Samuel Alito. As expected, it took away the right established nearly a half-century before. Women and men across the country took to social media to express both displeasure and happiness at the news. Some posts were written with complete ignorance about the history of feminism. In a few memes, they called for the use of coded language when discussing abortion. The speakouts in the 60s were about stopping such behavior.

The decision permitted states to outright ban abortion. No longer would there be a need to chip away at reproductive freedoms. Incrementalism was out. Now it was a full-on direct assault on and a complete restriction on women getting any form of abortion care.

Conservative state legislatures moved to outlaw abortion altogether, and clinics in those states stopped performing the procedure. Leading feminist leaders and intellectuals pondered the reasons why the protections for *Roe* had ended. They speculated about what to do next.

One of the initial efforts was to involve more religious people. In January 2021, the Sacred Gathering was held via Zoom. The two-day conference featured presentations from respected religious thinkers, leaders and theologians who discussed ways to attract more people of faith to the movement. The challenge of getting the larger abortion rights community to accept the role of religious people and organizations proved to be difficult as many people had been snookered into believing the false narrative that faith and belief in God were inherently anti-abortion.

Earlier in the year, Rev. Elle Dowd of Chicago had said that embracing religion would be vital to a successful reproductive rights movement going forward.

"The more that we talk about these very faith-based values, I think it can be more clear to people that there are many ways that our faith can inform our values around reproductive rights and reproductive freedoms," Dowd said.

Rev. Terry Williams is an ordained minister at the Orchard Hill United Church of Christ in Chillicothe, Ohio. He is also a leader within Faith Choice Ohio, which helps women travel out of state to get abortions. The organization engaged in other forms of advocacy at the grassroots level. After *Dobbs*, he explained what it was like for him and his staff.

"It's like we get up every single morning and we've been hit by a new round of tornadoes," Williams said to me. "It's like a tornado natural disaster every single day that we wake up because we just have this continuous struggle of trying to find ways to get people hundreds of miles to the care they used to only have to go 50 or 60 miles to get."

For the next few months, state legislatures sought to ban procedures altogether. States like Wisconsin and Michigan had pre-*Roe* bans come back into place and activists there had to put together plans to do something, including getting proposals on the ballot that would return a woman's right to determine her reproductive fate.

In Indiana, an OB/GYN named Dr. Caitlin Bernard performed an abortion on a 10-year-old rape victim. It later became a flashpoint of political debate, featured in *The New York Times* and several other outlets. Bernard is a fixture at pro-choice events. Many anti-abortion candidates and lobbyists harshly criticized her for doing the procedure.

In Chevy Chase, Maryland, protestors rallied outside the homes of Supreme Court justices John Roberts and Brett Kavanaugh. Among the groups who participated was Ruth Sent Us, an amalgamation of mostly middle-aged women who fought for people of color and LGBTQ+ groups. Congressional Republicans linked them to another organization called Jane's Revenge, which had claimed that they had attacked several crisis pregnancy centers. No one I spoke to at the rally had heard of Jane's Revenge, and there was speculation online that it was a shadow organization from the anti-abortion side designed to frame pro-abortion activists. Senators and House representatives from the GOP said both Ruth Sent Us and Jane's Revenge were examples of newfound terrorism on anti-abortion centers.

That was a complete misrepresentation of those groups from what I saw, and it was a false equivalency to bracket those marginal and arguably harmless groups with some of the more extreme anti-abortion movements currently mobilizing in the country. One such movement is the New Apostolic Reformation (NAR), which is an even more radical movement than most on the Christian right. According to an article in the Texas Observer, they were "Christian Nationalism on steroids."

The NAR, an increasingly politicized movement of Pentecostal and charismatic evangelicalism, demonizes people with whom they religiously and politically disagree as people seeking to stop God's will. The movement's fusion of messianism and theocratic compulsion harkens back to an earlier time of the abortion debate, when groups began looking for more militant and violent methods of deterring abortions.

As readers have seen in this book, most fringe groups resort to violence when they sense that they're losing the culture wars. As the abortion rights movement continues to succeed and gain power, I see these methods possibly coming back on a scale not seen since the 1980s.

A Shift in Care

While the decline in the number of abortion clinics in certain parts of the country has diminished access, women now have more options that don't require an in-person visit. During the pandemic, more women turned to telehealth services to get abortion care, according to Elizabeth Raymond, a senior medical associate at Gynuity Health Projects, a New York-based organization that pushes for advances in reproductive medical care. Her service mailed abortion medication to women who needed it.

"Suddenly it was really problematic for both patients and clinic staff to actually get in person to a clinic," Raymond said. "So the idea of using direct-to-patient telemedicine abortion along with mail suddenly became of huge interest all around the world."

Mifeprex, better known as mifepristone, formerly known as RU-486, is used together with another medication called misoprostol to end an early pregnancy. Mifeprex blocks the effects of progesterone, and misoprostol causes contractions to expel the embryo. If necessary, in a situation where the medication does not end the pregnancy, additional medication may be prescribed or a surgical abortion.

The FDA first approved Mifeprex in 2000. However, it wasn't smooth sailing, as it was restricted under Subpart H, later known as the Risk Evaluation and Mitigation Strategy (REMS) program for drug safety. This meant that typical retail pharmacies were not permitted to stock or distribute mifepristone. The drug was available only from a clinic, doctor's office or hospital registered with the manufacturer.

Due to such restrictions, someone seeking a medication abortion had to find a registered provider who had it in stock. The registration and stocking of mifepristone requirements are stringent and include completing a certification attesting to specific competencies and returning it to the manufacturer. But in 2021, to limit interaction and risk during the COVID-19 public health emergency, the FDA loosened the in-person dispensing requirement and permitted discretionary enforcement.

Social media users throughout the country spread misinformation about abortion medication, abortion reversal methods and herbal remedies they thought could induce abortion. Meedan, a think tank researching reproductive topics, issued a 62-page report. It revealed that anytime a claim or narrative is repeated, it is more likely to be seen as accurate by the consumer.

The move to medication abortion was, predictably, met with opposition. Sen. Bill Cassidy (R-LA) had introduced the Teleabortion Prevention Act to Congress the previous year. The bill would prevent chemical abortions without the presence of a health care provider. The Senate sponsors sought to require women to have in-person visits with doctors before getting the pill. The punishment they recommended for violations included a $1,000 fine and two years in prison for the prescriber. Fortunately, the bill went nowhere.

Even while the overall number of abortions declined, the number of medication abortions and the proportion of all abortions that were medication abortions increased, according to a 2017 study from the Guttmacher Institute. Researchers there found that about 60% of abortion patients who were less than 10 weeks pregnant chose medication abortion over suction or surgery. That same year, 89% of counties in the United States did not have a single clinic that provided abortion.[111]

After the Supreme Court overturned *Dobbs*, legal battles ensued over access to mifepristone. In Texas, Judge Matthew Kacsmaryk, a member of the U.S. District Court for the northern district of Texas, invalidated the Food and Drug Administration's longtime approval of mifepristone. His ruling was quickly invalidated by a Washington State judge who said that the pill could continue to be available. The case went to the Supreme Court to determine what to do with mifepristone access. The court ruled that the plaintiffs in the case, a group of anti-abortion doctors, didn't have legal standing, and therefore the drug could remain on the market.

During the hearing, however, Justice Clarence Thomas quizzed the lawyer for a drug manufacturer of mifepristone about whether the Comstock Act—the 19th-century law that forbids the mailing of abortifacients and contraceptives—legally prevents them from distributing it

---

111 Jones, R. K., Witwer, E., & Jerman, J. (2019). *Abortion incidence and service availability in the United States, 2017* (Guttmacher Institute report). Guttmacher Institute. https://www.guttmacher. org/report/abortion-incidence-service-availability-us-2017

now. When the Supreme Court legalized birth control in *Griswold*, abortion medication wasn't even an option. So, it wasn't a question that legal scholars or the justices considered. But the decisions made the Comstock laws moot anyway. However, Congress never repealed them.

Jessica Ellsworth presented the argument for the petitioners, Danco Laboratories, which produces Mifeprex. She said that ruling in favor of the doctors would upend all drug approval. Justice Thomas asked whether they would be subject to the Comstock Act. Ellsworth responded by disagreeing with the interpretation of the statute.

"This statute has not been enforced for nearly a hundred years, and I— I don't believe that this case presents an opportunity for this Court to opine on the reach of the statute," Ellsworth said.

So mifepristone remained legal for the time being. Yet there are looming threats and a possibility that a Republican presidency could restrict access through future decisions by the agency that sought to keep its authority to prescribe medication in this case.

Justice Brett Kavanaugh, in the unanimous decision, said as much. He characterized the regulation as "relaxed":

> *The plaintiffs may present concerns and objections to the President and FDA in the regulatory process or to Congress and the President in the legislative process. And they may also express their views about abortion and mifepristone to fellow citizens, including in the political and electoral processes.*

That was precisely what Republicans had said they would do. In a conservative manifesto, Project 2025, Republican intellectuals called for the FDA to rescind approval of mifepristone should they win this presidential election. Furthermore, the Justice Department may still enforce Comstock laws.

Democrats in Congress pushed back. Congresswoman Cori Bush introduced the Stop Comstock Act, a repeal of the archaic law. While Rep. Bush and Rep. Becca Balint championed efforts in the House to repeal Comstock, Minnesota Sen. Tina Smith did it in the other chamber.

Thus far, the Trump administration hasn't enforced the Comstock Act, despite encouragement to do so by the anti-abortion lobby. As long as the law is on the books, it's still a possibility down the road with future Republican administrations.

Other previously moot laws came into effect at the state level in the wake of *Dobbs*. In Arizona, the highest court determined that an 1864 ban could come back into effect since it hadn't been repealed. No one had tried to since *Roe* established a constitutional right to abortion, thereby making the ban dead letter. So, there has been precedent for reinstituting these laws, which Sanger and others fought against.

The Thin Line Between Legal and Illegal

Another critical case that happened in the aftermath of *Roe* was *Moyle v. United States*, a battle over whether federal law regarding care in emergencies trumped an Idaho state law that forbids abortions with certain exceptions to protect the life and health of the mother. The federal law, the Emergency Medical Treatment & Labor Act, was passed in 1986. One of the law's stipulations requires ER workers to provide all necessary care in their workplace. That includes abortions.

There were several amicus briefs in the case, including from district attorneys throughout America who said that the Idaho law placed medical decisions in the hands of prosecutors and police who had no medical training that would be needed to distinguish between legal and illegal abortions. Eli Savit, a prosecuting attorney in Washtenaw County, Michigan, explained how many district attorneys and similar offices feel about how jurisprudence and law enforcement have evolved since the Supreme Court eliminated abortion access as a constitutional right. Savit said they rely on doctor testimony in cases of rape and incest.

"Now they're thinking, 'If I am talking to law enforcement, if I'm corresponding with them, do I have to worry about being criminally charged myself?'" Savit said to me over the phone for an article I did for my newsletter, Repro Rights Now.

"That's going to kill relationships. That will make it less likely that stuff is reported and ultimately make us able to investigate and prosecute."

The Associated Press reported in April that a woman in Texas had been forced to have her miscarriage in the lobby restroom of a hospital after the front desk refused to check her in. In North Carolina, a woman gave birth in a car after an emergency room couldn't offer an ultrasound. The baby later died.

Federal investigators looked into just over a dozen pregnancy-related complaints in 19 states during the months leading up to *Dobbs*. But more than two dozen complaints about emergency pregnancy care were lodged in the months after the decision was unveiled, according to the AP.

In another Texas lawsuit, similar concerns appeared after a 31-year-old woman couldn't get an abortion after her child was diagnosed with full trisomy, which is nearly always fatal at birth. The woman, Kate Cox, sued Texas to get access to the abortion care she needed. She later went out of state to get the treatment she needed. In its decision, the state supreme court said that the statute doesn't require a woman's death to be imminent. It also said there didn't need to be a universal medical judgment on a woman in a situation where she needs an abortion. The Texas Supreme Court asked the Texas Medical Board to clarify its rules on exceptions.

A number of women joined as plaintiffs in another Texas case, *Zurawski v. State of Texas*. Among them was Lauren Miller, who had been trying to add another child to her family with her husband, Jason. After developing a sickness, Miller went to the doctor and discovered she was pregnant with twins.

At the 12-week ultrasound, she learned that there was something wrong with one of the fetuses. It had Trisomy 18 and several other fatal diagnoses. Doctors told her that it imperiled her life as well as that of the other fetus.

Because of the state's abortion ban and the fear of prosecution, doctors who cared for her didn't explicitly say that she needed an abortion. Miller remembers speaking with a maternal fetal medicine specialist.

"He just, in frustration, ripped off his gloves, he threw them at the trashcan, not even in, just at it, just so angry, and turned to us and said, 'I can't help you anymore. This baby isn't going to make it to birth. You need to leave the state," Miller recalled in a phone interview with me.

Miller flew to Colorado and had a fetal reduction procedure, which is when one of the fetuses in a pregnancy involving twins is subject to an abortion.

When the Texas Medical Board finally met to discuss the issues, activists on both sides took issue with what it proposed. Doctors were performing C-sections instead of D&E procedures to accomplish abortion. The latter method is far safer and less intrusive. Still, doctors have avoided it because it's exclusively used and associated with abortion, and they fear it would be more likely to lead to prosecution than the C-section procedure. It's an essential point of advocacy for leaders. Women are entitled to the safest possible medical care using the simplest method called for.

The organization that is pushing for the C-section approach is the American Association of Pro-Life OBGYNs. In a policy letter sent out, the organization referred to abortion as "feticide."

It recommends C-sections to remove stillborns because it is a morally acceptable procedure. They also recommend a salpingostomy, a surgical procedure that involves making an incision into a fallopian tube to remove an ectopic pregnancy while preserving the tube's patency. One of the chief proponents of the C-section method is Dr. Ingrid Skop, who testified before the Senate Committee on the Judiciary in April 2023. Skop enumerated a list of reasons why she felt D&E procedures were dangerous.

Amy Bresnen, who along with her husband, Steve, was chiefly responsible for lobbying the board to address the problem, explained to me the effect this reasoning has had on doctors in the state.

"If you're looking at the coding, and you can put in C-section versus D&E, you can probably … other than the fact that you just disemboweled a woman for no reason … you don't have to go to bed at night worrying if prosecutors are going to come after you," Bresnen said.

In a related case, Cox's doctor Damla Karsan was listed as a plaintiff in a seminal decision by the Texas Supreme Court. Twenty women had filed a complaint in the judicial system earlier in 2023. The case, *Zurawski v. Texas*, reached the highest court in Texas. Activists and lawyers in the state had sought to get clarification for doctors so that they could figure out safely and with impunity when they could perform abortions under the life-saving exception written into the law that forbids abortion. Two doctors had joined as plaintiffs.

The Human Life Protection Act, which makes abortion punishable by up to 99 years in prison in Texas, has a stipulation: a woman with a life-threatening physical condition and her physician have the legal authority to proceed with an abortion to save the woman's life or major bodily function.

The Center for Reproductive Rights brought the case, seeking action from the state medical board, the attorney general, and the state supreme court to protect doctors in these scenarios. The center argued that such a standard makes doctors susceptible to a battle of the experts when only some doctors might reach the same medical judgment in each case.

Amanda Zurawski, the lead plaintiff, had been informed by two doctors that her pregnancy would result in miscarriage, but her doctors refused to perform an abortion because the fetus had a heartbeat. Zurawski later developed septic shock. Doctors then induced a stillborn baby. Zurawski remained in emergency care for three days. Scarring from the infection was so severe that she required surgical reconstruction of her uterus and lost one of her fallopian tubes.

A medical expert had testified on the plaintiff's behalf earlier in the case that doctors in Texas had opted not to perform the abortion to err on the side of legal caution. The Supreme Court found that doctors listed as plaintiffs had legal standing because they could be prosecuted under the order. The woman didn't, though.

The state supreme court judges wrote in the majority opinion the burden is the state's to prove that *no* reasonable physician would have concluded that the mother had a life-threatening physical condition that placed her at risk of death or of substantial impairment of a major bodily function unless the abortion was performed.

That's worth exploring further because the court contends that prosecutors would have to show that there wouldn't be a single doctor who would perform the procedure in a given circumstance. In the event of a prosecution, doctors could summon other medical experts who could testify that they would also have performed an abortion. They can also cite peer-reviewed studies to justify their decision. Nonetheless, the potential legal expenses that would emerge from such a criminal defense are in and of itself a deterrent to performing necessary abortions.

Bresnen and her husband spent the next year lobbying for change at the Texas Board of Health and in the state legislature.

The Board of Health met in June 2024 to clarify that they permit abortions for ectopic pregnancies. That was received well by the abortion rights community. There were other decisions by the board that weren't as popular. Most people complained about the transfer provision, which required doctors to document whether they had tried to transfer the patient to a different facility to perform an abortion.

Dr. Sherif Zaafran, president of the Texas Medical Board, spoke at the meeting.

"There are certain things we can address," Zaafran said. "And there are certain things that we ultimately don't think we have the authority to address."

The board didn't list specific medical conditions that would serve as exceptions.

"The concern with a list is what if a situation arises where something is not on that list," Zaafran said.

The board's rules were much narrower than the protections provided by the *Zurawski* decision.

"The most important takeaway is that the medical board wanted to wait until the end of the litigation before they took to rulemaking," Bresnen said to me afterward. "They waited until the *Zurawski* opinion came out and then completely ignored the holding and the *Zurawski* opinion."

Later, Bresnen was involved in a state legislative effort to codify the *Zurawski* opinion. Eventually, the Texas legislature passed a bill that expanded protections for and provides training to doctors who perform abortions in life-threatening situations. Known as the Life of the Mother

Act, it clarifies when abortions are permitted in Texas to save the mother's life or prevent serious impairment of a major bodily function. The bill required the state bar to develop an education program by January 2026, focusing on updated abortion laws and medical emergencies.

Bresnen described a conservative movement that was divided. Some were abortion abolitionists who thought women should be prosecuted for getting abortions. Others believed that a woman's future fertility shouldn't be a concern when deciding whether to perform an abortion. Most supported some form of reform, though.

The state now needs to educate doctors about the updated definitions of medical emergency and what reasonable medical judgment means. The latter term came from the *Zurawski* decision, when the state supreme court held that the language in state abortion laws allowing abortions when the life of the mother is threatened was constitutional and adequate to protect the health of the patient.

In Tennessee, Kathryn Archer, a Nashville woman, was diagnosed with several anomalies in her pregnancy that made a miscarriage likely. She had to wait for three weeks to go out of state to get the abortion she needed. Archer and seven other women sued the state to ask it to clarify its exceptions.

Physicians for Human Rights, a group dedicated to advancing reproductive freedom, issued a study chock-full of medical perspectives on how a six-week abortion ban has affected women in Florida who need abortions. After the law went into effect, the researchers behind this study undertook fact-finding interviews from July to August 2024 with 25 clinicians and clinicians in training to document whether and, if so, how Florida's abortion ban is impacting patients, health care workers and access to health care.

They interviewed clinicians in obstetrics and gynecology, maternal-fetal medicine, family medicine, reproductive endocrinology and certified nurse midwifery as well as medical students and genetic counselors across the state, with representation in varied practice types that include public and private hospitals, academic medical centers, private practices and free-standing abortion-providing facilities.

In these interviews, clinicians described the serious and manifold harms the ban is causing pregnant people in the state who seek reproductive health care. The six-week ban is unclear in its guidelines and introduces barriers to care, delays in emergency reproductive services and deviations from standard medical care. Moreover, the steep penalties, particularly when combined with other laws, create intensified fear and confusion among health care providers, who do not know in what cases they legally can or cannot provide abortion care, creating strain in the patient-clinician relationship and inducing providers and trainees to leave the state.

Clinicians reported receiving warnings from hospital administrators, legislators and others that they may be targeted for providing necessary abortions and that these laws are being strictly enforced. That has had a chilling effect, according to the report.

The physicians also shared stories about how delayed care had imperiled people's lives and how an inability to pay for increasing costs had left many in precarious situations where they couldn't get the care they needed or wanted.

The report indicated that the day after the six-week ban went into effect, the Florida Agency for Health Care Administration (AHCA) released emergency rules stating that certain pregnancy terminations, including for premature preterm rupture of membranes (PPROM), ectopic pregnancy and trophoblastic tumors, should not be considered abortion for reporting purposes. These guidelines lack medical clarity, further confusing clinicians.

When the U.S. Supreme Court heard oral arguments in *Moyle*, Justice Barrett focused on whether different doctors could concentrate on different conclusions on whether abortion was merited in a hypothetical medical situation. She asked Idaho's counsel whether a prosecutor could reach a different conclusion than the doctor. Turner said the decision to charge someone was a matter of prosecutorial discretion.

One of the central arguments offered up by Solicitor General Elizabeth Prelogar in support of EMTALA was that the spending clause of the Constitution permits the federal government to make states comply with conditions attached to getting funding. Hospitals that accept Medicaid and money from the Department of Health & Human Services must provide the care directed by the law, including abortions.

The court's decision in *Moyle* permitted hospitals in Idaho to perform abortions in emergency settings. But the victory was temporary. Justice Elena Kagan wrote that the decision issued by the District Court could now go to the Court of Appeals. It remains to be resolved on its merits.

In Idaho, the impact was felt regardless of the decision. Susie Keller, chief executive officer of the Idaho Medical Association, told me that there was a high level of trepidation among physicians and doctors who don't want to face the sentences that come with violating the state's abortion ban. They face five years in prison for performing the procedure— less draconian than in Texas, which can dole out 99 years in prison for performing it against the state's ban, but still a powerful deterrent.

Exceptions

Also in Idaho, in April 2025, a state judge expanded the circumstances in which an abortion exception would work.

Judge Jason D. Scott issued the ruling in a case that involved a medical exception to Idaho's near-total ban, which permits abortion only to prevent death. Lawyers hoped clarifying the law's medical exceptions would allow physicians to provide life-saving care without waiting for patients to be near death.

The lawsuit sought to clarify and expand the exceptions under the two bans to ensure physicians can provide abortion care to preserve a pregnant person's health, including when the pregnant person has received a fatal fetal diagnosis. The plaintiffs included four women who couldn't get abortion care under the ban, two doctors who couldn't give it and a medical association concerned about the law.

The Center for Reproductive Rights filed this lawsuit on Sept. 11, 2024, challenging the limited scope of the medical exceptions to both of Idaho's abortion bans: a total trigger ban and a six-week ban that has "vigilante"-style civil liability provisions.

The court held hearings in November 2024 about the case. Jennifer

Adkins, the lead plaintiff, was pregnant with her second child when she learned at 12 weeks of pregnancy that her baby was unlikely to survive because of multiple conditions, including the likelihood of Turner syndrome, which usually results in miscarriage.

Adkins had been likely to develop mirror syndrome, which could lead to edema and preeclampsia, which are both life-threatening conditions if untreated. She got an abortion by traveling with her husband to Oregon with money she got from abortion funds.

Other plaintiffs included Jillaine St. Michel, Kayla Smith and Rebecca Vincen-Brown.

St. Michel, of Meridian, was pregnant with her second child when her 20-week ultrasound revealed that her baby had several severe developmental and chromosomal conditions affecting multiple organ systems and was unlikely to survive. After St. Michel and her husband had reached out to several out-of-state abortion clinics, she was able to get an abortion at a clinic in Seattle, Washington.

Smith, of Nampa, pregnant with her second child, learned at her 19-week ultrasound scan that her baby had a likely fatal and inoperable heart condition. Since she had previously developed preeclampsia during her first pregnancy, Smith had a heightened risk of developing preeclampsia again if she carried the pregnancy to term. She and her husband traveled to Seattle, Washington, to get an abortion. She had to take out a personal loan and get money from friends and family to pay for the trip, which cost thousands of dollars.

Vincen-Brown, of Ada County, pregnant with her second child, discovered at a 16-week anatomy scan that her baby had several fatal fetal conditions—including a chromosomal condition and significant cardiac conditions—and was unlikely to survive. She risked developing preeclampsia or severe hemorrhaging if she continued the pregnancy. Vincen-Brown, her husband and their daughter drove seven hours to Portland, Oregon, to get an abortion. After the first day of her abortion procedure, she passed her pregnancy in the hotel bathroom the next morning.

Emily Corrigan and Julie Lyons were the two doctors, and the organization was the Idaho Academy of Family Physicians. Dr. Corrigan specializes in treating patients with complicated pregnancies, including by performing a few abortions per year, both before and after Idaho's abortion laws took effect. Lyons was a physician from Blaine County, a rural area in Idaho.

When Lyons testified in November 2024, she said that the bans exacerbated a physician shortage, particularly affecting specialists like obstetricians. She detailed how the bans cause confusion, fear and delays in care, leading to increased patient harm and physician burnout. Lyons highlighted that 25–30% of her pregnant patients experience complications, often requiring travel for specialized care. She emphasized the need for clear medical exceptions to allow abortions in cases of fatal fetal diagnoses and to protect patient health.

Several other doctors had testified in the case that painted the dire picture in Idaho surrounding maternal care. They described specific circumstances where Idaho's abortion ban had hurt patients and affected medical decisions.

In April 2024, Judge Scott expanded the circumstances in which an abortion exception would work. The judge's ruling said physicians had been confused by the unclear language in the state's ban, which led to delays in needed care.

Criminal Prosecutions

The arrest of Maria Margarita Rojas in March 2025 marked a turning point in the post-*Dobbs* era. A licensed midwife known in her community as "Dr. Maria," she had long operated a network of modest clinics across northwest Houston that served primarily low-income, Spanish-speaking patients. When agents from the Texas attorney general's office raided her facilities, they carried away a small envelope of cash, a bottle of misoprostol tablets and a trove of clinic records.

That evidence formed the basis for charges of criminal abortion and practicing medicine without a license—allegations that carry the possibility of nearly two decades in prison. It was the first time since the early 1970s that Texas officials had used the state's criminal abortion statutes to pursue a provider, underscoring how swiftly the legal climate had shifted once federal constitutional protections were stripped away.

Alongside the criminal charges, Attorney General Ken Paxton pursued a civil lawsuit designed to make an example of Rojas. Invoking the Texas Human Life Protection Act and the Medical Practice Act, his office sought to shutter her clinics permanently and impose civil penalties of at least $100,000 per violation. Paxton's lawyers painted a picture of a shadow medical enterprise where unlicensed staff lured women into back-room procedures and Rojas procured abortion drugs under false identities.

In court, when asked whether she had administered misoprostol or performed abortions, Rojas invoked her Fifth Amendment rights more than 150 times. That silence was enough for a district judge to grant the state a sweeping injunction, forbidding her and her staff from "practicing medicine or performing abortions in violation of State law."

Her attorneys countered that the case was built on sand. Rojas was represented by the Center for Reproductive Rights and Arnold & Porter. They argued that Paxton had exceeded his statutory authority, pointing out that the legislature had empowered the Texas Medical Board—not the attorney general—to seek injunctions against unauthorized medical practice. They highlighted how misoprostol is routinely used for labor induction and miscarriage care and how the clinics relied on nurse practitioners working through telemedicine, supported by medical assistants.

To them, the state's investigation resembled the prosecutions of the pre-*Roe* era, when law enforcement scoured immigrant neighborhoods for signs of clandestine abortion, often mistaking legitimate reproductive care for crime. By resurrecting statutes long dormant, the state was not simply targeting one woman but signaling a new willingness to use the combined weight of criminal and civil law to police abortion in 21st-century Texas.

One of the men who was charged was later found to be a member of Doctors Without Borders, the humanitarian organization that sends medical staff into war-torn countries to provide care.

In October 2025, the Texas Attorney General's Office announced the arrest of eight additional individuals connected to the Houston-area network of clinics previously operated by Rojas. The arrests followed Rojas' earlier indictment on felony charges of performing an illegal abortion and practicing medicine without a license. According to the attorney general, the new defendants were unlicensed staff members who assisted in operating or managing clinics that provided abortion-related services without proper authorization. The state secured court orders barring those involved from continuing medical or abortion-related activity while the criminal proceedings are pending.

The announcement marked an expansion of the state's enforcement efforts in the Rojas investigation, shifting from prosecution of a single operator to dismantling the broader infrastructure surrounding her clinics. The attorney general characterized the arrests as part of Texas's ongoing commitment to enforcing its abortion restrictions and medical-licensing laws, framing the operation as necessary to protect patients and uphold "pro-life" statutes. The action reflects the state's use of coordinated criminal enforcement and public messaging to deter similar unlicensed or unauthorized medical practices while signaling the government's broader intent to pursue those associated with illegal abortion networks.

In the summer of 2024, a Louisiana grand jury indicted Dr. Margaret Carpenter, a New York–based physician and cofounder of the Abortion Coalition for Telemedicine. Carpenter had become a visible advocate for expanding access to abortion medication through telehealth, but that role placed her squarely in the crosshairs of states determined to criminalize such care. Grand jurors in West Baton Rouge Parish unanimously charged her, her company (Nightingale Medical), and the mother of a pregnant teenager with the felony of criminal abortion by means of abortion-inducing drugs. Authorities swiftly arrested the mother, who turned herself in, and issued a warrant for Carpenter, who remained in New York.

District Attorney Tony Clayton alleged that the mother had submitted only an online questionnaire to obtain the medication and that Carpenter had prescribed the drugs without ever speaking directly to the girl herself.

According to Louisiana prosecutors, Carpenter mailed a "cocktail of pills" that the mother then instructed her daughter to take. When the teenager experienced a medical emergency alone, she dialed 911 and was rushed to the hospital for treatment. A responding police officer learned about the medication, which launched a broader investigation and eventually pointed back to Carpenter's practice in New York. Louisiana law carried stiff penalties—up to five years in prison and a $50,000 fine for the basic offense—but a separate statute threatened a sentence of as much as 50 years if injury to a minor could be shown.

Almost immediately, the case ignited political fire. Louisiana Attorney General Liz Murrill engaged in heated commentary on social media, sparring with critics on X in ways that legal observers suggested could compromise the integrity of the proceedings. Reproductive rights advocates decried the prosecution as a test case for states seeking to extend their abortion bans beyond their own borders.

In New York, the response was unequivocal. Gov. Kathy Hochul announced that she would not allow Carpenter to be extradited, citing the state's shield law designed to protect abortion providers from out-of-state investigations. Attorney General Letitia James issued a sharp statement, declaring that "abortion care is health care" and condemning Louisiana's indictment as a brazen attempt to weaponize the law against providers. New York's leaders signaled that they saw Carpenter's case not just as an attack on one doctor but as a threat to the ability of providers everywhere to practice medicine across state lines.

Even as the Louisiana case drew national headlines, Carpenter faced another legal battle in Texas, where Paxton filed a civil lawsuit accusing her of prescribing abortion-inducing drugs to a Collin County woman. The complaint claimed the medication led to serious complications and emergency hospital care, and Paxton sought a $250,000 civil penalty. The case was framed in unusual terms, focusing less on the woman's experience than on the man who had impregnated her. According to filings, he discovered her pregnancy only after accompanying her to the hospital, later finding pill containers for mifepristone and misoprostol at her home.

The Abortion Coalition for Telemedicine, which Carpenter co-founded, issued a forceful statement in her defense. The group argued that these prosecutions jeopardized reproductive access nationwide and represented a disturbing escalation of state efforts to criminalize abortion. "Make no mistake," the coalition warned, "this state-sponsored effort to prosecute a doctor providing safe and effective care should alarm everyone."

The civil case is worth exploring. When the civil motions from Texas first arrived in Ulster County, New York, Taylor Bruck had been clerk for only a few months. I spoke to him after a suggestion from a follower of mine on Bluesky.

The job, as he understood it, was largely ministerial: If a document met the filing requirements, it was filed, no questions asked. But the New York telehealth shield law complicated that routine. Its language was broad, declaring that no government employee should comply with an out-of-state proceeding tied to health care services legal in New York.

That left Bruck facing a dilemma for which there was no precedent. Filing the judgment risked violating state law and exposing him to lawsuits at home, while rejecting it meant inviting litigation from Texas. After reviewing the statute with attorneys and finding no guidance in prior cases, he chose to reject the filing, leaving it to the courts to decide whether the shield law applied to clerks.

Bruck insisted the decision was rooted in duty rather than politics. Though he was the first Democrat to hold the clerk's office in nearly a century, he described himself as following the letter of the law, not an ideological impulse. Yet he acknowledged to me over the phone that the politics could not be ignored. A Republican clerk, he admitted, might well have filed the judgment and stepped aside.

For him, the calculation was straightforward: protect local constituents from the reach of Texas enforcement. The law was vague enough to permit different readings, but his reading carried the least risk to those he served. That choice, however, pushed a quiet local office into the center of a national conflict, with Bruck himself becoming a symbol of resistance.

The collision of roles was jarring. Bruck had run for clerk out of a love of history and archives, never imagining that he would be pulled into one of the country's fiercest debates. At home, he was a new father,

still adjusting to sleepless nights. At work, he was suddenly facing reporters' questions, lawsuits from a distant attorney general and the unset-
tling knowledge that his office was part of a constitutional test case. He
described the experience as surreal.

Messages poured in—letters and emails of encouragement from
across the country, but also the occasional threat from strangers who
accused him of betraying life itself. The words of Paxton, who cast New
York officials as radicals bent on killing children, he found particularly
alarming, the kind of rhetoric that could endanger his family. Yet the
immediate backing of Gov. Hochul and Attorney General Letitia James
steadied him; their public statements of support gave him the confidence
that he would not be left to fight alone.

As the legal battle unfolded, Bruck pieced together resources for
his defense. Ulster County authorized $50,000 from its surplus fund to
retain outside counsel, and once that sum was exhausted, his attorneys
agreed to continue pro bono. The arrangement underscored the fragility
of the position he was in, and the ease with which future clerks might be
dissuaded by legal costs from making a similar stand. Bruck, for his part,
began to reflect more deeply on what the shield law represented.

He saw both its promise and its perils, imagining how different states
might twist such laws to their own ends. He also noted the irony: New
York was now mounting a states' rights argument to defend reproductive
health care, a reversal of the usual political script. What had begun as a
decision in a small county office had widened into a test of federalism in
the digital age, with telehealth at its center. Bruck continued to describe
his role modestly—he was just doing his job, he said—but he understood
that history might remember it very differently.

James intervened in the *Texas v. Bruck* case by filing notice that her
office would join the defense, signaling New York's direct involvement
in a case testing whether one state can punish conduct that is legal in
another. The move was both symbolic and strategic, positioning New
York as a defender of reproductive access against states seeking to impose
extraterritorial bans. It represents a broader legal turning point, one that
could define how far individual states can go in enforcing their abortion

restrictions beyond their borders — and how firmly others will stand in protecting their own laws and providers.

Together, the Louisiana indictment and the Texas civil suit underscored the precarious terrain of post-*Roe* America. Carpenter's prosecution illustrated how states hostile to abortion were no longer content to regulate within their borders; they sought to punish providers elsewhere, threatening not only one physician's career but the very future of telemedicine as a vehicle for reproductive freedom.

To understand how this might unfold, I began speaking with scholars who have written about conflicts of law. My interview with Professor Lea Brilmayer of Yale underscored the constitutional tensions at play. She explained how the full faith and credit clause, which obligates states to honor judgments from elsewhere, could collide with New York's shield law, which refuses to enforce civil liability or extradition tied to reproductive health care. The result, she told me, is a standoff between constitutional obligation and state sovereignty. In her words, conflicts of law are often thought of as technical or obscure, but Carpenter's prosecution has made them immediate and deeply political.

My conversation with Professor Roderick Hills of NYU Law added another layer. He cautioned that if mailing abortion pills is treated as establishing jurisdiction in the patient's home state, telemedicine providers would effectively be barred from serving anyone in abortion-ban states. In contrast, providing abortions in New York to residents who travel there remains on firm legal ground.

Professor Paul Schiff Berman of George Washington University took the hypothetical further, imagining what might happen if federal courts ordered Gov. Kathy Hochul to extradite Carpenter. Courts, he pointed out, lack their own enforcement power. Unless a president intervenes with federal law enforcement or the National Guard—as Eisenhower did to enforce desegregation—such an order could go unheeded, raising profound questions about the survival of the rule of law.

What emerged from these conversations is that Carpenter's prosecution is legally unprecedented and fraught with uncertainty. Washington University's Susan Appleton later told me that if cases like this succeed, they will chill telehealth abortion nationwide, deterring providers through threats of criminal liability, civil penalties and endless retaliatory suits. Yet Carpenter has never set foot in Louisiana or Texas, and historically, abortion prosecutions have often faltered before juries unwilling to convict.

Shield laws, though untested, represent a deliberate stand by states like New York. Whether they can withstand constitutional challenge remains unknown. What is certain is that Carpenter's prosecution is more than a case against one doctor—it is a test of interstate conflict, reproductive rights and the stability of American federalism itself. Shield laws that states have passed have not yet been deemed constitutional by the U.S. Supreme Court. Judges in that institution have defended extradition, which is enumerated in the Constitution as an obligation of governors. So, there is a conflict between extradition precedents and shield laws, which judges must adjudicate.

Aiding and Abetting

In Alabama, a federal judge ruled that the state's attorney general can't prosecute or sue abortion fund organizations for helping women in the state get abortions elsewhere.

Yellowhammer Fund v. Attorney General of Alabama was a civil rights action asking a federal court to prevent Alabama Attorney General Steve Marshall from making good on his threats to criminalize people who help pregnant Alabamians leave the state to access legal abortion.

U.S. District Judge Myron Thomson said that Marshall would violate the First Amendment rights and the constitutional right to travel of citizens if he tried to bring criminal charges against abortion funds. Thomson's decision acknowledged the logistical and economic barriers that Alabama women faced in getting abortions and cited the indispensable role that abortion funds played in helping them get the reproductive care they needed. He wrote:

The court has found that the Attorney General's threatened prosecutions violate the right to travel and the First Amendment. But the broader, practical implications of the Attorney General's threats should not be overlooked. If Alabama held the power its Attorney General asserts here, it is hard to envision a limiting principle besides what the Attorney General personally sees as permissible and impermissible.

It is one thing for Alabama to outlaw by statute what happens in its own backyard. It is another thing for the State to enforce its values and laws, as chosen by the Attorney General, outside its boundaries by punishing its citizens and others who help individuals travel to another State to engage in conduct that is lawful there but the Attorney General finds to be contrary to Alabama's values and laws.

The attorney general's threats specifically targeted helpers like the Yellowhammer Fund, an organization that seeks to resume providing funding and practical support to pregnant Alabamians who are forced to leave their home state and travel, often hundreds of miles, to access legal abortion care, according to the Lawyering Project's description of the case.

In 2022, State Rep. Chris England, D-Huntsville, who doubles as the chairman of the Alabama Democratic Party, posted a photo on social media of a section of Alabama law separate from the abortion ban to argue that helping someone to get an abortion or plan one in another state was a felony.[112]

Marshall later said he would look into England's point and went on radio programs to push it to justify prosecuting abortion funds for forming a conspiracy to violate the state's ban.

At the end of March 2025, a federal judge ruled that Alabama's attorney general can't prosecute or sue abortion funds for helping women in the state get abortions elsewhere. Tia Freeman, the organization's spokeswoman, spoke to me about the development.

"Finally being able to have that decision, and it had been so long awaited, and knowing that we can finally start to support our community in totality again, felt really exciting," Freeman said.

These questions over free speech appeared elsewhere. The Tennessee

112 England, C. (2022, June 6). *If Republicans want a law-enforcement government, they should stop attacking law enforcement* [Tweet]. X. https://x.com/RepEngland70/status/1540482376014462977

legislature's Underage Abortion Trafficking Act, enacted in May 2024, made it a crime for adults to "recruit, harbor, or transport" unemancipated minors for the purpose of concealing or facilitating an abortion without parental consent.

Violations carried penalties of nearly a year in jail. While parents and guardians were exempt, the law targeted teachers, lawyers, clergy and advocates who might provide guidance or assistance to minors. With its vague language—particularly the word "recruit"—the measure left citizens uncertain about what speech or conduct could lead to prosecution, creating what opponents described as a deliberate chilling effect.

Two Tennesseans led the legal challenge: State Rep. Aftyn Behn, a Nashville Democrat and former social worker, and attorney Rachel Welty, who worked in family law. They argued the statute infringed on their First Amendment rights by criminalizing their ability to share accurate information about abortion access or help minors navigate out-of-state care. In federal court, both testified that the law chilled their advocacy, even constraining Behn's speech as a legislator. In September 2024, U.S. District Judge Aleta Trauger granted a preliminary injunction, temporarily halting enforcement.

The case culminated in July 2025, when the district court granted summary judgment for Behn and Welty. The judge struck down the law's "recruitment" provision on First Amendment grounds, issuing a permanent injunction that prohibited enforcement. Though the court declined to rule the statute void for vagueness, its free-speech violation was enough to invalidate the central section.

With the permanent ruling in place, the Sixth Circuit dismissed Tennessee's pending appeal of the injunction as moot, since the final judgment resolved the matter. The decision marked a rare post-*Dobbs* victory for abortion rights advocates in a deeply conservative state.

Even so, the outcome remains unsettled. Tennessee has the option to appeal the final judgment, and other lawsuits are still in motion, including cases brought by clergy members and abortion funds challenging additional provisions under the interstate commerce clause. Those cases will determine whether states can penalize individuals who aid in securing lawful abortions across state lines.

Behn, who launched a congressional campaign amid the litigation, framed the ruling as part of a larger struggle against legislative overreach in Tennessee. The case highlights the continuing tension between states' efforts to restrict abortion after *Roe* and the enduring constitutional limits that protect speech and advocacy

In Vitro Fertilization

Alabama's Supreme Court recently ruled that embryos can be considered children under state law after six people sued a reproductive medicine clinic following the unintentional destruction of embryos stored cryogenically.

The case revolved around the concerns of IVF parents James and Emily LePage and William and Caroline Fonde, two couples that reside in the state. Another case that was joined in the decision was that of Felicia Burdick-Aysenne and Scott Aysenne, who were in the same situation. All were prospective parents of destroyed petri dishes that contained embryos. The defendant in the case was The Center for Reproductive Medicine, located in Mobile.

In December 2020, according to the opinion, a patient wandered into the center's fertility clinic through an unsecured doorway and removed several embryos. The subzero temperatures at which the embryos were stored freeze-burned the patient's hand, causing the patient to drop the embryos on the floor.

A lower court had ruled that the embryos could not be considered people. They also dismissed the plaintiff's other complaints of wantonness and negligence.

While the court reasoned in its decision that there was precedent supporting its claim, neither the Supreme Court and nor virtually any other court within the tradition of English common law has ever established fetal or embryonic personhood, which is when legal protections begin.

The center contended in its briefs that ruling against them would make IVF treatments cost-prohibitive, if not impossible. The Supreme Court judges said that would be an issue left to the legislature. Chief Justice Tom

Parker, who is aligned with the New Apostoic Reformation, cited religious texts and the Bible to justify his views in his concurring opinion.[113]

Frozen embryos, created through IVF procedures, are a crucial aspect of fertility treatments, offering hope to individuals and couples struggling with infertility. From a scientific perspective, embryos represent a stage in the continuum of human development, but they do not possess the attributes of personhood.

Anti-abortion activists and leaders have long sought to establish fetal personhood as a manner to make abortions illegal under all circumstances. It's usually done indirectly, with the opposition using the example of a pregnant woman who is assaulted and who loses her pregnancy as a reason for why the perpetrator should be charged with manslaughter. The hope is to use that example as an indirect justification to end the right to abortion altogether.

Harvard Law Professor Glenn Cohen spoke to me about the issue.

"That would make abortion now subject to the same criminal penalties we have for killing adults or killing children," Cohen said.

After the *Dobbs* decision, the anti-abortion movement shifted its strategy. Now, its goal is to build precedent at the state level to eventually make the case for the U.S. Supreme Court to acknowledge fetal and embryonic personhood.

"They recognize that the more states and places start saying this, the easier it is to treat this as an idea that goes from off the wall to on the wall if you will," Cohen said. "And so this is part of that process."

Following the Alabama Supreme Court's decision to grant personhood to embryos that hadn't been planted, state legislators nationwide scrambled to introduce and pass protections for IVF.

Cohen said the people in Alabama have little legal recourse on the IVF decision. The U.S. Supreme Court doesn't typically review cases they think are on adequate and independent state grounds. The only thing they can do is go to the legislature. That's precisely what they've done, but it may be insufficient protection.

---

113 Clarkson, F. (2023, June 17). *"Unfriending" America: The Christian right is coming for the enemies of God — like you and me.* Salon. Retrieved from https://www.salon.com/2023/06/17/unfriending-america-the-christian-right-is-coming-for-the-enemies-of-god-like-you-and-me/

"There might be other places where the holding of the state supreme court would still apply or certainly portends future decisions in this direction," Cohen said.

Of course, Congress could do something to protect IVF treatments nationwide. Sen. Tammy Duckworth introduced a bill establishing a federal right to IVF treatments. Senate Republicans rejected it for a vote. In his State of the Union address, President Joe Biden called on representatives and senators to create federal protections for the procedure.

"It didn't go anywhere," Cohen said. "And I don't know whether it will go anywhere in the future. I think it will depend on whether there are Democrats who can make a case that there's a credible threat to IVF coming from another place now that Alabama has tried to tie the knot quickly on the issue."

A similar case appeared in the court system in Texas—a lawsuit pitting a wife against her husband. According to a news site, Live Action, Caroline Antoun sued her husband, Gaby Antoun, who has custody of the embryos, as part of their divorce agreement. Caroline wanted possession of the embryos. A lower court had ruled for her husband. The Texas Supreme Court is currently considering the case.

More than 7,500 IVF children are born each year in Texas.

Lawyers for the American Society for Reproductive Medicine (ASRM) filed an amicus brief arguing that such rights do not exist for embryos or fetuses. Many people don't understand how embryonic personhood, if established, would affect IVF availability and treatment. If unused, embryos would have to be stored indefinitely, which is so cost-prohibitive that it may make IVF an impossibility altogether.

"A frozen embryo is not a legal 'person' under a plain reading of Texas laws," the ASRM brief contends. "As such, parents' rights over the care and custody of their children do not apply to frozen embryos stored at a facility. Granting 'personhood' status to a frozen embryo would upend IVF treatment in the State of Texas."

IVF patients agree to certain conditions that address their wishes for the disposal or preservation of embryos. Those agreements protect IVF providers from litigation.

The courts aren't the only threat to IVF treatment in Texas. Recently, the state Republican party's platform committee narrowly rejected a proposal to establish embryonic personhood, according to the *Austin American-Statesman*. They referred to embryos as "snowflake babies."

The term has its roots in the George W. Bush "culture of life" era; government officials argued that the government should preserve embryos until they were donated for adoption. The Bush administration spent millions to promote the effort, according to an academic paper written by Jaime Conde that appeared in the *William & Mary Journal of Race, Gender, and Social Justice* in 2006.

It originated with the Snowflakes Frozen Embryo Adoption Program, run by Nightlight Christian Adoptions, an influential organization pushing for embryonic personhood in the early 2000s. The organization began in 1997 and, according to its current website, has been responsible for 1,300 IVF adoptions.

IVF adoption—also known as embryo adoption—is the practice of transferring cryopreserved embryos created through IVF to a woman who is not the embryos' genetic mother, so that she can carry the pregnancy to term. Supporters frame it as a life-affirming alternative to discarding, indefinitely freezing, or experimenting on embryos.

Nightlight Christian Adoptions says on its website that it counsels women against abortions. It lists adverse health side effects and says women can experience depression after abortion.

As these cases play out, we should expect more state governments to push for embryo adoption. We will also have to conduct studies about how commonplace embryo adoption is in proportion to how many embryos are stored medically. If it's only a minute amount, then the concerns about storage costs would still be of significant concern and a central point of argument against embryonic personhood.

With all the threats to reproductive care at the state political level, activists and observers have questioned what, if anything, the federal government can do to protect treatments and procedures like in vitro fertilization and abortion.

In general, the federal government has done "precious little," as Sean

Tipton, chief advocacy and policy officer at the American Society of Reproductive Medicine, has described it.

"One of the lessons from the Alabama decision is that these things can happen quickly," Tipton. "And while we were tracking that case, we did not expect the kind of decision that came down."

Federal legislators on both sides of the political aisle have suggested bills that would address some of the legal threats appearing at lower government levels. There are essential distinctions when comparing what Republicans have offered as solutions to those proposed by Democrats.

Texas Sen. Ted Cruz, facing a tough reelection campaign, sought to moderate his position on reproductive rights by publicly endorsing IVF and introducing a bill that would protect it. There are significant problems with it, though. If a state bans IVF, it will lose access to its Medicaid funding. That creates a situation that adds to the challenges women face in getting reproductive care. The ASRM opposed the bill.

"We certainly are not going to promote access to needed reproductive treatments on the backs of poor women," Tipton said. "We think that's a morally offensive choice."

Illinois Sen. Tammy Duckworth introduced a separate bill that took a different tack. In January 2024, she and others introduced the Right to Build Families Act, which would establish a statutory right to access IVF and other ART services, thereby pre-empting any state effort to limit such access and ensuring no hopeful parents—or their doctors—are punished for trying to start or grow a family. Republicans shot down that bill because they said it went beyond protecting IVF.

Later that year, Duckworth introduced a similar piece of legislation, the Access to Family Building Act, which would prevent an all-out ban or restrictions on IVF.

Anti-abortion activists and leaders proposed new medical approaches in response to these developments. A concept known as restorative reproductive medicine (RRM) has emerged as a policy framework promoted by anti-abortion organizations, one that deliberately sidelines IVF under the guise of offering less invasive, more natural approaches to fertility care. Groups like the Heritage Foundation and the Ethics and Public

Policy Center frame RRM as a cost-effective alternative that treats under-lying conditions such as polycystic ovary syndrome or endometriosis.

Yet reproductive specialists note that these conditions are already addressed within standard fertility treatment. The crucial difference is RRM's refusal to include IVF, which for many patients remains the only viable pathway to parenthood. By withholding this option, advocates argue, RRM effectively denies access to science-based care while quietly advancing an ideological agenda against IVF and abortion.

The political momentum behind RRM has intensified in recent years, coinciding with Donald Trump's return to the presidency. While Trump publicly promised to expand access to IVF, his administration dismantled reproductive health initiatives, froze grant funding, and allowed anti-abortion allies to promote fertility education centered on RRM. States such as Arkansas have already enacted measures declaring infertility not to be a disease, a stance aligned with insurance companies seeking to avoid coverage for IVF.

This legislative wave exposes the contradiction at the heart of the movement: IVF remains broadly popular with the public, yet it conflicts with the anti-abortion claim that life begins at conception. IVF's biolog-ical reality—that most fertilized eggs do not result in pregnancy—under-mines the premise that every embryo must be granted full legal rights.

The consequences for patients could be profound if RRM supplants IVF in policy and practice. Fertility seekers would spend years cycling through less effective treatments while advancing in age, reducing their chances of successful pregnancies by the time IVF was finally considered. The result, as reproductive medicine advocates stress, would be fewer families formed and more suffering for those struggling with infertility. Critics liken RRM's approach to that of crisis pregnancy centers, which withhold information to steer patients toward ideologically acceptable choices.

In this case, patients might believe they were receiving compre-hensive care without realizing that IVF—the most effective treatment available—was intentionally excluded. For groups like the American Society for Reproductive Medicine, the central fight is ensuring that evidence-based fertility care remains accessible, and that medical decisions rest with patients and physicians rather than political movements

Ballot Initiatives

Two paths have emerged to protect abortion access across the country since the *Dobbs* decision. In 26 states, voters can pass ballot initiatives to amend state constitutions.

In 2024, several states were able to get ballot initiatives before voters to enshrine abortion rights in state constitutions before voters. Among them were Florida, Arkansas, Ohio and Arizona. Groups like Ohio Physicians for Reproductive Rights and Arizonans for Reproductive Freedom were pivotal in accomplishing that.

Lauren Beene, co-founder of Ohio Physicians for Reproductive Rights, is a rising star in the abortion rights movement. I spoke to her about her memories of the successful campaign to pass it there. One of her starker memories was when they turned in the signatures needed for the ballot initiative. There was a giant U-Haul truck in which they packed the petitions that they dropped off at the secretary of state's office. News crews from national television stations were there to capture the moment. Beene remembers what she thought.

"This is the power of democracy right here," she said. "And I'm looking at it."

During the Ohio campaign, I drove into the state to accompany doctors who knocked on doors. Beene and others walked through a neighborhood in their medical coats and spoke with voters. It was indisputable that seeing doctors on their front steps affected those they talked to. One woman started crying when she walked to the door.

"That, to me, was really an incredible movement or moment where we made a connection with this person we would have never met before," Beene said.

Anti-abortion activists in Ohio sought to make it more difficult to pass a ballot initiative by trying to raise the threshold of support to 60% for voters to be able to change the state constitution. The amendment passed after that effort was defeated.

The most significant dispute currently in the abortion rights movement is whether to include viability clauses or limits, as their opponents call them, in ballot initiatives that would enshrine abortion rights in state constitutions. Viability was the basis for the *Roe V. Wade* decision. According to that decision, no state legislature could regulate abortion until after that point. Generally speaking, most doctors consider lung development around the 22nd week of pregnancy as the point of viability.

In Ohio, the recent success of its ballot initiative came with wording that regulation was permitted after the point of viability. Activists had sought to word the initiative in such a way as to return the state's abortion care to what it had been before the Supreme Court overturned *Roe.*

Opponents of viability clauses have pointed to the case of a woman in Ohio who was cleared by a grand jury of abusing a corpse after she left a nonviable fetus at home following a miscarriage. Reproductive rights activists criticized the prosecutor who convened the grand jury. It had implications for abortion rights because the judge who presided cited the ballot initiative's language during proceedings.

Activists in South Dakota said it would be virtually impossible to pass a ballot initiative there without that wording. One group called Dakotans for Health has pushed for the same legal framework governing abortion regulation even before the *Dobbs* decision. Most other groups that operate in the state have had their leaders say they didn't think the protections in either *Roe* or the ballot initiative went far enough. Rick Weiland, co-founder of Dakotans for Health, explained the tension between the pro-viability and anti-viability factions of the movement.

"There was this idea that you could go beyond *Roe,*" Weiland said of the reaction. "That *Roe* was always just the floor, that we could do better. Well, the first thing I say is you don't live and work in South Dakota. You don't have a clue of what it's going to take to get it done out here."

Groups like the South Dakota Justice Empowerment Network and Planned Parenthood South Dakota Advocate distanced themselves from the ballot initiative. Kim Floren, the empowerment network's cofounder, said many activists have problems with the amendment because it permits regulation in the second and third trimesters.

"If we're gonna throw our weight behind something and put all of our efforts into an amendment that's going to be in our constitution forever, it needs to be better than just *Roe*, which most reproductive justice organizations have recognized is not enough in the last ten years," Floren said.

As the activists approached the November election in South Dakota, opponents of the ballot initiative attempted to use the courts to prevent it from going before voters. The anti-abortion group Life Defense Fund said Dakotans for Health, the pro-choice group, had committed several wrongs in securing the signatures needed to get it up for a vote. A South Dakota judge ruled it could go forward. Anti-abortion plaintiffs in the case appealed to the state supreme court in a last-ditch effort to prevent the amendment from going before voters. The state supreme court reversed the lower court ruling. However, the ballot initiative still failed to pass.

Similar attempts to prevent ballot initiatives came in Arkansas and Montana.

Arkansas State Attorney General Tim Griffin approved the language for a proposed amendment in January 2024. They had to collect 90,000 signatures, with a certain percentage for at least 50 counties represented on their final tally. They managed to get more than 101,000 signatures.

The legal battle was over whether or not to count roughly 14,000 signatures collected by paid canvassers (rather than volunteers) and whether the leading abortion rights group in the state should have extended time to correct any issues with the signatures. Arkansas Secretary of State John Thurston wanted to disqualify the signatures gathered by the paid people. Arkansans for Limited Government, a pro-choice group, filed a brief for the pro-choice side.

It went before the Supreme Court, which disqualified the signatures collected by paid canvassers. The state supreme court ruled 4–3 against the pro-choice side. The decision didn't permit activists to correct the problems with the petition either. That was strange because when errors were detected with two other ballot initiatives involving marijuana and casinos, the people who had gathered the signatures were allowed to correct the problems pointed out by state authorities.

Now, Arkansas activists must wait until 2026 to try again for a ballot initiative, as stipulated by state law. Another aspect worth mentioning is the need for more support from national leaders. There had been an unwillingness on the part of national organizations like Planned Parenthood to endorse this initiative and to provide support for the effort because the wording, which allowed abortions up to the 18th week, wasn't robust enough in its protections. Rebecca Bobrow, Arkansans for Limited Government's spokeswoman, spoke to me about that aspect.

"I feel very strongly that 18 weeks is better than zero weeks," Bobrow said. "So I think, personally, in my opinion, the national organizations were wrong on this one, and this would have passed if it had made the ballot and made a really tangible difference in the lives of a lot of women in the state."

The legal shenanigans took place elsewhere. The Nebraska State Supreme Court ruled that two competing abortion ballot initiatives— one protecting and one limiting—could proceed after challenges to disqualify the pro-choice one came from a resident and a doctor.

The proposed pro-choice amendment states that all people shall have a fundamental right to abortion until fetal viability or when needed to protect the life or health of the pregnant patient, without interference from the state or its political subdivisions. Fetal viability means the point in pregnancy when, in the professional judgment of the patient's treating health care practitioner, there is a significant likelihood of the fetus's sustained survival outside the uterus without the application of extraordinary medical measures.

One of the relators—or someone who brought a complaint on someone else's behalf—in the lawsuit was Dr. Catherine Brooks, a neonatologist in Lincoln. She challenged the law under the belief that it violated the single subject requirement, which means that a proposed law has multiple aspects to vote on instead of one issue. Her lawyers also said the terms used in the ballot initiative were too vague and would mislead voters.

The other relator, an anti-abortion resident named Carolyn LaGreca, was a registered voter and resident of Douglas County. Her lawyers argued that the amendment would give virtually an unlimited right to abortion after viability, according to the ruling.

The court ruled against both by saying the amendment didn't violate the single-subject rule.

In a separate lawsuit, 29 current or retired physicians challenged the Protect Women and Children initiative, which sought to enshrine the 12-week abortion ban in the state constitution. The competing ballot initiative says, "Except when a woman seeks an abortion necessitated by a medical emergency or when the pregnancy results from sexual assault or incest, unborn children shall be protected from abortion in the second and third trimesters."

The doctors had argued that the initiatives should rise or fall together. Either both or neither should appear on the ballot. The state supreme court justices addressed that in their decision by saying they had effectively admitted that neither initiative violated the single-subject rule.

Montana activists spent 80 days collecting signatures, needing around 60,000, stipulating that they required 40% of the electorate in 40 of 100 House districts. They amassed 117,000 signatures in support of CI-128, the name for the initiative, which is the most ever collected for a ballot initiative in Montana history.

But it wasn't without difficulty. Montana Secretary of State Christi Jacobsen had sought to reduce the time activists had to collect signatures. Later, in July, there was a court battle when Jacobsen attempted to disqualify inactive voters, including registered voters who had moved to different addresses, from signing. During a scheduled district court hearing, Montanans Securing Reproductive Rights and Montanans for Election Reform successfully defended the rights of Montana voters. They obtained a court order to ensure all signatures from registered voters—including those previously erroneously removed for being "inactive"—were counted.

Ashley All, spokesperson for Montanans Securing Reproductive Rights, discussed their training of volunteers and the hurdles they faced as they pushed for the amendment's passage.

"It was a lot of work and a lot of challenges that were thrown in our way," All said. "But ultimately, we were able to make the ballot and successfully win in quite a dramatic fashion on election day in November."

Akilah Deernose, executive director of the ACLU in Montana, said all that was unjust.

"We had so many unnecessary legal battles that we've never seen for any other group that was trying to get a ballot initiative onto the ballot," Deernose said. "And so the day-to-day was like, 'Let's see what attacks are going to come, and figure out how we fight back against them.'"

Activists heard heartfelt stories from women about needing care when their health had been threatened. They heard about the back alley. One of the more memorable things for Kiersten Iwai, executive director of Forward Montana, was counting the signatures for Montana's smaller counties, whose populations were only in the hundreds.

"Here we are about to do this thing and turn in all these signatures, but that also we truly were able to connect with voters and collect signatures from every corner of the state and some of the most unexpected or surprising places," Iwai said. "That was a huge highlight for me."

In Florida, there was brazen voter intimidation. Florida Gov. Ron DeSantis called on police to interrogate voters who signed a petition for an abortion rights ballot initiative. Several news outlets reported that DeSantis intended to send a special contingent of officers to thousands of voters' homes before the election.

In April 2024, Florida's state supreme court ruled that the ballot initiative could go before voters. Known as Amendment 4, it stated that no law should prohibit or restrict abortion before viability or when necessary to protect the mother's health. The amendment specifically laid out that it did not address parental notification.

The recent tactic had its seed planted years ago when the state legislature passed a bill that gave the governor broad discretionary power to oversee campaigns. The Office of Election Crimes and Security was established in 2022 after the wave of accusations by former President Donald Trump about how he was cheated out of a victory in his 2020 campaign. The unit investigates election fraud allegations.

Another aspect of DeSantis' effort was the use of a government-funded website for the Agency for Health Care Administration to spread disinformation about the ballot initiative. It characterized abortion rights activists as "fear-mongers."

"We must keep Florida from becoming an abortion tourism destination," the website said.

Ultimately, Florida's ballot initiative failed to meet the required 60% threshold.

In the 24 states that don't allow for ballot initiatives, the other approach is challenge abortion bans before state supreme courts. This strategy originated out of Alaska, which provided legal protections for abortion in the 1990s that went beyond what *Roe* gave. It based the right to abortion access on the right to privacy guaranteed in the state constitution. In South Carolina, this strategy worked. Wisconsin activists also employed this method. Much of this success depends on how state supreme court justices are selected. If it's up to voters, then judges may be able to campaign by promising to protect abortion access. In other states, the governor or legislature appoints justices.

Arizona's legislature recently had two bans in effect. Its state supreme court upheld an 1864 Civil War-era ban that restricted most abortions. A 15-week ban was also in place. Rep. Stephanie Stahl Hamilton led the effort to repeal the 1864 law.

Throughout six legislative sessions, the senators and representatives in Arizona's government had been deliberating a repeal, a journey that began in 2019. Rep. Athena Salman, who championed the cause until her resignation in 2024, spearheaded the effort. At her departure, she entrusted the responsibility of continuing the fight to Hamilton, who took up the mantle and carried the torch forward.

The repeal was one of Gov. Katie Hobbs' primary objectives for this session. Hamilton dropped three pieces of legislation about it in the hopper, one of the first processes in getting a bill passed.

The legislative process in Arizona requires a multi-step journey for a bill to become law. It begins with developing the bill's language and lawmakers securing sponsors. The bill is then placed in the hopper, and a unique bill number is assigned. It undergoes a first read on the floor, followed by a second read on a consecutive day. The bill then proceeds to a committee for in-depth study and discussion.

Once it gets heard, then it goes to the rules committee, after which it goes to each caucus in the legislature. Then, it goes to the committee, and it's debated on the floor. Along the process, the bill could be amended. It receives a third read. After that, it then goes to the Senate, where the process repeats itself. It comes back to the House for a final read. Once the Senate's changes are accepted, the bill goes to the governor's desk for signature or veto.

"Any point in that process can get interrupted," Hamilton said. "So anything that absolutely lands on the governor's desk and then gets a signature is nothing short of a pretty incredible feat, to be quite honest."

The state supreme court's decision to uphold the ban was a galvanizing factor. The decision in Alabama to establish embryonic personhood also motivated the members of the Arizona legislature.

"A lot of this stuff has been brewing and churning," Hamilton said.

They knew they would need and would get support from the Republicans in the legislature too.

"It's just a matter of figuring out who's going to fall on the sword for the Republicans and who is going to end up having to take the heat from their party," Hamilton said. But the politics of it all is that there were some districts where my Republican colleagues needed to vote yes on that repeal, no matter what they needed to vote."

The repeal effort succeeded. The victory is significant because it shows repeal is possible, and it has to be in some states where ballot initiatives aren't feasible. In 24 states, that's the case. So, the only recourse is to flip the state legislature and then repeal whatever bans or limits they have in place about abortion.

Arizona's abortion rights community didn't stop there, though. Amy Fitch-Heacock was one of the major leaders in two ballot initiative efforts. Activists had sought unsuccessfully immediately after the *Dobbs* decision to get a ballot initiative but fell short because of time constraints and looming deadlines.

They began another campaign in 2023—starting with polls and focus groups to determine the wording of the amendment. By September, they had the amendment written and then began the signature-gathering phase. They filed 823,685 signatures, though they only needed less than 384,000. Arizona certified those signatures in August 2024.

Fitch-Heacock remembers some heart-wrenching stories that strengthened her resolve to push for abortion law reform. One soldier living on a base messaged her online and told Fitch-Heacock that his wife needed an abortion after a fetal anomaly that would have caused death. She gave him resources on where to get an abortion out of state.

Fitch-Heacock also remembered a case in which a 10-year-old girl was impregnated by her father and couldn't get permission from her parents to get an abortion.

But it wasn't just saddening stories; it was also ones that uplifted people by finding common causes. One woman was reluctant to sign the petition for the initiative while with her church group, but they later met her at her house, and she signed it. The woman pointed out the pro-choice homes in the area, including the ones belonging to Republicans, and canvassers gathered more signatures that way.

"Those are three really poignant stories that really have sat heavy with me but also have given me the hope to continue to do this work," Fitch-Heacock said.

One of the things people need to realize about the abortion rights movement is that it's pluralistic. Many leaders and activists don't agree. That's where politicians come in. Fitch-Heacock said Arizona Gov. Katie Hobbs played that role.

"She was instrumental in sort of creating a bridge between repro groups," Fitch-Heacock said. "We didn't all see eye to eye, and really nationwide, we don't. We are all very different in terms of the work that we do. But she was instrumental in creating a bridge for us and putting resources into this."

The measure passed with nearly 62% of voters supporting it.

Missouri had an almost complete abortion ban that prevented the procedure from occurring after six weeks, with no rape or incest exceptions. In certain situations, abortion was permissible if a mother's life was in what was characterized as "immediate" danger—but not for "potential" danger, a fine line that created a precarious atmosphere for medical professionals.

Missouri women had different experiences depending on the part of the state they lived in. If they were close to the Illinois border, there were many clinics that organizations like Planned Parenthood had set up to be close to them. However, in the western part of the state, the situation was more complicated. Nearby states like Tennessee and Oklahoma don't allow abortions. In Kansas, abortion was legal up to 22 weeks after a woman's last period. Nebraska, as previously mentioned, was considering a ballot initiative itself.

In September 2024, more than 800 Missouri doctors signed a letter supporting the passage of an amendment that would protect abortion up to viability. They emphasized the need to have abortions available for life-threatening circumstances:

As a result, Missourians are being denied abortions and forced to continue life-threatening pregnancies, risking their health and lives. Doctors can't treat patients with heartbreaking pregnancy complications until they are on the brink of death. Otherwise, they could be put in jail.

This leaves pregnant patients with few options. It forces many to leave the state to receive care, while others are forced to carry a pregnancy against their will. No one should ever have their health deteriorate or need to flee to receive care, nor should anyone have to carry a pregnancy against their will.

The effort wasn't without legal hurdles either. In March, Missouri Attorney General Andrew Bailey sought to make it seem that the initiative would cost more than expected and said he wouldn't sign the fiscal note permitting it to appear on the ballot. The state supreme court rejected that argument in July. In September, Missouri Secretary of State Jay Ashcroft decertified the ballot initiative, claiming the language wasn't clear on what law it was repealing. The state supreme court overruled him.

One of the key activists in the Missouri campaign was Karen Francis, president of Women's Voices Raised, a reproductive justice organization in the state. She had a unique vantage point in that she was involved in the abortion rights movement even before *Roe v. Wade* was decided. All of those years of activism helped her lead a successful effort. Francis spoke to me about her memories of the campaign.

They collected more than 400,000 signatures in three months to get the amendment before voters. They held training sessions on Zoom for petitioners and people canvassing for support. Thousands of people went out throughout communities to do it. Missouri has eight congressional districts, and they had to get a certain number of signatures from each district.

Television and social media ads also played a key role. Many of them featured heart-wrenching stories of women who needed to get abortions after doctors detected a fetal anomaly. Another aspect that worked was drive-through signature locations, where they had notaries stationed to approve the signed documents voters submitted to support the petition.

"People were going down the road honking their horns in support," Francis said.

The efforts paid off. In November 2024, Missouri passed a ballot initiative that protected abortion rights up until the point of fetal viability in the state constitution.

How Will the Amendments be Interpreted?

Anti-abortion officeholders want the recently passed constitutional amendments protecting abortion rights to be interpreted as narrowly as possible when it's time to review the existing abortion laws under the new protections.

Conservative attorneys general and legal scholars have pointed to how abortion was adjudicated at the federal level when *Roe* was the law of the land. Even then, when it was guaranteed as a right, the Supreme Court upheld restrictions and regulations that limited abortion rights and made it so expensive to operate that clinics went out of business. Why can't state judges take the same approach now? That's their rhetorical question.

As such, state supreme court races are of vital importance to how extensive the protections will become. The next few years will see one courtroom battle after another as state judges interpret constitutional amendments to review whether existing bans and regulations violate them. Penn State professor Michael Nelson, co-author of *Judging Inequality: State Supreme Courts and the Inequality Crisis*, spoke to me about the nature of abortion litigation going forward.

"This is where all the action is, right now," he said. "The U.S. Supreme Court is going to be involved a little bit, but all of the action in terms of abortion access is really in these state races. And they really don't get the attention that they deserve."

The political makeup and sensibilities of the courts matter. So does how the judges come to fill those seats. In some states, governors and legislatures can appoint judges for a specific term, such as four or eight years. They may serve until age 70 in states with an age limit. Other states may use the Missouri Plan, a merit system in which a committee of lawyers or experts convenes to recommend judges to a governor, who then appoints one of the people from the list. Judges can also be selected through an election by popular vote, with some states listing the party affiliation and others not.

Each method has a benefit, but the judicial selection method means that candidates or officials respond to different political pressures. If a politician fills those seats, judges will react to what the politician wants. If it's done through popular vote, public opinion will matter the most, Nelson said. While courts may advance abortion rights because of constitutional amendments specifically addressing it, they may also find that abortion rights are protected under other aspects of its state constitution, including the right to privacy. The *Roe v. Wade* decision had been based on that right. The actual U.S. Constitution doesn't mention abortion specifically. Supreme Court justices interpreted *Roe* based on the *Griswold* decision establishing privacy as a fundamental right.

The cost of elections could continue to rise as these judicial seats play a more significant role in determining how expansive abortion rights are across the country.

"The races might become more expensive because abortion makes more people see the value of their state supreme court," Nelson said.

"And therefore, there's more attention to those races, which attracts more money."

Federal Politics

At the 2024 Democratic National Convention, Kamala Harris accepted the nomination after a controversial process that saw her secure it without winning a primary contest. Throughout the week leading up to the convention, feminist groups held events throughout Chicago to discuss abortion rights.

Abortion politics had shifted how Democratic candidates pursued power in the general election, as well as primary contests. Before, they had sought to get through the Democratic primary, convincing feminist leaders they would advance their cause, only to have the candidate downplay the issue in the general election because political operatives advised them it would lose votes. However, with the success of the recent ballot initiatives, candidates were eager to endear themselves with the groups that suddenly had the most significant sway in the party.

The Feminist Majority Foundation held an event that featured appearances by Nancy Pelosi, former U.S. Sen. Carol Moseley Braun and U.S. Rep. Ayanna Pressley. Though the rally had more to do with a new effort to pass the Equal Rights Amendment, abortion was a major topic of discussion for the 300 people who attended.

A day later, the women's caucus was held. I spoke with its chairwoman, Lois Frankel, whom I spoke to about the Comstock Act, which Democrats in Congress had sought to repeal after it became apparent that it was a central part of the anti-abortion movement's plan to limit abortion medication. She told me what it was like dealing with Republicans in Congress.

"When you talk about reproductive freedom, it's like you're talking to settlers from another planet," Frankel said. "I mean, it is just cold."

She remembered a meeting, at one point in the last few years, in which the pro-choice caucus was about to meet. A conservative Georgia congressman saw her in the hallway and conversed. When she told him the meeting was about abortion, he lectured her about reading the Bible.

"It went downhill from there," Frankel said.

At a DNC event held by All In Together, a nonprofit focused on advocating for young women politically, three executives—New York Gov. Hochul, New Mexico Gov. Michelle Lujan Grisham and Kansas Gov. Laura Kelly—spoke about the collaboration liberal states have had in protecting abortion rights.

They didn't focus on the flip side of that—the tension that exists between powerful leaders in pro-choice states versus those in control of anti-abortion ones. What types of things will Democratic governors and attorney generals do to thwart politicians like Alabama Attorney General Marshall, who wants to treat abortion funds as accessories to the crime of violating the state's ban on the procedure?

Those funds are used to pay for abortions out of state, which means that Marshall considers it a violation of the law based on the person's residency instead of the jurisdiction where the incident occurred. There's no precedent for that in American legal history.

NOW held a mixer too. One of the more interesting people I met there was Anji Gandhi, an assistant prosecutor from Jefferson City, Missouri. One of the amicus briefs filed in *Moyle v. United States* dealt with how the abortion bans had complicated the jobs of district attorneys and their staff.

Gandhi told me another aspect of criminal justice that hadn't been mentioned in that filing. When a woman needs an abortion after rape, the fetus becomes evidence against the accused person. Before *Dobbs*, that was a lot easier to do. Now, if the woman goes to another state to get an abortion, prosecutors from Missouri have a more challenging time getting the evidence they need because it's not within their jurisdiction.

Outside the United Center, where the speeches were held, anti-abortion protestors held signs comparing abortion to murder and saying gay sex was evil.

At the convention, former Planned Parenthood president Cecile Richards and current President Alexis McGill Johnson implored the attendees to support abortion rights. Richards mentioned a 13-year-old rape victim in Mississippi who was forced to carry on a pregnancy.

Johnson spoke about a Georgia woman who drove through the South, repeatedly being denied an abortion, until she flew to California to get the care she needed.

"We cannot call ourselves a free nation when women are not free," Johnson said.

Of the remaining people who took the stage, Oprah Winfrey's speech most directly addressed abortion rights.

"The women and men who don't want us going back to a time of desperation, shame and stone-cold fear, they are the new freedom fighters, and make no mistake, they are the best of America," Winfrey said.

The convention's final night featured Harris, who had toured the country as part of a campaign effort to get Joe Biden re-elected before he dropped out of the race following a bad debate performance in which he seemed incoherent.

In her speech, Harris emphasized reproductive rights, which capped off her acceptance of the Democratic nomination:

> *Many women are not able to make those decisions. And let's be clear about how we got here. Donald Trump handpicked members of the United States Supreme Court to take away reproductive freedom, and now he brags about it in his words, "I did it, and I'm proud to have done it."*
>
> *Well, I'll tell you, over the past two years, I've traveled across our country, and women have told me their stories. Husbands and fathers have shared their stories of women miscarrying in a parking lot, developing sepsis, losing the ability to ever again have children, all because doctors are afraid they may go to jail for caring for their patients. Couples just trying to grow their family cut off in the middle of IVF treatment. Children who have survived sexual assault potentially being forced to carry a pregnancy to term.*
>
> *This is what's happening in our country because of Donald Trump. And understand he is not done. As a part of his agenda, he and his allies will limit access to birth control, ban medication abortion, and enact a nationwide abortion ban, with or without Congress. And get this. He*

plans to create a national anti-abortion coordinator and force states to report on women's miscarriages and abortions. Simply put, they are out of their minds.

She continued after the audience jeered:

They don't trust women. Well, we trust women, and when Congress passes a bill to restore reproductive freedom, as president of the United States, I will proudly sign it into law.

One of the biggest problems with the convention was the absence of the grassroots activists who had played a part in getting the ballot initiative passed in Ohio. None of the organizers from Florida, South Dakota, Missouri, Arkansas or any other states were represented as speakers or presenters at the arena or related events.

Here the party was emphasizing its championing of reproductive rights, and yet none of the people on the front lines were there. Several women who had been hurt by abortion bans were present. These grassroots activists were potential leaders of the party down the road. While speaking about passing the torch, the Democrats hadn't included the idealistic young people fighting for reproductive justice.

Men and women who had been in the movement for a long time listened to that and wondered why the party hadn't done that before *Roe* had fallen. For the two years following its demise, countless journalists sought to diagnose why the movement sputtered. The primary reason was the Democratic Party's reluctance to embrace the issue fully.

They had sought to downplay it and hadn't fought for difficult progress, like eliminating parental consent laws and the Hyde Amendment. Yet, they now realized that it was a winning issue. So there was a sense that much of this was expedient and done in the interest of political careers instead of out of sincerity.

For the remaining months that passed between the convention and the election, Donald Trump avoided discussing abortion altogether. When asked by anti-abortion leaders about what he would do, he told them that he had been the one responsible for *Roe*'s overturning, but that he couldn't emphasize an abortion ban because Republicans had to win elections. It was a sign of shifting strategy among Republicans. Some within the party wanted to push for a national ban but characterized it instead as an agreed-upon "standard," a misleading term that tested better in polling and merely meant that they would restrict abortions past a certain point.

The election was a mixed success for the abortion rights movement. As had been described earlier, they had victories in Arizona, Montana and Missouri. They lost in Florida by a small margin, needing 60% but bringing in 57% of the vote. Nebraska narrowly passed an abortion ban.

But the biggest news was that Trump, despite a year in which he was in federal and state court and was convicted of a felony, won the presidency in a contest that wasn't even close electorally, though it was tighter in the popular vote. It was an indication of another failure of the Democratic Party to assess what the American public wanted, which was a Democratic primary to select a candidate of its own choosing.

Immediately upon assuming office, Trump pardoned 23 people who had violated the FACE Act. It was part of a movement within the Trump administration and Justice Department to downplay the significance of the law that had been passed during the Clinton administration to deter violence and harassment of women and abortion workers. The Associated Press reported that they would only prosecute people who violated the law in "extraordinary circumstances."

Many of those pardoned were serving prison sentences for physically blocking patients from accessing their doctors. Some of the offenses committed include breaking into clinics, stealing fetal tissue and accosting pregnant patients. Six of the people pardoned had blocked patients from entering a Michigan health care clinic that the Center for Reproductive Rights represents, according to the Center for Reproductive Rights.

Trump also issued an executive order to enforce the Hyde Amendment's ban on using federal taxpayer money on abortion. Trump's executive order read:

For nearly five decades, the Congress has annually enacted the Hyde Amendment and similar laws that prevent Federal funding of elective abortion, reflecting a longstanding consensus that American taxpayers should not be forced to pay for that practice. However, the previous administration disregarded this established, commonsense policy by embedding forced taxpayer funding of elective abortions in a wide variety of Federal programs.

It is the policy of the United States, consistent with the Hyde Amendment, to end the forced use of Federal taxpayer dollars to fund or promote elective abortion.

Trump also revoked two executive orders issued by President Joe Biden. One was Executive Order 14076, titled Protecting Access to Reproductive Health Services. It had directed the Department of Health and Human Services to expand access to contraceptives, requested that the Federal Trade Commission protect patients' reproductive health privacy, and directed the Department of Justice to organize a group of pro bono lawyers to defend women charged with having an abortion.

Another order he rescinded was Executive Order 14079, known as Securing Access to Reproductive and Other Healthcare Services. That had allowed Medicaid to pay for abortions in situations where a woman traveled to a state where the state had opted to submit its own money to pay for poor people's reproductive care.

Trump recorded a video that was broadcast at the annual March for Life, a few days after his inauguration. He said that his Justice Department would investigate attacks on churches and crisis pregnancy centers, again conflating the infrequency with which that occurred with the constant attacks on abortion clinics.

"Never again will religious persecution be allowed to happen in America," Trump said.

As this happened, the pro-choice movement mourned the death of Cecile Richards, who had died the day before Trump was sworn in after a battle with incurable brain cancer. She had been the most influential woman in the reproductive rights movement, both during her time as

Planned Parenthood's president and after she left that position. Many described her as a four-star general with how involved she was in the movement's direction. Within the movement, the loss of its ostensible figurehead forced many to ponder what was next and who would be given the prevailing influence.

Pill Bills

In August, a debate began in the Texas Senate with Senate Bill 6, formally titled the Texas Women and Child Protection Act. Introduced in a special session, the measure was pitched as a bold new strategy to stop abortion pills from being mailed into the state. Lawmakers argued that while clinics had closed under earlier bans, tens of thousands of pills still entered Texas each year. SB 6 would let private citizens sue out-of-state manufacturers and distributors, extending the civil enforcement model pioneered by the Heartbeat Act. Supporters presented it as both the strongest abortion pill law in the country and a test case for how far Texas could go in the post-*Dobbs* era.

The Senate hearing quickly revealed the divide. Anti-abortion advocates said pills endangered women's health and enabled abusers, urging new civil tools to punish traffickers. Critics countered that the act blurred critical medical lines, targeting drugs also used for miscarriage care and treatment of hemorrhage. Doctors warned that liability fears could worsen Texas's already high maternal mortality rate. Despite those concerns, the Senate advanced the bill swiftly, with little sign of hesitation.

The measure resurfaced in the House as HB 7, still carrying the Women and Child Protection Act title. Rep. Jeff Leach called it the "strongest bill in the nation" against abortion pills, stressing that women themselves would not face penalties. Yet questions mounted. Could a Texan order pills just to trigger a lawsuit? Why did the text override "any other law" more than a dozen times? And why were defendants barred from recouping legal fees even if they prevailed? For critics, the bill looked less like careful lawmaking than a weapon of intimidation.

Public testimony in the House amplified these tensions. Supporters of the bill insisted pills were unsafe and unregulated, while opponents told wrenching stories of delayed miscarriage care, pregnancies turned life-threatening and pharmacies refusing prescriptions. Faith leaders warned that exempting abortion from the state's Religious Freedom Restoration Act set a dangerous precedent. Medical groups said the act would undercut protections established in the Life of the Mother Act, passed earlier the same year. The conflicting accounts highlighted the bill's core contradiction: A law touted as protecting women could in practice deprive them of life-saving care.

By the close of both hearings, the outlines of the strategy were clear. The Senate had already moved SB 6 forward, and Leach promised revisions to HB 7 before a floor vote. But the essence of the Texas Women and Child Protection Act remained: a sweeping attempt to police abortion pills beyond Texas' borders through private lawsuits.

To anti-abortion advocates, it was the next frontier of their movement; to opponents, it was unconstitutional overreach. In its path through both chambers, the act crystallized Texas' determination to push abortion enforcement into new, untested territory—no matter the risks for women or doctors caught in the crossfire.

Texas' role in shaping abortion law in the post-*Roe* era cannot be understood without considering the quiet but transformative influence of Jonathan F. Mitchell. Unlike the loud voices of street protestors or elected officials, Mitchell has operated from the shadows of academia, state government and private litigation, devising strategies that have redefined how states could regulate abortion.

His tenure as Texas solicitor general from 2010–2015 introduced him to the political and legal networks that would later sponsor his most audacious innovations. But it was after he left public office that his full impact on abortion law emerged: Mitchell became the architect of a new model for restricting reproductive rights by exploiting procedural loopholes and resurrecting long-dormant statutes.

The turning point was Senate Bill 8, the Texas Heartbeat Act of 2021. Traditional abortion bans were routinely blocked in federal courts before they took effect. Mitchell engineered a workaround: outsourcing enforcement to private citizens who could sue providers and anyone aiding an abortion. This design effectively insulated the state from pre-enforcement lawsuits and forced abortion opponents into a new posture of private vigilance.

The Supreme Court's refusal to block SB 8 on Sept. 1, 2021, allowed the law to take immediate effect while *Roe v. Wade* was still formally the law of the land. For almost a year, abortion after six weeks was virtually eliminated in Texas, not by a direct legislative repeal of *Roe* but by Mitchell's procedural ingenuity. To supporters, he had cracked the code on how to sidestep federal courts; to critics, he had shown how constitutional rights could be nullified without a single legislator casting a vote to ban abortion outright.

Mitchell's ambitions, however, extended beyond Texas. He began to promote the revival of the Comstock Act, the 1873 federal anti-vice law that bans mailing abortion drugs and instruments. By inserting Comstock provisions into local "sanctuary city for the unborn" ordinances and citing it in wrongful-death lawsuits against abortion pill providers, Mitchell sought to position the statute as a de facto national abortion ban.

His strategy was clear: provoke litigation that could eventually bring Comstock before the Supreme Court, forcing the justices to decide whether a 150-year-old law could close down abortion access nationwide. To Mitchell, this was proof that sweeping new legislation was unnecessary; the tools for prohibition were already hiding in the U.S. Code.

In this way, Texas became both a laboratory and launching pad. Mitchell's theories provided the blueprint for a wave of copycat measures in other states, and his litigation tactics were eagerly adopted by anti-abortion groups nationwide. He filed briefs urging the Court not only to overrule *Roe v. Wade* in *Dobbs v. Jackson Women's Health Organization* but also to question the legitimacy of other privacy-related precedents, from contraception to same-sex marriage. For legislators and activists, Mitchell became the indispensable strategist, the man who showed how to transform ideological opposition to abortion into enforceable law. Texas may have supplied the political will, but Jonathan Mitchell supplied the legal brain.

If Mitchell supplied the legal brain behind Texas' abortion restrictions, the resistance was carried by a coalition of providers, advocates and lawyers scrambling to counter his procedural maneuvers. Organizations like Planned Parenthood of Greater Texas, the Center for Reproductive Rights and the ACLU immediately recognized SB 8 not only as a direct attack on abortion rights but as a precedent-shattering legal model. Their first move was to challenge the law in *Whole Woman's Health v. Jackson*, but the Supreme Court's refusal to enjoin it showed how effectively Mitchell had insulated the statute from judicial review.

Critics of SB 8 argued that Mitchell had designed a blueprint for nullifying constitutional rights—one that could be copied to undermine not just abortion, but gun rights, free speech or any constitutional protection disfavored by a state legislature. Justice Sonia Sotomayor, dissenting in *Jackson*, warned that the law's "breathtaking act of defiance" of precedent would not end with abortion alone. For abortion providers in Texas, this meant immediate peril: Lawsuits threatened not only physicians but nurses, staff and even drivers who might transport patients to clinics.

The opposition also focused on public messaging. Alexis McGill Johnson pointed to Mitchell's filings in *Dobbs*—in which he argued that women could "control their reproductive lives" by abstaining from sex—as proof of the cruelty at the core of his vision. For advocates, this bluntness clarified the stakes: Mitchell was not only dismantling abortion access through procedural law, he was advancing a worldview that rejected modern understandings of gender equality and privacy.

Litigators quickly pivoted to defensive innovation. If Mitchell revived the Comstock Act, his opponents moved to delegitimize it, lobbying Congress to pass the Stop Comstock Act and framing the law as a relic of Victorian censorship. They also argued in federal court that mailing abortion medication remained lawful under FDA authority, directly countering Mitchell's wrongful-death suits and municipal Comstock ordinances. This strategy aimed to prevent Comstock from reaching the Supreme Court on Mitchell's terms.

Clinics, meanwhile, adapted on the ground. Networks of abortion funds sprang up to shuttle patients across state lines, openly defying the chilling effect of SB 8's bounty system. Their leaders—often young women of color—described Mitchell's scheme as a reminder that the fight over reproductive rights was as much about democratic account-ability as about procedure. "If they can take away abortion this way," one advocate said, "they can do it to anything."

Ultimately, Texas became a battleground of asymmetry: Mitchell and his allies advancing lawsuits and ordinances with surgical precision while abortion rights advocates raced to block, blunt or out-organize him. Each move by Mitchell's camp forced an improvisational counter-move by the opposition. And while *Dobbs* in 2022 formally ended the federal constitutional right to abortion, the fight in Texas crystallized the larger lesson: the future of abortion law would not be decided only by elected officials or Supreme Court rulings, but in the skirmishes between creative legal entrepreneurs like Jonathan Mitchell and the equally determined advocates resisting them.

Mitchell has been involved in all the legislative efforts in Texas since then, including the Women and Child Protection Act. Amy Bresnen describes Mitchell as the central figure driving Texas' increasingly aggres-sive abortion restrictions. While lawmakers like Jeff Leach and activists such as Mark Lee Dickson have received public attention, Amy Bresnen argues that they were secondary players compared to Mitchell.

In her view, Mitchell has planted himself deeply in the state gov-ernment of Texas despite living in Washington State, using Texas as the proving ground for legal strategies that could reverberate nationwide. She emphasizes that nobody else is producing such novel approaches with the potential to reshape abortion law across the country.

"You cannot mention abortion without Jonathan Mitchell any lon-ger," she said, framing him as the legal architect behind Texas'—and potentially the nation's—new reproductive regime.

The latest Texas legislation marks a new turn in the use of civil enforcement against abortion. Earlier measures like SB 8 already dep-utized private citizens to sue providers, but the new bill goes further by building a financial incentive system that critics warn transforms enforce-ment into a fundraising tool. It creates two tracks: one for family mem-bers of a pregnant person and another for outsiders.

The family track allows relatives to sue and claim damages. The second, described to me by Amy Bresnen as a "grifter track," lets third parties with no personal connection to the pregnancy sue. In that scenario, the plaintiff receives only a small share of damages, while the majority flows to a nonprofit organization tied to the anti-abortion movement. This structure effectively institutionalizes profit-driven litigation.

Crisis pregnancy centers—already heavily funded by the state—stand to gain the most from this system. These centers often present themselves as medical facilities while discouraging abortion, and the bill now places them at the center of enforcement. A pregnant woman might visit for a free sonogram, mention having ordered abortion pills, and unknowingly trigger a lawsuit. The center could link her disclosure to a plaintiff, generating damages that return to anti-abortion organizations. In this way, ordinary health decisions become opportunities for litigation, and CPCs function less as care providers than as surveillance and enforcement hubs.

Equally troubling are the bill's gaps in oversight. It does not specify how nonprofit recipients must use recovered funds, leaving open the possibility that state-enforced damages could flow into lobbying or campaign activity. Common carriers like postal services and delivery companies are left vulnerable under a vague negligence standard, despite having no way to monitor the contents of packages.

While the bill gestures toward privacy protections, it includes no meaningful penalties for violations. Taken together, these provisions encourage frivolous lawsuits and political profiteering, while offering little accountability. Far from a carefully designed enforcement tool, the legislation creates a system that monetizes private behavior and destabilizes the legal framework it seeks to strengthen.

The debates in the House chamber revealed sharp divisions. Republican leaders celebrated the bill as compassionate and consistent with a moral duty to defend unborn life, while some of their colleagues on the party's right flank argued that it did not go far enough, preferring total abolition. Democrats countered with warnings about the dangers of unsafe abortions, the chilling effect on medical practice, and the constitutional flaws of outsourcing law enforcement to private individuals.

They argued that HB 7 would empower abusers, destabilize the courts and return women to the precarious conditions of the pre-*Roe* era.

During the hearing, Texas Democratic Rep. Donna Howard lambasted the bill as a "big brother, nanny state, Wild Wild West piece of shit" when speaking at the podium. She directed her fire not only at the bill but at Mitchell himself. She argued that the measure was less about protecting women than about advancing Mitchell's agenda, calling it a recycled bounty-hunter scheme designed to bypass the courts.

In her view, HB 7 offered a $100,000 slush fund for Mitchell's allies while shredding constitutional protections and encouraging entrapment suits. Howard reminded colleagues that during her early years in the Legislature, bipartisanship was possible on issues of public concern, but she believed measures like HB 7 reflected a new hyper-partisan strategy. To her, the bill was not a compassionate policy but a dangerous departure from both constitutional norms and the lived reality of women's health.[114]

By the time the legislature advanced HB 7 at the end of August, Texas had once again positioned itself at the forefront of abortion politics. Just as the state's earlier "heartbeat" law had reshaped national debate, this new statute signaled that medication abortion—the most common method in the United States—would be the next frontier.

The measure reflected not only the priorities of Texas lawmakers but also the broader strategy of testing legal boundaries in hopes of setting precedents for the nation. With HB 7, the Legislature demonstrated its willingness to expand enforcement powers beyond the state itself, embedding citizen lawsuits into the machinery of reproductive governance in the post-*Dobbs* era.

In the Texas Senate chamber, the deliberation over HB 7 unfolded as a stark clash between two visions of the state's role in reproductive health. Democratic senators warned that the measure's private enforcement provisions would expand the culture of suspicion already seeded by earlier laws, effectively turning neighbors and delivery drivers into informants. Sen. Carol Alvarado described the bill as "surveillance, not

---

114 Texas House of Representatives. (2025, August 27). Hearing on House Bill 7: *Texas Woman and Child Protection Act* [Legislative hearing]. *USLege.* https://app.uslege.ai/share/c4c4c2ea-1e47-45ab-840e-5b606cb8ae30

safety," invoking cases like Shelley Hall's, where miscarriage care was delayed after her prescription was flagged. Her warning framed the bill not merely as policy, but as a direct intrusion into the most private medical circumstances of women across Texas.

Sen. Nathan Johnson deepened the critique, recasting the legislation as a constitutional affront rather than a localized skirmish. He insisted that HB 7 trampled over the commerce clause and due process protections while tying its origins to Mitchell. Johnson's attack was personal as well as legal: He accused Mitchell of manipulating Texans as pawns in a broader ideological campaign. To Johnson and his allies, the bill represented not just an expansion of abortion restrictions, but a deliberate attempt to test the outer limits of state power in defiance of federal principles.

Republican backers, led by Sen. Bryan Hughes, countered with language steeped in moral urgency. Hughes rejected the charge that HB 7 sought to punish women, instead framing the law as a shield for both mothers and their unborn children. He read from testimony alleging the dangers of medication abortion, highlighting instances where pills were administered without consent, and argued the law was necessary to prevent further harm. "We can love and protect them both," Hughes concluded, casting the legislation as a balance of compassion and accountability. That framing, however, did little to soften the partisan split: The Senate advanced HB 7 over Democratic protest, setting the stage for Gov. Greg Abbott's signature and inevitable courtroom battles.

The legal battles commenced almost immediately. Marine Captain Christopher Cooprider was, by most accounts, an unlikely figure to find himself at the center of a political storm. A decorated aviator in training, he lived quietly in Corpus Christi until his neighbor, Liana Davis, accused him of surreptitiously slipping abortion pills into her hot chocolate while she was eight weeks pregnant.

In a 33-page wrongful-death complaint filed in federal court on Aug. 11, 2025, Davis alleged that the poisoning caused her miscarriage, citing both the Texas Wrongful Death Act and the Comstock Act. The charge was sensational enough to capture headlines, but its significance deepened when Davis retained Jonathan Mitchell as her attorney.

The timing was no accident. That same morning, the Texas Senate was debating SB 6, a measure to expand civil liability for the distribution of abortion pills. Davis' complaint, with its dramatic allegations of chemical sabotage, mirrored the logic of the bill: that abortion-inducing drugs posed dangers that civil courts should punish, and that ordinary citizens could serve as enforcers.

In this way, Mitchell's role spanned both chambers of power—he was pressing lawmakers in Austin while simultaneously pressing the judiciary in Corpus Christi. For Cooprider, this convergence meant his personal reputation and military career were suddenly entangled with the state's abortion wars, his name invoked not only in legal filings but in legislative testimony. Cooprider's attorneys responded forcefully. In September, Mikal Watts, joined by James "Rick" Holstein and Beth Klein, denounced the lawsuit as a "political assassination."[115]

Watts presented medical and pharmaceutical evidence that he said rendered Davis' account impossible, arguing instead that her miscarriage was more likely the result of drinking, infections, untreated health problems and medication risks. In countering Mitchell's narrative, Cooprider's legal team reframed the case not as a story of betrayal and violence, but as a cautionary tale of how personal situations could be weaponized for legislative ends.

California's lawmakers reacted to what was happening in Texas. The Golden State responded with its own battery of bills. These proposals were not improvised gestures but carefully drafted defenses: a set of statutes that, taken together, attempted to blunt the extraterritorial reach of Texas law. At their core lay questions of sovereignty—whether one state could project its prohibitions across borders, and whether another could erect shields strong enough to keep them out.

The first of these, Assembly Bill 45, struck at the tools of surveillance. In an August committee hearing, senators weighed its prohibition of "geofencing," the collection of location data around health clinics that could be sold to hostile actors. The bill also barred releasing personally identifying research data in response to out-of-state subpoenas.

---

115 Press conference – *Davis v. Cooprider: response to allegations in lawsuit filed August 11, 2025* [Video]. YouTube. https://www.youtube.com/watch?v=KoMjC0dCNxg

After testimony and discussion, the measure was placed on the suspense file, a procedural purgatory reserved for bills with potential fiscal impact. The decision did not kill AB 45, but it underscored the cost of privacy—California was willing to protect its residents, but only after its accountants had calculated the price.

AB 54 and AB 260 went to the heart of medication access. AB 54, also moving through committee in mid-August, reaffirmed that shipping and receiving abortion medication remained lawful in California, explicitly shielding patients and providers alike. AB 260, debated and passed on the Assembly floor in May, extended that protection directly to clinicians and pharmacists, insulating them from prosecution or professional discipline even if their practice differed from FDA labeling or restrictions.

In committee deliberations, members highlighted the bill's provision allowing pharmacists to dispense medication without recording identifiers that could be pried loose by out-of-state investigators. These measures declared openly that California would not be a passive bystander; it would defend its practitioners against incursions from beyond its borders.

The final measure, AB 551, aimed less at legal theory than at capacity. It sought to create a Reproductive Health Emergency Preparedness Program, mandating grants to emergency departments to expand miscarriage care, contraception and abortion services. But in May the committee held it under submission, halting its progress before it reached the floor.

That stall illustrated a paradox of California's defensive stance: the state could draft elaborate protections against Texas lawsuits, but funding the hospital care necessary to absorb patients in need proved politically and fiscally harder. Still, the combined trajectory of these hearings revealed a legislature intent on drawing a bright line—Texas may pursue its bounty system, but California would answer with shields, silence and readiness, setting up a collision of statutes that would inevitably find its way into the courts.

Spying on the Enemy

Donald Trump had never been one for subtlety. In the fall of 2025, as the campaign trail heated up, he promised crowds that the "radical left" would be crushed, that Antifa would be branded a terrorist organization and that the financiers of dissent—whoever they might be—would be hunted down.

Antifa—short for "anti-fascist"—is not a single organization but a loose, decentralized network of activists and groups united by their opposition to fascism, racism and far-right extremism. As Stanislav Vysotsky explains in his analysis for Ontario Tech University's Centre on Hate, Bias and Extremism, Antifa activists engage in research, community defense and public education as much as, if not more than, street confrontation. They define fascism broadly—as systems of social or biological inequality maintained through violence—and see their activism as a form of prevention against such movements rather than unprovoked aggression.

Vysotsky also dispels the widespread misconception that Antifa is a disciplined paramilitary or domestic terrorist organization. In reality, it lacks centralized leadership, operates through autonomous local networks and makes decisions collectively rather than hierarchically. Much of what outsiders interpret as chaos or militancy, he argues, is better understood as self-organized, community-based resistance to organized hate groups.[116]

I'm aware that some people would compare that leaderless structure to the anti-abortion terror cells mentioned earlier in this book. But I'm sharing the explanation of the group from a sociologist who has studied them closely.

Trump's allies in the White House echoed the theme. They spoke of dismantling a "vast domestic terror movement," and the implication was that it reached into neighborhoods, nonprofits and even reproductive rights networks.

The applause lines were not new. They belonged to a lineage of suspicion stretching back half a century, a lineage in which women's voices were once treated as threats, and the very act of demanding reproductive freedom was enough to put a person under government watch.

116 Vysotsky, S. (2021, May 26). *Persistent myths about Antifa*. Centre on Hate, Bias and Extremism, Ontario Tech University. https://socialscienceandhumanities.ontariotechu.ca/centre-on-hate-bias-and-extremism/blog/dr.-stainslav-vysotsky.php

Three years earlier, in June 2022, Sen. Charles Grassley had set the tone. The Supreme Court's decision in *Dobbs v. Jackson Women's Health Organization* loomed, and protests gathered outside courthouses and in leafy suburban streets. Grassley, then the senior Republican on the Senate Judiciary Committee, fired off a letter to FBI Director Christopher Wray warning of what he called "pro-abortion violent extremism." He pointed to groups with militant-sounding names—Jane's Revenge, Ruth Sent Us—and described a nation on the verge of firebombings and riots.

The words conjured images of coordinated terror. Flyers, Grassley said, called for a "night of rage" if *Roe* fell. He urged the FBI to prepare for another long summer of unrest, likening abortion rights supporters to the extremists who had battled police in Portland in 2020. But on the ground, the story looked far different.

As I wrote about earlier in the book, I spent time with women who had claimed some knowledge of Ruth Sent Us as they protested outside the homes of Justices Brett Kavanaugh and John Roberts. Sometimes there were as few as seven of them—middle-aged women, young professionals, a retired teacher. They held cardboard signs, sang chants and, in one whimsical moment, blew bubbles into the humid air. The state's response was out of proportion to the scene. One night, 53 police officers arrived clad in bulletproof vests and backed by canine units. The imbalance was surreal: an armed phalanx confronting a handful of neighbors with placards.

Grassley's letter had warned that Ruth Sent Us was a violent group. In reality, the organization was tied to local organizers in that very community—people whose activism extended to racial justice and LGBTQ+ rights as much as reproductive freedom. They were not extremists but citizens exercising a right older than the republic itself. Most of the marchers had never even heard of Jane's Revenge, the shadowy name repeated in op-eds and cable news chyrons. Online, speculation grew that the group might be an invention, or at least an exaggeration, crafted to smear the movement.

The irony was brutal. For decades, the real violence in the abortion wars had come from the other side: Doctors gunned down in parking lots. Clinics bombed. Nurses stalked. Entire communities terrorized by the fury of anti-abortion radicals. Yet here was a senior senator warning that pro-choice activists were the extremists, their chants and marches a prelude to terror.

The inversion mattered. Once dissent is branded as extremism, the machinery of surveillance can be switched on. Categories are created, files are opened, and soon the act of holding a sign or raising funds for a clinic becomes suspicious. Grassley praised the FBI for already tracking "pro-abortion violent extremism." That phrase, dry as it sounded, carried a heavy charge: it placed abortion rights activism in the same breath as terrorism. And once such a label takes hold, history shows it rarely stays confined to those who commit crimes. It spreads outward until dissent itself is suspect.

The echoes led back to another season of American paranoia. In the 1970s, the Senate's Church Committee revealed what the FBI had been doing in secret under the name COINTELPRO. What had begun in the 1950s as a project to monitor the Communist Party had metastasized into a dragnet. Civil rights leaders, Black nationalists, antiwar organizers—all were drawn in. So too were women's liberation groups.

The government files told the story. Agents collected newsletters and leaflets, reported on meetings in Baltimore where women spoke of family life and abortion, and kept dossiers on national organizations like NOW. The suspicion was not based on evidence of violence; it was rooted in ideology. To J. Edgar Hoover, a gathering of women discussing equality was destabilizing in itself.

The Church Committee condemned this posture. In a democracy, they said, the order should be clear: evidence first, surveillance second. But the FBI had inverted the logic. It treated dissent as danger and ideology as evidence.

The parallels were hard to ignore. In the 1970s, feminists were watched because they questioned norms and fought for abortion rights. In 2022, a senator exaggerated threats to paint abortion rights activists as extremists. In 2025, a president promised to brand entire networks of the "radical left" as terrorists. The continuity was not just rhetorical. It carried practical consequences.

The post-*Dobbs* landscape has made these stakes immediate. Before *Roe*, underground networks like Jane in Chicago arranged abortions at great personal risk. Members were surveilled and arrested. Now, as states impose new bans, similar networks are emerging. If government agencies adopt Grassley's framing or Trump's promises, these groups could once again be treated as extremists—not for violence, but for defying unjust laws.

The lessons, written in government ink, are plain. Surveillance must be anchored in evidence of crime, not in ideology. Transparency and oversight are essential to keep abuses in check. And above all, dissent must remain protected. Yet the trajectory of recent years suggests otherwise. Grassley's exaggerations created the predicate. Trump's rhetoric threatens to institutionalize it. And the continuity with COINTELPRO is unmistakable: when those in power feel threatened, dissent becomes danger, and files fill up once more.

The history of reproductive rights is a history of surveillance as much as it is a history of law and medicine. The lesson for activists today is urgent. What is exaggerated in headlines can become justification in memos. What is justified in memos can become surveillance in practice. And what begins with names on a list can end with democracy itself diminished.

Gloria Feldt and the Future of the Movement

My conversation with Gloria Feldt took place on an early autumn afternoon, and she spoke with the same plainspoken candor that has long defined her career. She was warm but deliberate, willing to pause and turn a question over in her mind before answering, then delivering her response with the precision of someone who has spent decades in public life.

Feldt's career reflects both the battles of her time and the broader arc of women's rights. As president of Planned Parenthood Federation of America, she navigated some of the fiercest political struggles over reproductive freedom at the turn of the 21st century, insisting that access to contraception and abortion be recognized as fundamental rights rather than negotiable policies.

When her tenure ended, she did not retreat from public life. Instead, she shifted her focus to the issue that had always driven her work: women's ability to claim an equal share of power. To advance that goal, she co-founded Take The Lead, an organization dedicated to preparing women for leadership across every sector. In this role, Feldt has sought not only to defend past gains but to build the conditions for lasting equality, training a new generation to step into positions once closed to them.

Feldt began by challenging the familiar shorthand of an "abortion rights movement." She argued that the stakes were always larger: whether women would be recognized as full and equal citizens, entrusted with moral authority over their own bodies. That conviction drove her efforts as president of Planned Parenthood to reimagine the Freedom of Choice Act as a civil rights act—a declaration that deciding whether and when to have children was not a matter of privacy alone but a fundamental human right.

The Freedom of Choice Act, first introduced in 1989, sought to enshrine abortion rights in federal law at a moment when *Roe v. Wade* seemed vulnerable. It would have guaranteed access before viability and when a woman's life or health was at risk, sweeping aside many state restrictions such as waiting periods and parental consent laws. Supporters saw it as a safeguard against shifting courts; opponents decried it as federal overreach. Though reintroduced several times and briefly revived when Barack Obama endorsed it in 2007, FOCA never advanced. Its failure exposed the difficulty of defending abortion rights through Congress, yet its vision endured in later proposals like the Women's Health Protection Act.

"It is about whether women are going to have an equal place in the world," Feldt told me. "It is going to be about whether women have equal moral authority over their own bodies. It is not just about abortion."[117]

This insistence on reframing the struggle echoed a pattern visible in earlier chapters of this book. The Civil Rights Movement did not define itself narrowly as a battle against segregated lunch counters, but as a

---

117 McDevitt, C. (2025, September 25). *Interview with Gloria Feldt* [Personal interview].

campaign to redefine the American promise. Labor activists in the 1930s did not fight solely for wages, but for dignity and a new social contract. In the same way, Feldt urged that reproductive freedom must be asserted as a broad moral and civic principle, not confined to a single procedure.

She was quick to remind me that complacency has always been the enemy of progress. After *Roe*, many leaders assumed the battle was settled, just as reformers after the Civil Rights Act of 1964 or the New Deal believed their victories had permanently changed the landscape. Each time, opponents regrouped, weaponized backlash, and exploited the tendency of movements to drift into defense rather than offense.

Her analysis also turned to the mechanics of organizing. She worried that the consolidation of Planned Parenthood affiliates over the past decades had weakened bonds with local communities. Real power, she believed, comes from the slow, unglamorous work of building trust—knocking on doors, attending local meetings, supporting candidates long before they appear on a ballot.

Feldt contrasted this with the strategy of the religious right, which painstakingly built influence precinct by precinct over a 30-year horizon. Their success, she argued, was not mysterious: They understood democracy as a system of relentless participation. The parallel is striking to the way industrial unions grew in the early 20th century—less through grand strikes than through countless shop-floor relationships that, knitted together, produced national momentum.

But Feldt did not romanticize grassroots energy as sufficient on its own. She argued that successful movements must weave bottom-up activism with top-down coherence. The Civil Rights Movement paired church-based organizing with the national litigation strategy of the NAACP. Conservatives used ALEC's model legislation to funnel local efforts into a unified agenda. The fight for reproductive rights, she suggested, requires the same blend of spontaneity and discipline—young activists organizing in their own idioms, supported by a national vision that ties local struggles into a shared story.

Her urgency sharpened when we discussed authoritarian threats. Women forced to travel for abortion care already live under suspicion, she noted, a reality reminiscent of COINTELPRO surveillance of feminist and civil rights organizations. She feared that revived Comstock-era restrictions and new forms of digital monitoring could transform private health decisions into matters of state scrutiny. History shows that repression often accompanies backlash, but Feldt insisted that anticipation and resilience—not denial—are the only defenses.

She refused to end in despair. She emphasized that the ferocity of the backlash itself is proof of the movement's past success: near-universal access to birth control, the rise of women into leadership positions once thought impossible, and the ballot initiative victories in states long assumed to be hostile terrain. The challenge, she argued, is helping younger generations understand these gains as fragile achievements, not permanent fixtures. Just as earlier movements advanced by marrying the fuel of anger with the spark of aspiration, reproductive freedom will endure only if it can inspire people to believe in something larger than resistance.

As our conversation closed, Feldt admitted fatigue with politics after decades in the trenches. Yet she returned to one final lesson: participation cannot be optional. Victories fade when movements mistake them for permanence. They endure when people keep showing up—at doors, at meetings, at rallies, at the polls—refusing to leave the field. That is the thread linking the victories of labor, civil rights, feminism and now reproductive freedom. For Feldt, the future of the movement depends not on waiting for leaders to deliver salvation, but on the willingness of ordinary people to remain in the game, pressing forward and refusing to yield.

She also noted that within any strong movement, local and lower-level leaders inevitably carve out space to operate with their own autonomy. This, she said, is both a challenge and a strength. It can create friction, as local leaders pursue strategies that don't always align neatly with national agendas. Yet it also keeps the movement dynamic, responsive and alive to the needs of particular communities. In her view, the messiness of such autonomy should not be feared; it is precisely what distinguishes a genuine grassroots movement from a managed campaign.

The key, she believed, is not to stifle that independence but to connect it to a larger framework that amplifies rather than dilutes its impact.

"It's going to be a little messy, because movements are inherently messy," Feldt said. "At least the ones on our side are inherently messy, because our people don't just do as they're told.

"They want to make sure that what they're told is correct, and so they challenge it, and they all think they can do it better. And you have to just let that happen."

Real World Consequences

More than 23 million American women of childbearing age now live in states with abortion bans. Though the protections of *Roe* have ended, the history of the abortion rights movement is still being written. The massive protests and extensive coverage surrounding the *Dobbs* decision show how central the issue remains to progressives and supporters of women's rights. How the movement evolves will be shaped by the next generation of feminist leaders. It is an exciting and pivotal moment—one that will define many of their lives. One can only hope they look to history for lessons and inspiration as they fight once again to secure the right to self-determination.

The last few years have galvanized the abortion rights movement, but advocates have lost far more than they've gained. Twelve states now enforce total bans. Women are forced to drive across multiple states for essential medical care. Some have been harmed; some have died. One of them was Porsha Ngumezi.

Porsha was expecting a child with her husband, Hope Ngumezi. She was only 35.

The couple met at Lamar University, where she studied marketing and business management. They began dating in 2008 and married in 2016. They had two boys, ages 7 and 4. Porsha worked as a finance manager at a charter school. Hope was an aircraft engineer for an airline.

In mid-2023, Porsha began experiencing complications in her pregnancy, including vaginal bleeding, or spotting. The condition worsened during a vacation to Austin, and when they returned home, they went to

Houston Methodist Sugar Land Hospital.

Porsha had suffered a miscarriage, but it was incomplete. Doctors administered a blood transfusion. The recommended course of care was a D&C—dilation and curettage—a procedure that is also classified as an abortion.

Throughout the ordeal, Hope and Porsha tried to keep each other calm. They talked about their vacation and anything unrelated to the hospitalization.

"She was really scared. Of course, I was scared too," Hope said. "I think what I was trying to do was keep her calm. So we would talk about other stuff."

Hope trusted the doctor.

"I think my trigger words were when he told me this is routine," he said. "Once he told me that, I felt like it confirmed they had seen this before and knew how to treat it."

What neither realized was that physicians in Texas had become reluctant to provide necessary care because of the state's restrictive abortion ban. Many doctors avoided performing abortions—even when medically indicated—due to fear of legal consequences.

Without the D&C she needed, Porsha went into cardiac arrest. Doctors attempted to save her, but it happened so quickly that Hope could hardly comprehend what was unfolding.

Porsha died on June 11, 2023.

Hope waited two days before telling their children. He recalls feeling as if he were outside his own body when he approached his wife's coffin at the funeral.

"I just could not believe this is where we were in our life, especially since everything was going so well," Hope said. "And all of a sudden, we go to the hospital for care, and my wife leaves in a body bag. I just never understood it."

AFTERWORD

I started this journey as a journalist who was interested in writing a newspaper article about a coroner who had performed autopsies on women who died during back-alley abortions. As newspapers have disappeared nationwide, few outlets were willing to take such a story. Undeterred, I spent the next several years reading books on the entire sweep of history to write a work of my own.

I'm aware that I'm as much an activist on the issue as a chronicler of the movement. Until this moment, I tried to merely observe what other people had done before me while I was alive. But I can't ignore some of the impacts that my work and research have had because of my newsletter, Repro Rights Now, published on Substack. I've also built a storytelling platform on Facebook that has served as a template for other abortion rights pages. That can be seen by searching for *Given No Choice: A History of Abortion Rights*, which now has nearly 30,000 followers.

I don't see myself as a leader of anything, but I know my work influences those who are. As a man who is involved in the movement, I have no rightful claim to the highest positions of leadership within the abortion rights movement. But I play an essential support role.

Both men and women have a place in this movement going forward. But first we need to develop an understanding of all the history and developments that came before our involvement. That's what the purpose of this book was, and what I hope readers take away from it. As we've seen, those who don't know history are doomed to repeat it.

I don't know what the future will bring for women's rights or for abortion access. I don't know which side will prevail. The battle will rage for as long as all of us are alive. It won't go anywhere. As such it's important to remain vigilant against and adaptive to any challenges that come our way. If there's one thing I've learned in studying this, it's that you don't know what will come next.

It's hard enough to understand the history of abortion, let alone predict its future. The activists I've interviewed, followed and accompanied these last few years have given me hope that a new wave of feminists has emerged and will continue to advance the cause. Hopefully, we can connect with longtime leaders and draw from their understanding and experience to develop a compelling message and movement.

I will continue to document the evolution of abortion rights in the coming years for my newsletter *Repro Rights Now,* which is available on Substack. The information will be used for future editions of this book.

Some have been on this road for decades, and their time on it is nearing its end. Others have just joined the journey. What unites those who have traveled on it before and those who are on it now is a common belief that women need to have the same choices, freedom and rights as men. They are equal in every way, and should have domain over their body. Hopefully this book will serve to advance that idea.

ACKNOWLEDGMENTS

I want to thank my family members, which include Jerry McDevitt, Hilary McDevitt, Casey McDevitt, Kelly McDevitt, Andrew Montanaro, Kristine Connell, Holly Frank, Lori McDevitt and all their children. My father played an important role in explaining the evolution of reproductive rights jurisprudence. My sisters and mother instilled in me an appreciation for feminist viewpoints.

I'd like to thank all the women and men who granted me interviews to recount this crucial historical movement.

I have grown due to this work, and I can now speak with expertise about one of America's most critical social issues. Hearing poignant abortion stories moved me to give my best effort with the research and composition of this work. It also opened my eyes to why women should maintain the right to choose.

I'd like to thank Jenny Brown, a noted abortion rights researcher. I appreciated her referring me to the Redstockings Women's Liberation Archives for Action (www.redstockings.org).

So many others played an important role, including Frederick Clarkson, who graciously edited the early drafts of the book and drew on his considerable knowledge to improve all chapters. Hattie Fletcher, a brilliant editor in Pittsburgh, provided the final touches and improvements.

Karen Mulhauser has been a champion of my work throughout all my research and journalism. I appreciate all her insights and support. I wouldn't have had the access or reputation I have without her vouching for me. Her foreword was moving and poignant.

Many feminist leaders have given this book credibility by agreeing to do an interview about the direction and future of the reproductive rights movement. Patricia Ireland, Kathy Spillar and Gloria Feldt are a few.

I've had many friends and supporters along the way in my writing career. I don't personally know what's next. But I recently took a trip to Greece that left an impression on me. One of the things I learned was the importance of not resting on your laurels, an ancient expression meaning that you shouldn't become complacent with one achievement of which you're proud. We should continue to strive to do our best. I have many more books, plays and screenplays to write. And many more stories to tell. But I hope that readers appreciate all that went into this book. I certainly did.

ABOUT THE AUTHOR

Cody McDevitt is an award-winning journalist and author whose work explores the intersections of history, law and social justice. His reporting on reproductive rights, civil liberties and political movements has appeared in national and regional outlets, and his Substack newsletter, *Repro Rights Now*, chronicles ongoing battles over abortion access in America.

McDevitt has spent years researching *Given No Choice: A History of Abortion Rights*, uncovering forgotten stories from archives, interviews and court records to illuminate the people and forces that have shaped reproductive freedom. His work combines investigative rigor with a storyteller's empathy, situating the modern abortion debate within a century-long struggle for bodily autonomy and equality.

Based in Pennsylvania, McDevitt is also developing a series of plays and screenplays drawn from historical events, including *Banished: The Story of a Great Injustice* and a dramatization of the Aleck Bourne abortion trial. He continues to write and speak on issues of human rights, gender and democracy.

ENDNOTES

Preface

Chessen, Sherri. Interview. Conducted by Cody McDevitt. May 11, 2020.

Anonymous. (1962, August) The Drug that Left a Trail of Heartbreak. *Life Magazine*, 53(6), 26-33.

Chessen, Sherri. "The Lesser of Two Evils," *The Case for Legalized Abortion Now.* Diablo Press, Berkeley, 1967. Pg. 15-25.

Guttmacher, A. (1967). *The Case for Legalized Abortion Now* (pp. 15-25). Diablo Press.

Gale, John. "Thalidomide Baby Fund Launched," *The Observer,* Oct. 21, 1962. Pg. 3. (Accessed via newspapers.com on July 26, 2022)

Chapter 1

Taussig, F. J. (1936). *Abortion: Spontaneous and Induced: Medical and Social Aspects* (p. 31). C.V. Mosby Company.

Bates, J. E., & Zawadski, E. S. (1964). *Criminal Abortion: A Study in Medical Sociology* (pp. 15-21). Charles C. Thomas.

Huser, R. J. (1942). *The Crime of Abortion in Canon Law* (p. 31). The Catholic University of America Press.

Riddle, J. (1992). *Contraception and Abortion in the Ancient World to the Renaissance* (p. 8). Harvard University Press.

(1871). One More Unfortunate. *Harper's Weekly, XV*(768), 1.

Parry, L. A. (1932). *Criminal Abortion* (pp. 91-100). John Bale, Sons and Danielsson.

Duffy, Mary Alice. "The Law on Abortion." 13th Annual Bench-Bar Conference, Sept. 10, 1971.

Lakey, Gene. "Winds of Change: The Problem of Abortion," Medico-Legal Bulletin, March 1968, Bulletin No. 179

Rosen, H. (1954). *Therapeutic Abortion* (p. 175). Julian Press.

Rosen, H. (1954). *Abortion in America: Medical, Psychiatric, Legal, Anthropological and Religious Considerations* (pp. 175-186). Beacon Press.

Mohr, J. C. (1979). *Abortion in America: The Origins and Evolution of National Policy* (pp. 3-20). Oxford University Press.

Brodie, J. F. (1994). *Contraception and Abortion in Nineteenth-Century America* (pp. 50-54). Cornell University Press.

Devereux, G. (1955). *Abortion in Primitive Societies* (p. 10). The Julian Press.

Watke, Bruce. "Old Testament texts bearing on the problem of the control of human reproduction," *Birth Control and the Christian,* Tyndale House Publishers. Wheaton, Illinois. 1969. Pg. 7-23.

Biale, R. (1995). *Women and Jewish Law: The Essential Texts, Their History, and Their Relevance for Today.* Schocken.

Callahan, D. (1970). *Abortion: Law, Choice & Morality* (p. 411). The Macmillan Company.

Maguire, Daniel. Interview. Conducted by Cody McDevitt. June 29, 2021.

Reagan, L. (1997). *When Abortion Was a Crime: Women, Medicine and the Law in the United States, 1867-1973.* (pp. 6-50). The University of California Press.

Davis, A. (1982). *Women, Race and Class* (pp. 202-271). The Women's Press.

Von Bar, C. L. (1916). *A History of Continental Criminal Law* (pp. 165-167). Little, Brown, and Company.

Taylor, H. (1944). *The Abortion Problem.* The Williams and Wilkins Company.

Reagan, L. (1991). About to Meet her Maker: The State's Investigation of Abortion in Chicago, 1867-1940. *Journal of American History, 77*(March 1991), 1240-1260. https://doi.org/10.2307/2078347

Browder, C. (1988). *The Wickedest Woman in New York: Madame Restell, The Abortionist* (p. 1). Archon Books.

Tietze, C., & Lewit, S. (1940, April 1). Abortion. *Scientific American, 220*(1), 21-27.

Dorsett, W. B. (1908). "Criminal Abortion in its Broadest Sense." *The Journal of the American Medical Association, LI*(12), 957-961.

Maguire, Daniel. Interview. Conducted by Cody McDevitt. June 29, 2021.

Sauer, R. "Attitudes to abortion in America: 1800-1973." *Population Studies.* Vol. 28, No. 1. March 1974.

Fadiman, Dorothy. "When Abortion Was Illegal," Bullfrog Films, 2019.

Davis, A. Y. (1981). *Women, race & class.* New York, NY: Random House.

Morgan, J. L. (2015). *Reckoning with slavery: Gender, kinship, and capitalism in the early Black Atlantic.* Durham, NC: Duke University Press.

Morgan, J. L. (2004). *Laboring women: Reproduction and gender in New World slavery.* Philadelphia, PA: University of Pennsylvania Press.

Lowcountry Digital History Initiative. (n.d.). *Hidden voices: Enslaved women and reproductive resistance.* College of Charleston. Retrieved from https://ldhi.library.cofc.edu/exhibits/show/hidden-voices

Chapter 2

Alfred, Bruce. *Margaret Sanger.* Films Media Group. 2011.

Miller, Lois Mattox. "Margaret Sanger: Mother of Planned Parenthood," *Readers Digest*, July 1941. Pg. 27-29

Chesler, E. (2007). *Woman of Valor: Margaret Sanger and the Birth Control Movement in America*. Simon & Schuster.

Sanger, Margaret. "Love or Babies: Must Negro Mothers Choose," *Negro Digest*, August 1946. Pg. 3-8.

Grant, G. (1995). *Killer Angel: A Short Biography of Planned Parenthood's Founder Margaret Sanger* (pp. 91-95). Highland Books.

Lader, L. (1955). *The Margaret Sanger Story*. Greenwood Press Publishers.

Reed, J. (1978). *From Private Vice to Public Virtue: The Birth Control Movement and American Society Since 1830* (pp. 118-120). Basic Books.

Sanger, M. (1926). *The Sixth International Neo-Malthusian and Birth Control Conference, Volume 2: Problems of Overpopulation*. The American Birth Control League.

Rongy, A. (1933). *Abortion: Legal or Illegal* (pp. 118-120). Vanguard Press.

Jenkins, A. (1960). *Law for the Rich*. Victor Gollancz, LTD.

Davis, T. (2005). *Planned Parenthood and its Clergy Alliances*. Rutgers University Press.

Barbas, S. (2021). *The Rise and Fall of Morris Ernst, Free Speech Renegade*. The University of Chicago Press.

Tallman, J. Q. (2011). *The notorious Dr. Flippin: Abortion and consequence in the early twentieth century* (H. A. Washington, Foreword). Texas Tech University Press.

Lader, Lawrence. *The Margaret Sanger Story*. Doubleday and Company, New York. 1955. Pg. 266-267.

"Mrs. Sanger Proposes Limitation of Babies as Antidote for War," Ashville Citizen-Times, May 23, 1938. Pg. 2. (Accessed via newspapers.com on May 8, 2022)

Grossman, Anita. *Reforming Sex: The German Movement for Birth Control and Abortion Reform*. Oxford University Press. 1997. .

Grant, George. *Killer Angel: A Short Autobiography of Planned Parenthood's Founder Margaret Sanger,* Highland Books,Nashville. 1995. Pg. 95-105. https://georgegrant.net/margaret-sanger-in-her-own-words/ (accessed on March 23, 2022)

Sanger, Margaret. *The Sixth International Neo-Malthusian and Birth Control Conference: Volume 3, Medical and Eugenic Aspects of Birth Control,* New York, 1926. American Birth Control League. Pg. 129.

32. Parker, Kim. "The Legacy of Planned Parenthood," *Concerned Women*, June 1988. Pg. 3.

Garrow, D. (1998). *Liberty and Sexuality: The Right to Privacy and the Making of Roe v. Wade* (pp. 12-14). Macmillan Publishing Company.

Tone, A. (2001). *Devices and Desires: A History of Contraception in America* (pp. 177-179). Hill & Wang.

Sanger, M. (2004). *The Autobiography of Margaret Sanger*. Dover Publications.

Sanger, M. (1922). *The Pivot of Civilization*. Astounding Stories.

Tolnai, B. B. (1935, July 1). The Abortion Racket. *The Forum, XCIV*, 175-180.

Davis, D. S. (1938). Law of Abortion and Necessity. *Modern Law Review*, (September), 126-138.

Bourne, A. (1962). *A Doctors creed: The memoirs of a gynaecologist* (pp. 88-108). Victor Gollancz.

William Porter v. Commonwealth of Pennsylvania. County of Somerset. (1939)

Finger, Anne. Interview. Conducted by Cody McDevitt. Dec. 14, 2022.

Bourne, Dr. Aleck W.: Abortion. DPP2- Director of Public Prosecutions: Case Papers, New Series. The National Archives. (https://discovery.nationalarchives.gov.uk/results/r?_q=aleck+bourne&_sd=&_ed=&_hb=)

Valenza, Charles. "Was Margaret Sanger a Racist?" *Family Planning Perspectives*, Vol. 17, No. 1. Jan-Feb. 1985. P. 44-46.

Johnson, Alexis McGill. "I'm the head of Planned Parenthood. We're done making excuses for our founder," The New York Times. April 17, 2021. (Accessed via https://www.nytimes.com/2021/04/17/opinion/planned-parenthood-margaret-sanger.html on July 31, 2022)

Solinger, Rickie. *The Abortionist: A Woman Against the Law*. University of California Press: Oakland. 1995. P. 5.

Hargrove, David. *"Mississippi Federal Courts: A History," University Press of Mississippi. December 2018. (accessed via https://books.google.com/books?id=lah8DwAAQBAJ&pg=PT183&lpg=PT183&dq=gov.+%22lee+russell%22+abortion+mississippi&source=bl&ots=-jA4RY7ZziV&sig=ACfU3U2zt-u-0tfr5-UFGE_2gY50ytjAsA&hl=en&sa=X&ved=2ahUKEw-jAwKS6-aP5AhWbFlkFHdAcCi0Q6AF6BAgUEAM#v=onepage&q=gov.%20%22lee%20russell%22%20abortion%20mississippi&f=false on July 31, 2022)*

Browne, F.W. Stella. "The Right to an Abortion" in "Sexual Reform Congress," Kegan, Paul, Trench, Trubner & Co. London, P. 178- 181. (Accessed on https://www.lesleyahall.net/stella29.pdf on Oct. 15, 2020)

Davis, Tom. *Sacred Work: Planned Parenthood and its Clergy Alliances*. Rutgers University Press, New Brunswick, 2005. Pg. 37.

Tolnai. B.B. "The Abortion Racket," *The Forum, July-December 1935. Pg. 177-181.*

Bates, Jerome. "The Abortion Mill: An Institutional Study," The Journal of Criminal Law, Criminology and Police Science, July-Aug. 1954. Pg. 157-160.

"About abortion in Britain," *Journal of Medical Ethics, Vol. 27*. Pg. 27. 2007.

Chapter 3

Women Face Jury in Chicago Abortion Ring," *New York Daily News,* Nov. 30, 1941. (accessed via newspapers.com on Dec. 9, 2020)

People of the State of Illinois v. Ada Martin and Josephine Kuder. Reply Brief for Plaintiffs in Error, Supreme Court of Illinois, September term, 1942.

Connolly, V. (1944, January 22). Death Before Birth. *Collier's, 113*(4), 11, 45-46.

(1940, April 1). What Can America Do to Stop the Abortion Racket? *True Pictorial Stories, 1*(2), 20-23.

"The Abortion Menace," *Ebony* 6 (January 1951)

Lochridge, P. (1947, June 1). Abortion Is an Ugly Word. *Reader's Digest*, *50*(302), 31-32.

Miller, P. (1993). *The Worst of Times: Illegal Abortion--Survivors, Practitioners, Coroners, Cops and Children of Women Who Died Talk About Its Horrors*. Harper Perennial.

Vaughn, P. (1970). *The Pill on Trial*. Tower Publications.

Ramirez de Arellano, A. B. (1983). *Colonialism, Catholicism and Contraception: A History of Birth Control in Puerto Rico*. The University of North Carolina Press.

Blumenthal, K. (2022). *Jane Against the World: Roe v. Wade and the Fight for Reproductive Rights* (p. 40). Square Fish.

Havemann, E. (1958, March 1). The New Kinsey Institute Report: Pregnancy, Birth and Abortion. *McCall's*, *LXXXV*(6), 34-35, 90-94, 98-102.

Williams, D. (2019). *Defenders of the Unborn: The Pro-Life Movement before Roe v. Wade*. Oxford University Press.

Means, C., Jr. (1968). *The Morality of Abortion: The Case for Legal Reform*. The Governor's Commission to Review New York State's Abortion Law.

Calderone, M. S. (1958). *Abortion in the United States*. Planned Parenthood Federation of America.

Leavy, Zad, and Jerome M. Kummer. "Criminal Abortion: A Failure of Law." *American Bar Association Journal 50*, no. January (1964): 52-55. Accessed November 12, 2020.

Martin, J. B. (1961, May 20). Abortion. *The Saturday Evening Post*, *234*(20), 19-21, 72-74.

Martin, J. B. (1961, May 27). Abortion. *The Saturday Evening Post*, *234*(21), 20-21, 49-56.

Martin, J. B. (1961, June 3). Abortion. *The Saturday Evening Post*, *234*(22), 25, 91-92.

Lochridge, P. (1947, March 1). Abortion Is an Ugly Word. *Companion*, 4, 164.

No author is listed. (1957, September 1). Abortion Butchers; Exposing the Medical Quacks who Prey on Desperate Girls! *Expose Detective*, *1*(4), 18-21.

Muhauser, Karen. Interview. Conducted by Cody McDevitt. July 24, 2021.

Wecht, Cyril. Interview. Conducted by Cody McDevitt. May 14, 2021.

Whitman, Alden. "Alan Guttmacher, Pioneer In Family Planning, Dies," *New York Times*, March 19, 1974. (Accessed via nytimes.com on May 6, 2021)

"Dr. Edgar Keemer Performed First Abortion in 1937," *The News-Palladium*, March 7, 1973, Pg. 24. (Accessed via newspapers.com on May 7, 2021)

Martin, John Bartlow. "Abortion," *Saturday Evening Post, May 20, 1961. Pg. 19-21, 72.*

Martin, John Bartlow. "Criminal Abortionists," *Saturday Evening Post*, May 27, 1961, Pg. 20, 21, 49, 52, 55, 56.

Friedman, Daniel; Grimberg, Sharon. *Back-Alley Detroit: Abortion Before Roe v. Wade*, Filmmakers Library, New York, 1992.

Fadiman, Dorothy. "When Abortion Was Illegal: Untold Stories," Bullfrog Films, 2019.

Chapter 4

Callahan, Daniel. "Abortion: Law Choice & Morality," The Macmillan Company: London. 1970. P. 297.

Gustafson, J. (1970). *The Sixties: Radical Change in American Religion* (pp. 109-117). The American Academy of Political and Social Science.

Kaplan, L. (2019). *The Story of Jane: The Legendary Underground Feminist Abortion Service.* The University of Chicago Press.

Beito, D. T., & Beito, L. R. (2018). *T.R.M. Howard: Doctor, Entrepreneur, Civil Rights Pioneer* (pp. 226-227, 320). Independent Institute.

Hall, R. (1970, January 1). The Abortion Revolution. *Playboy, 17*(9), 112-114, 150, 272-276.

Messer, E., & May, K. (1988). Back Rooms: *Voices from the Illegal Abortion Era.* St. Martin's Press.

Friedan, B. (2000). *Life So Far: A Memoir.* Simon & Schuster.

Zarnow, L. R. (2019). *Battling Bella: The Protest Politics of Bella Abzug.* Harvard University Press.

Ziegler, M. (2015). *After Roe: The Lost History of the Abortion Debate.* Harvard University Press.

Carmen, A., & Moody, H. (1973). *Abortion Counseling and Social Change: The Story of the Clergy Consultation Service on Abortion.* Judson Press.

Phelan, Lana C. "The Cruel Fraud." Speech at California Conference on Abortion, Santa Barbara, February 10, 1968.

Lader, L. (1969, January 21). First Exclusive Survey of Non-Hospital Abortions. *Look, 33*(2), 63-64.

NBC Evening News. "SOUTH VIETNAM TAXES / ARMORED CAR / LONDON ABORTIONS." Reported by David Brinkley. Vanderbilt TV News Archive. https://tvnews.vanderbilt.edu/broadcasts/448008. Accessed April 12, 2021.

Fleischman, S., Friendly, F., & Sevareid, E. (Directors). (2000). *Birth control and the law* [Film]. CBS.

Cronkite, W., Lowe, D., & Williams, P. (Directors). (2004). *Abortion and the Law* [Film]. CBS.

Kaufman, M. T. (1989, July 1). Abortion Doctor. *Lear's.* 2(5), 85-87.

Brownmiller, S. (1999). *In Our Time: Memoir of a Revolution.* The Dial Press.

Kaufman, M. T. (1989, July 1). Abortion Doctor. *Lear's.*, 85-87.

Brownmiller, S. (1969, January 30). When an Abortionist Dies. *The Village Voice, XIV*(16). https://www.villagevoice.com/when-an-abortionist-dies/

Krassner, P. (1998, June 1). The Saintly Abortionist. *Playboy Magazine.*

Dispaci, M. I. (1969, June 1). Prominent Doctors Admit Performing 60,000 Abortions. *Uncensored,* 44.

No author listed. (1969, February 17). King of the Abortionists. *Newsweek.*

(Note: Many of these documents and stories about Robert Spencer were kept at the offices of his lawyer's firm, Strouse Law, located in Ashland, Pa. I visited the office and took pictures of the case file and other documents and photos pertaining to his life.)

Turk, K. *(2023). The Women of NOW: How Feminists Built an Organization That Transformed America.* Farrar, Straus and Giroux.

Lutz, Ron. Interview. Conducted by Cody McDevitt. Aug. 24, 2020.

Traupman, Mary Ann. Interview. Conducted by Cody McDevitt. Nov. 9, 2022

Scott, Martha. Interview. Conducted by Cody McDevitt. April 27, 2020.

Frank, Gillian. Interview. Conducted by Cody McDevitt. Dec. 28, 2021.

Quintanilla, Ray. "Puerto Ricans recall being guinea pigs for magic pill,'" Chicago Tribune, April 11, 2004. (Accessed via https://www.chicagotribune.com/news/ct-xpm-2004-04-11-0404110509-story.html on Jan. 11, 2022)

Gebhard, Paul; Pomeroy, Wardell; Martin, Clyde; Christenson, Cornelia. "Pregnancy, Birth and Abortion." Harper and Brothers: Bloomington. 1958. Pg. 195.

Friedman, Daniel; Grimberg, Sharon. *Back-Alley Detroit: Abortion Before Roe v. Wade,* Filmmakers Library, New York, 1992.

Fadiman, Dorothy. "When Abortion Was Illegal: Untold Stories," Bullfrog Films, 2019.

Fleischman, Stephen; Friendly, Fred. "Birth Control and the Law," CBS News, 1962.

Carter, Stan. "High Court Told Birth Law Spies on Boudoir," *New York Daily News, March 30, 1965. Pg.* Fiske, Edward.

"Clergymen Offer Abortion Advice," *The New York Times,* May 22, 1967. Pg. 1, 36. (accessed via nytimes.com on Dec. 16, 2020)

Lauta, Thomas. "Dr. Robert Douglas Spencer: A Man of Risks and Courage," *Historical Methods,* December 4, 1992.

Browmiller, Susan. "When an Abortionist Dies," Jan. 30, 1969. Vol. XIV, No. 16.

Davis, Tom. *Sacred Work: Planned Parenthood and Its Clergy Alliances.* Rutgers University Press, New Brunswick. 2005. Pg. 27.

Williams, Daniel K. *Defenders of the Unborn: The Pro-Life Movement before Roe v. Wade.* Oxford University Press, New York. 2016.

Clarkson, Frederick, *An Annotated Directory of the Prochoice Religious Community in the United States,* Political Research Associates, 2020.

Edmonds, Patty. "Birthright: Helping Mother, Child," *National Catholic Reporter,* July 2, 1976.

Callahan, Daniel. "Contraception and Abortion: American Catholic Response." *The Sixties: Radical Change in American Religion.* The American Academy of Political and Social Science. New York. 1970. Pg. 112-113.

"A Protestant Affirmation on the Control of Human Reproduction: A Theological Basis," *Birth Control and the Christian,* Tyndale House Publishers. Wheaton Illinois. 1969. Pg. XXII-XXXI.

Koppel, Ted, "Gloria Steinem: The Accidental Activist," Nightline, ABC News, 2004.

"Our Bodies, Ourselves: A Book By and For Women," Boston Women's Health Collective. Simon and Schuster: New York. 1971. P. 13.

Fadiman, Dorothy. *The Fight for Safe Abortion,* 1995. Cocentric Films

Chapter 5

Brown, J. (2019). *Without Apology: The Abortion Struggle Now.* Verso.

Ehrlich, P. (1971). *The population bomb.* Ballantine Books.

Tate, Cassandra. "Koome, Adrian Frans (1929-1978)," History Link, Sept. 14, 2000. (Accessed via historylink.org on March 29, 2021)

"Bill to Legalize Abortions Clears Hawaii Legislature." *The New York Times*, 25 Feb. 1970, www.nytimes.com/1970/02/25/archives/bill-to-legalize-abortions-clears-hawaii-legislature-bill-on.html.

Diamond, M., et al. "Abortion in Hawaii." *Family planning perspectives* vol. 5,1 (1973): 54-60.

Wetherby, P. (1968, May 1). The Mexican Abortion Trip. *Cheetah, 1*(8), 61, 66-69.

Star, J. (1967, July 11). "We'll Be the Abortion Mecca for the Nation." *Look, 31*(14), 67-69.

Rickerby, A. (1970, April 17). The Two Apostles of Control. *Life, 68*(14), 33-37.

NBC Nightly News. "Dr. Frans Koome." Reported by Chet Huntley. Aired on Dec. 18, 1969, on NBC. Vanderbilt TV News Archive. https://tvnews.vanderbilt.edu/broadcasts/443777. Accessed April 12, 2021.

ABC Evening News. "Maryland/Abortion." Reported by Stephen Geer and Howard K. Smith. Aired on March 31, 1970. Vanderbilt TV News Archive. https://tvnews.vanderbilt.edu/broadcasts/9785. Accessed April 12, 2021.

Murphy, Bruce Allen. *The Legend and Life of William O. Douglas: America's Most Controversial Supreme Court Justice.* Random House: New York. 2003. P. 384-388.

Cronkite, Walter. 1965. "Abortion and the Law," CBS News. Lowe, David; Williams, Palmer, CBS News.

Montgomery, Lewis & Hammersby, Maternal Deaths in California, 1957-1962, 100 CAL. Medicine. 412, 415 (1964).

Steinhoff, P., & Diamond, M. (1977). *Abortion Politics: The Hawaii Experience.* The University of Hawaii Press.

NBC Evening News. "Abortion/New York/Chicago." Reported by Catherine Mackin and David Brinkley. Aired on April 9, 1970. Vanderbilt Television News Archive. https://tvnews.vanderbilt.edu/broadcasts/451023. Accessed on June 26, 2021.

Diamond, M., James, P., Smith, R., & Steinhoff, P. (1973). Abortion in Hawaii. *Family Planning Perspectives, 5*(1), 54-60.

CBS Evening News. "New York/Abortion/Michaels." Reported by Ben Silver and Harry Reasoner. Aired on April 10, 1970. Vanderbilt Television News Archive. https://tvnews.vanderbilt.edu/broadcasts/209166. Accessed on June 26, 2021.

NBC Evening News. "New York/Abortion/Michaels." Reported by Chet Huntley. Aired on April 10, 1970. Vanderbilt Television News Archive. https://tvnews.vanderbilt.edu/broadcasts/450637. Accessed on June 26, 2021.

ABC Evening News. "New York Abortion." Reported by Marlene Sanders. Aired July 1, 1970. Vanderbilt Television News Archive. https://tvnews.vanderbilt.edu/broadcasts/11045. Accessed April 12, 2021

CBS Evening News. "New York/Abortion." Reported by Morton Dean and Harry Reasoner. Aired on July 2, 1970. Vanderbilt Television News Archive. https://tvnews.vanderbilt.edu/broadcasts/211032. Accessed on April 12, 2021.

No author is listed. (1970, February 27). Abortion Comes out of the Shadows. *Life Magazine, 68*(7), 20-29.

NBC Evening News. "Abortion/Military/New York City." Reported by John Chancellor and Liz Trotta. Aired Aug. 18, 1970. Vanderbilt Television News Archive, https://tvnews.vanderbilt.edu/broadcasts/452684 Accessed April 19, 2021.

NBC Evening News. "Women/Protests." Reported by John Chancellor. Aired Aug. 26, 1970. Vanderbilt Television News Archive. https://tvnews.vanderbilt.edu/broadcasts/452841. Accessed April 12, 2021.

NBC Evening News. "New York/Abortion Agency." Reported by David Brinkley and Liz Trotta. Aired Sept. 24, 1970. Vanderbilt Television News Archive. https://tvnews.vanderbilt.edu/broadcasts/453328. Accessed April 12, 1970.

NBC Evening News. "New York/Commercial Abortion Referral Agencies." Reported by Ken Alvord. Aired June 8, 1971. Vanderbilt Television News Archive. https://tvnews.vanderbilt.edu/broadcasts/458651. Accessed April 12, 2021.

NBC Evening News. "New York City/Abortions." Reported by Ken Alvord and John Chancellor. Aired June 29, 1971. Vanderbilt Television News Archive. https://tvnews.vanderbilt.edu/broadcasts/458531. Accessed April 12, 2021.

NBC Evening News. "Abortions/West Germany/France." Reported by John Chancellor, Robert Hager and David Burrington. Aired July 14, 1971. Vanderbilt Television News Archive. https://tvnews.vanderbilt.edu/broadcasts/458774. Accessed April 12, 1971.

NBC Evening News. "Hawaii/Abortion." Reported by Frank Bourgholtzer and John Chancellor. Aired Sept. 21, 1971. Vanderbilt Television News Archive. https://tvnews.vanderbilt.edu/broadcasts/459984. Accessed April 12, 2021.

CBS Evening News. "Population Control." Reported by Daniel Schorr. Aired March 16, 1972. Vanderbilt Television News Archive. https://tvnews.vanderbilt.edu/broadcasts/222070. Accessed April 12, 2021.

CBS Evening News. "Campaign '72/Demo. Women." Reported by Marya McLaughlin and Walter Cronkite. Aired July 14, 1972. Vanderbilt Television News Archive. https://tvnews.vanderbilt.edu/broadcasts/223904. Accessed on April 12, 2021.

NBC Evening News. "Campaign '72/Republican Platform Campaign." Reported by Douglas Kiker. Aired Aug. 14, 1972. Vanderbilt Television News Archive. https://tvnews.vanderbilt.edu/broadcasts/465587. Accessed April 12, 2021.

CBS Evening News. "Campaign '72/Republicans and Women." Reported by Michele Clark and Walter Cronkite. Aired on Aug. 16, 1972. Vanderbilt Television News Archive. https://tvnews.vanderbilt.edu/broadcasts/224346. Accessed April 12, 2021.

ABC Evening News. "Maryland/Abortion." Reported by Stephen Geer and Howard K. Smith. Aired on March 31, 1970. Vanderbilt Television News Archive. https://tvnews.vanderbilt.edu/broadcasts/9785. Accessed on April 22, 2021.

ABC Evening News. "Women's Lib. Magazine." Reported by Howard K. Smith and Gregory Jackson. Aired on Jan. 25, 1972. Vanderbilt Television News Archive. https://tvnews.vanderbilt.edu/broadcasts/17679. Accessed on March 29, 2021.

No Author listed. (1972, October 1). Abortion Law Repeal: Ms. Report. *Ms. Magazine, 1*(4), 116-120.

Lamm, Richard. Interview. Conducted by Cody McDevitt. March 21, 2021.

Ehrlich, Paul. Interview. Conducted by Cody McDevitt. June 8, 2021.

Reimers, Paula. Interview. Conducted by Cody McDevitt. Oct. 26, 2021.

Kritzler, Helen. Interview. Conducted by Cody McDevitt. April 16, 2021.

Baird, Bill. Interview. Conducted by Cody McDevitt. July 21, 2021.

Willis, Ellen. "Hearing," *The New Yorker,* Feb. 14, 1969. Accessed via newyorker.com.

Wallach, Janet. "Cardinal of Choice," Washington Post Magazine, Aug. 24, 1986.

Kerr, James. "Aborted Abortion Ads May Have a Rebirth Soon," *Fort Lauderdale News,* July 27, 1971. Pg. 4. (Accessed via newspapers.com on April 1, 2021)

Dillon, Valerie Vance. "Birthright," *The Sign,* July 1971, Pg. 27-29.

Greenhouse, Linda. "Dr. Milan Vuitch, 78, Fighter for Abortion Rights," *The New York Times,* April 11, 1993, Pg. 30.

"Critics Hit Abortion Proposals," *Press and Sun Bulletin,* March 17, 1972, Pg. 28. (Accessed via newspapers.com on April 2, 2021)

Box 65, folder "August 11, 1972 - H.R. Haldeman - Abortion" of the Robert Teeter Papers at the Gerald R. Ford Presidential Library.

Los Angeles Times. (1995, Nov. 30). *Lawrence Lader, abortion rights advocate, dies at 86. The Los Angeles Times*, p. 63.

Los Angeles Times. (1995, Nov. 30). *Obituaries: Lawrence Lader; champion of abortion rights movement. The Los Angeles Times*, p. 73.

The Bulletin (Bend, Ore.). (2006, May 12). *Lawrence Lader helped start abortion rights movement*, p. 22.

Chapter 6

Gebhard, P. H., Pomeroy, W. B., Martin, C. E., & Christenson, C. V. (1958). *Pregnancy, Birth and Abortion* (p. 238). Harper and Brothers.

Stern, S., & Wermeil, S. (2010). *Justice Brennan: Liberal Champion* (pp. 372-377). Houghton Mifflin Harcourt.

Faux, M. (2000). *Roe v. Wade: The Untold Story of the Landmark Supreme Court Decision That Made Abortion Legal.* Cooper Square Press.

Greenhouse, L. (2006). *Becoming Justice Blackmun: Harry Blackmun's Supreme Court Journey.* Times Books.

Woodward, B., & Armstrong, S. (2005). *The Brethren: Inside the Supreme Court.* Simon & Schuster.

NBC Evening News. "Abortion." Reported by Andrea Mitchell and John Chancellor. Aired on Jan. 22, 1979. Vanderbilt Television News Archive. https://tvnews.vanderbilt.edu/broadcasts/501120. Accessed on March 29, 2021.

Harry Blackmun. Abortion–Law and legislation–United States. [Correspondence: Abortion Mail]. Harry Blackmun Papers. (Box 68-85, Supreme Court File)

Harry Blackmun. Abortion–Law and legislation–United States. [Abortion] Harry Blackmun Papers. Library of Congress, Manuscript Division. (Box 1355, Subject File)

Farmer, Joyce. Interview. Conducted by Cody McDevitt. Feb. 27, 2021.

McCorvey, Norma; Meisler, Andy. *I am Roe: My Life, Roe v. Wade and Freedom of Choice*, New York: HarperCollins Publishers, 1994.

Kirtz, Kate; Lundy, Nell. "Jane: An Abortion Service," Women Make Movies, San Francisco. 1996.

Fancher, Mike; Bowers, Elaine; Gosa, Geri; Morgan, Sally. "Illegal Operations Still Taking Toll," *The Kansas City Star*, Aug. 2, 1970, Pg 1-2. (Accessed via newspapers.com on March 1, 2021)

Fancher, Mike; Bowers, Elaine; Gosa, Geri; Morgan, Sally. "Not all women accepted under new Kansas Law," *The Kansas City Star*, Aug. 3, 1970, Pg. 1-2. (Accessed via newspapers.com on March 1, 2021)

Fancher, Mike; Bowers, Elaine; Gosa, Geri; Morgan, Sally. "Change in Attitudes Sweeping States," *The Kansas City Star*, Aug. 4, 1970. Pg. 1-2. (Accessed via newspapers.com on March 1, 2021)

"Abortion Ruling Begot League," *National Catholic Reporter*, June 21, 1985, Vol. 21, No. 33. "Court Strikes Down State Abortion Law," *The Sunday News and Tribune*, May 20, 1973. Pg. 5. (Accessed via newspapers.com on March 1, 2021).

Chapter 7

Nolen, W. (1978). *The Baby in the Bottle*. Coward, McCann & Geoghegan.

ABC Evening News. "Senate Subcommittee/Abortion Hearing." Reported by Harry Reasoner. Aired on March 7, 1974. Vanderbilt Television News Archive. https://tvnews.vanderbilt.edu/broadcasts/30833. Accessed April 12, 2021.

CBS Evening News. "Boston Trial/Edelin/Abortion." Reported by Robert Schakne and Walter Cronkite. Aired on Feb. 14, 1975. Vanderbilt Television News Archive. https://tvnews.vanderbilt.edu/broadcasts/238607. Accessed on April 12, 2021.

Edelin case (records pertaining to Ken Edelin case. Religious Coalition for Reproductive Choice Records. Wisconsin Historical Society, Madison, Wisc. (Box 16, Folder 36-37)

ABC Evening News. "Edelin/Abortion Case." Reported by Harry Reasoner. Aired Feb. 18, 1975. Vanderbilt Television News Archive. https://tvnews.vanderbilt.edu/broadcasts/35890. Accessed April 12, 1975.

CBS Evening News. "Dr. Edelin Returns to Work." Reported by Betty Ann Bowser and Walter Cronkite. Aired on Feb. 19, 1975. Vanderbilt Television News Archive. https://tvnews.vanderbilt.edu/broadcasts/238695. Accessed April 12, 2021.

NBC Evening News. "Special Report/Abortion." Reported by Betty Rollin. Aired on Feb. 27, 1975. Vanderbilt Television News Archive. https://tvnews.vanderbilt.edu/broadcasts/481515. Accessed April 12, 2021.

ABC Evening News. "Abortions/Edelin Follow-Up." Reported by Lem Tucker and Howard K. Smith. Aired on Dec. 1, 1975. Vanderbilt Television News Archive. https://tvnews.vanderbilt.edu/broadcasts/35204. Accessed April 12, 2021.

Alpern, D. (1975, March 3). Abortion and the Law. *Newsweek, LXXXV*(9), 19-30.

Early Days of RCAR. Annual Reports. Religious Coalition for Reproductive Choice Records. Wisconsin Historical Society. (M93-025, Box 4, Folder 1)

Pierce, H. W. (1974, Nov. 1). Dr. Laufe Cleared as Inquest Finds Baby a Stillborn. *Pittsburgh Post-Gazette*, 1, 5.

Susman, Frank. Interview. Conducted by Cody McDevitt. June 19, 2020.

Donnally, Jennifer. "The Edelin Manslaughter Trial and the Anti-Abortion Movement," Massachusetts Historical Review, Vol. 20, 2018, Pg. 1-32.

Boston City Council Committee on Public Health transcript, Sept. 18, 1973.

Pilati, Joe. "Edelin says, 'Die was cast when jurors were picked,' " *Boston Globe*, Feb. 17, 1975, Pg. 32. (Accessed on newspapers.com on Dec. 30, 2020)

Rubin, Eva. R. "The Edelin Case," *The Abortion Controversy, A Documentary History,* Greenwood Press: Westport, 1994, Pg. 186-188.

"Dr. Kenneth Edelin symbol of unresolved abortion issue," *The Journal Times,* Sept. 28, 1975, Pg. 9. (Accessed via newspapers.com on Dec. 30, 2020)

Internal Information Bulletin, *Socialist Workers Party,* Socialist Workers Party Convention, August 1975.

Karagianis, Maria. "Decision seen curtailing later abortions," *Boston Globe, Feb. 19, 1975, Pg. 3. (Accessed via newspapers.com on Dec. 30, 2020)*

McLaughlin, Loretta. "Dr. Edelin's Odyssey," *Boston Globe,* Sept. 23, 1979, Pg. 102. (Accessed via newspapers.com on Dec. 30, 2020)

"The Edelin Trial," Boston: Legal-Medical Studies, 1975. *Reprint of the Commonwealth v. Edelin Trial Transcript)*

Chapter 8

Garcia-Ditta, Alexa. "Reckoning With Rosie," *Texas Observer*, Nov. 3, 2015. Accessed via texasobserver.org.

Stanley-Becker, Isaac. "Henry Hyde—Abortion Amendment's Namesake, was a culture warrior with some surprising causes," *Washington Post*, June 7, 2019. (Accessed via washingtonpost.com on June 24, 2021)

Astor, Maggie. ""What is the Hyde Amendment? A look at its impact as Biden reverses his stance," *The New York Times,* June 7, 2019. (Accessed via newspapers.com on Dec. 26, 2020)

"Firebrand Image Lingers From Watergate, War," *The Dispatch*, Sept. 1, 1977, Pg. 16. (Accessed via newspapers.com on May 6, 2021)

Fling, Sarah. "Betty Ford, Activist First Lady," (found on https://www.whitehousehistory.org/betty-ford-activist-first-lady) (Accessed on Oct. 17, 2022)

Cooper, Candy. "Rosie and the Medicaid Cutoff," *Detroit Free Press*, Sept. 23, 1979. (accessed via newspapers.com on Dec. 26, 2020)

CBS Evening News. "Congress/Abortion/Medicaid." Reported by Steve Young. Aired on Aug. 22, 1976. Vanderbilt Television News Archive. https://tvnews.vanderbilt.edu/broadcasts/247584. Accessed on March 19, 2021.

NBC Evening News. "Abortion/Supreme Court/Medicaid/Catholic Bishops Conference." Reported by David Brinkley and Ford Rowan. Aired on Nov. 8, 1976. Vanderbilt Television News Archive. https://tvnews.vanderbilt.edu/broadcasts/486496. Accessed on March 19, 2021.

CBS Evening News. "Supreme Court/Abortion and Welfare Payments." Reported by Fred Graham. Aired on June 20, 1977. Vanderbilt Television News Archive. https://tvnews.vanderbilt.edu/broadcasts/252703. Accessed on March 19, 2021.

ABC Evening News. "Abortion Funding." Reported by Harry Reasoner and Vic Ratner. Aired on Nov. 29, 1977. Vanderbilt Television News Archive. https://tvnews.vanderbilt.edu/broadcasts/46721. Accessed on March 19, 2021.

Martin, W. (1996). *With God on Our Side: The Rise of the Religious Right in America.* Broadway Books.

Fitzgerald, F. (2017). *The Evangelicals: The Struggle to Shape America.* Simon & Schuster.

Liebman, R. C., & Wuthnow, R. (1983). *The New Christian Right: Mobilization and Legitimation.* Aldine Publishing Company.

Flippen, J. B. (2011). *Jimmy Carter, the Politics of Family and the Rise of the Religious Right* (pp. 56-57). The University of Georgia Press.

Schaeffer, F. (2007). *Crazy for God: How I Grew Up as One of the Elect, Helped Found the Religious Right, and Lived to Take All (or Almost All) of It Back.* Carroll & Graf.

Ziegler, M. (2020). *Abortion & The Law in America: Roe v. Wade to the Present* (p. 206). Cambridge University Press.

Wattleton, F. (1996). *Life on the Line.* Ballantine Books.

NBC Evening News. "Special Segment (Abortion and Rape). Reported by Chris Wallace. Aired on July 1, 1981. Vanderbilt Television News Archive. https://tvnews.vanderbilt.edu/broadcasts/517819. Accessed on April 12, 2021.

Flippen, Brooks. *Jimmy Carter: The Politics of Family and the Rise of the Religious Right.* University of Georgia Press, Athens. 2011.

Balmer, Randall. "The Real Origins of the Religious Right," *Politico Magazine,* May 27, 2014. (Accessed via politico.com on Dec. 27, 2020)

Fitzgerald, Frances. *The Evangelicals: The Struggle to Shape America,*" Simon & Schuster: New York, 2017. Pg. 303.

Hook, Janet. "On abortion, many have flip-flopped," *Los Angeles Times,* March 11, 2007, Pg. A22-23. (Accessed via newspapers.com on Dec. 27, 2020)

CBS Evening News. "Ford/Abortion." Reported by Walter Cronkite. Aired on Feb. 3, 1976. Vanderbilt Television News Archive. https://tvnews.vanderbilt.edu/broadcasts/244606. Accessed on March 20, 2021.

NBC Evening News. "Abortion/Ford/Reagan/Poll." Reported by John Chancellor and Tom Brokaw. Aired on Feb. 3, 1976. Vanderbilt Television News Archive. https://tvnews.vanderbilt.edu/broadcasts/487273. Accessed on March 20, 2021.

ABC Evening News. "Campaign 1976/Ford/Abortion." Reported by Tom Jarriel and Harry Reasoner. Aired on Sept. 10, 1976. Vanderbilt Television News Archive. https://tvnews.vanderbilt.edu/broadcasts/45225. Accessed on March 20, 2021.

ABC Evening News. "Campaign 1976/Carter/Abortion." Reported by Frank Reynolds and Harry Reasoner. Aired on Sept. 10, 1976. Vanderbilt Television News Archive. https://tvnews.vanderbilt.edu/broadcasts/45226. Accessed on March 20, 2021.

Carter Meeting–1977. Women of Color Partnership Program. Religious Coalition for Reproductive Choice Records. Wisconsin Historical Society. (M93-025, Box 8, Folder 21)

Medicaid Strategy. Women of Color Partnership Program. Religious Coalition for Reproductive Choice Records. Wisconsin Historical Society. (M93-025, Box 13, Folder 16)

Edelin. Women of Color Partnership Program. Religious Coalition for Reproductive Choice Records. Wisconsin Historical Society. (M93-025, Box 16, Folder 32)

RCAR Action. Edelin. Women of Color Partnership Program. Religious Coalition for Reproductive Choice Records. Wisconsin Historical Society. (M93-025, Box 6, Folder 36)

RCAR: An Analysis of Its Role In the Pro-Choice Movement. Women of Color Partnership Program. Religious Coalition for Reproductive Choice Records. Wisconsin Historical Society. (M2010-020, Box 6, Folder 29)

RCAR Press, 1979. Religious Coalition for Reproductive Choice Records. Wisconsin Historical Society. (M93-025, Box 1, Folder 23)

Media Relations, 1979. Religious Coalition for Reproductive Choice Records. Wisconsin Historical Society. (M93-025, Box 1, Folder 24)

RCAR Press, 1978. Religious Coalition for Reproductive Choice Records. Wisconsin Historical Society. (M93-025, Box 1, Folder 25)

RCAR Press, 1978. Religious Coalition for Reproductive Choice Records. Wisconsin Historical Society. (M93-025, Box 1, Folder 26)

RCAR Press, 1977. Religious Coalition for Reproductive Choice Records. Wisconsin Historical Society. (M93-025, Box 1, Folder 27)

RCAR Newsletter, 1973-circa 1990s) Religious Coalition for Reproductive Choice Records. Wisconsin Historical Society. (M93-025, Box 1, Folder 28)

RCAR Publications, 1974-circa 1990s. Religious Coalition for Reproductive Choice Records. Wisconsin Historical Society. (M93-025, Box 1, Folder 29)

Mills, S. (1991). Abortion and Religious Freedom: The Religious Coalition for Abortion Rights (RCAR) and the Pro-Choice Movement, 1973-1989. *Journal of Church and State*, *33*(3), 569-594.

Avery, Byllye. Interview. Conducted by Cody McDevitt. March 27, 2021.

Daynes, Byron W.; Tatalovich, Raymond. "Presidential Politics and Abortion," Presidential Studies Quarterly, Vol. 22, No. 3, Summer 1992, Pg. 545-561

News release, Religious Coalition for Abortion Rights. Feb. 24, 1977. Religious Coalition for Abortion Rights Records, Wisconsin Historical Society, Box 1.

Herbers, John. "Ultraconservative evangelicals a surging new force in politics," *The New York Times*. Aug. 17, 1980.

"The Religion Lobby," *Newsweek, July 18, 1979.*

Liebman, Robert; Wuthnow, Robert. *The New Christian Right: Mobilization and Legitimation,* Aldine Publishing Company: New York. 1983. Pg. 31-35.

Chapter 9

Baird-Windle, P., & Bader, E. (2001). *Targets of Hatred: Anti-abortion Terrorism*. Palgrave.

Jefferis, J. (2011). *The Army of God and Anti-Abortion Terror in the United States*. Praeger.

Reagan, R. S. (1984). *Abortion and the Conscience of a Nation*. Thomas Nelson Publishers.

Ballmer, R. (2014, May 27). The Real Origins of the Religious Right. *Politico Magazine*. https://www.politico.com/magazine/story/2014/05/religious-right-real-origins-107133/

Culver, S. (2007). *Steeplejacking: How the Christian Right is Hijacking Mainstream Religion* (p. 35). IG Publishing.

Grimes, D. A., & Shields, W. C. (1989). Violence against abortion providers. *Journal of the American Medical Association, 262*(24), 3444–3449. https://doi.org/10.1001/jama.1989.03430240060030

Medoff, M. H. (2011). The impact of anti-abortion activities on abortion providers. *Social Science Research, 40*(1), 151–163. https://doi.org/10.1016/j.ssresearch.2010.08.001

National Bureau of Economic Research. (2010). *Abortion Clinic Violence and the Supply of Abortion Services*. NBER Working Paper No. 16603. https://www.nber.org/papers/w16603

Southern Poverty Law Center. (n.d.). *A violent history: Anti-abortion extremists and clinic violence.* https://www.splcenter.org/resources/reports/violent-history/

NBC Evening News. "Abortion/Akron Ordinance." Reported by Eric Burns and David Brinkley. Aired on Feb. 28, 1978. Vanderbilt Television News Archive. https://tvnews.vanderbilt.edu/broadcasts/497686. Accessed on Feb. 28, 2022.

NBC Evening News. "Campaign 80/The Issues: Abortion." Reported by John Chancellor. Aired on Feb. 21, 1980. Vanderbilt Television News Archive. https://tvnews.vanderbilt.edu/broadcasts/508957. Accessed on March 19, 2021.

CBS Evening News. "Florida/Abortion Bombings." Reported by Dan Rather. Aired on Feb. 24, 1985. Vanderbilt Television News Archive. https://tvnews.vanderbilt.edu/broadcasts/303192. Accessed on March 19, 2021.

No Author Listed. (1981, Jan. 1). Abortion: Women Speak Out, an Exclusive Poll. *Life, 4*(11), 45-54.

CBS Evening News. "Illinois/Couple's Disappearance." Reported by Meredith Viera and Dan Rather. Aired on Aug. 19, 1982. Vanderbilt Television News Archive. https://tvnews.vanderbilt.edu/broadcasts/285457. Accessed on April 12, 2021.

CBS Evening News. "Senate/Abortion/School Prayer." Reported by Dan Rather. Aired on Sept. 15, 1982. Vanderbilt Television News Archive. https://tvnews.vanderbilt.edu/broadcasts/285878. Accessed on Feb. 28, 2022.

NBC Evening News. "Supreme Court/Abortions." Reported by Carl Stern and Roger Mudd. Aired on Nov. 30, 1982. Vanderbilt Television News Archive. https://tvnews.vanderbilt.edu/broadcasts/521060. Accessed on Feb. 28, 1982.

ABC Evening News. "Supreme Court/Abortion." Reported by Tim O'Brien, Bettina Gregory and David Brinkley. Aired on June 15, 1983. Vanderbilt Television News Archive. https://tvnews.vanderbilt.edu/broadcasts/84878. Accessed on Feb. 28, 2022

ABC Evening News. "Senate/Abortion Debate." Reported by Max Robinson and Brit Hume. Aired on June 27, 1983. Vanderbilt Television News Archive. https://tvnews.vanderbilt.edu/broadcasts/85136. Accessed on Feb. 28, 2022.

ABC Evening News. "Campaign '80/Moral Majority." Reported by Frank Reynolds and Susan King. Aired on July 7, 1980. Vanderbilt Television News Archive. https://tvnews.vanderbilt.edu/broadcasts/66905. Accessed on March 24, 2022.

NBC Evening News. "Special Segment (Born-Again Politics)." Reported by Mark Nancannon and John Chancellor. Aired on Aug. 19, 1980. Vanderbilt Television News Archive. https://tvnews.vanderbilt.edu/broadcasts/512071. Accessed on March 24, 2022.

CBS Evening News. "Moral Majority." Reported by Rita Flynn and Ed Bradley. Aired on Nov. 9, 1980. Vanderbilt Television News Archive. https://tvnews.vanderbilt.edu/broadcasts/268165. Accessed on March 24, 2022.

NBC Evening News. "Supreme Court/Abortion." Reported by Carl Stern and Roger Mudd. Aired on June 15, 1983. Vanderbilt Television News Archive. https://tvnews.vanderbilt.edu/broadcasts/531058. Accessed on Feb. 28, 2022.

CBS Evening News. "Illinois/Kidnapped Dr." Reported by Meredith Viera and Dan Rather. Aired on Aug. 20, 1982. Vanderbilt Television News Archive. https://tvnews.vanderbilt.edu/broadcasts/285493. Accessed on April 12, 2021.

ABC Evening News. "Special Assignment Abortion Clinics and Terrorism." Reported by Peter Lance. Aired on July 13, 1984. Vanderbilt Television News Archive. https://tvnews.vanderbilt.edu/broadcasts/90755. Accessed on April 22, 2021.

ABC Evening News. "Supreme Court Justice Threatened." Reported by Tim O'Brien and Peter Jennings. Aired on Oct. 10, 1984. Vanderbilt Television News Archive. https://tvnews.vanderbilt.edu/broadcasts/87216. Accessed on March 29, 2021.

Silent Scream. Women of Color Partnership Program. Religious Coalition for Reproductive Choice Records. Wisconsin Historical Society. (M93-025, Box 6, Folder 26)

ABC Evening News. "Blackmun/Gun Attack." Reported by Tim O'Brien and Peter Jennings. Aired on March 4, 1985. Vanderbilt Television News Archive. https://tvnews.vanderbilt.edu/broadcasts/95231. Accessed on March 29, 2021.

NBC Evening News. "Abortion Wars." Reported by Dennis Murphy. Aired on July 5, 1984. Vanderbilt Television News Archive. https://tvnews.vanderbilt.edu/broadcasts/538449. Accessed on April 12, 2021.

ABC Evening News. "Special Assignment (Abortion Clinics and Terrorism." Reported by Peter Lance. Aired on July 13, 1984. Vanderbilt Television News Archive. https://tvnews.vanderbilt.edu/broadcasts/90755. Accessed on April 12, 2021.

NBC Evening News. "Maryland/Terrorism." Reported by Robert Hager. Aired on Nov. 19, 1984. Vanderbilt Television News Archive. https://tvnews.vanderbilt.edu/broadcasts/534502. Accessed on April 12, 2021.

ABC Evening News. "Abortion Clinic Bombings/Reagan Statement." Reported by Carole Simpson. Aired on Jan. 3, 1985. Vanderbilt Television News Archive. https://tvnews.vanderbilt.edu/broadcasts/92395. Accessed on April 12, 2021.

NBC Evening News. "Abortion Anniversary." Reported by Carl Stern and Roger Mudd. Aired on Jan. 22, 1986. Vanderbilt Television News Archive. https://tvnews.vanderbilt.edu/broadcasts/546497. Accessed on March 19, 2021.

ABC Evening News. "Abortion Ruling Anniversary." Reported by Barry Serafin, Lark McCarthy, Peter Jennings and Sam Donaldson. Aired on Jan. 22, 1986. Vanderbilt Television News Archive. https://tvnews.vanderbilt.edu/broadcasts/99099. Accessed on March 19, 2021.

CBS Evening News. "Campaign '88/Dukakis/Debates/Anti-Abortion Protestors." Reported by Bob Schieffer, Dan Rather and Bruce Morton. Aired on Sept. 6, 1988. Vanderbilt Television News Archive. https://tvnews.vanderbilt.edu/broadcasts/323500. Accessed on March 19, 2021.

ABC Evening News. "Atlanta, Georgia/Abortion Protests." Reported by Rebecca Chase and Sam Donaldson. Aired on Aug. 25, 1988. Vanderbilt Television News Archive. https://tvnews.vanderbilt.edu/broadcasts/117592. Accessed on June 2, 2021.

ABC Evening News. "Atlanta, Georgia/Anti-Abortion Protest." Reported by Mark Potter and Peter Jennings. Aired on Oct. 4, 1988. Vanderbilt Television News Archive. https://tvnews.vanderbilt.edu/broadcasts/112706. Accessed on June 2, 2021.

NBC Evening News. "Atlanta, Georgia/ Anti-Abortion Protests." Reported by Kenley Jones and Tom Brokaw. Aired on Oct. 4, 1988. Vanderbilt Television News Archive. https://tvnews.vanderbilt.edu/broadcasts/559533. Accessed on June 2, 1988.

CBS Evening News. "PTL Controversy." Reported by Bob Schieffer and Bruce Hall. Aired on May 27, 1987. Vanderbilt Television News Archive. https://tvnews.vanderbilt.edu/broadcasts/315888. Accessed on March 24, 2022.

NBC Evening News. "PTL/Falwell's Resignation." Reported by Kenley Jones and Tom Brokaw. Aired on Oct. 8, 1987. Vanderbilt Television News Archive. https://tvnews.vanderbilt.edu/broadcasts/553532. Accessed on March 24, 2022.

CBS Evening News. "Falwell." Reported by Lem Tucker and Dan Rather. Aired on Nov. 3, 1987. Vanderbilt Television News Archive. https://tvnews.vanderbilt.edu/broadcasts/313660. Accessed on March 24, 2022.

CBS Special. "48 Hours: Abortion Battle." Various reporters. Aired on Oct. 20, 1988. Vanderbilt Television News Archive. https://tvnews.vanderbilt.edu/broadcasts/659348. Accessed on June 2, 2021.

Magnuson, E. (1985, January 14). Explosions Over Abortion. *Time* magazine, *125*(2), 10-11.

Operation Rescue (records regarding Operation Rescue Organization). Religious Coalition for Reproductive Choice Records. Wisconsin Historical Society, Madison, Wisc. (Box 3, Folder 4-5)

Anti-Abortion Organizations, 1974-1988 (records regarding all anti-abortion organizations between 1974 and 1988) Religious Coalition for Reproductive Choice Records. Wisconsin Historical Society, Madison, Wisc. (Box 4, Folders 31-52, Box 5, 1-28)

Goldberger, Norma. Interview Conducted by Cody McDevitt. Dec. 19, 2021.

Anti-Choice Groups. Religious Coalition for Reproductive Choice Records. Wisconsin Historical Society. (M93-146, Box 4, Folder 31)

Americans Against Abortion/Walk America for Life. Annual Reports. Religious Coalition for Reproductive Choice Records. Wisconsin Historical Society. (M93-146, Box 4, Folder 32)

American Citizens Concerned for Life. Annual Reports. Religious Coalition for Reproductive Choice Records. Wisconsin Historical Society. (M93-146, Box 4, Folder 33)

American Life Lobby. Annual Reports. Religious Coalition for Reproductive Choice Records. Wisconsin Historical Society. (M93-146, Box 4, Folder 34)

Birthright. Annual Reports. Religious Coalition for Reproductive Choice Records. Wisconsin Historical Society. (M93-146, Box 4, Folder 35)

Catholic Pro-Life Resources. Annual Reports. Religious Coalition for Reproductive Choice Records. Wisconsin Historical Society. (M93-146, Box 4, Folder 36)

Robert Destro/Catholic League. Annual Reports. Religious Coalition for Reproductive Choice Records. Wisconsin Historical Society. (M93-146, Box 4, Folder 37)

Catholics United for Life-Sidewalk Counselors. Annual Reports. Religious Coalition for Reproductive Choice Records. Wisconsin Historical Society. (M93-146, Box 4, Folder 38)

Christian Action Council. Annual Reports. Religious Coalition for Reproductive Choice Records. Wisconsin Historical Society. (M93-146, Box 4, Folder 39)

Christians Against Abortion. Annual Reports. Religious Coalition for Reproductive Choice Records. Wisconsin Historical Society. (M93-146, Box 4, Folder 40)

Christian Voice. Annual Reports. Religious Coalition for Reproductive Choice Records. Wisconsin Historical Society. (M93-146, Box 4, Folder 41)

Concerned Women for America. Annual Reports. Religious Coalition for Reproductive Choice Records. Wisconsin Historical Society. (M93-146, Box 4, Folder 42)

Eagle Forum. Annual Reports. Religious Coalition for Reproductive Choice Records. Wisconsin Historical Society. (M93-146, Box 4, Folder 43)

Feminists for Life. Annual Reports. Religious Coalition for Reproductive Choice Records. Wisconsin Historical Society. (M93-146, Box 4, Folder 44)

Human Life Foundation. Annual Reports. Religious Coalition for Reproductive Choice Records. Wisconsin Historical Society. (M93-146, Box 4, Folder 45)

Human Life International. Annual Reports. Religious Coalition for Reproductive Choice Records. Wisconsin Historical Society. (M93-146, Box 4, Folder 46)

Intercessors for America. Annual Reports. Religious Coalition for Reproductive Choice Records. Wisconsin Historical Society. (M93-146, Box 4, Folder 47)

Just Life. Annual Reports. Religious Coalition for Reproductive Choice Records. Wisconsin Historical Society. (M93-146, Box 4, Folder 48)

LAPAC/National Pro-LIFEPAC. Annual Reports. Religious Coalition for Reproductive Choice Records. Wisconsin Historical Society. (M93-146, Box 4, Folder 49)

Last Days of Ministries. Annual Reports. Religious Coalition for Reproductive Choice Records. Wisconsin Historical Society. (M93-146, Box 4, Folder 50)

Liberty Lobby. Annual Reports. Religious Coalition for Reproductive Choice Records. Wisconsin Historical Society. (M93-146, Box 4, Folder 51)

Moral Majority/Jerry Falwell. Annual Reports. Religious Coalition for Reproductive Choice Records. Wisconsin Historical Society. (M93-146, Box 4, Folder 52)

National Right to Life (NRL) News. Religious Coalition for Reproductive Choice Records. Wisconsin Historical Society. (M93-146, Box 5, Folder 1).

The Pearson Foundation. Religious Coalition for Reproductive Choice Records. Wisconsin Historical Society. (M93-146, Box 5, Folder 2)

Prolifers for Survival. Religious Coalition for Reproductive Choice Records. Wisconsin Historical Society. (M93-146, Box 5, Folder 3)

Rutherford Institute. Religious Coalition for Reproductive Choice Records. Wisconsin Historical Society. (M93-146, Box 5, Folder 4)

March for Life-Nellie Gray. Religious Coalition for Reproductive Choice Records. Wisconsin Historical Society. (M93-146, Box 5, Folder 5)

National Committee for Human Life Amendment. Religious Coalition for Reproductive Choice Records. Wisconsin Historical Society. (M93-146, Box 5, Folder 6)

National Federation of Decency. Religious Coalition for Reproductive Choice Records. Wisconsin Historical Society. (M93-146, Box 5, Folder 7)

National Federation of Priests Council. Religious Coalition for Reproductive Choice Records. Wisconsin Historical Society. (M93-146, Box 5, Folder 8)

Pro-Life Action League: Joseph Scheidler, Chicago. Religious Coalition for Reproductive Choice Records. Wisconsin Historical Society. (M93-146, Box 5, Folder 9)

U.S. Coalition for Life. Religious Coalition for Reproductive Choice Records. Wisconsin Historical Society. (M93-146, Box 5, Folder 10)

Women Exploited by Abortion. Religious Coalition for Reproductive Choice Records. Wisconsin Historical Society. (M93-146, Box 5, Folder 11)

White House Working Groups on Family Report, 1986 November. Religious Coalition for Reproductive Choice Records. Wisconsin Historical Society. (M93-146, Box 5, Folder 12)

Washington March for Jesus. Religious Coalition for Reproductive Choice Records. Wisconsin Historical Society. (M93-146, Box 5, Folder 13)

Film–Silent Scream, 1985. Religious Coalition for Reproductive Choice Records. Wisconsin Historical Society. (M93-146, Box 5, Folder 14)

Reagan-National Sanctity of Human Life Day. Religious Coalition for Reproductive Choice Records. Wisconsin Historical Society. (M93-146, Box 5, Folder 15)

Political Consultant. Religious Coalition for Reproductive Choice Records. Wisconsin Historical Society. (M93-146, Box 5, Folder 16)

Political Action Material. Religious Coalition for Reproductive Choice Records. Wisconsin Historical Society. (M93-146, Box 5, Folder 17)

Catholic Organizations. Religious Coalition for Reproductive Choice Records. Wisconsin Historical Society. (M93-146, Box 5, Folder 18)

Life Letter. Religious Coalition for Reproductive Choice Records. Wisconsin Historical Society. (M93-146, Box 5, Folder 19)

Publications. Religious Coalition for Reproductive Choice Records. Wisconsin Historical Society. (M93-146, Box 5, Folder 20)

Operation Avalanche. Religious Coalition for Reproductive Choice Records. Wisconsin Historical Society. (M93-146, Box 5, Folder 21)

Assault on Clinic Day, 1980 August 9. Religious Coalition for Reproductive Choice Records. Wisconsin Historical Society. (M93-146, Box 5, Folder 22)

Visuals. Religious Coalition for Reproductive Choice Records. Wisconsin Historical Society. (M93-146, Box 5, Folder 23)

Debate Foundation. Religious Coalition for Reproductive Choice Records. Wisconsin Historical Society. (M93-146, Box 5, Folder 24)

Religion and Society Report. Religious Coalition for Reproductive Choice Records. Wisconsin Historical Society. (M93-146, Box 5, Folder 25)

Right Wing-Group Research Report. Religious Coalition for Reproductive Choice Records. Wisconsin Historical Society. (M93-146, Box 5, Folder 26)

Life Letter. Religious Coalition for Reproductive Choice Records. Wisconsin Historical Society. (M93-146, Box 5, Folder 27)

Miscellaneous Pamphlets. Religious Coalition for Reproductive Choice Records. Wisconsin Historical Society. (M93-146, Box 5, Folder 28)

Religious Denominational Media. Religious Coalition for Reproductive Choice Records. Wisconsin Historical Society. (M93-025, Box 1, Folder 1)

Women of Color. Religious Coalition for Reproductive Choice Records. Wisconsin Historical Society. (M93-025, Box 1, Folder 2)

Affiliate Ads. Religious Coalition for Reproductive Choice Records. Wisconsin Historical Society. (M93-025, Box 1, Folder 3)

Press Conference. Religious Coalition for Reproductive Choice Records. Wisconsin Historical Society. (M93-025, Box 1, Folder 4)

Media Relations, 1989. (Collected speeches and congressional testimony). Religious Coalition for Reproductive Choice Records. Wisconsin Historical Society. (M93-025, Box 1, Folder 5)

Religious Coalition for Abortion Rights Clips, 1988. Religious Coalition for Reproductive Choice Records. Wisconsin Historical Society. (M93-025, Box 1, Folder 6)

Operation Rescue Press Conference. Religious Coalition for Reproductive Choice Records. Wisconsin Historical Society. (M93-025, Box 1, Folder 7)

Media Relations, 1988. Religious Coalition for Reproductive Choice Records. Wisconsin Historical Society. (M93-025, Box 1, Folder 8)

RCAR Press, 1987. Religious Coalition for Reproductive Choice Records. Wisconsin Historical Society. (M93-025, Box 1, Folder 9)

Media Relations, 1987. Religious Coalition for Reproductive Choice Records. Wisconsin Historical Society. (M93-025, Box 1, Folder 10

RCAR Press Vogue, Christianity and Crisis, 1986. Religious Coalition for Reproductive Choice Records. Wisconsin Historical Society. (M93-025, Box 1, Folder 11)

Bogus Clinics Press Conference. Religious Coalition for Reproductive Choice Records. Wisconsin Historical Society. (M93-025, Box 1, Folder 12)

Media Relations, 1986. Religious Coalition for Reproductive Choice Records. Wisconsin Historical Society. (M93-025, Box 1, Folder 13)

RCAR Press, 1985. Religious Coalition for Reproductive Choice Records. Wisconsin Historical Society. (M93-025, Box 1, Folder 14)

Media Relations, 1985. Religious Coalition for Reproductive Choice Records. Wisconsin Historical Society. (M93-025, Box 1, Folder 15)

RCAR Press, 1984. Religious Coalition for Reproductive Choice Records. Wisconsin Historical Society. (M93-025, Box 1, Folder 16)

Media Relations, 1984. Religious Coalition for Reproductive Choice Records. Wisconsin Historical Society. (M93-025, Box 1, Folder 17)

RCAR Press, 1983. Religious Coalition for Reproductive Choice Records. Wisconsin Historical Society. (M93-025, Box 1, Folder 18)

Media Relations, 1983. Religious Coalition for Reproductive Choice Records. Wisconsin Historical Society. (M93-025, Box 1, Folder 19)

RCAR Press, 1982. Religious Coalition for Reproductive Choice Records. Wisconsin Historical Society. (M93-025, Box 1, Folder 20)

RCAR Press, 1981. Religious Coalition for Reproductive Choice Records. Wisconsin Historical Society. (M93-025, Box 1, Folder 21)

Coalition Press Conference, Religious Coalition for Reproductive Choice Records. Wisconsin Historical Society. (M93-025, Box 1, Folder 22)

1984. Religious Coalition for Reproductive Choice Records. Wisconsin Historical Society. (M93-025, Box 1, Folder 30)

Background Material. Religious Coalition for Reproductive Choice Records. Wisconsin Historical Society. (M93-025, Box 1, Folder 31)

Abortion: Why Religious Organizations ..., 1986. Religious Coalition for Reproductive Choice Records. Wisconsin Historical Society. (M93-025, Box 1, Folder 32)

Point/Counterpoint supporting research. Religious Coalition for Reproductive Choice Records. Wisconsin Historical Society. (M93-025, Box 1, Folder 33)

Annual Reports. Religious Coalition for Reproductive Choice Records. Wisconsin Historical Society. (M93-025, Box 1, Folder 34)

RCAR-UMC Relationship Materials. Annual Reports. Religious Coalition for Reproductive Choice Records. Wisconsin Historical Society. (M93-025, Box 4, Folder 2)

RCAR Staff Structure. Annual Reports. Religious Coalition for Reproductive Choice Records. Wisconsin Historical Society. (M93-025, Box 4, Folder 3)

Board of Directors Mailing List. Annual Reports. Religious Coalition for Reproductive Choice Records. Wisconsin Historical Society. (M93-025, Box 4, Folder 4)

Board of Directors Biographies. Annual Reports. Religious Coalition for Reproductive Choice Records. Wisconsin Historical Society. (M93-025, Box 4, Folder 5)

RCAR Program Director's Positions. Annual Reports. Religious Coalition for Reproductive Choice Records. Wisconsin Historical Society. (M93-025, Box 4, Folder 6)

Personnel Committee. Annual Reports. Religious Coalition for Reproductive Choice Records. Wisconsin Historical Society. (M93-025, Box 4, Folder 7)

RCAR Statement of Purpose. Annual Reports. Religious Coalition for Reproductive Choice Records. Wisconsin Historical Society. (M93-025, Box 4, Folder 8)

Family Planning Resolution. Annual Reports. Religious Coalition for Reproductive Choice Records. Wisconsin Historical Society. (M93-025, Box 4, Folder 9)

Advisory Council–statement of purpose, 1978. Annual Reports. Religious Coalition for Reproductive Choice Records. Wisconsin Historical Society. (M93-025, Box 4, Folder 10)

Program Documents, 1988, 1989. Annual Reports. Religious Coalition for Reproductive Choice Records. Wisconsin Historical Society. (M93-025, Box 4, Folder 11)

Budget Revisions, 1988, April. Annual Reports. Religious Coalition for Reproductive Choice Records. Wisconsin Historical Society. (M93-025, Box 4, Folder 12)

Retreat-Program Documents. Annual Reports. Religious Coalition for Reproductive Choice Records. Wisconsin Historical Society. (M93-025, Box 4, Folder 13)

RCAR/Education–budgets, 1987. Annual Reports. Religious Coalition for Reproductive Choice Records. Wisconsin Historical Society. (M93-025, Box 4, Folder 14)

1982. Religious Coalition for Reproductive Choice Records. Wisconsin Historical Society. (M93-025, Box 1, Folder 20)

Gauen, P. (1983, Feb. 11). Zevallos Abductor gets 30-year term. *St. Louis Globe-Democrat*, 1A-22A.

Bosworth, C., & Steichen, G. C. (1984, Aug. 12). Recruits in the Army of God. *St. Louis Post-Dispatch*, 1A-22A.

Frances, Gail. Interview. Conducted by Cody McDevitt. March 16, 2022.

Taft, Charlotte. Interview. Conducted by Cody McDevitt. Sept. 13, 2021.

Harrington, Walt. "Judie Brown: Sex, Politics and Religion in the anti-abortion crusade," *The Washington Post Magazine,* Jan. 5, 1986.

Daynes, Byron W.; Tatalovich, Raymond. "Presidential Politics and Abortion," Presidential Studies Quarterly, Vol. 22, No. 3, Summer 1992, Pg. 545-561

Wattleton, Faye. *Life on the Line.* Ballantine Books: New York. Pg. 192.

Collins, Gail. "The Last of Her Kind," Dec. 30, 2007, *New York Times Magazine.* (Accessed via nytimes.com on May 28, 2021)

Liebman, Robert; Wuthnow, Robert. *The New Christian Right: Mobilization and Legitimation,* Aldine Publishing Company: New York. 1983.

Culver, S., & Dorhauer, J. (2007). Steeplejacking: How the Christian right is hijacking mainstream religion (p. 35). IG Publishing.

"Mixing Politics and Religion," *Mansfield News-Journal,* Nov. 28, 1981. Pg. 4.

Clarkson, Frederick. "The Battle for Mainline Churches," *The Public Eye*, Spring 2006. https://politicalresearch.org/2006/03/05/battle-mainline-churches

Sharpe, Jerry. "Churches answer mission critics," *The Pittsburgh Press,* Feb. 6, 1983, Pg. 27. (Accessed via newspapers.com on April 15, 2022)

Clarkson, Frederick, "The Prochoice Religious Community May Be the Future of Reproductive Rights, Access, and Justice," Political Research Associates, Sept. 28, 2020. https://politicalresearch.org/2020/09/28/prochoice-religious-community-may-be-future-reproductive-rights-access-and-justice

Dewar, Helen. "Toughest Curbs on Abortion Funds voted by Senate," *Washington Post,* May 22, 1981. (Accessed via washingtonpost.com on April 7, 2021)

A Religious Statement on Abortion: A Call to Commitment, The Religious Coalition for Abortion Rights, Inc., 1981.

UPI. "Abortion Foe is Convicted in Couple's Abduction," *The New York Times,* Jan. 28, 1983. (Accessed via nytimes.com on April 8, 2021)

Bosworth, Charles; Steichen, Girard. "Recruits in the Army of God," *St. Louis Post Dispatch.* Aug. 12, 1984. Pg 1, 5, 6.

Jackson, Lawton L.; Malladi, Lakshmeeramya. "City of Akron v. Akron Center for Reproductive Health," *The Embryo Project Encyclopedia.* (Accessed via https://embryo.asu.edu/pages/city-akron-v-akron-center-reproductive-health-1983 on Feb. 18, 2022)

Franklin, Ben. "Shot fired through window of Blackmun Home," *The New York Times,* March 5, 1985. Pg. 1A. (accessed via nytimes.com on March 18, 2021)

"Terror on Trial," *The Miami Herald,* April 29, 1985, Pg. 12. (Accessed via newspapers.com on Dec. 28, 2020).

Liff, Robert A. "Bombing Suspects Aren't Sorry," *The Orlando Sentinel,* Jan. 6, 1985, Pg. 1, A20. (Accessed via newspapers.com on Dec. 28, 2020)

Liff, Robert. "Pensacola Residents Forgive Suspects," *The Orlando Sentinel,* Jan. 6, 1985, Pg. A20.

Mason, Carol. *Killing for Life: The Apocalyptic Narrative of Pro-Life Politics,* Cornell University Press, Ithaca, 2002. Pg. 21

Sweeney, Paul. "Joe Scheidler: Fighting TV-Imposed Morality," *About Issues: For God, For Life, For the Family, For The Nation,* June 1982. Vol. 4, No. 6.

Risen, James; Thomas, Judy L. *Wrath of Angels: The American Abortion War.* Basic Books, New York, 1998. Pg 101.

Winter, Aaron. "Anti-abortion extremism and violence in the United States," *Extremism in America,* University Press of Florida, Gainesville, 2014. Pg. 218-248.

Sekulow, Logan. "Choosing Life: A History of the Prolife Movement," ACLJ Films, 2009.

Falwell signs contract to make and distribute 50,000 "Silent Scream" Films," RCAR Records, Wisconsin Historical Society, Box 4.

Carnahan, Ann. "5,000 anti-abortionists from city to demonstrate in D.C. Tuesday," *The Pittsburgh Press,* Jan. 20, 1985, Pg. 1, 4. (Accessed via newspapers.com on Jan. 1, 2021)

"Religious Group Shuns 'Pastors Protest,'" Religious Coalition for Abortion Rights Records, Wisconsin Historical Society, Box 1.

Albrecht, Marsha. "Churches should make stands on abortion clear, speaker says," *The Argus Leader.* Oct. 9, 1987.

Smeal, Eleanor. "Anti-abortionists use old ploy," *Clarion-Ledger.* March 16, 1986. Page 103 (Accessed via newspapers.com on Feb. 17, 2022)

Medicaid Abortion Scrapped," *Latrobe Bulletin,* Sept. 14, 1988. Pg. 23. (Accessed via newspapers.com on Feb. 16, 2022)

"Enemy of Abortions is also taking issue with protest tactics," *The New York Times,* Aug. 31, 1988. Section A, Page 14. (Accessed via nytimes.com on Feb. 16, 2022).

Wallach, Janet. "Cardinal of Choice," *Washington Post Magazine,* Aug. 24, 1986.

Harder, J. D. (2014). *"Heal Their Land": Evangelical political theology from the Reagan era to the Trump era* (Doctoral dissertation, University of Nebraska–Lincoln). University of Nebraska–Lincoln.

People for the American Way. (2012, Feb. 21). *Washington for Jesus returns as the America for Jesus prayer rally in Philadelphia.* Right Wing Watch.

Rolsky, L. B. (2021). *Producing the Christian Right: Conservative activism and political realignment. MDPI Religions.*

Christianity Today. (1980, May). *Washington for Jesus: Revival fervor and political maneuvering.*

First Amendment Encyclopedia. (2023, Aug. 5). *Religious Right movement and key figures.* Middle Tennessee State University.

Critchlow, D. T. (1996). *Intended consequences: Birth control, abortion, and the federal government in modern America.* Oxford University Press.

Ginsburg, F. D. (1989). *Contested lives: The abortion debate in an American community.* University of California Press.

National Catholic Reporter. (2012, April 17). *DFLA calls for big tent in Democratic platform.* [Blog post]. https://www.ncronline.org/blogs/distinctly-catholic/dfla-calls-big-tent-dem-platform

First Things. (2020, Oct. 6). *The last pro-life Democrat president.* https://www.firstthings.com/web-exclusives/2020/10/the-last-pro-life-democrat-president

Chicago Tribune. (2005, Jan. 5). *Army ready to march, CWA says. Chicago Tribune,* p. 8–7. https://www.newspapers.com/image/231367479/

Chapter 10

Bell, Bill and Karen. Interview. Conducted by Cody McDevitt. June 2, 2021.

Sherman, Mark. "Pro-Lifers vow to pack jails in city," *Atlanta Journal Constitution,* Aug. 5, 1988. Pg. 1.

Jefferis, J. (2011). *The Army of God and Anti-Abortion Terror in the United States.* Praeger.

Wong, F. (2011). *Christian Extremism as a Domestic Terror Threat* [A Monograph, United States Army Command and General Staff College].

Program Packet. Women of Color Partnership Program. Religious Coalition for Reproductive Choice Records. Wisconsin Historical Society. (M93-146, Box 6, Folder 1)

Articles. Women of Color Partnership Program. Religious Coalition for Reproductive Choice Records. Wisconsin Historical Society. (M93-146, Box 6, Folder 6)

Press Releases. Women of Color Partnership Program. Religious Coalition for Reproductive Choice Records. Wisconsin Historical Society. (M93-146, Box 6, Folder 7)

Letters. Women of Color Partnership Program. Religious Coalition for Reproductive Choice Records. Wisconsin Historical Society. (M93-146, Box 6, Folder 32)

ABC Evening News. "Supreme Court/Abortion." Reported by Tim O'Brien. Aired on April 9, 1989. Vanderbilt Television News Archive. https://tvnews.vanderbilt.edu/broadcasts/121934. Accessed on April 12, 2021.

CBS Evening News. "Supreme Court/Abortion Ruling/Reaction." Reported by Wyatt Andrews, Dan Rather and Richard Schlesinger. Aired on July 3, 1989. Vanderbilt Television News Archive. https://tvnews.vanderbilt.edu/broadcasts/328244. Accessed on March 19, 2021.

ABC Evening News. "Supreme Court/Abortion." Reported by Tim O'Brien. Aired on July 2, 1989. Vanderbilt Television News Archive. https://tvnews.vanderbilt.edu/broadcasts/123185. Accessed on April 12, 2021.

ABC Evening News. "Supreme Court/Abortion Ruling/Missouri Case/The States." Reported by Chris Bury, Mike Von Fremd and Barry Serafin. Aired on July 3, 1989. Vanderbilt Television News Archive. https://tvnews.vanderbilt.edu/broadcasts/123397. Accessed on April 12, 2021.

NBC Evening News. "New York/Abortion Case." Reported by Stan Bernard and Tom Brokaw. Aired on Feb. 9, 1989. Vanderbilt Television News Archive. https://tvnews.vanderbilt.edu/broadcasts/567264. Accessed on April 22, 2021.

ABC Special. "Nightline." Reported by Ted Koppel. Aired on Feb. 10, 1989. Vanderbilt Television News Archive. https://tvnews.vanderbilt.edu/broadcasts/646369. Accessed on April 22, 2021.

ABC Evening News. "Florida/Abortion Debate." Reported by Mike Von Fremd and Diane Sawyer. Aired on Oct. 9, 1989. Vanderbilt Television News Archive. https://tvnews.vanderbilt.edu/broadcasts/119402. Accessed on March 19, 2021.

CBS Evening News. "'89 Elections/Bush/Abortion Issue." Reported by Lesley Stahl and Dan Rather. Aired on Nov. 3, 1989. Vanderbilt Television News Archive. https://tvnews.vanderbilt.edu/broadcasts/324862. Accessed on March 19, 2021.

Ross, Loretta. Interview. Conducted by Cody McDevitt. March 26, 2021.

Kissling, Frances. Interview. Conducted by Cody McDevitt. Aug. 8, 2020.

Dixon Diallo, Dazon. Interview. Conducted by Cody McDevitt. Jan. 2, 2022.

Keyes, Claire. Interview. Conducted by Cody McDevitt. May 9, 2015.

Kolata, Gina. "Self-help abortion movement gains momentum," *The New York Times,* October 23, 1989, P. 7

Hiris, Lori. *In Defense of Roe.* 1989. (Available on https://www.youtube.com/watch?v=30j0FPK-bCA)

Protect Freedom of Choice Rally, Boston, Massachusetts–May 1, 1990, Religious Coalition for Abortion Rights Records, Wisconsin Historical Society, Box 1.

Clarkson, Frederick, An Annotated Directory of the Prochoice Religious Community in the United States, Political Research Associates, Sept. 28, 2020. https://politicalresearch.org/2020/09/28/annotated-directory-prochoice-religious-community-united-states

Daly, Lewis. *A Moment to Decide: The Crisis in Mainstream Presbyterianism.* Institute for Democracy Studies, 2000. Pg. 41-53.

"Becky's Story," 60 Minutes, originally aired on Feb. 24, 1991. Accessed via cbs.com.

Chapter 11

Wilkerson, Isabel. "Drive against abortion finds a symbol: Wichita." *The New York Times,* Aug. 4, 1991. Pg. 20.

Schrage, L. (2003). *Abortion and Social Responsibility: Depolarizing the Debate.* Oxford University Press.

Singular, S. (2011). *The Wichita Divide: The Murder of George Tiller and the Battle Over Abortion.* St. Martin's Press.

"If all human cells are human beings, are all acorns oak trees," Religious Coalition for Abortion Rights Records, Wisconsin Historical Society, Box 1.

"35 Major Religious Groups Support Abortion Rights," Religious Coalition for Abortion Rights Records, Wisconsin Historical Society, Box 1.

"Operation Rescue's 'Religious Behavior' Challenged by Pro-choice Clergy and People of Faith," Religious Coalition for Abortion Rights Records, Wisconsin Historical Society, Box 1

CBS Evening News. "Abortion/Louisiana, Wichita, Kansas." Reported by Bruce Morton and Dan Rather. Aired on Aug. 7, 1991. Vanderbilt Television News Archive. https://tvnews.vanderbilt.edu/broadcasts/340111. Accessed on March 19, 2021.

ABC Evening News. "Wichita, Kansas/Anti-abortion Protests." Reported by Mike Von Fremd and Carole Simpson. Aired on Aug. 9, 1991. Vanderbilt Television News Archive. https://tvnews.vanderbilt.edu/broadcasts/136809. Accessed on March 19, 2021.

CBS Evening News. "Wichita, Kansas/Anti-Abortion Protests/Pro-Choice Rally." Reported by Bob Schieffer and Bob McNamara. Aired on Aug. 24, 1991. Vanderbilt Television News Archive. https://tvnews.vanderbilt.edu/broadcasts/339912. Accessed on March 19, 2021.

CBS Evening News. "Supreme Court/Abortion Pill." Reported by Dan Rather and Rita Braver. Aired on July 17, 1992. Vanderbilt Television News Archive. https://tvnews.vanderbilt.edu/broadcasts/345400. Accessed on March 20, 2021.

ABC Evening News. "Supreme Court/Abortion." Reported by Tim O'Brien and Peter Jennings. Aired on Nov. 7, 1991. Vanderbilt Television News Archive. https://tvnews.vanderbilt.edu/broadcasts/132543. Accessed on March 29, 2021.

ABC Evening News. "Supreme Court/Abortion." Reported by Tim O'Brien and Peter Jennings. Aired on June 8, 1992. Vanderbilt Television News Archive. https://tvnews.vanderbilt.edu/broadcasts/142181. Accessed on March 29, 2021.

NBC Evening News. "Supreme Court/Abortion/Pennsylvania." Reported by Garrick Utley and Carl Stern. Aired on June 28, 1992. Vanderbilt Television News Archive. https://tvnews.vanderbilt.edu/broadcasts/587296. Accessed on March 29, 2021.

ABC Special. "Nightline." Reported by Nina Totenberg and Ted Koppel. Aired on Dec. 2, 1993. Vanderbilt Television News Archive. https://tvnews.vanderbilt.edu/broadcasts/647470. Accessed on March 29, 2021.

ABC Evening News. "Supreme Court/Abortion Blockades." Reported by Tim O'Brien and Peter Jenningers. Aired on Dec. 8, 1993. Vanderbilt Television News Archive. https://tvnews.vanderbilt.edu/broadcasts/145864. Accessed on March 29, 2021.

NBC Evening News. "Campaign '96/Religious Right." Reported by Lisa Myers and Tom Brokaw. Aired on Sept. 10, 1983. Vanderbilt Television News Archive. https://tvnews.vanderbilt.edu/broadcasts/595099. Accessed on March 24, 2022.

CBS Evening News. "Supreme Court/Abortion/RICO Laws." Reported by Eric Engberg and Connie Chung. Aired on Dec. 8, 1993. Vanderbilt Television News Archive. https://tvnews.vanderbilt.edu/broadcasts/348850. Accessed on March 29, 2021.

Maddux, B. (1992, July 1). The Great Divide. *Life Magazine, 15*(7), 32-42.

Ireland, Patricia. Interview. Conducted by Cody McDevitt. March 21, 2021

Lennon, Thomas; Zwonitzer, Mark; Sheff, Jody; Strathairn, David; Rosen, Jeffrey, *The Supreme Court, 2007. Ambrose Video: New York.*

Sack, Kevin. "Under the Big Top: The Candidate; Protestors thrusts fetus at surprised Clinton," *The New York Times,* July 15, 1992. A11. (Accessed via nytimes.com on May 28, *2021)*

"Goldwater Opposes GOP on Abortion," *Los Angeles Times,* Aug. 7, 1992. (Accessed via latimes.com on May 28, 2021)

"Anti-abortion protester shows fetus to Clinton," UPI, July 14, 1992. (Accessed via https://www.upi.com/Archives/1992/07/14/Anti-abortion-protester-shows-fetus-to-Clinton/6865711086400/)

The Orlando Sentinel. (1991, Nov. 22). *[Article on Bill Clinton's abortion stance as Arkansas governor and early campaign messaging]. The Orlando Sentinel,* p. 4. https://www.newspapers.com/image/231030663/

The Orlando Sentinel. (1991, Dec. 15). *[Article on Democratic primary positioning and abortion rights groups' pressure on Clinton]. The Orlando Sentinel*, p. 271. https://www.newspapers.com/image/231208440/

North County Times. (1992, July 15). *[Article on Clinton using abortion as a contrast with George H.W. Bush during the 1992 campaign]. North County Times*, p. 8. https://www.newspapers.com/image/573175006/

Bryan-College Station Eagle. (1992, Sept. 24). *[Article on late 1992 campaign abortion rhetoric and reactions from both sides]. Bryan-College Station Eagle*, p. 6. https://www.newspapers.com/image/1002793657/U.S. House of Representatives. (1994, March 17).

U.S. Government Publishing Office. (1994). *Freedom of Access to Clinic Entrances Act of 1994, Public Law No. 103-259.* https://www.congress.gov/bill/103rd-congress/senate-bill/636/text

Chapter 12

Mason. Carol. *Killing for Life: The Apocalyptic Narrative of Pro-Life Politics.* Cornell University Press, Ithaca, 2002. Pg. 46-58

Jefferis, Jennifer. *Armed for Life: The Army of God and Anti-abortion Terror in the United States,* ABC-CLIO: Santa Barbara. Pg. 22.

"Religious Leader denounces Army of God manual." RCAR Records, Wisconsin Historical Society, Box 5.

Clarkson, F. (1997). *Eternal Hostility: The Struggle Between Theocracy and Democracy.* Common Courage Press.

Booth, William. "Doctor Killed During Abortion Protest," *Washington Post,* March 11, 1993, Pg. A01.

Reiter, Jerry. *Live From the Gates of Hell: An Insider's Look at the Anti-abortion Underground.* Prometheus Books, Amherst, 2000. Pg. 72, 75.

Martin, William. *With God on Our Side: The Rise of the Religious Right in America.* Broadway Books, New York. Pg. 330.

No Author. "Two Cities Feel Friction over Abortion," *Tampa Bay Times,* Aug. 20, 1994. Pg. 45. (Accessed via newspapers.com on April 7, 2022)

Lamb, Sara. "Women to be Guided Elsewhere," *Pensacola News Journal,* March 12, 1993. Pg. 1. (Accessed via newspapers.com on March 2, 2021)

Kallio, Nikki. "Responses to Preborn Rally Mixed," *Marshfield News-Herald.* July 24, 1996. Pg. 1-2. (Accessed via newspapers.com on April 13, 2022)

Scott, Janny. "Radical anti-abortion Alliance Described," *The New York Times,* Aug. 18, 1994. (Accessed via nytimes.com on April 13, 2022)

Lamb, Sara; Basiouny, Angie. "Doctor cared about people, friends say," *Pensacola News Journal,* March 12, 1993. Pg. 1, 10A. (Accessed via newspapers.com on March 2, 2021)

Gunn Jr., David. Interview. Conducted by Cody McDevitt. Jan. 24, 2022.

Fitzsimmons. Ron. Interview. Conducted by Cody McDevitt. April 27, 2021.

ABC Evening News. "Pensacola/Florida/Abortion Doctor Murder/Violence." Reported by Mark Potter, Peter Jennings and Karen Burnes. Aired on March 11, 1993. Vanderbilt Television News Archive. https://tvnews.vanderbilt.edu/broadcasts/146444. Accessed on March 19, 2021.

CBS Evening News. "Supreme Court/Abortion/Clinic Protests." Reported by Dan Rather, Eric Engberg and Connie Chung. Aired on Jan. 24, 1994. Vanderbilt Television News Archive. https://tvnews.vanderbilt.edu/broadcasts/353268. Accessed on April 12, 2021.

CBS Evening News. "Abortion Funding/Clinton." Reported by Susan Spencer and Dan Rather. Aired on March 30, 1993. Vanderbilt Television News Archive. https://tvnews.vanderbilt.edu/broadcasts/349731. Accessed on March 19, 2021.

ABC Evening News. "Melbourne, Florida/Abortion Protests." Reported by Mark Potter and Peter Jennings. Aired on April 9, 1993. Vanderbilt Television News Archive. https://tvnews.vanderbilt.edu/broadcasts/147510. Accessed on March 19, 2021.

NBC Evening News. "Politics and Religion: Christian Coalition/Reed." Reported by Bob Kur, Gwen Ifill and Tom Brokaw. Aired on Sept. 8, 1995. Vanderbilt Television News Archive. https://tvnews.vanderbilt.edu/broadcasts/608743. Accessed on March 24, 2022.

ABC Evening News. "The 94 Vote (Christian Coalition)." Reported by Peggy Wehmeyer and Peter Jennings. Aired on Nov. 3, 1994. Vanderbilt Television News Archive. https://tvnews.vanderbilt.edu/broadcasts/151518. Accessed on March 24, 2022.

ABC Evening News. "Supreme Court/Abortion Protests." Reported by Tim O'Brien and Peter Jennings. Aired on June 30, 1994. Vanderbilt Television News Archive. https://tvnews.vanderbilt.edu/broadcasts/154613. Accessed on April 12, 2021.

NBC Evening News. "Pensacola,Florida/Abortion Doctor Murder Trial." Reported by Deborah Roberts and Noah Nelson. Aired on Feb. 20, 1994. Vanderbilt Television News Archive. https://tvnews.vanderbilt.edu/broadcasts/597856. Accessed on March 19, 2021.

ABC Evening News. "Pensacola, Florida/Abortion Doctor Murder Trial." Reported by Mark Potter and Catherine Crier. Aired on Feb. 21, 1994. Vanderbilt Television News Archive. https://tvnews.vanderbilt.edu/broadcasts/152278. Accessed on March 19, 2021.

CBS Evening News. "Pensacola, Florida/Abortion Doctor Murder Trial." Reported by Diana Gonzalez and Catherine Crier. Aired on Feb. 21, 1994. Vanderbilt Television News Archive. https://tvnews.vanderbilt.edu/broadcasts/355198. Accessed on March 19, 2021.

ABC Evening News. "Birmingham, Alabama/Anti-abortion protests." Reported by Kathy Wolff and Renee Poussaint. Aired on March 26, 1994. Vanderbilt Television News Archive. https://tvnews.vanderbilt.edu/broadcasts/152875. Accessed on March 19, 2021.

ABC Evening News. "Pensacola, Florida/Abortion Doctor Murder Trial." Reported by Mark Potter and Aaron Brown. Aired on March 5, 1994. Vanderbilt Television News Archive. https://tvnews.vanderbilt.edu/broadcasts/153031. Accessed on March 19, 2021.

CNN Evening News. "Abortion Lawsuit." Reported by Judy Woodruff and Patty Davis. Aired on April 20, 1998. Vanderbilt Television News Archive. https://tvnews.vanderbilt.edu/broadcasts/423713. Accessed on April 12, 2021.

CNN Special. "Freedom of Access to Clinic Entrances Act Signing." Reported by Wolf Blitzer. Aired on May 26, 1994. Vanderbilt Television News Archive. https://tvnews.vanderbilt.edu/broadcasts/840392. Accessed on March 19, 2021.

NBC Evening News. "Pensacola, Florida/Abortion Clinics." Reported by Pete Williams and Brian Williams. Aired on Aug. 5, 1994. Vanderbilt Television News Archive. https://tvnews.vanderbilt.edu/broadcasts/601623. Accessed on March 19, 2021.

NBC Evening News. "Brookline, Massachusetts/Abortion Clinic Attacks/Salvi Arrest." Reported by Sara James and Brian Williams. Aired on Dec. 31, 1994. Vanderbilt Television News Archive. https://tvnews.vanderbilt.edu/broadcasts/726784. Accessed on March 19, 2021.

ABC Evening News. "Brookline, Massachusetts and Virginia/Abortion Clinic Shootings." Reported by Lisa Stark and Peter Jennings. Aired on Jan. 3, 1995. Vanderbilt Television News Archive. https://tvnews.vanderbilt.edu/broadcasts/156608. Accessed on March 19, 2021.

CBS Evening News. "Eye on America (Abortion Clinic Shootings/Salvi). Reported by Jim Stewart and Dan Rather. Aired on Jan. 13, 1995. Vanderbilt Television News Archive. https://tvnews.vanderbilt.edu/broadcasts/359403. Accessed on March 19, 2021.

NBC Evening News. "Abortion/Doctor's Fear." Reported by Tom Brokaw. Aired on March 1, 1995. Vanderbilt Television News Archive. https://tvnews.vanderbilt.edu/broadcasts/604835. Accessed on March 19, 2021.

ABC Evening News. "Massachusetts/Salvi Abortion Murder Trial." Reported by James Walker and Peter Jennings. Aired on March 18, 1996. Vanderbilt Television News Archive. https://tvnews.vanderbilt.edu/broadcasts/165246. Accessed on March 19, 2021.

ABC Evening News. "'96 Vote/Dole/Abortion Issue." Reported by Peter Jennings and John Cochran. Aired on June 6, 1996. Vanderbilt Television News Archive. https://tvnews.vanderbilt.edu/broadcasts/167338. Accessed on March 19, 2021.

ABC Evening News. "'96 Vote/Dole/Abortion Issue." Reported by Peter Jennings and John Cochran. Aired on June 7, 1996. Vanderbilt Television News Archive. https://tvnews.vanderbilt.edu/broadcasts/167356. Accessed on March 19, 2021.

CBS Evening News. "Republicans/Abortion/Christian Coalition." Reported by Harry Smith and Phil Jones. Aired on July 1, 1996. Vanderbilt Television News Archive. https://tvnews.vanderbilt.edu/broadcasts/370369. Accessed on March 24, 2022.

CBS Evening News. "Birmingham, Alabama/Abortion Clinic Bombing." Reported by Dan Rather and Byron Pitts. Aired on Jan 29, 1998. Vanderbilt Television News Archive. https://tvnews.vanderbilt.edu/broadcasts/378375. Accessed on March 19, 2021.

CBS Evening News. "Birmingham, Alabama/Abortion Clinic Bombing/Manhunt." Reported by Jim Stewart and Dan Rather. Aired on Feb. 11, 1998. Vanderbilt Television News Archive. https://tvnews.vanderbilt.edu/broadcasts/379946. Accessed on March 19, 2021.

CNN Evening News. "Birmingham, Alabama/Abortion Clinic Bombing/Search." Reported by Gene Randall and Brian Cabell. Aired on Feb. 14, 1998. Vanderbilt Television News Archive. https://tvnews.vanderbilt.edu/broadcasts/422037. Accessed on March 19, 2021.

CBS Evening News. "Birmingham, Alabama/Clinic Bombing/Evidence." Reported by Jim Stewart and Dan Rather. Aired on Feb. 24, 1998. Vanderbilt Television News Archive. https://tvnews.vanderbilt.edu/broadcasts/380180. Accessed on March 19, 2021.

CNN Evening News. "Birmingham, Alabama/Clinic Bombing/Link/Evidence." Reported by Pierre Thomas and Bernard Shaw. Aired on Feb. 27, 1998. Vanderbilt Television News Archive. https://tvnews.vanderbilt.edu/broadcasts/422398. Accessed on March 19, 2021.

NBC Evening News. "Amherst, New York/Abortion/Slepian Murder." Reported by Pete Williams and Tom Brokaw. Aired on Nov. 4, 1998. Vanderbilt Television News Archive. https://tvnews.vanderbilt.edu/broadcasts/622103. Accessed on March 19, 2021.

CBS Evening News. "Abortion/Shooting/Investigation." Reported by Dan Rather and Diana Olick. Aired on Nov. 5, 1998. Vanderbilt Television News Archive. https://tvnews.vanderbilt.edu/broadcasts/379357. Accessed on March 19, 2021.

CBS Evening News. "New York/Slepian Murder/Kopp Manhunt." Reported by Jim Stewart and Dan Rather. Aired on Oct. 22, 1999. Vanderbilt Television News Archive. https://tvnews.vanderbilt.edu/broadcasts/384747. Accessed on March 19, 2021.

NBC Evening News. "Anti-Abortion Underground/Kopp Arrest." Reported by John Seigenthaler and Norah O'Donnell. Aired on March 31, 2001. Vanderbilt Television News Archive. https://tvnews.vanderbilt.edu/broadcasts/637886. Accessed on March 19, 2021.

CBS Evening News. "France/Kopp Court Hearing." Reported by Jim Stewart and Dan Rather. Aired on June 7, 2001. Vanderbilt Television News Archive. https://tvnews.vanderbilt.edu/broadcasts/398912. Accessed on March 19, 2021.

CNN Evening News. "Buffalo, New York/Abortion Doctor's Murder/Kopp Trial." Reported by Jamie Colby and Aaron Brown. Aired on May 9, 2003. Vanderbilt Television News Archive. https://tvnews.vanderbilt.edu/broadcasts/728121. Accessed on March 19, 2021.

ABC Evening News. "Medicine: Abortion/Drugs." Reported by George Strait and Catherine Crier. Aired on Aug. 30, 1995. Vanderbilt Television News Archive. https://tvnews.vanderbilt.edu/broadcasts/161830. Accessed on March 20, 2021.

CBS Evening News. "Medicine: Abortion/Drugs." Reported by Richard Threlkeld and Harry Smith. Aired on Aug. 30, 1995. Vanderbilt Television News Archive. https://tvnews.vanderbilt.edu/broadcasts/365109. Accessed on March 20, 2021.

Clarkson, Frederick. Interview. Conducted by Cody McDevitt. March 4, 2021.

Cohen, David; Connon, Kristen. "Strikethrough (Fatality): The Origins of Online Stalking of Abortion Providers," Slate Magazine, May 21, 2015. (accessed slate.com on March 12, 2021)

Siemaszko, Corky. "Slain Doc Remembered," *New York Daily News,* Oct. 26, 1998, Pg. 111. (accessed via newspapers.com on March 14, 2021)

Goodman, Ellen. "Doctors now targets of terrorism," *The Post-Star,* Oct. 30, 1998. Pg. 4. (accessed via newspapers.com on March 14, 2021)

Mason, Carol. *Killing for Life: The Apocalyptic Narrative of Pro-Life Politics.* Cornell University Press, Ithaca, 2002. Pg. 46-47.

Associated Press. (1994, November 2). *Hill questions no witnesses in murder trial. Florida Today* (Cocoa, FL), p. 18. Retrieved from https://www.newspapers.com/image/177184192/

Associated Press. (1994, November 2). *Prosecutors to rest case. Florida Today* (Cocoa, FL), p. 22. Retrieved from https://www.newspapers.com/image/177184218/

Clary, M. (1994, November 3). Paul Hill convicted of murder: Jury deliberates less than half-hour. *Valley News* (West Lebanon, NH), p. 10. Retrieved from https://www.newspapers.com/image/833969449/

Hall, M. (1994, December 7). 'Martyr' or murderer? Abortion protester's death sentence ignites debate. *USA Today* (McLean, VA), p. 3. Retrieved from https://www.newspapers.com/image/1143012432/

Chapter 13

Singular, S. (2011). *The Wichita Divide: The Murder of George Tiller and the Battle Over Abortion.* St. Martin's Press.

Metzloff, Thomas. "Stenberg v. Carhart," Duke University School of Law, Voice of American Law.

NBC Evening News. "Campaign 2000 (New Hampshire/McCain/Abortion." Reported by Tom Brokaw and David Bloom. Aired on Jan. 26, 2000. Vanderbilt Television News Archive. https://tvnews.vanderbilt.edu/broadcasts/631856. Accessed on March 29, 2000.

NBC Evening News. "Supreme Court/Abortion Case." Reported by Pete Williams and Tom Brokaw. Aired on June 28, 2000. Vanderbilt Television News Archive. https://tvnews.vanderbilt.edu/broadcasts/635112. Accessed on March 19, 2021.

ABC Evening News. "Campaign 2000–Abortion." Reported by John Yang and Aaron Brown. Aired on July 1, 2000. Vanderbilt Television News Archive. https://tvnews.vanderbilt.edu/broadcasts/193204. Accessed on March 19, 2021.

NBC Evening News. "In Depth (Campaign 2000: Gore V. Bush: Supreme Court/Abortion)." Reported by Pete Williams, Lisa Myers and Tom Brokaw. Aired on Oct. 30, 2000. Vanderbilt Television News Archive. https://tvnews.vanderbilt.edu/broadcasts/632362. Accessed on March 19, 2021.

CBS Evening News. "Bush/Transition of Power/Abortion." Reported by Dan Rather and Bill Plante. Aired on Jan. 19, 2001. Vanderbilt Television News Archive. https://tvnews.vanderbilt.edu/broadcasts/396328. Accessed on March 19, 2021.

CNN Evening News. "Abortion/Roe v. Wade/30th Anniversary." Reported by Candy Crowley and Aaron Brown. Aired on Jan. 22, 2003. Vanderbilt Television News Archive. https://tvnews.vanderbilt.edu/broadcasts/720197. Accessed on March 19, 2021.

CBS Evening News. "Abortion/Partial-Birth Ban." Reported by Elizabeth Kaledin and Dan Rather. Aired on Oct. 21, 2003. Vanderbilt Television News Archive. https://tvnews.vanderbilt.edu/broadcasts/740255. Accessed on March 19, 2021.

CNN Special. "George W. Bush Statement RE: Late-term Abortion Ban." Reported by Dana Bash. Aired on Nov. 5, 2003. Vanderbilt Television News Archive. https://tvnews.vanderbilt.edu/broadcasts/976634. Accessed on March 19, 2021.

ABC Evening News. "Supreme Court/Abortion Battle." Reported by Jake Tapper and Elizabeth Vargas. Aired on Feb. 21, 2006. Vanderbilt Television News Archive. https://tvnews.vanderbilt.edu/broadcasts/819746. Accessed on March 19, 2021.

Gerstenzang, James; Gold, Matea. "Gore Explains Change in Abortion Stand," *Los Angeles Times,* Jan. 30, 2000. (Accessed via latimes.com on March 29, 2021)

No author. "Departing Head of Planned Parenthood faults Kerry," *Sioux City Journal,* Feb. 4, 2005. Pg. 23.

Chapter 14

CNN Evening News. "Sept. 10, 2008." Reported by Gary Tuchman and Anderson Cooper. Aired on Sept. 10, 2008. Vanderbilt Television News Archive. https://tvnews.vanderbilt.edu/broadcasts/904108. Accessed on March 20, 2021.

ABC Evening News. "Abortion/Rate." Reported by Dan Harris and Charles Gibson. Aired on Jan. 17, 2008. Vanderbilt Television News Archive. https://tvnews.vanderbilt.edu/broadcasts/883014. Accessed on March 20, 2021.

ABC Evening News. "Obama/Culture Wars/Abortion." Reported by Sharyn Alfonsi and Dan Harris. Aired on Jan. 25, 2009. Vanderbilt Television News Archive. https://tvnews.vanderbilt.edu/broadcasts/920278. Accessed on March 20, 2021.

ABC Evening News. "Notre Dame/Obama Address/ Abortion Issue/Protests/Catholics." Reported by David Wright, John Hendren and Dan Harris. Aired on May 17, 2009. Vanderbilt Television News Archive. https://tvnews.vanderbilt.edu/broadcasts/932870. Accessed on March 20, 2021.

CBS Evening News. "Philadelphia, Pennsylvania/Abortion Murder." Reported by Elaine Quijano and Katie Couric. Aired on Jan. 19, 2011. Vanderbilt Television News Archive. https://tvnews.vanderbilt.edu/broadcasts/985599. Accessed on April 12, 2021.

CNN Evening News. "Wichita, Kansas/Tiller Murder/Abortion/Waddington Interview." Reported by Anderson Cooper. Aired on June 1, 2009. Vanderbilt Television News Archive. https://tvnews.vanderbilt.edu/broadcasts/934640. Accessed on March 20, 2021.

CNN Evening News. "Wichita, Kansas/Tiller Clinic/Roeder, Carhart Interviews." Reported by Ted Rowland and Anderson Cooper. Aired on June 9, 2009. Vanderbilt Television News Archive. https://tvnews.vanderbilt.edu/broadcasts/935548. Accessed on March 20, 2009.

CNN Evening News. "Kansas/Roeder Murder Trial/Carhart Interview." Reported by Soledad O'Brien. Aired on Jan. 29, 2010. Vanderbilt Television News Archive. https://tvnews.vanderbilt.edu/broadcasts/957848. Accessed on March 20, 2021.

CNN Evening News. "Campaign 2012/Obama VS. Romney/Romney on Abortion/A Discussion." Reported by Anderson Cooper. Aired on Oct. 10, 2012. Vanderbilt Television News Archive. https://tvnews.vanderbilt.edu/broadcasts/1032073. Accessed on March 20, 2021.

CNN Evening News. "Congress/Planned Parenthood." Reported by John Berman. Aired on Sept. 29, 2015. Vanderbilt Television News Archive. https://tvnews.vanderbilt.edu/broadcasts/1090153. Accessed on March 29, 2015.

CNN Evening News. "Colorado/Planned Parenthood Shooting/Richards Interview." Reported by Pamela Brown and Anderson Cooper. Aired on Nov. 30, 2015. Vanderbilt Television News Archive. https://tvnews.vanderbilt.edu/broadcasts/1092528. Accessed on March 29, 2021.

Sadler, Marva. Interviewed by Cody McDevitt on Dec. 12, 2021.

Williams, Seth. Report of the Grand Jury. Court of Common Pleas: First Judicial District of Pennsylvania, Criminal Trial Division. Commonwealth of Pennsylvania v. Gosnell.

Frederick Clarkson, "Anti-Abortion Strategy in the Age of Obama," *The Public Eye*, Winter 2009/Spring 2010. https://politicalresearch.org/2009/12/01/anti-abortion-strategy-in-the-age-of-obama-2

Clarkson, Frederick. "Anti-abortion strategy in the age of Obama," Political Research Associates. (Dec. 1, 2009)

Daynes, Byron W.; Tatalovich, Raymond. "Presidential Politics and Abortion," Presidential Studies Quarterly, Vol. 22, No. 3, Summer 1992, Pg. 545-561

Crary, David. "Feminists Too, Divided Between Clinton-Obama," *The Cincinnati Enquirer*, May 11, 2018. Pg. 10.

Playing the Long Game: How the Christian Right Built Capacity to Undo Roe State By State, Political Research Associates, June 30, 2019. https://politicalresearch.org/2019/06/30/playing-the-long-game

Dowd, Maureen. "Trump Does it His Way," *The New York Times,* April 2, 2016. (Accessed via nytimes.com on March 23, 2021)

Whole Woman's Health vs Hellerstedt, 579 U.S. ___ (2016).

Mangan, Dan. "Trump: I'll Appoint Justices to Overturn Roe v. Wade Case," CNBC, Oct. 16, 2016. (Accessed via cnbc.com on March 24, 2021)

Chapter 15

Khazan, Olga. "Why Christians Overwhelmingly Backed Trump," *The Atlantic,* Nov. 9, 2016. (Accessed via theatlantic.com on March 24, 2021)

Kuruvilla, Carol. "After Trump's Win, White Evangelical Christians Face a Reckoning," *Huffington Post,* Nov. 11, 2016. (Accessed via huffpost.com on March 24, 2021)

Richards, C. (2019). *Make Trouble: Stand up, Speak Out, and Find the Courage to Lead.* Gallery Books.

ABC Evening News. "Campaign 2016/Trump Firestorm." Reported by David Muir. Aired on March 30, 2016. Vanderbilt Television News Archive. https://tvnews.vanderbilt.edu/broadcasts/1097003. Accessed on March 29, 2021.

ABC Evening News. "Campaign 2016/Trump & Abortion." Reported by Devin Dwyer and Cecilia Vega. Aired on April 2, 2016. Vanderbilt Television News Archive. https://tvnews.vanderbilt.edu/broadcasts/1097126. Accessed on March 29, 2021.

ABC Evening News. "Supreme Court/Texas Abortion Case." Reported by Mary Bruce and George Stephanopoulos. Aired on June 27, 2016. Vanderbilt Television News Archive. https://tvnews.vanderbilt.edu/broadcasts/1100402. Accessed on March 29, 2021.

CBS Evening News. "Abortion/Planned Parenthood/Demonstrations." Reported by Tony Dokoupil and Reena Ninan. Aired on Feb. 11, 2017. Vanderbilt Television News Archive. https://tvnews.vanderbilt.edu/broadcasts/1106948. Accessed on March 29, 2021.

CNN Evening News. "Planned Parenthood/Republican Defunding/A Discussion." Reported by Jeff Zeleny and Anderson Cooper. Aired on Jan. 5, 2017. Vanderbilt Television News Archive. https://tvnews.vanderbilt.edu/broadcasts/1106062. Feb. 11, 2021.

CNN Evening News. "Trump/Supreme Court/Richards Interview/A Discussion." Reported by Anderson Cooper. Aired on July 9, 2018. Vanderbilt Television News Archive. https://tvnews.vanderbilt.edu/broadcasts/1127258. Accessed on March 29, 2021.

CNN Evening News. "Campaign 2020/Biden on Abortion/Impeachment." Reported by Arlette Saenz and Jim Sciutto. Aired on June 6, 2019. Vanderbilt Television News Archive. https://tvnews.vanderbilt.edu/broadcasts/1138090. Accessed on March 29, 2021.

ABC Evening News. "Abortion/Planned Parenthood." Reported by David Muir. Aired on Aug. 19, 2019. Vanderbilt Television News Archive. https://tvnews.vanderbilt.edu/broadcasts/1140440. Accessed on Feb. 11, 2021.

CBS Evening News. "Connecticut/George Selim/Tristan Wix/James Reardon." No reporter is listed. Aired on Aug. 19, 2019. Vanderbilt Television News Archive. https://tvnews.vanderbilt.edu/broadcasts/1256452. Accessed on Feb. 11, 2022.

Suchanow, Klementyna. Interview. Conducted by Cody McDevitt. Dec. 30, 2022.

Hancock, Derenda. Interview. Conducted by Cody McDevitt. June 16, 2022.

Dowd, Elle. Interview. Conducted by Cody McDevitt. March 3, 2022.

Lerer, Lisa. "When Joe Biden Voted to Let States Overturn Roe v. Wade," *The New York Times,* March 29, 2019. (Accessed via nytimes.com on March 25, 2021)

Haberkorn, Jennifer. "Biden pledged to end an abortion funding ban. Will he start with his budget?" *Los Angeles Times,* April 7, 2021. (Accessed via latimes.com on April 9, 2021)

"Texas governor signs law banning abortions after as early as 6 weeks," *Los Angeles Times,* May 19, 2021. (Accessed via latimes.com on May 19, 2021)

INDEX